How to use this book:

This is a word search coloring book. Using the letters, find the words listed in the puzzle. You can simply draw a line through the words or get as creative and creative as coloring each letter.

For an extra challenge, we recommend use an old fashion turn-the-page dictionary and write the definitions of the words in the margins. This will expand your vocabulary.

Because this calendar has 366 puzzles, there is a quick learning activity to look forward to every day.

Find the letters, color the words

For more information, search us out at:
www.whimsywordsearch.com
Claire@whimsywordsearch.com

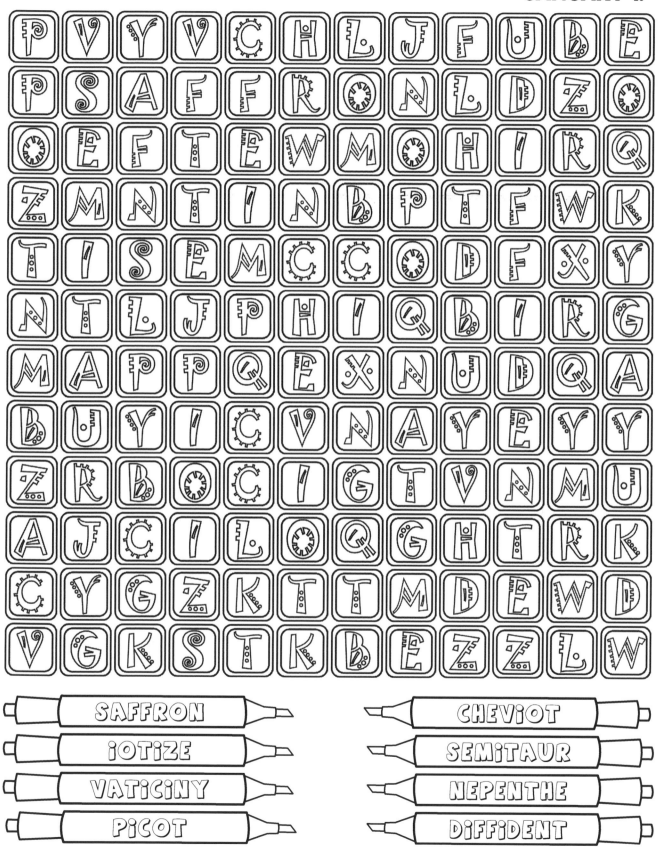

SAFFRON

CHEVIOT

IOTIZE

SEMITAUR

VATICINY

NEPENTHE

PICOT

DIFFIDENT

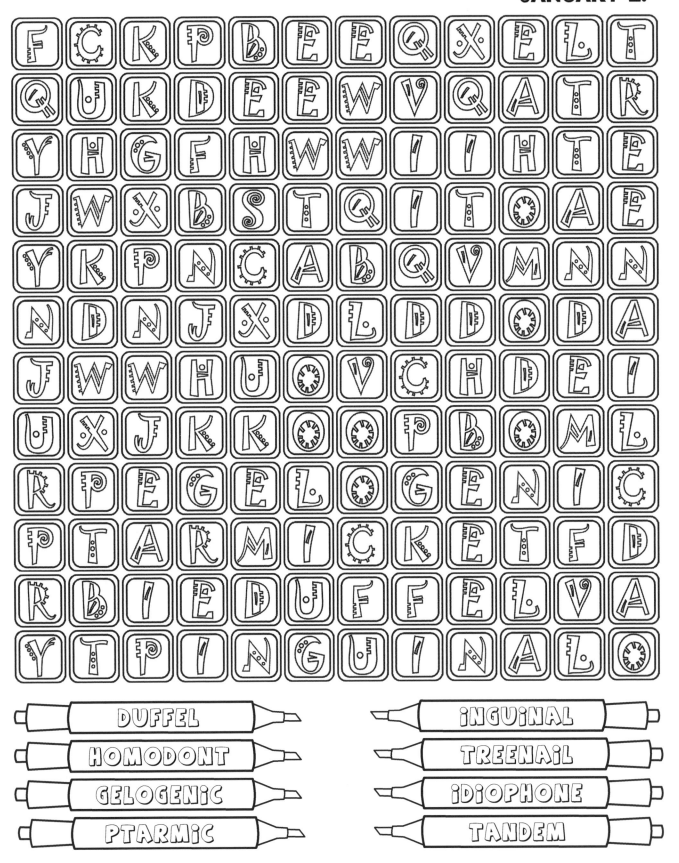

DUFFEL

HOMODONT

GELOGENIC

PTARMIC

INGUINAL

TREENAIL

IDIOPHONE

TANDEM

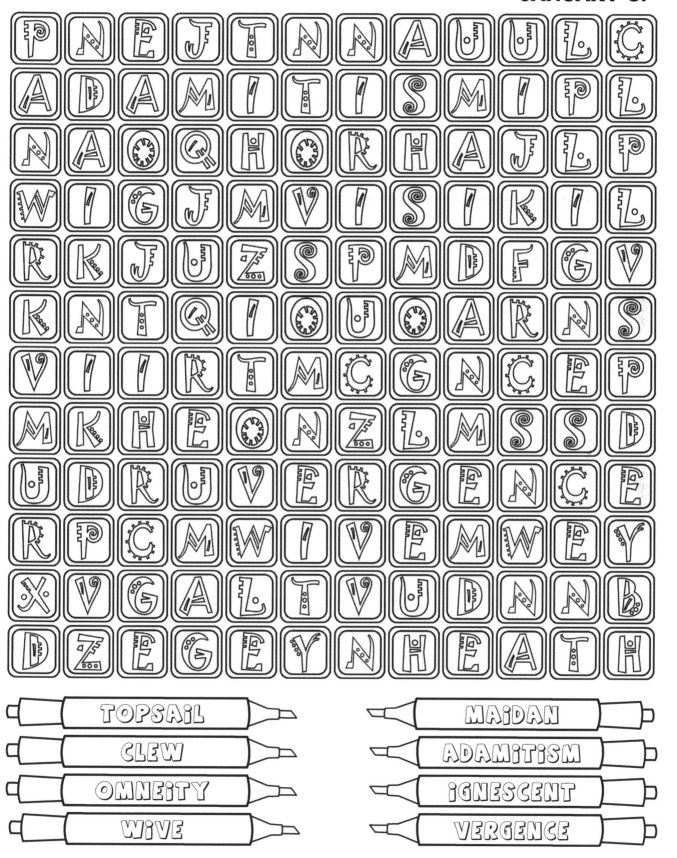

TOPSAIL

MAIDAN

CLEW

ADAMITISM

OMNEITY

IGNESCENT

WIVE

VERGENCE

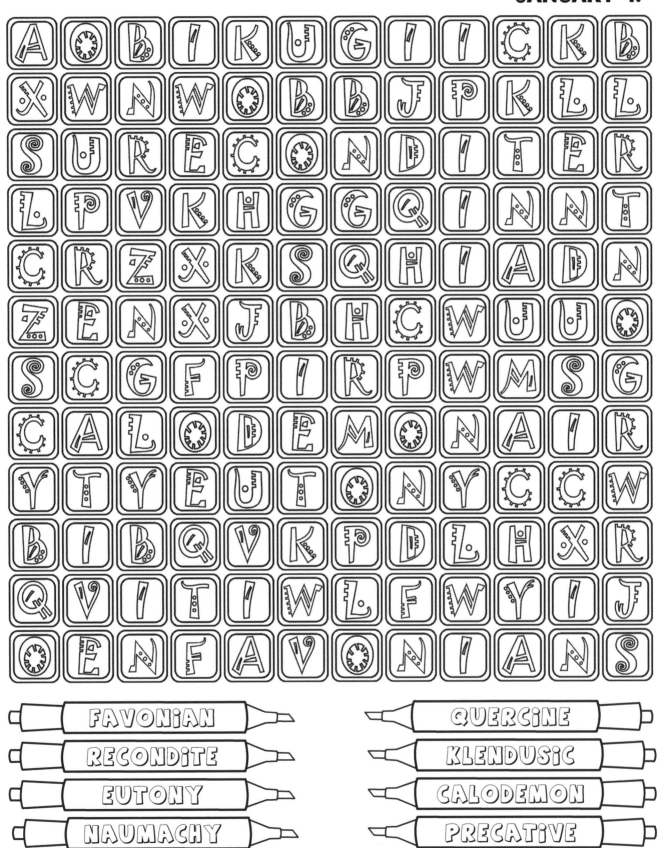

FAVONIAN

RECONDITE

EUTONY

NAUMACHY

QUERCINE

KLENDUSIC

CALODEMON

PRECATIVE

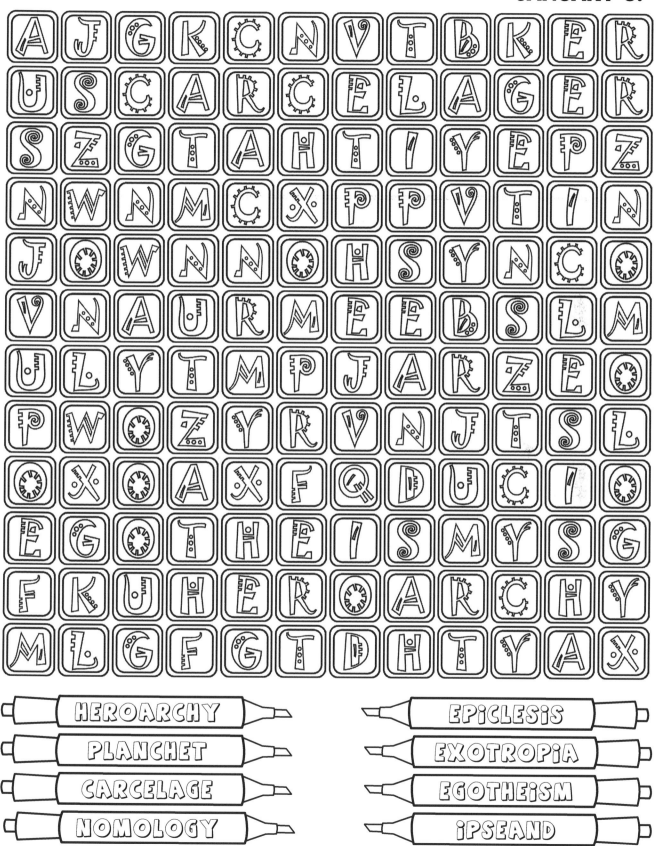

HEROARCHY

PLANCHET

CARCELAGE

NOMOLOGY

EPICLESIS

EXOTROPIA

EGOTHEISM

IPSEAND

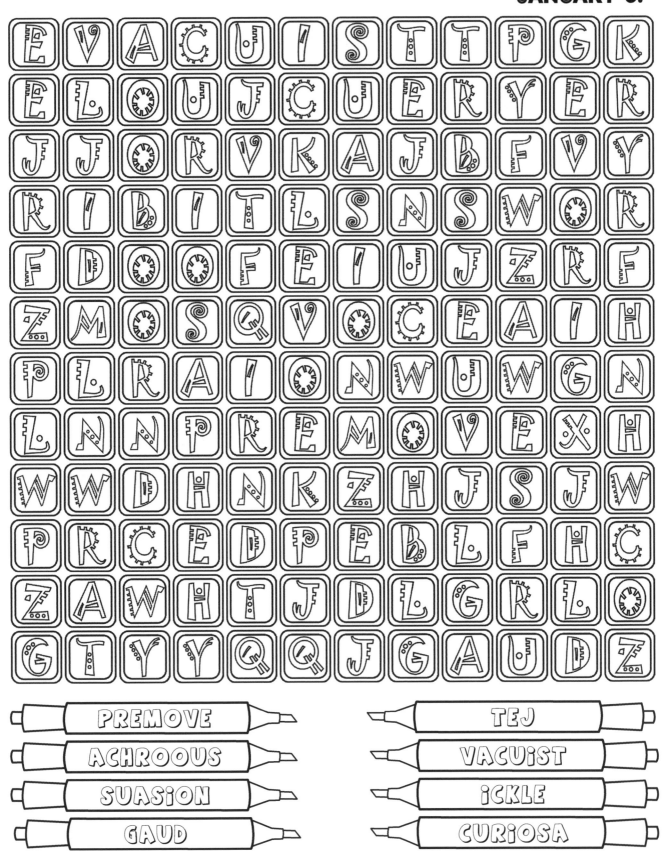

PREMOVE

ACHROOUS

SUASION

GAUD

TEJ

VACUIST

ICKLE

CURIOSA

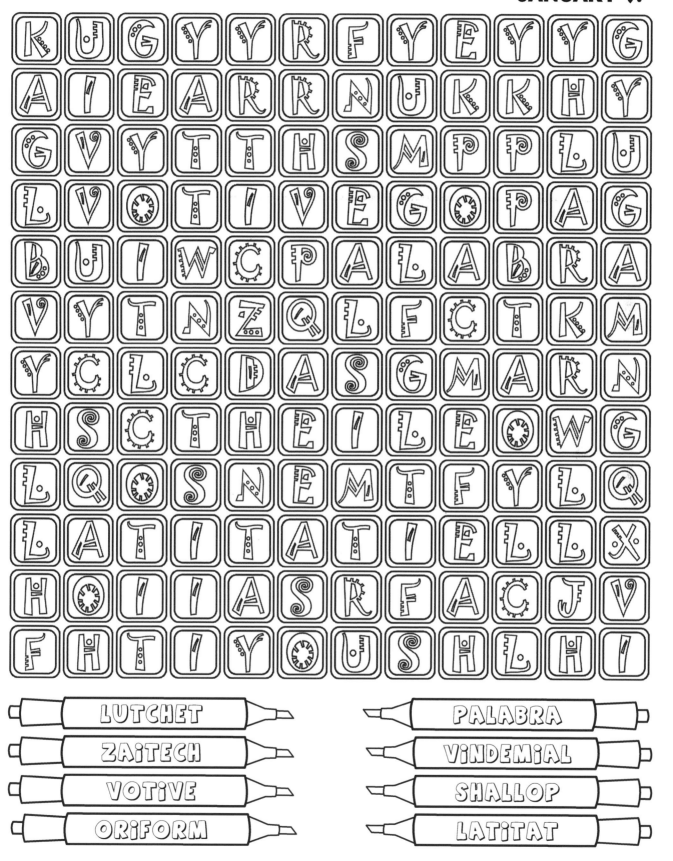

LUTCHET

ZAITECH

VOTIVE

ORIFORM

PALABRA

VINDEMIAL

SHALLOP

LATITAT

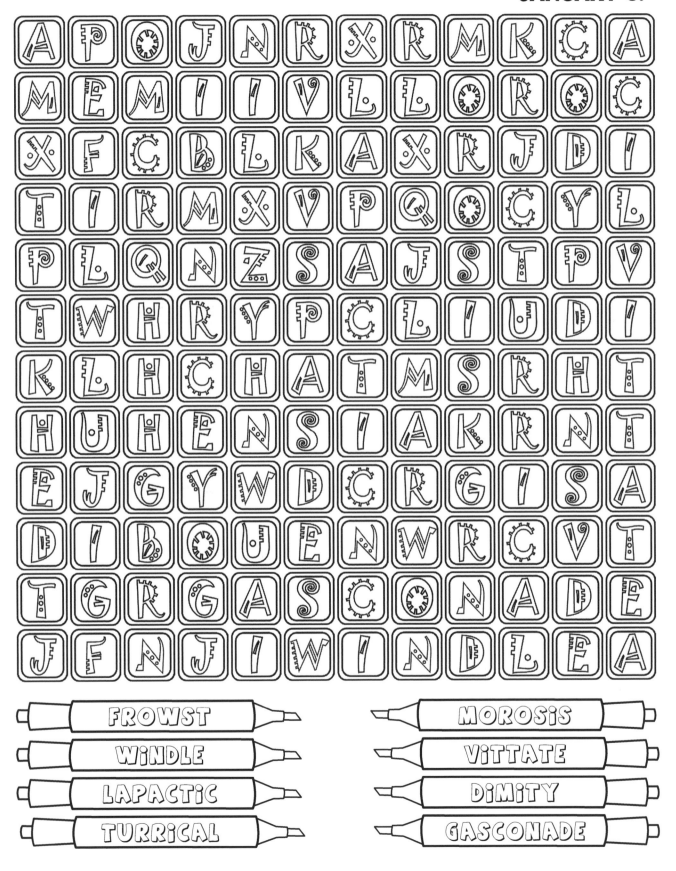

FROWST

WINDLE

LAPACTIC

TURRICAL

MOROSIS

VITTATE

DIMITY

GASCONADE

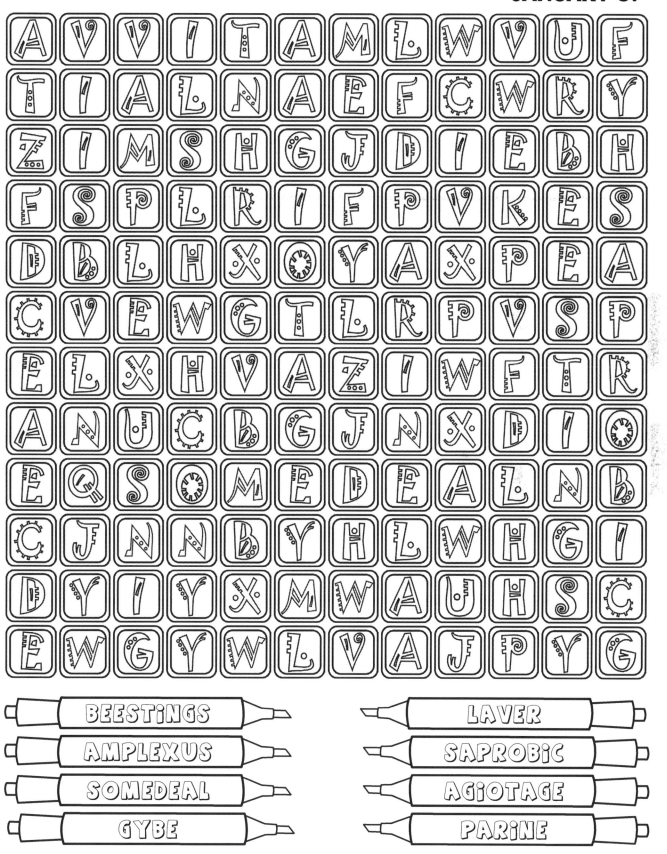

BEESTINGS

AMPLEXUS

SOMEDEAL

GYBE

LAVER

SAPROBIC

AGIOTAGE

PARINE

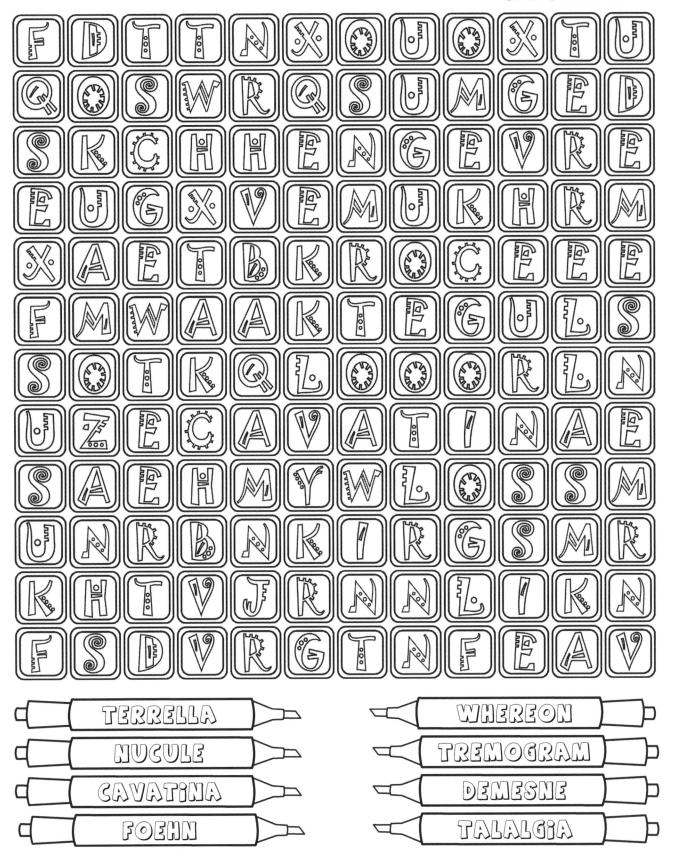

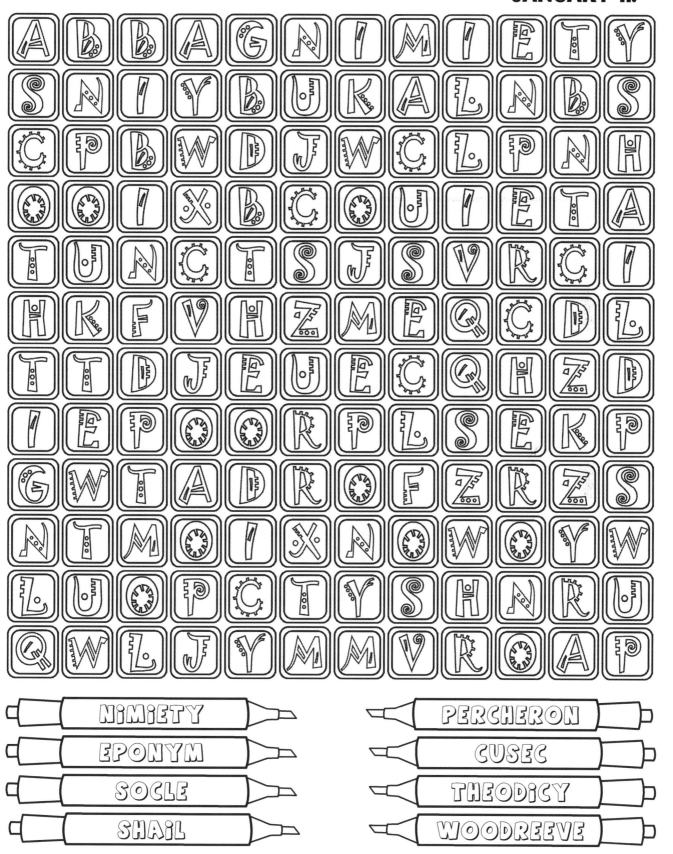

NIMIETY

EPONYM

SOCLE

SHAIL

PERCHERON

CUSEC

THEODICY

WOODREEVE

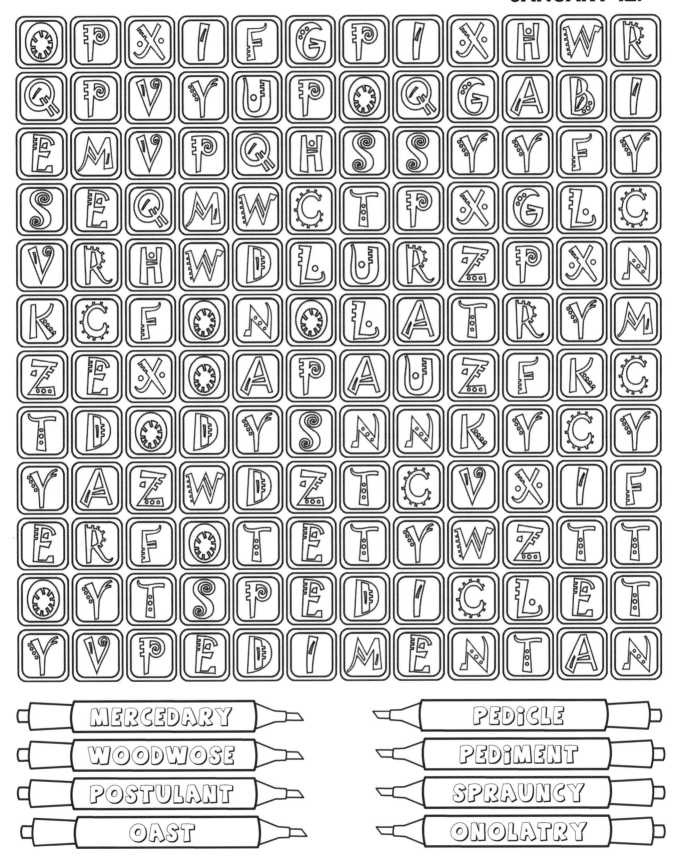

MERCEDARY

WOODWOSE

POSTULANT

OAST

PEDICLE

PEDIMENT

SPRAUNCY

ONOLATRY

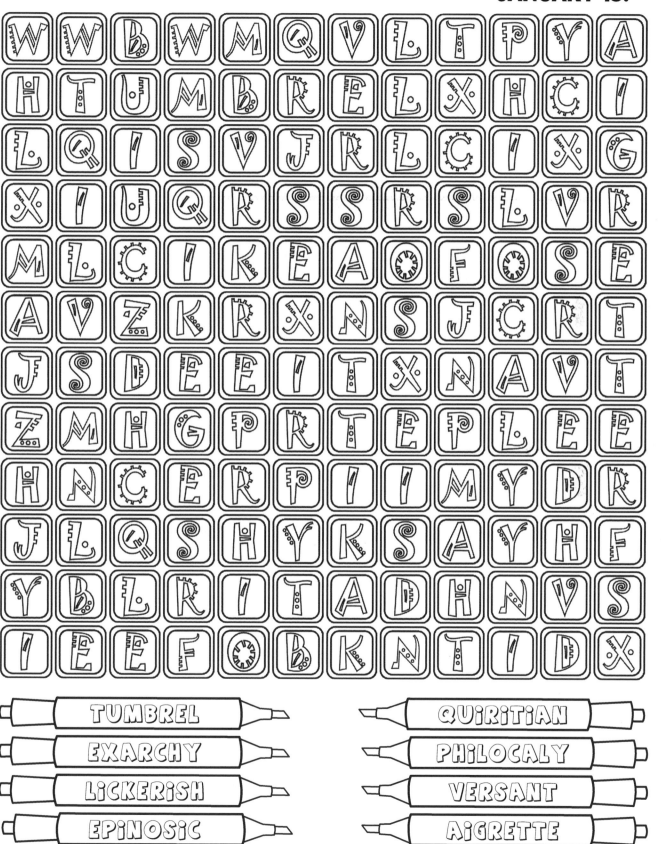

TUMBREL

QUIRITIAN

EXARCHY

PHILOCALY

LICKERISH

VERSANT

EPINOSIC

AIGRETTE

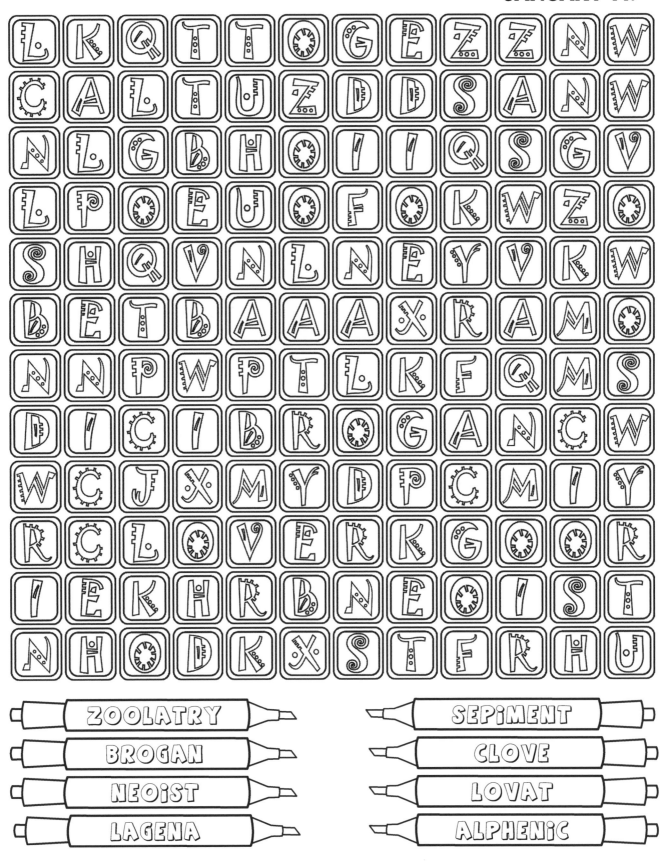

ZOOLATRY
BROGAN
NEOIST
LAGENA

SEPIMENT
CLOVE
LOVAT
ALPHENIC

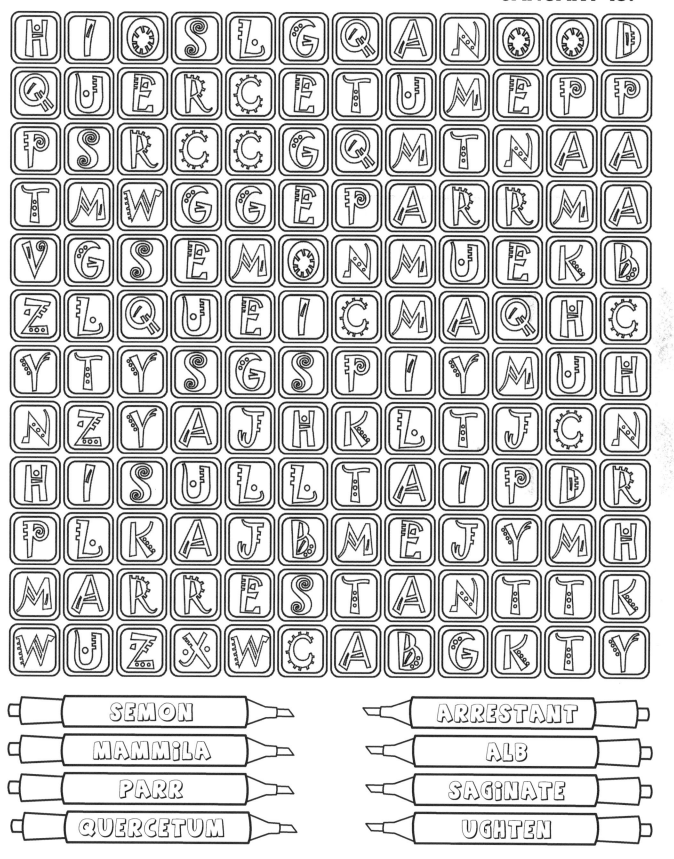

SEMON

MAMMILA

PARR

QUERCETUM

ARRESTANT

ALB

SAGINATE

UGHTEN

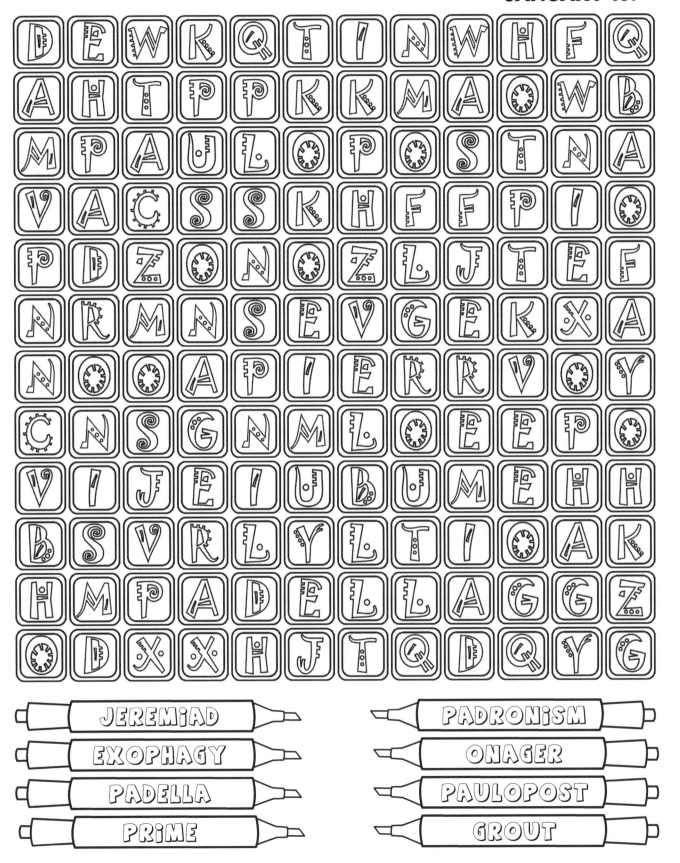

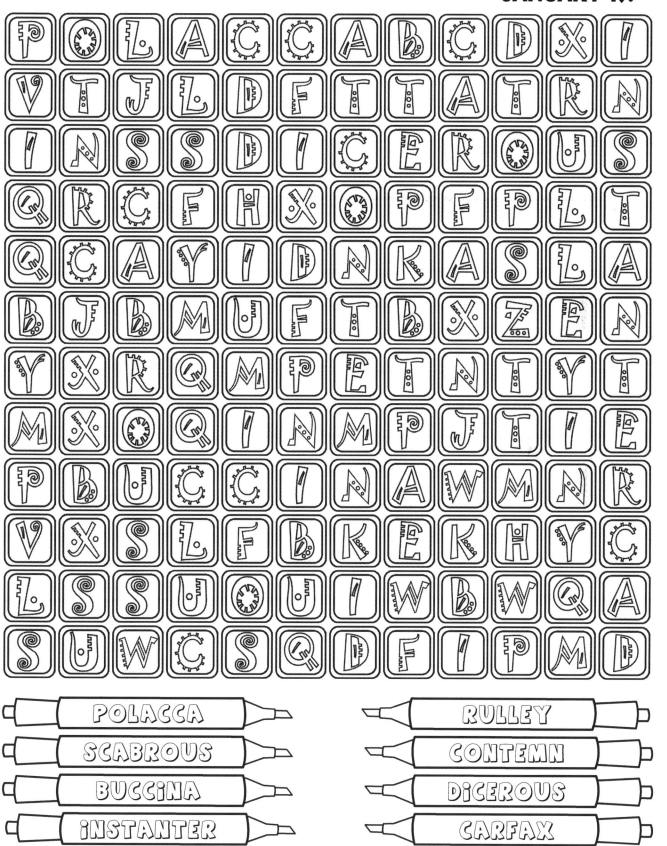

POLACCA

SCABROUS

BUCCINA

INSTANTER

RULLEY

CONTEMN

DICEROUS

CARFAX

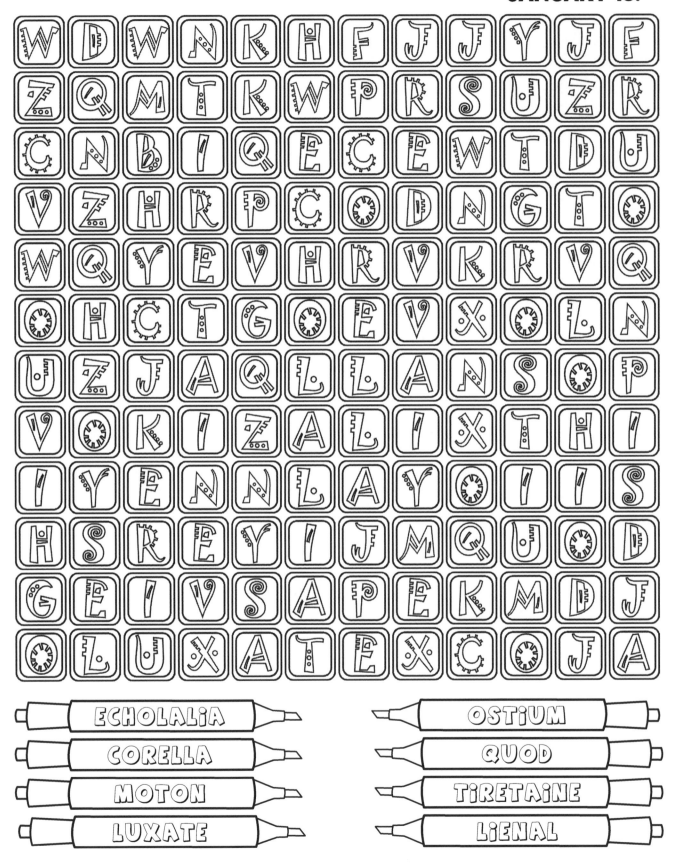

ECHOLALIA

CORELLA

MOTON

LUXATE

OSTIUM

QUOD

TIRETAINE

LIENAL

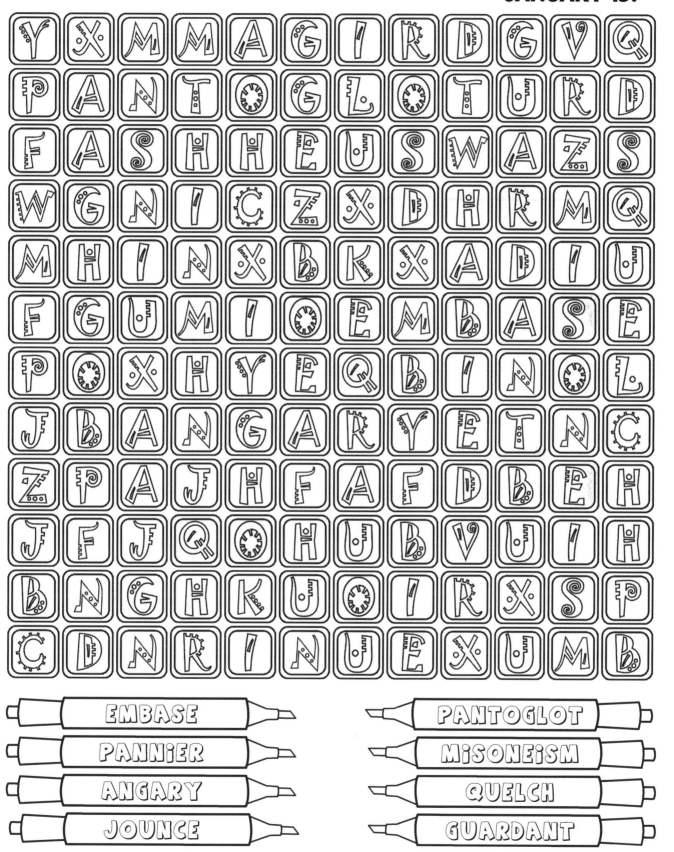

EMBASE

PANNIER

ANGARY

JOUNCE

PANTOGLOT

MISONEISM

QUELCH

GUARDANT

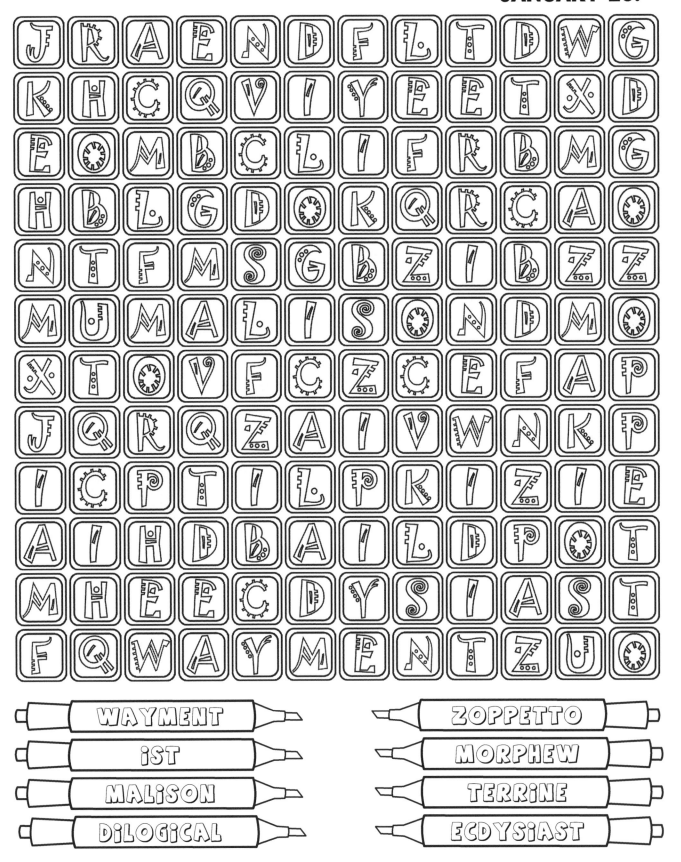

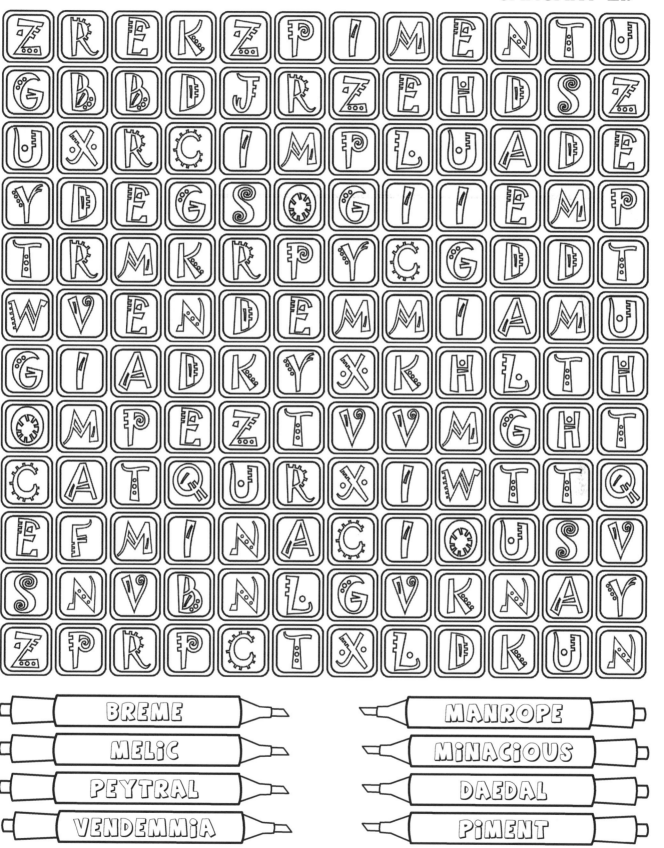

BREME

MELIC

PEYTRAL

VENDEMMIA

MANROPE

MINACIOUS

DAEDAL

PIMENT

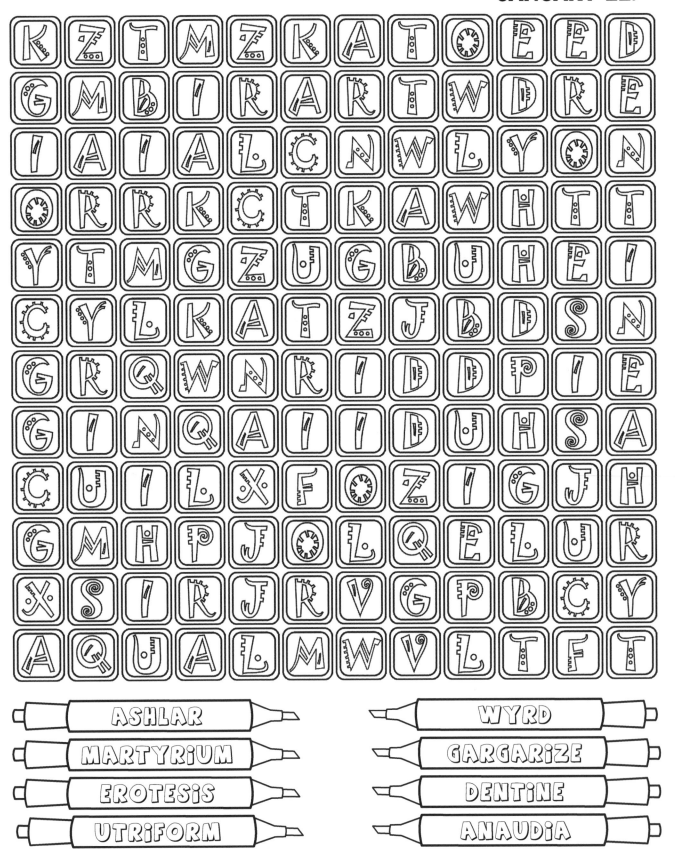

ASHLAR

MARTYRIUM

EROTESIS

UTRIFORM

WYRD

GARGARIZE

DENTINE

ANAUDIA

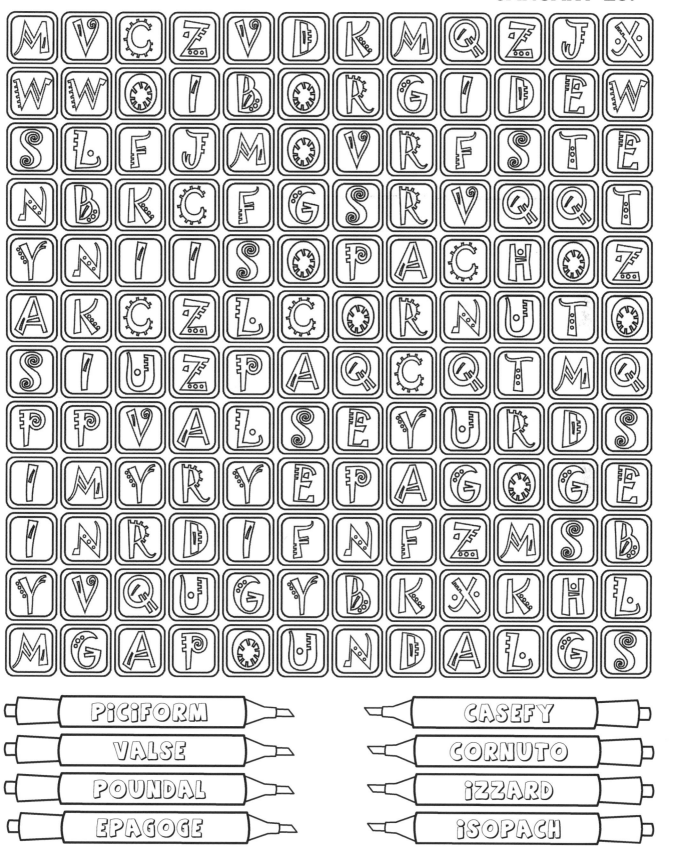

PICIFORM

VALSE

POUNDAL

EPAGOGE

CASEFY

CORNUTO

IZZARD

ISOPACH

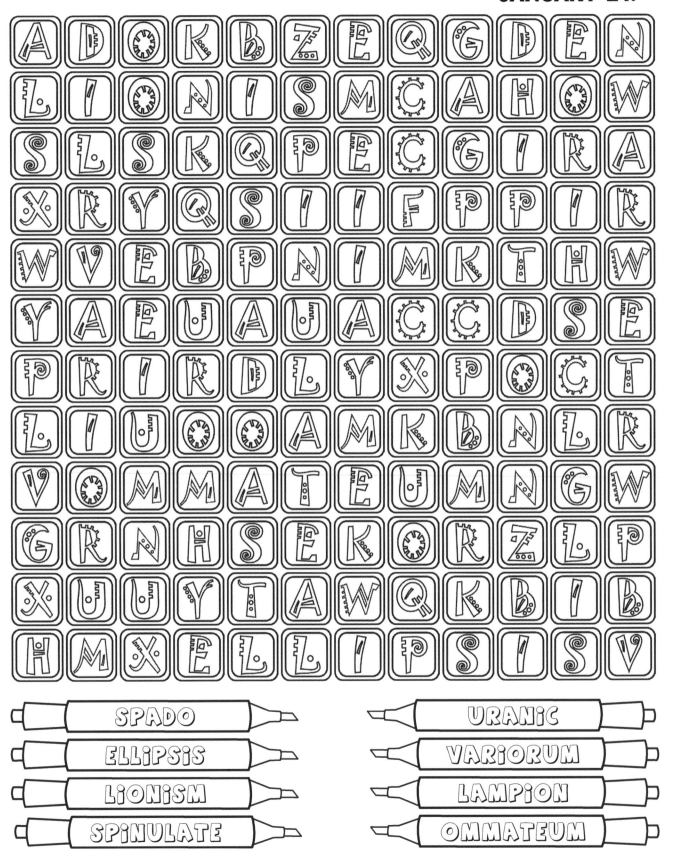

SPADO
ELLIPSIS
LIONISM
SPINULATE

URANIC
VARIORUM
LAMPION
OMMATEUM

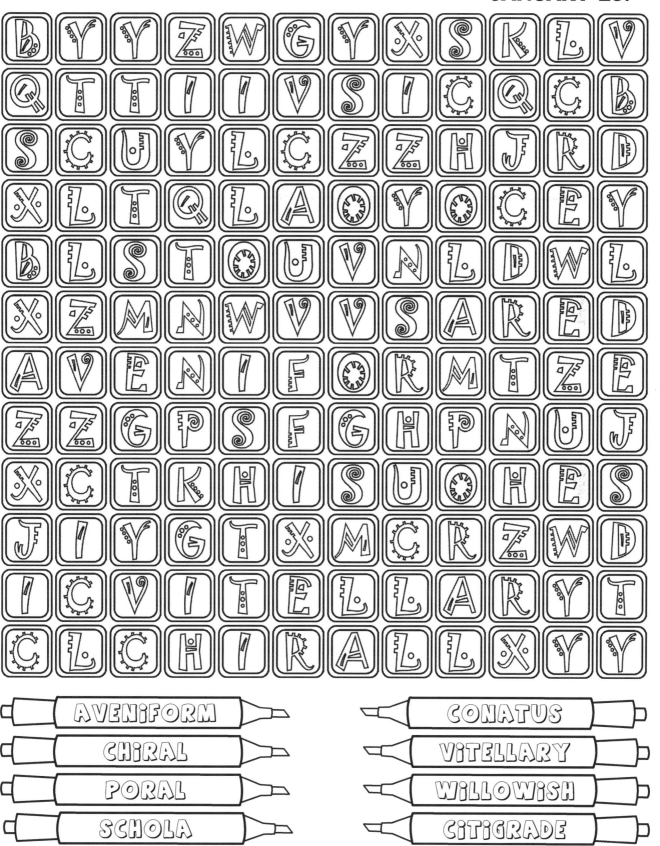

JANUARY 26:

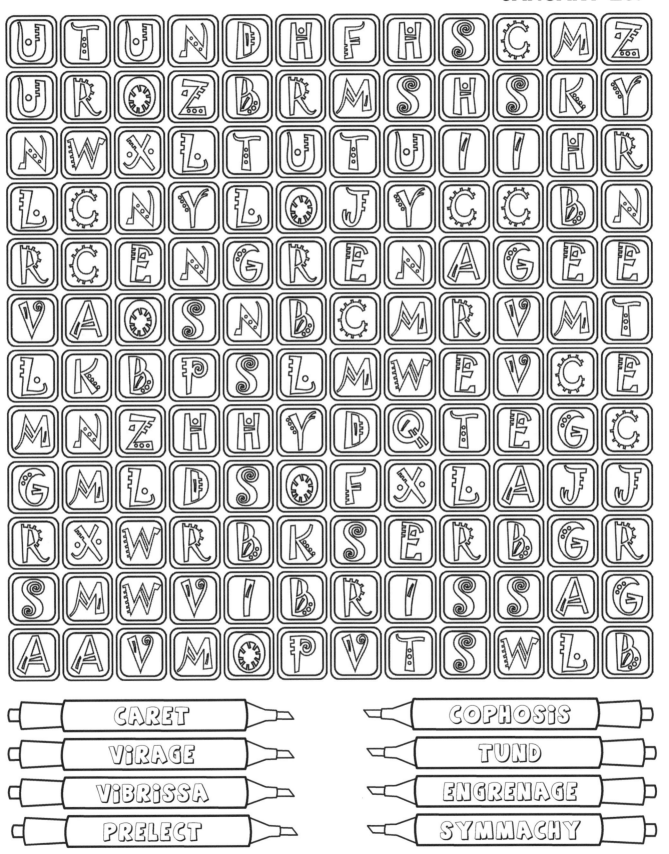

CARET

VIRAGE

VIBRISSA

PRELECT

COPHOSIS

TUND

ENGRENAGE

SYMMACHY

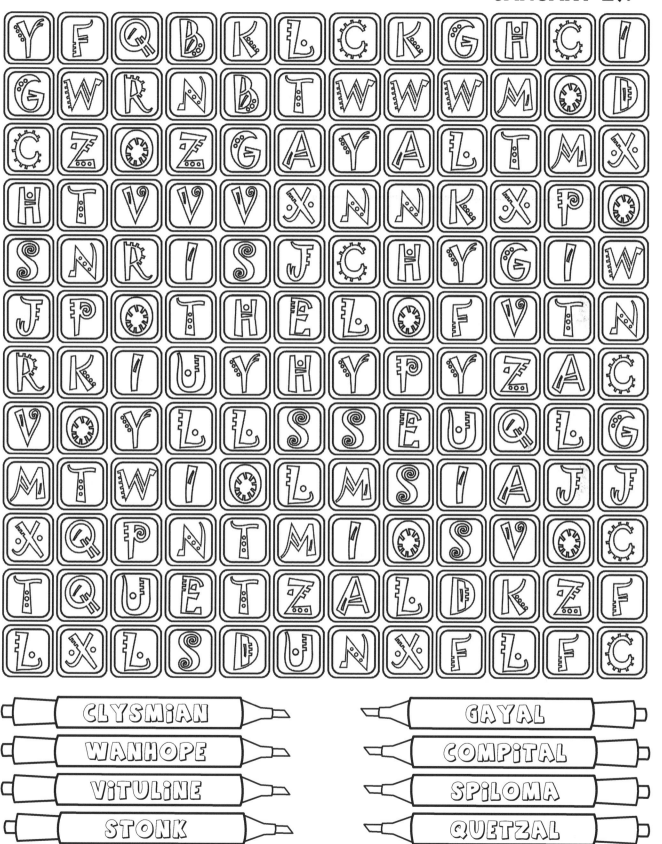

CLYSMIAN

WANHOPE

VITULINE

STONK

GAYAL

COMPITAL

SPILOMA

QUETZAL

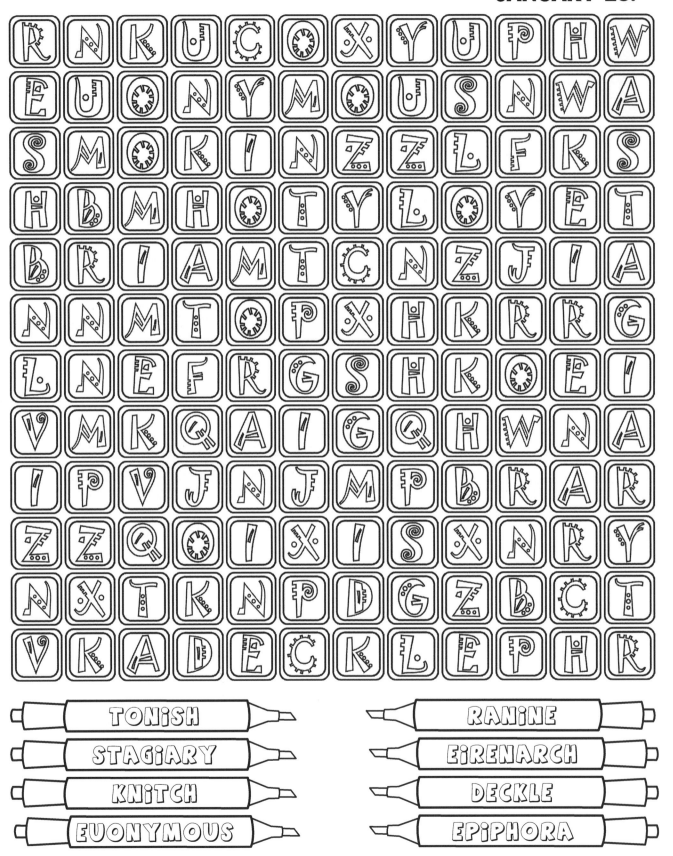

TONISH

STAGIARY

KNITCH

EUONYMOUS

RANINE

EIRENARCH

DECKLE

EPIPHORA

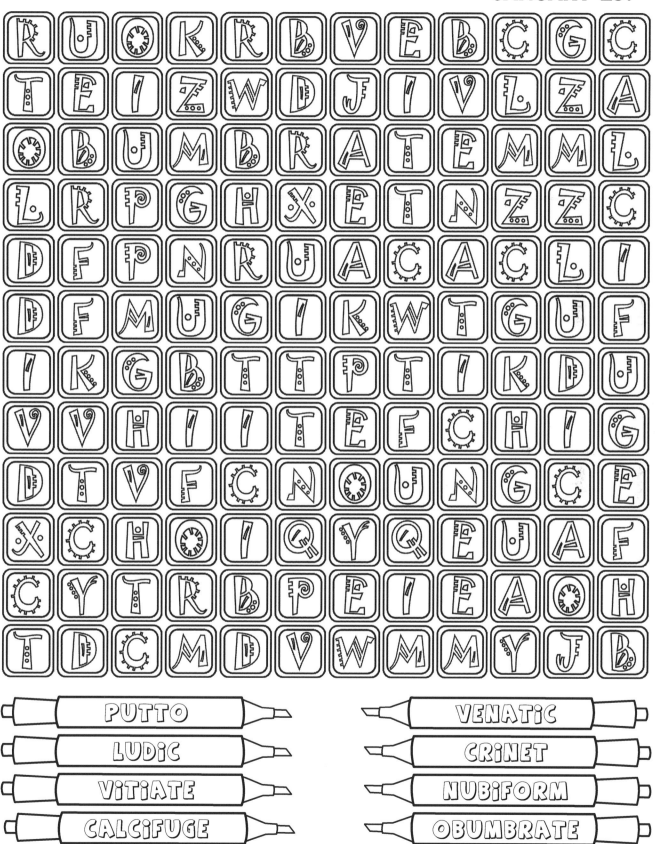

PUTTO

LUDIC

VITIATE

CALCIFUGE

VENATIC

CRINET

NUBIFORM

OBUMBRATE

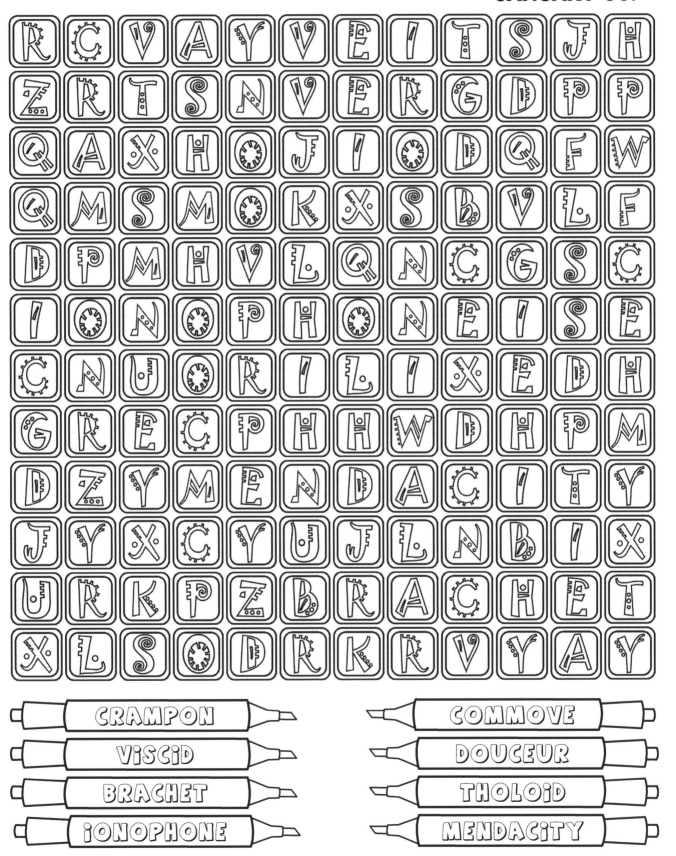

CRAMPON

COMMOVE

VISCID

DOUCEUR

BRACHET

THOLOID

IONOPHONE

MENDACITY

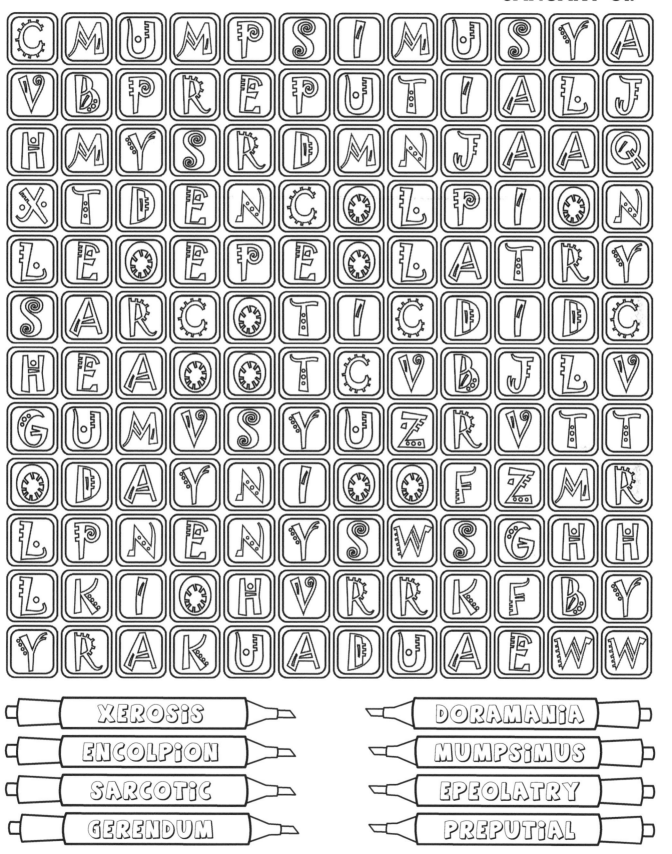

XEROSIS

ENCOLPION

SARCOTIC

GERENDUM

DORAMANIA

MUMPSIMUS

EPEOLATRY

PREPUTIAL

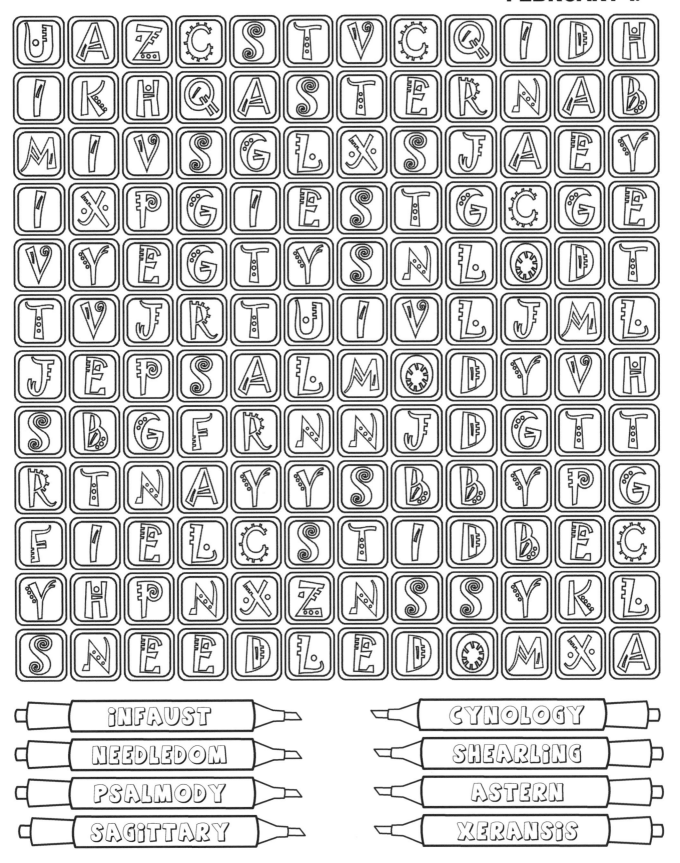

INFAUST

NEEDLEDOM

PSALMODY

SAGITTARY

CYNOLOGY

SHEARLING

ASTERN

XERANSIS

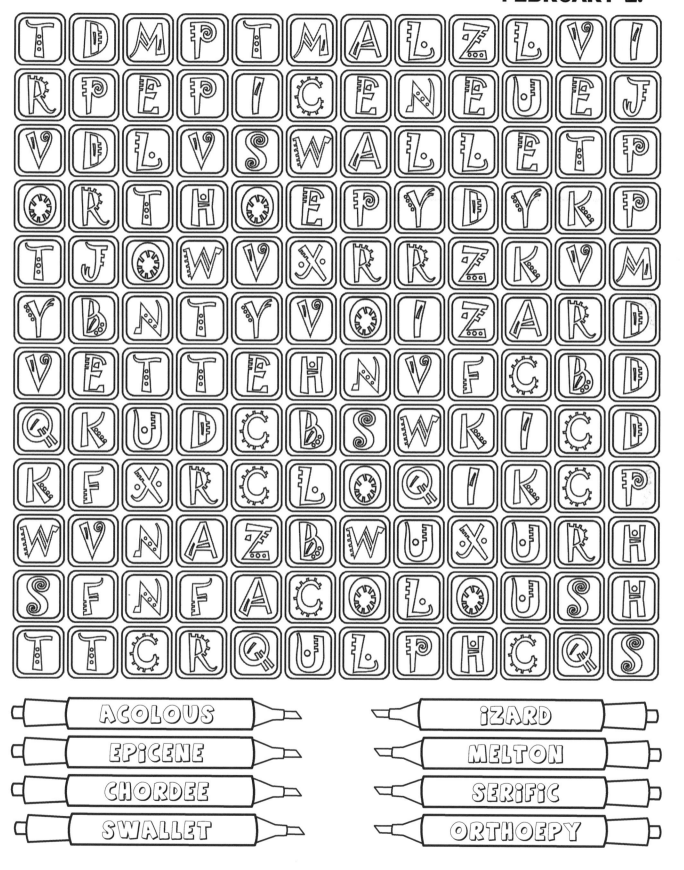

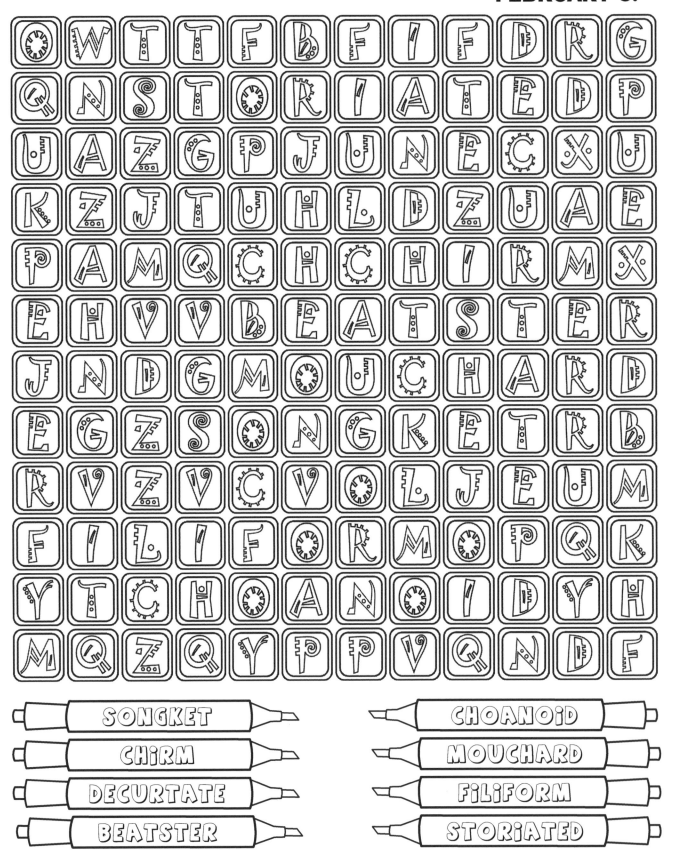

SONGKET

CHIRM

DECURTATE

BEATSTER

CHOANOID

MOUCHARD

FILIFORM

STORIATED

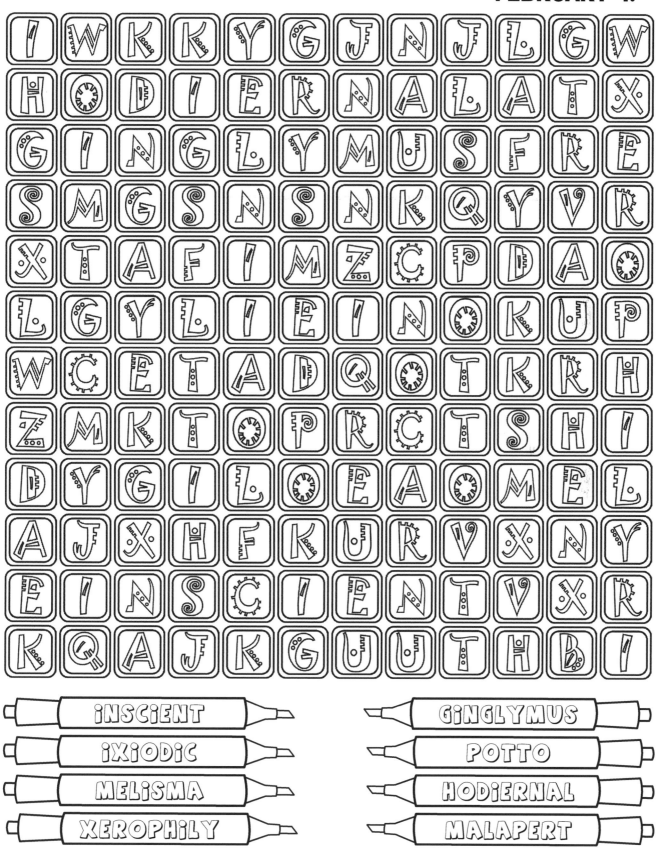

INSCIENT
IXIODIC
MELISMA
XEROPHILY

GINGLYMUS
POTTO
HODIERNAL
MALAPERT

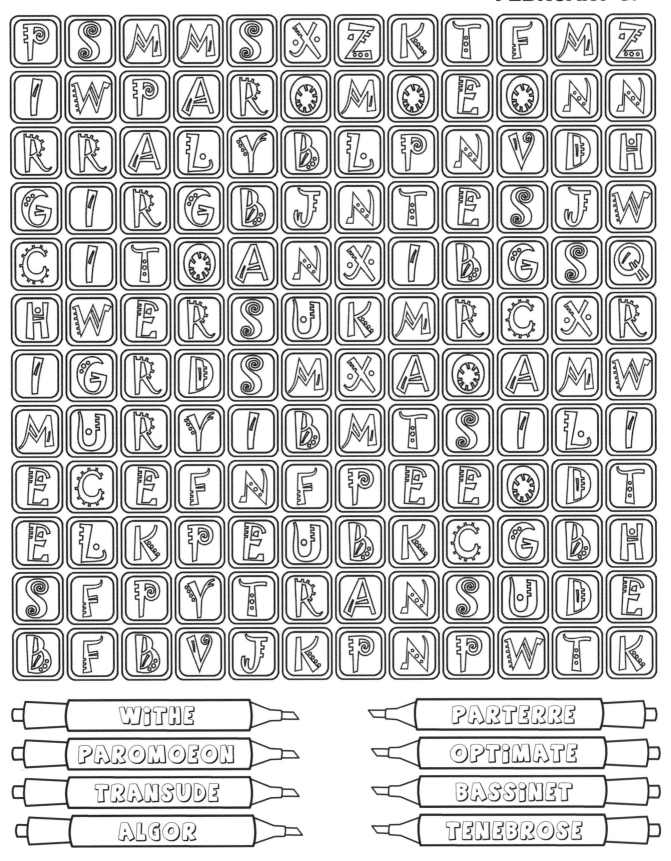

WITHE

PAROMOEON

TRANSUDE

ALGOR

PARTERRE

OPTIMATE

BASSINET

TENEBROSE

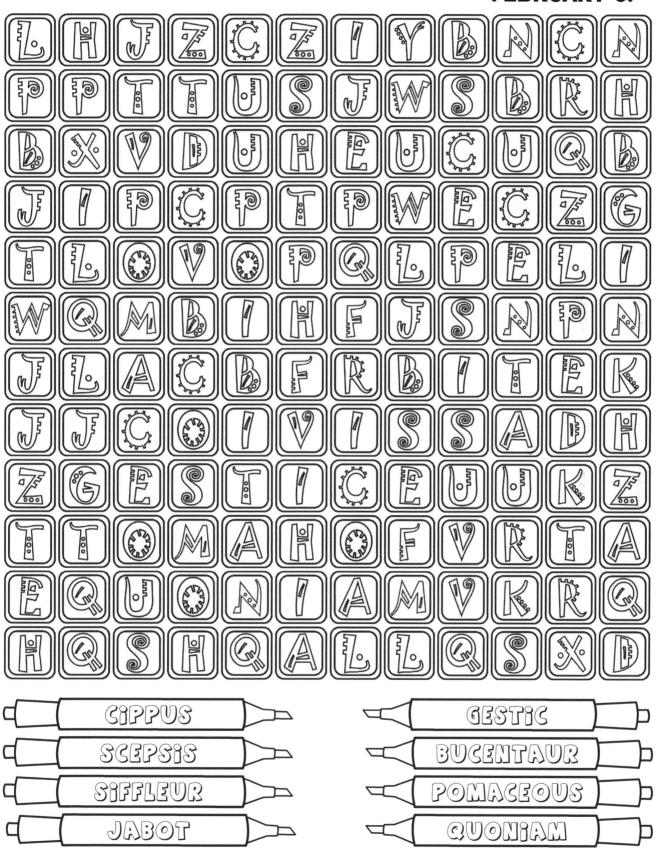

CIPPUS

SCEPSIS

SIFFLEUR

JABOT

GESTIC

BUCENTAUR

POMACEOUS

QUONIAM

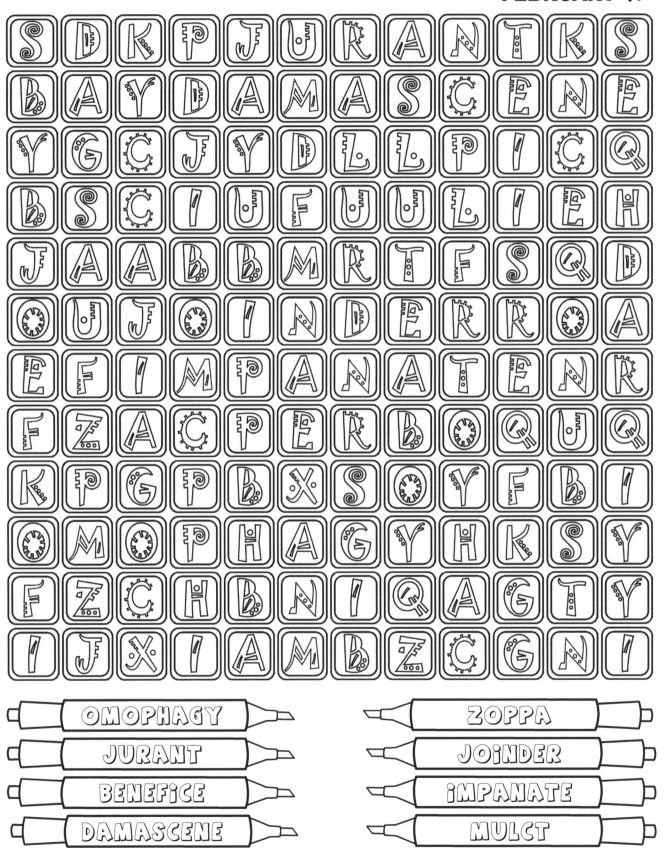

OMOPHAGY

ZOPPA

JURANT

JOINDER

BENEFICE

IMPANATE

DAMASCENE

MULCT

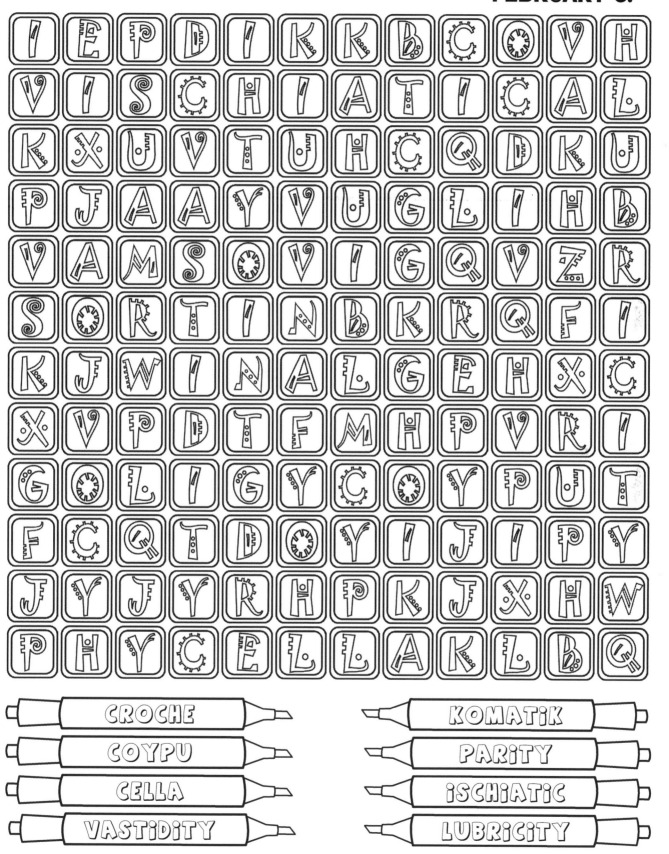

CROCHE

KOMATIK

COYPU

PARITY

CELLA

ISCHIATIC

VASTIDITY

LUBRICITY

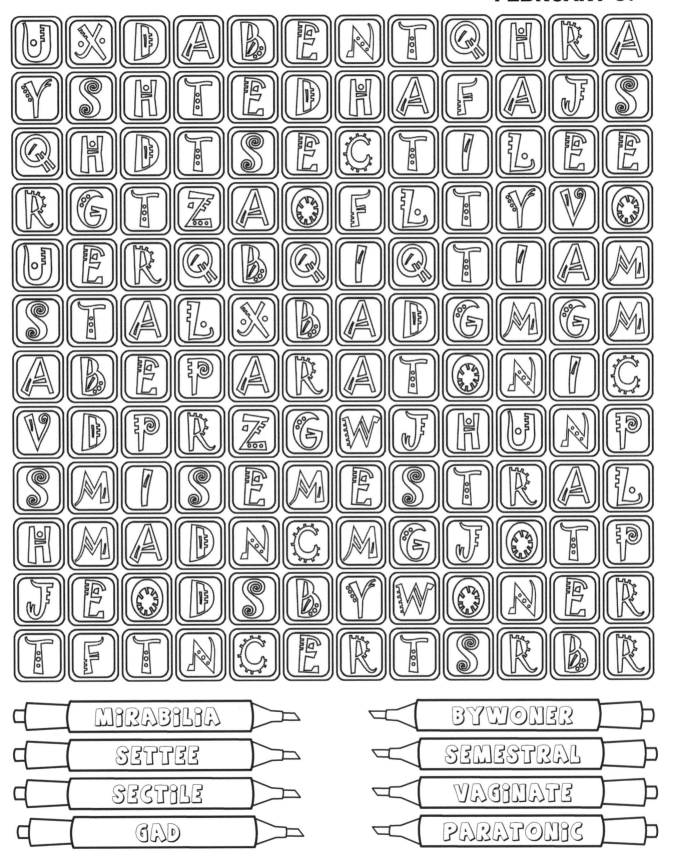

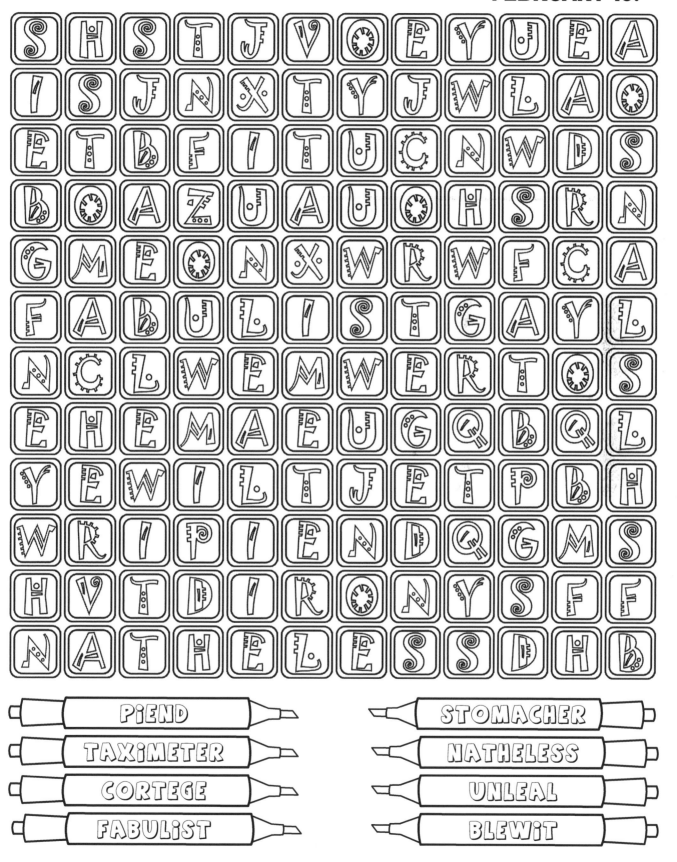

PIEND

TAXIMETER

CORTEGE

FABULIST

STOMACHER

NATHELESS

UNLEAL

BLEWIT

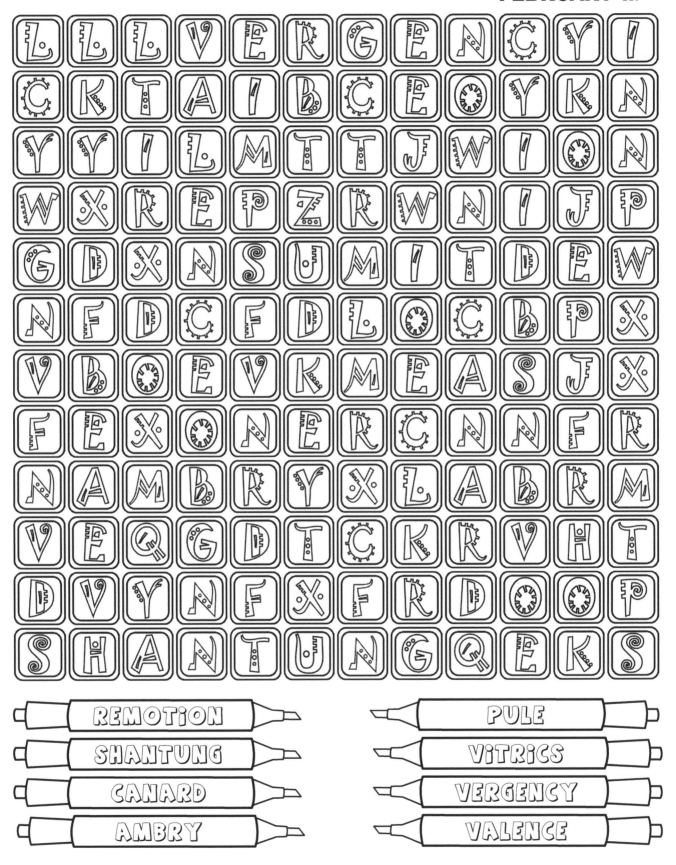

LLLVERGENCYI
CKTAIBCEOYKN
YYILMTTJWION
WXREPZRWNJP
GDXNSUMITDEW
NFDCFDLOCBPX
VBOEVKMEASJX
FEXONERCNNFR
NAMBRYXLABRM
VEQGDTCKRVHT
DVYNFXFRDOOP
SHANTUNGQEKS

REMOTION

SHANTUNG

CANARD

AMBRY

PULE

VITRICS

VERGENCY

VALENCE

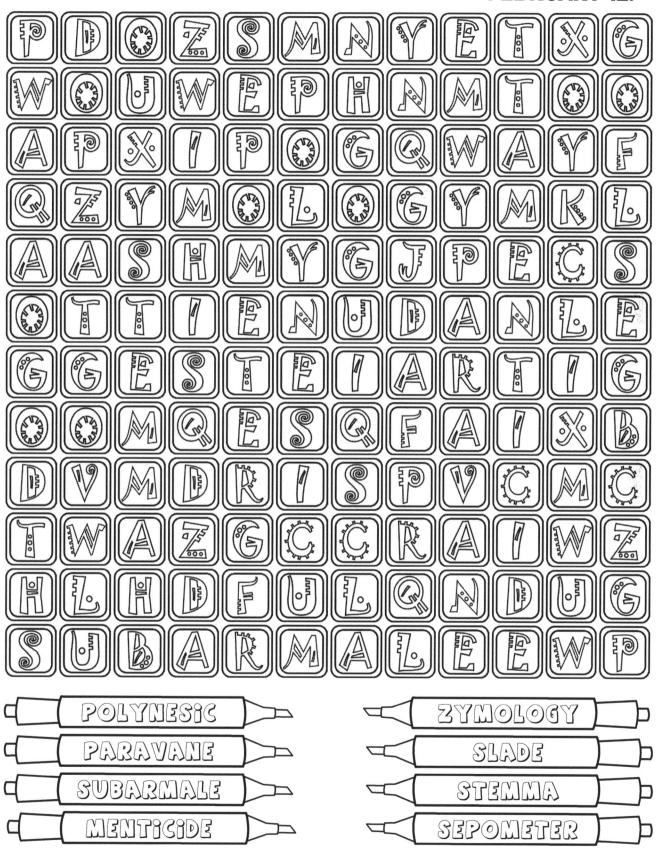

POLYNESIC

PARAVANE

SUBARMALE

MENTICIDE

ZYMOLOGY

SLADE

STEMMA

SEPOMETER

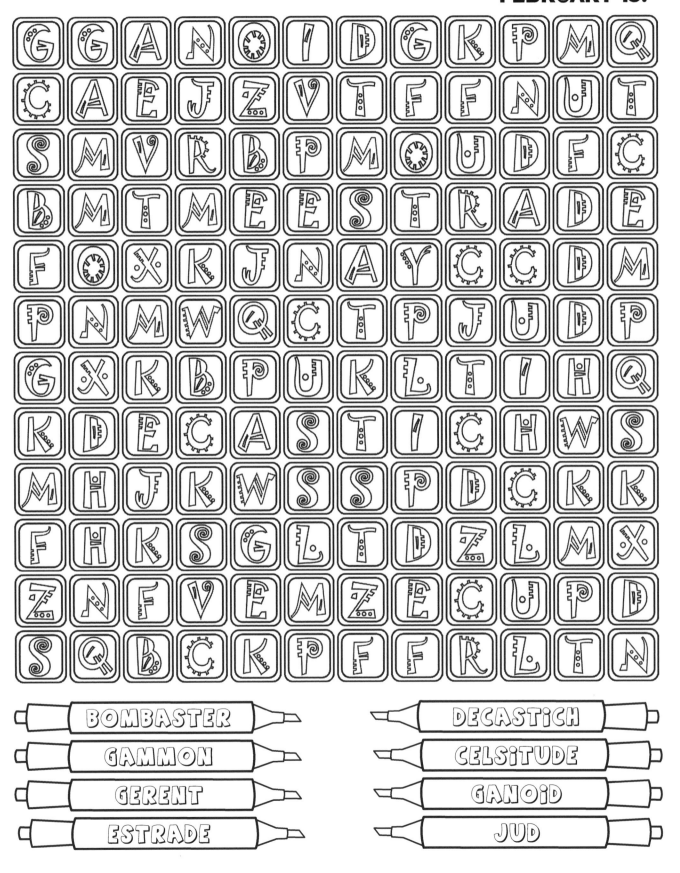

BOMBASTER

GAMMON

GERENT

ESTRADE

DECASTICH

CELSITUDE

GANOID

JUD

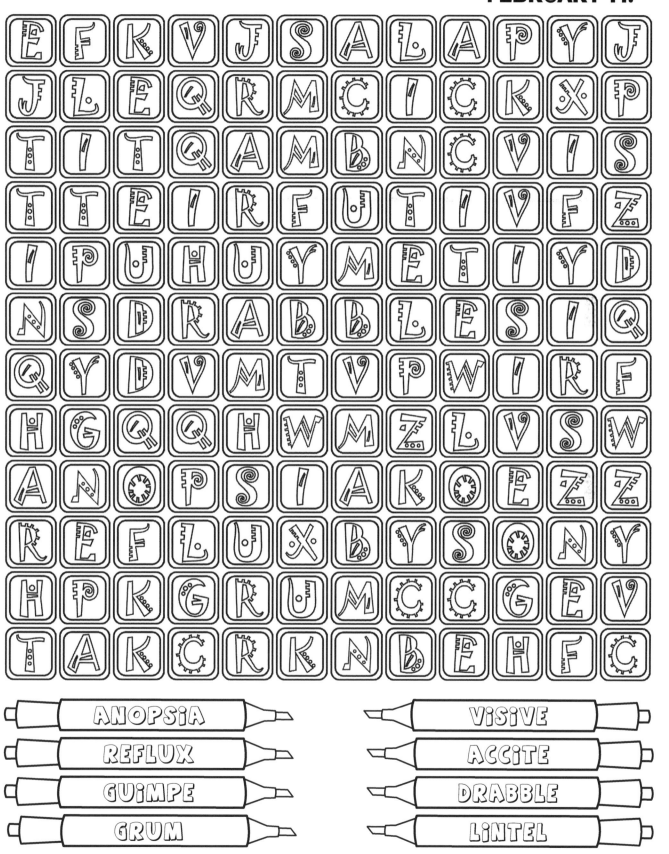

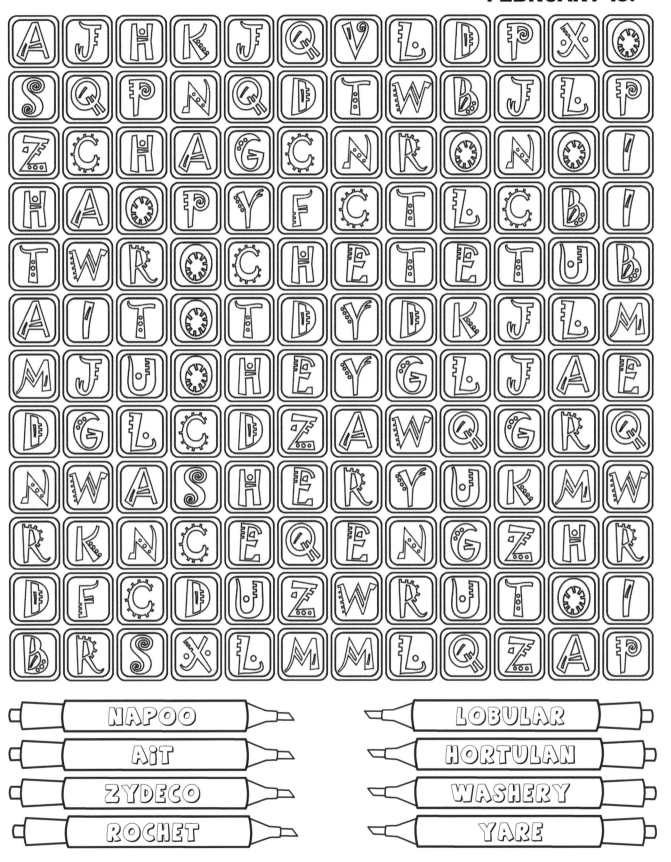

NAPOO

AIT

ZYDECO

ROCHET

LOBULAR

HORTULAN

WASHERY

YARE

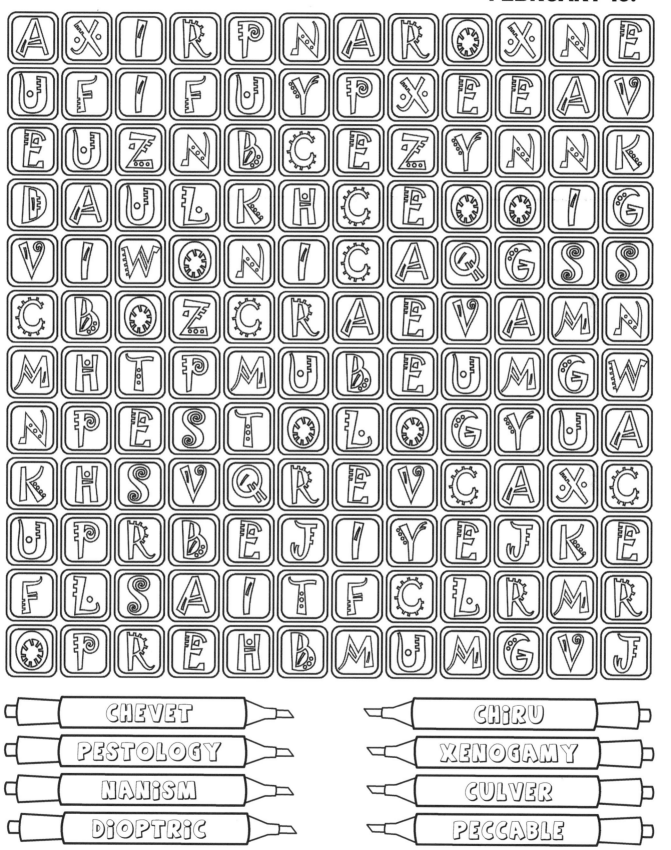

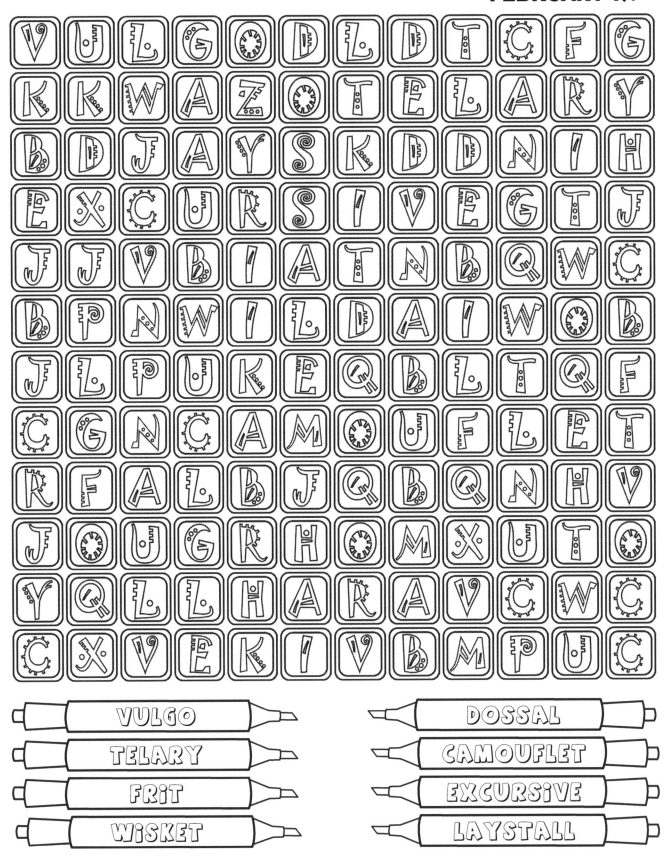

VULGO

TELARY

FRIT

WISKET

DOSSAL

CAMOUFLET

EXCURSIVE

LAYSTALL

FEBRUARY 18:

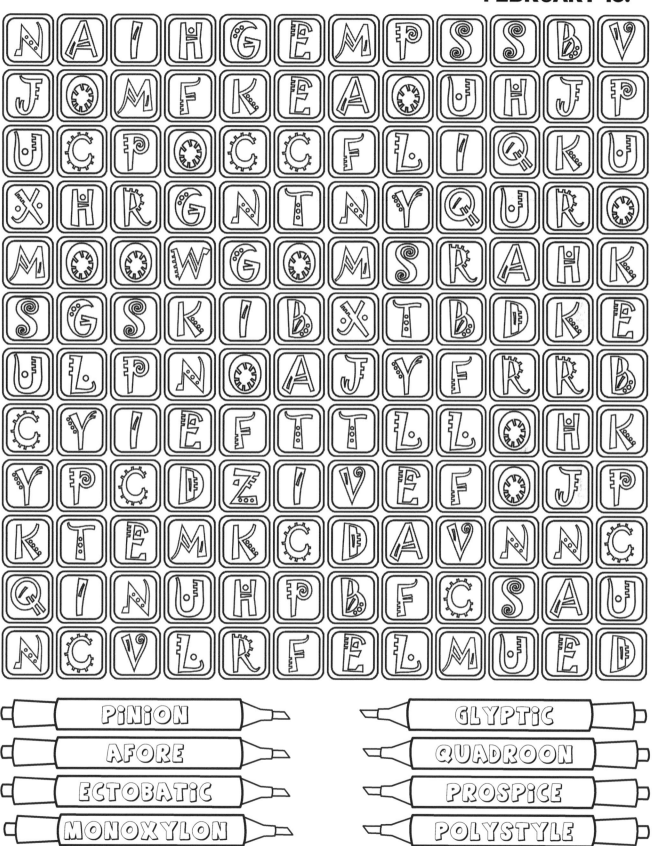

PINION

AFORE

ECTOBATIC

MONOXYLON

GLYPTIC

QUADROON

PROSPICE

POLYSTYLE

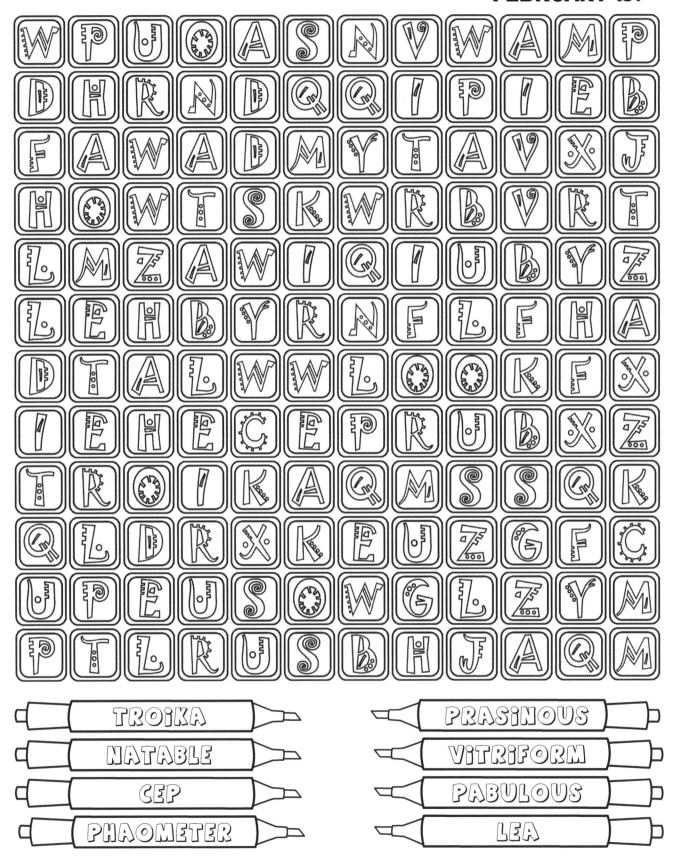

TROIKA

NATABLE

CEP

PHAOMETER

PRASINOUS

VITRIFORM

PABULOUS

LEA

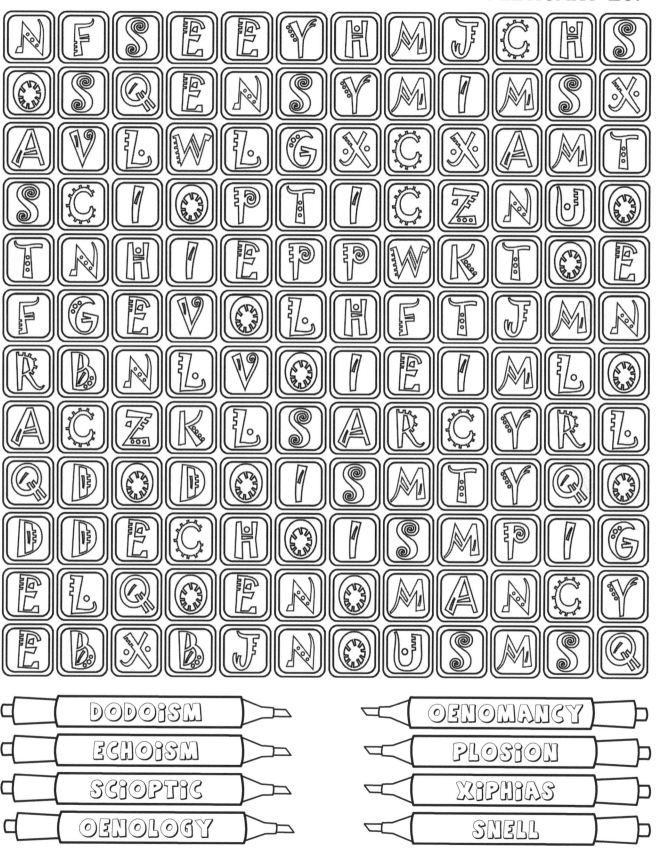

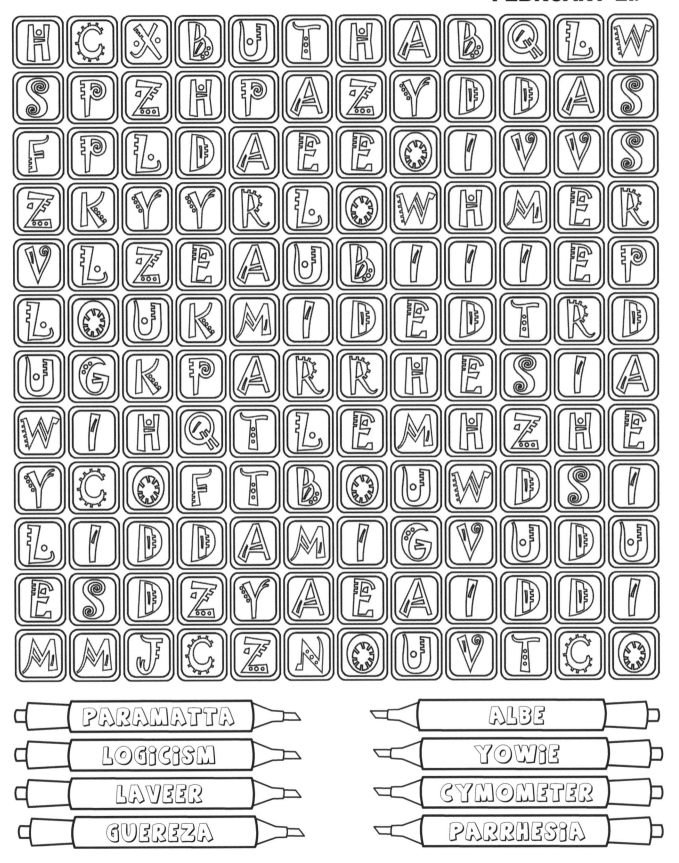

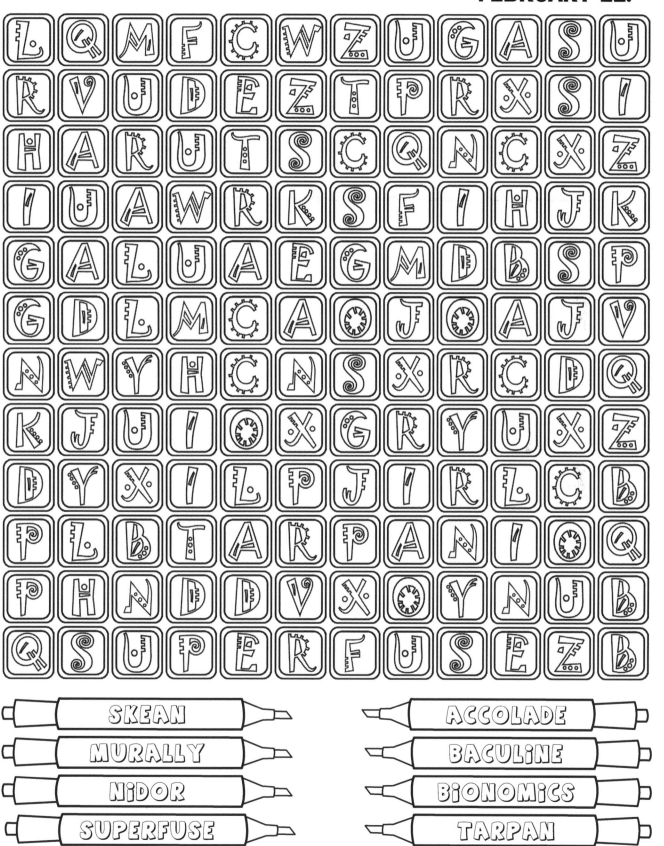

SKEAN

MURALLY

NIDOR

SUPERFUSE

ACCOLADE

BACULINE

BIONOMICS

TARPAN

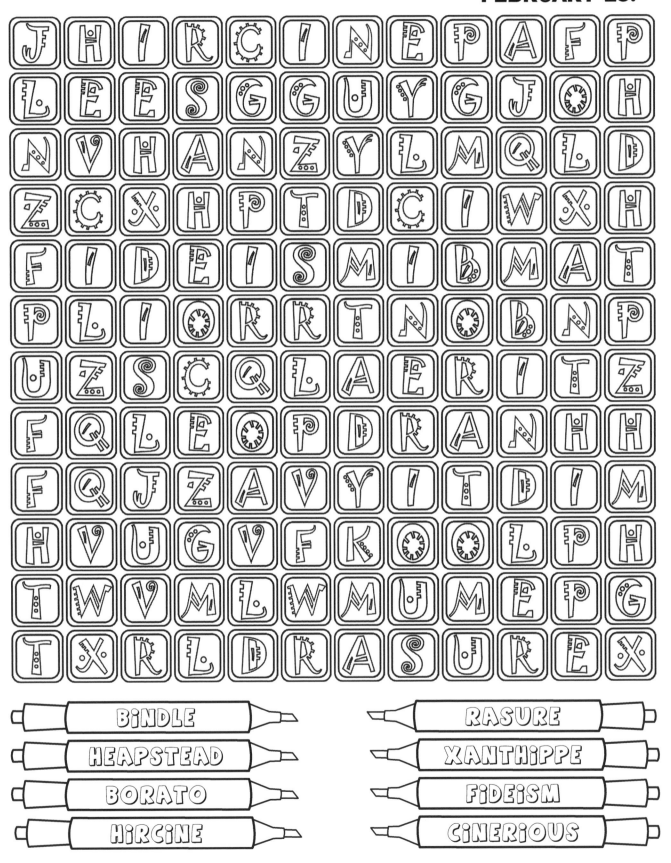

BINDLE

HEAPSTEAD

BORATO

HIRCINE

RASURE

XANTHIPPE

FIDEISM

CINERIOUS

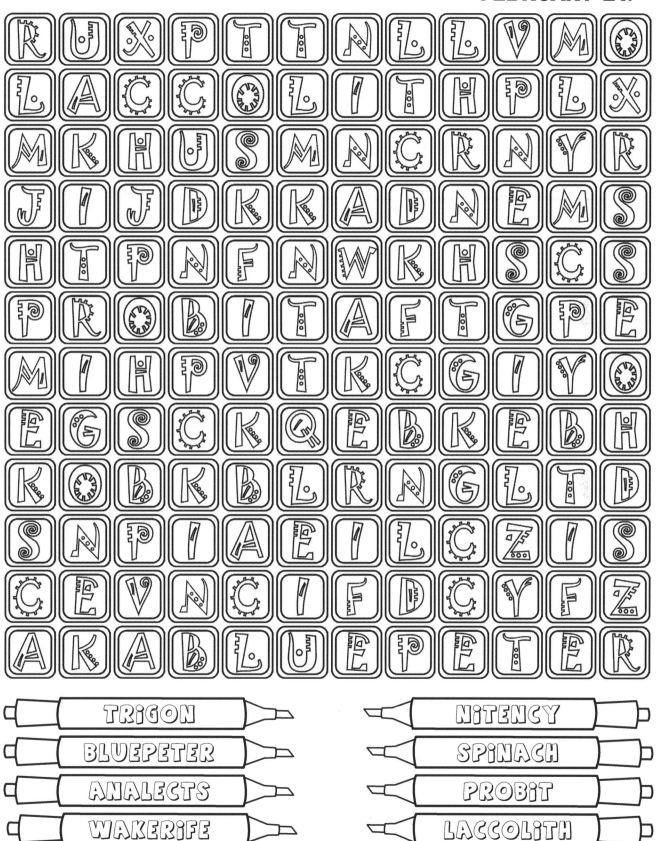

TRIGON

BLUEPETER

ANALECTS

WAKERIFE

NITENCY

SPINACH

PROBIT

LACCOLITH

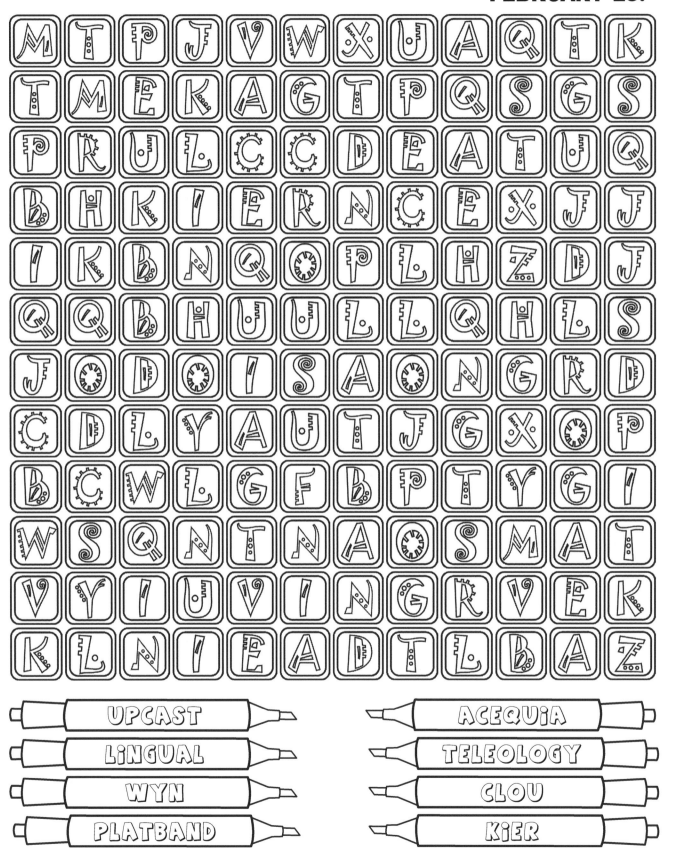

UPCAST

LINGUAL

WYN

PLATBAND

ACEQUIA

TELEOLOGY

CLOU

KIER

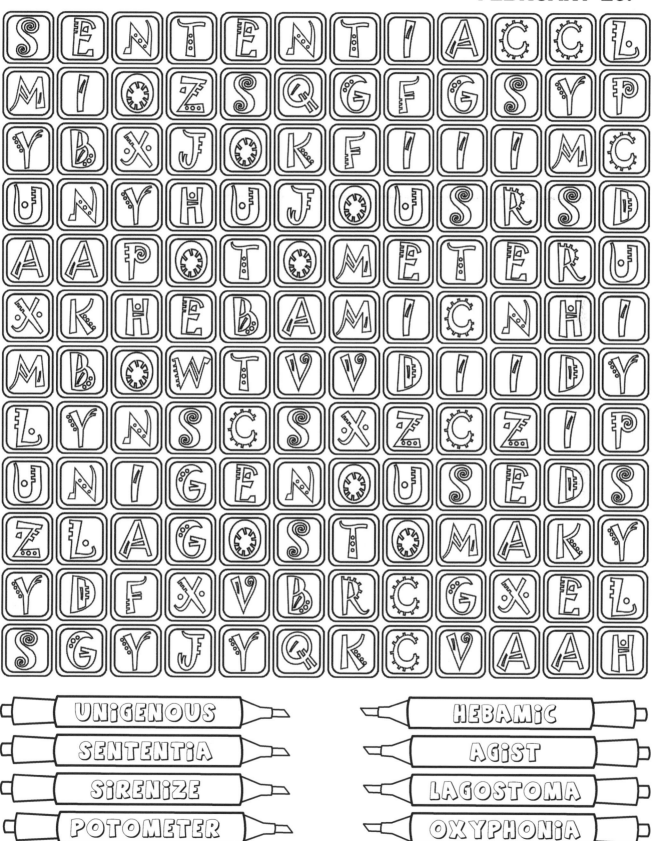

UNIGENOUS

SENTENTIA

SIRENIZE

POTOMETER

HEBAMIC

AGIST

LAGOSTOMA

OXYPHONIA

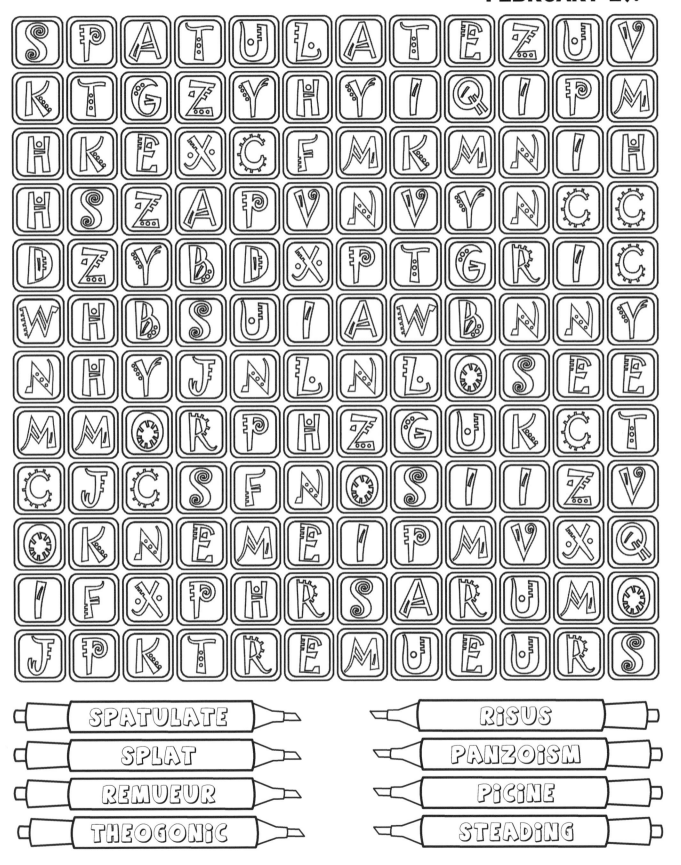

SPATULATE

SPLAT

REMUEUR

THEOGONIC

RISUS

PANZOISM

PICINE

STEADING

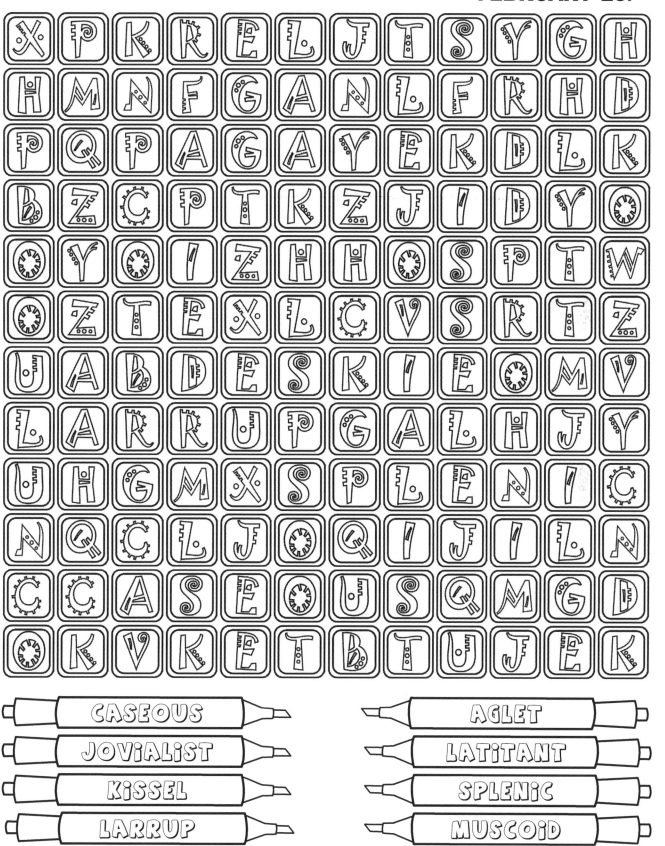

CASEOUS

JOVIALIST

KISSEL

LARRUP

AGLET

LATITANT

SPLENIC

MUSCOID

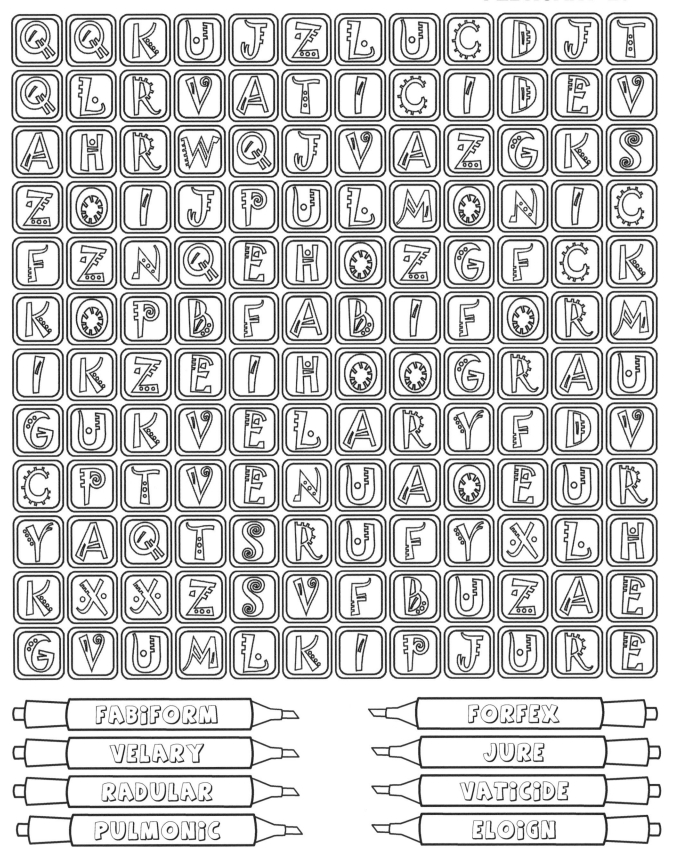

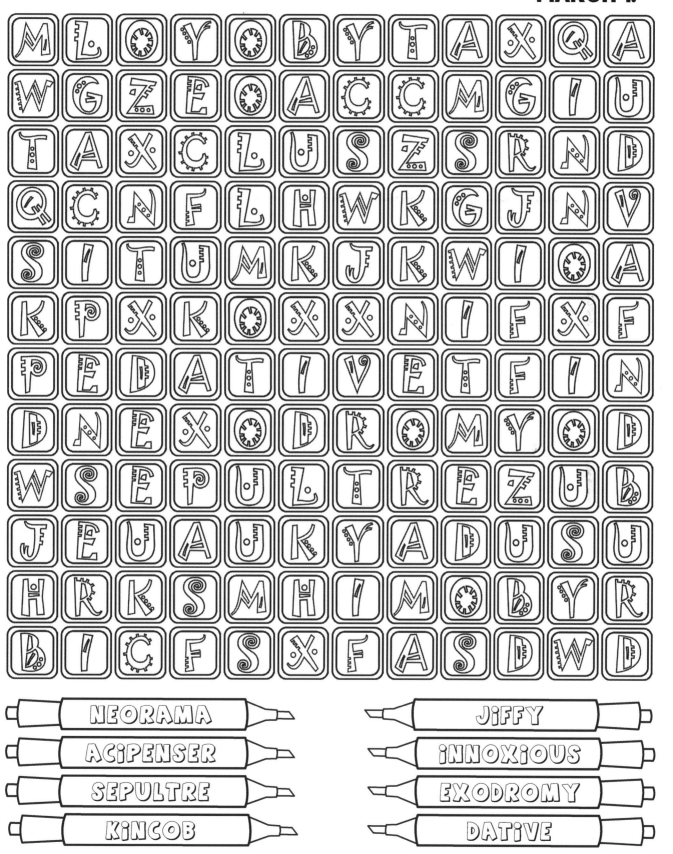

NEORAMA

JIFFY

ACIPENSER

INNOXIOUS

SEPULTRE

EXODROMY

KINCOB

DATIVE

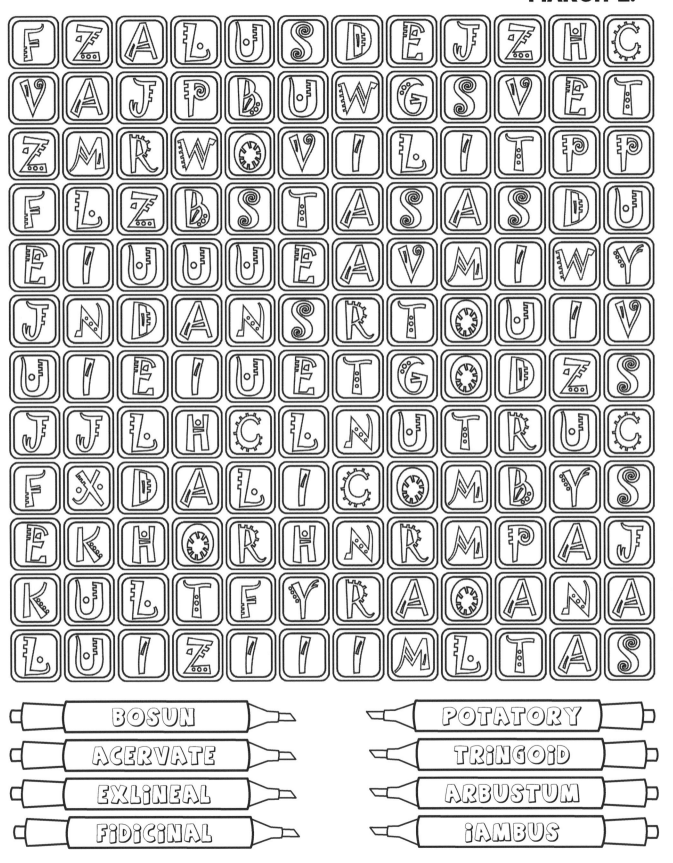

BOSUN

POTATORY

ACERVATE

TRINGOID

EXLINEAL

ARBUSTUM

FIDICINAL

IAMBUS

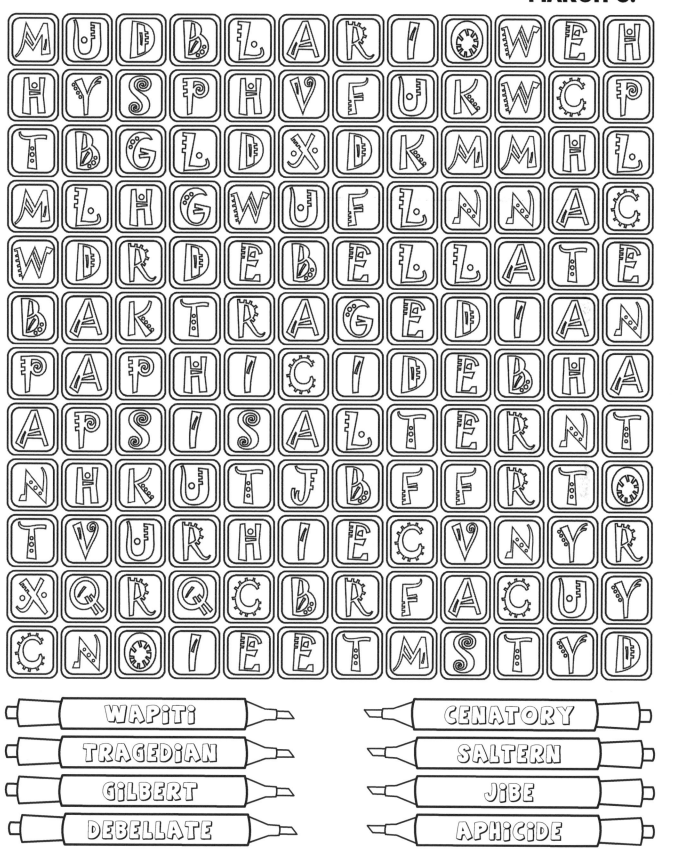

WAPITI

TRAGEDIAN

GILBERT

DEBELLATE

CENATORY

SALTERN

JIBE

APHICIDE

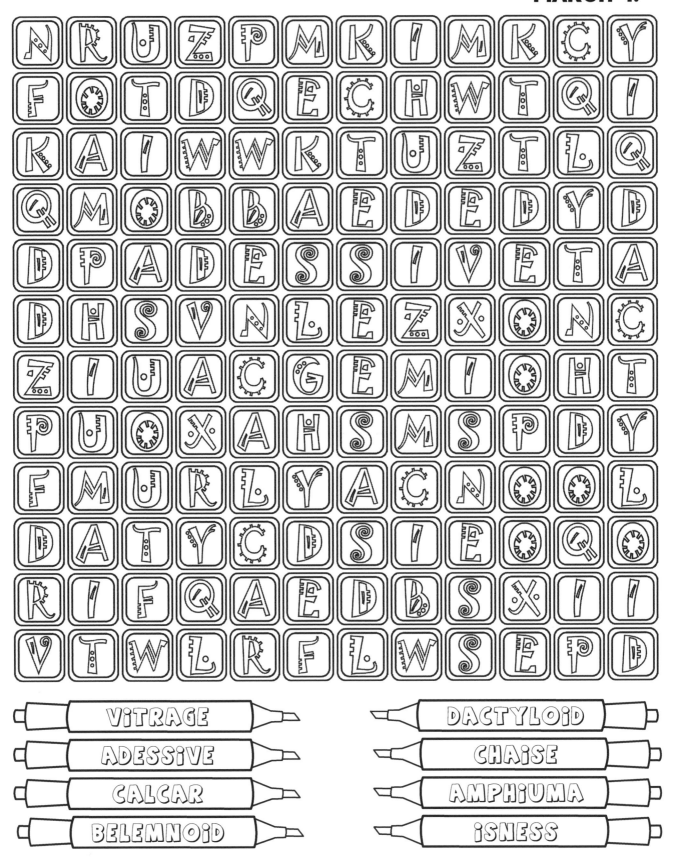

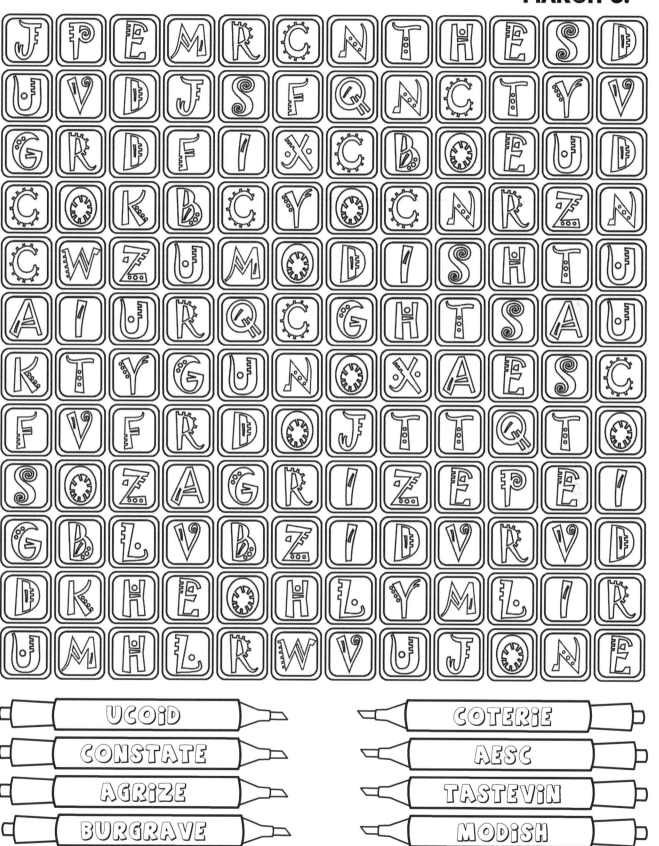

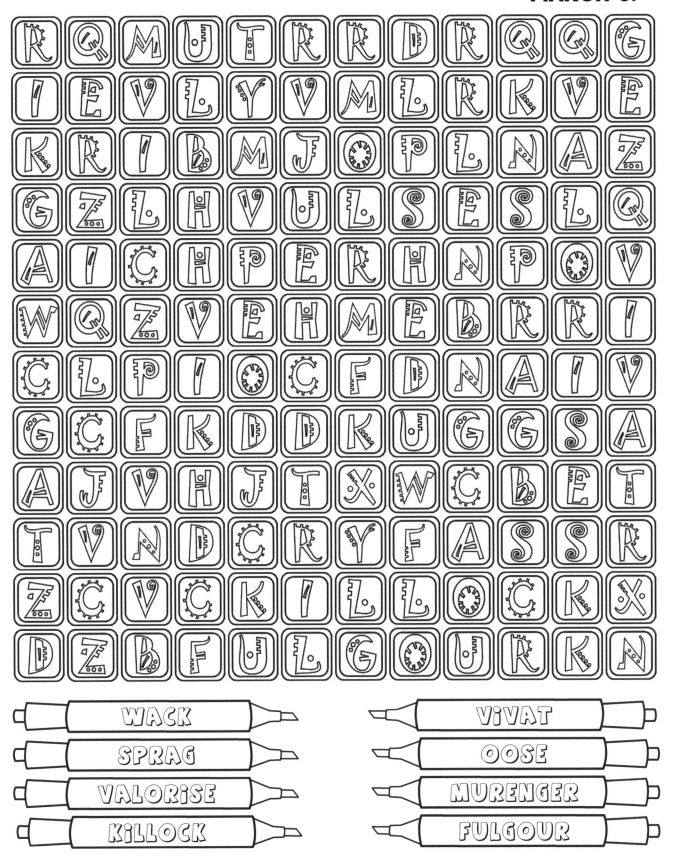

WACK

SPRAG

VALORISE

KILLOCK

VIVAT

OOSE

MURENGER

FULGOUR

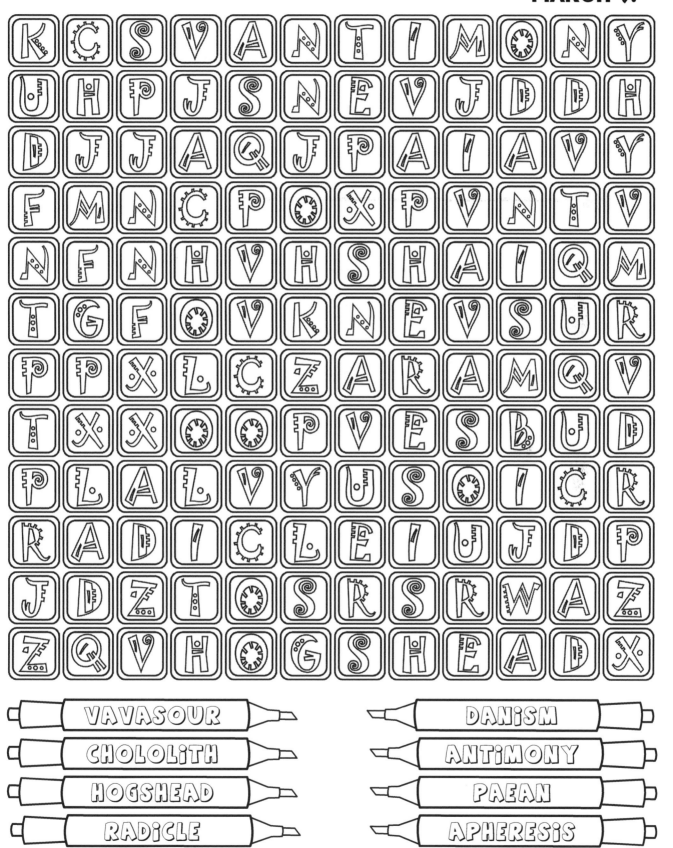

VAVASOUR

CHOLOLITH

HOGSHEAD

RADICLE

DANISM

ANTIMONY

PAEAN

APHERESIS

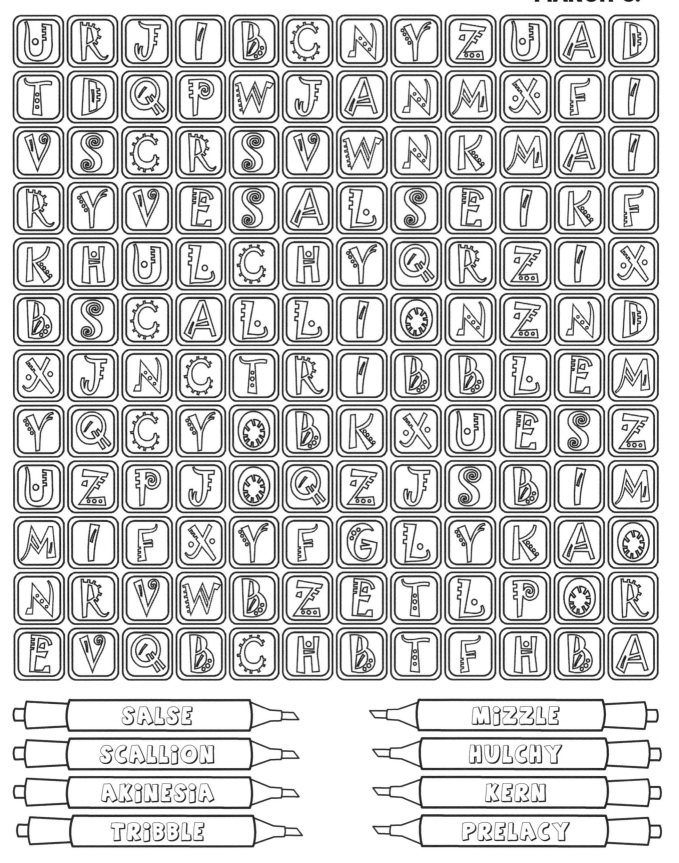

SALSE

SCALLION

AKINESIA

TRIBBLE

MIZZLE

HULCHY

KERN

PRELACY

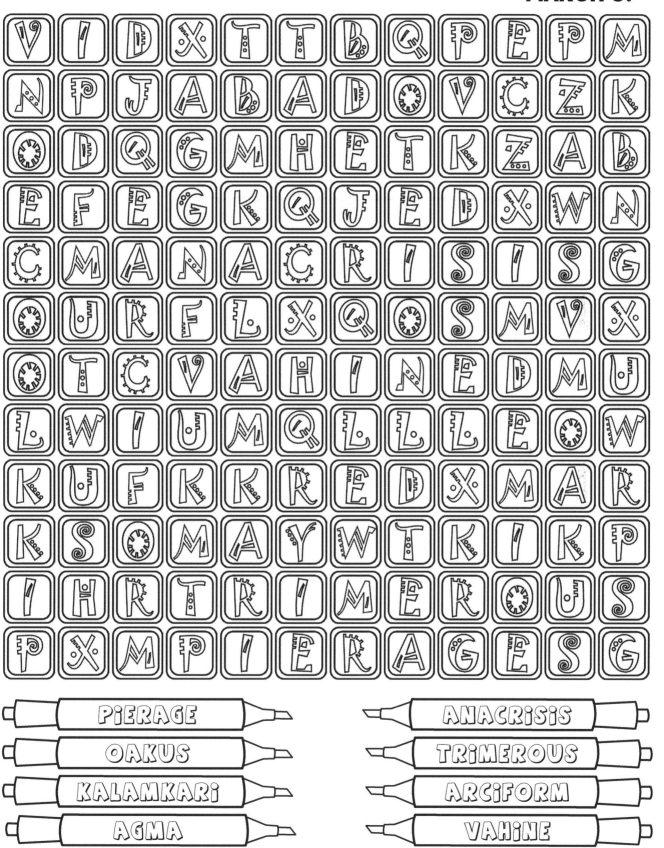

PIERAGE

OAKUS

KALAMKARI

AGMA

ANACRISIS

TRIMEROUS

ARCIFORM

VAHINE

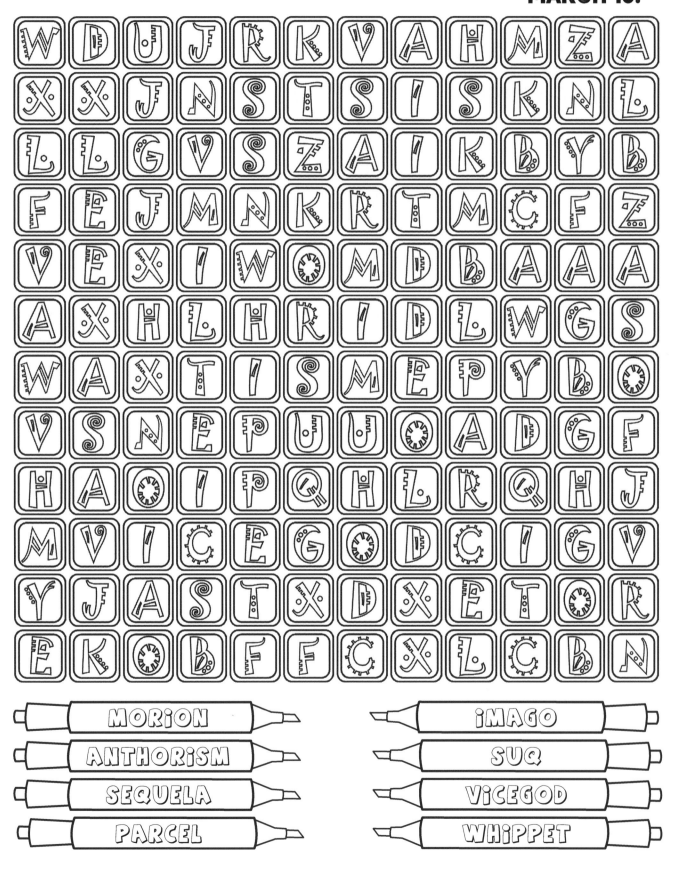

MORION

ANTHORISM

SEQUELA

PARCEL

IMAGO

SUQ

VICEGOD

WHIPPET

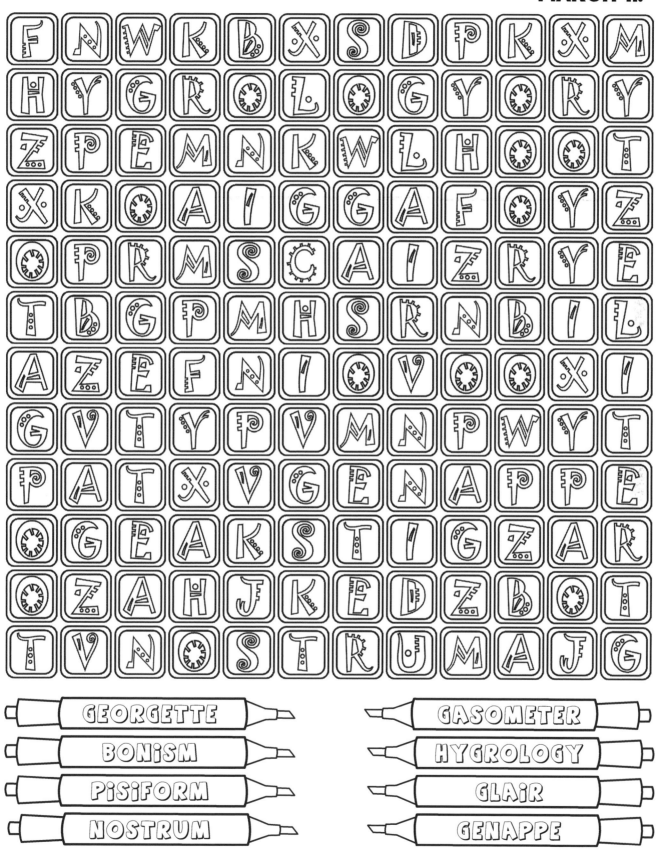

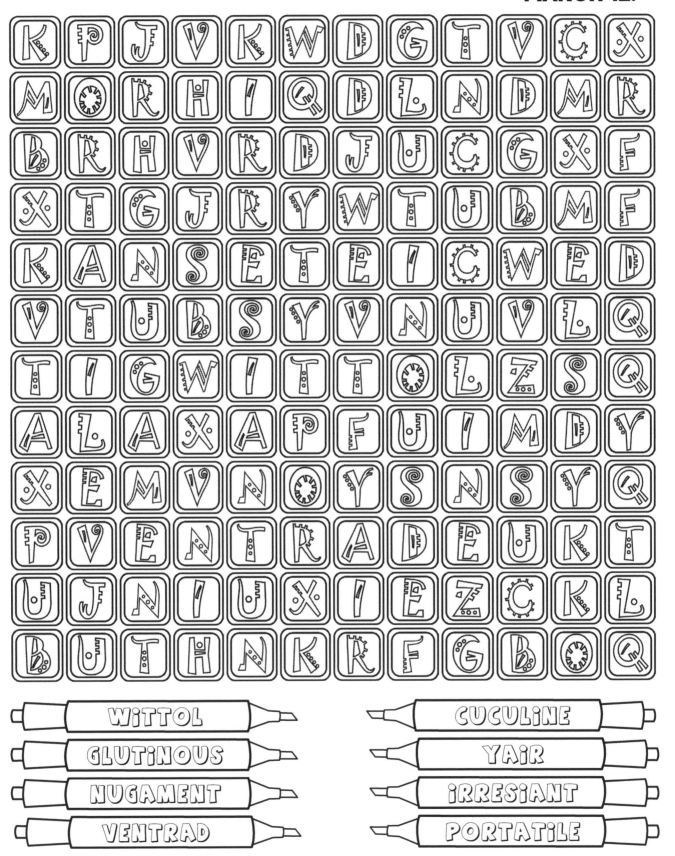

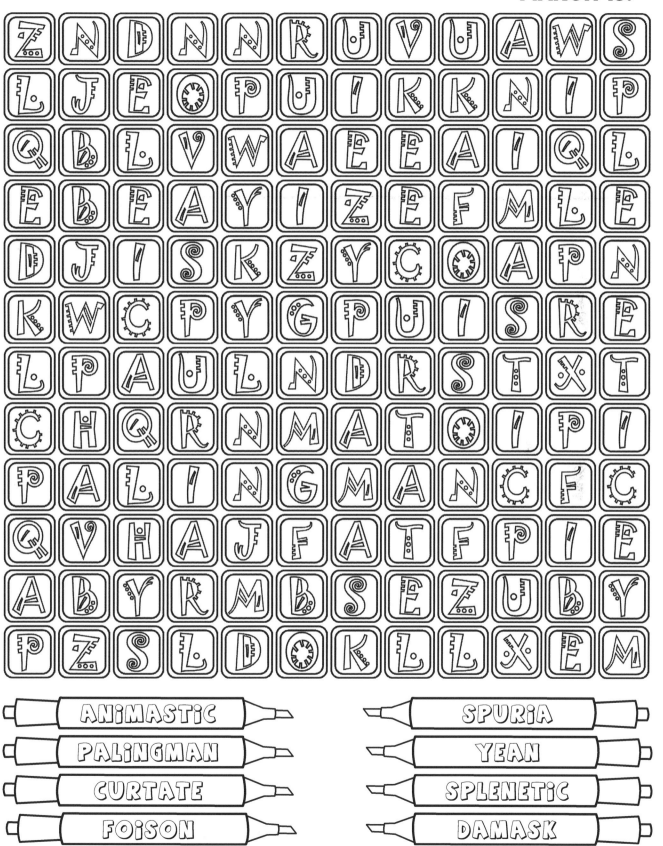

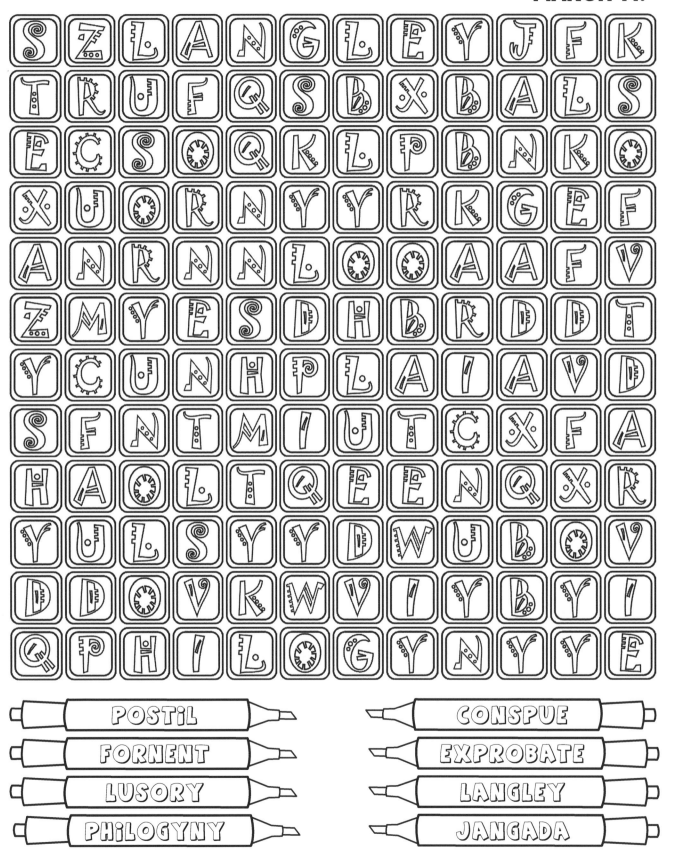

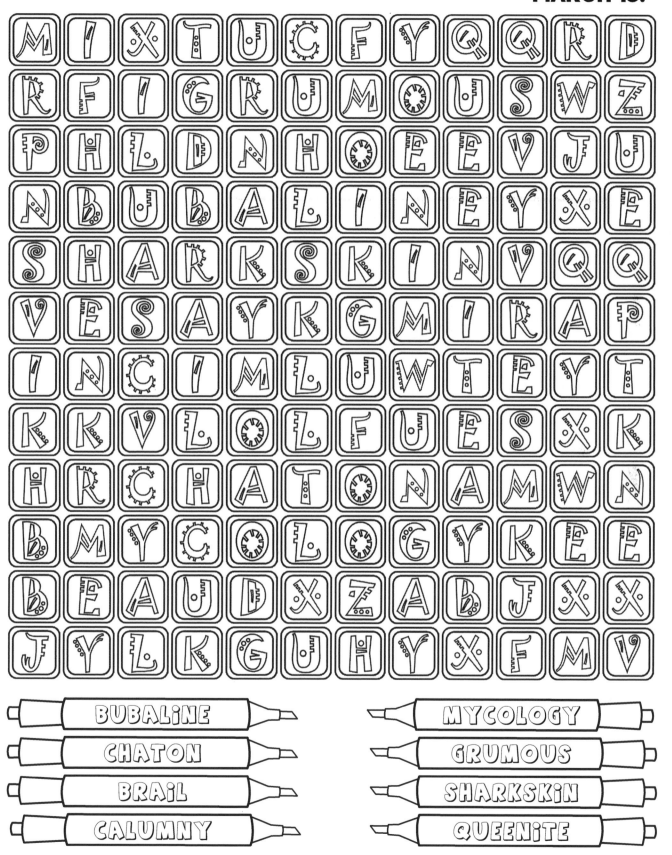

BUBALINE

CHATON

BRAIL

CALUMNY

MYCOLOGY

GRUMOUS

SHARKSKIN

QUEENITE

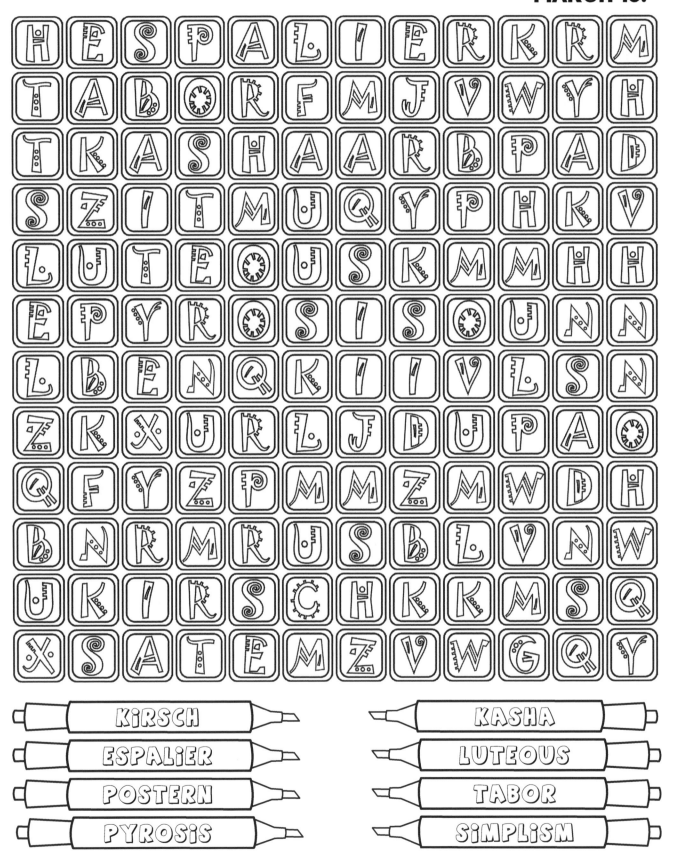

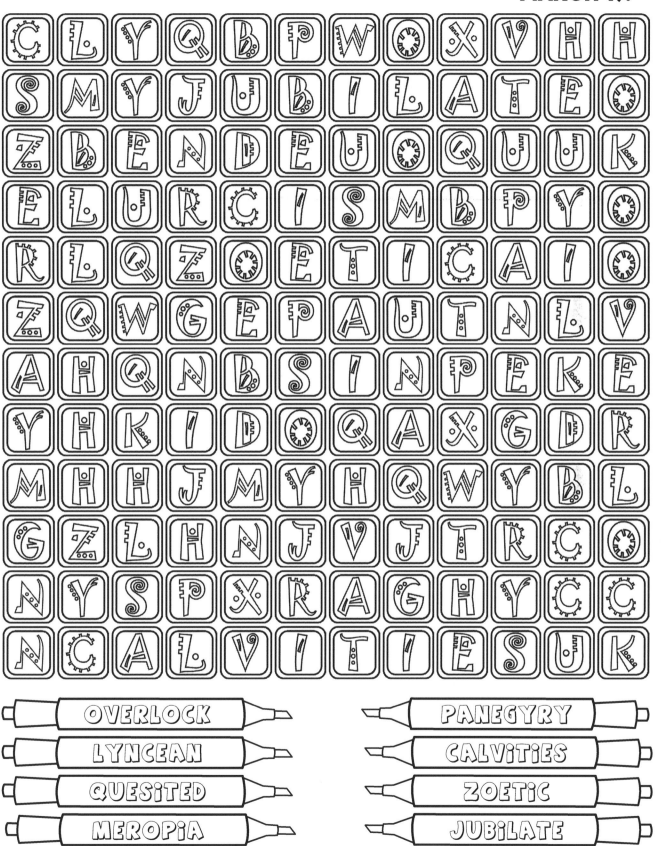

OVERLOCK

PANEGYRY

LYNCEAN

CALVITIES

QUESITED

ZOETIC

MEROPIA

JUBILATE

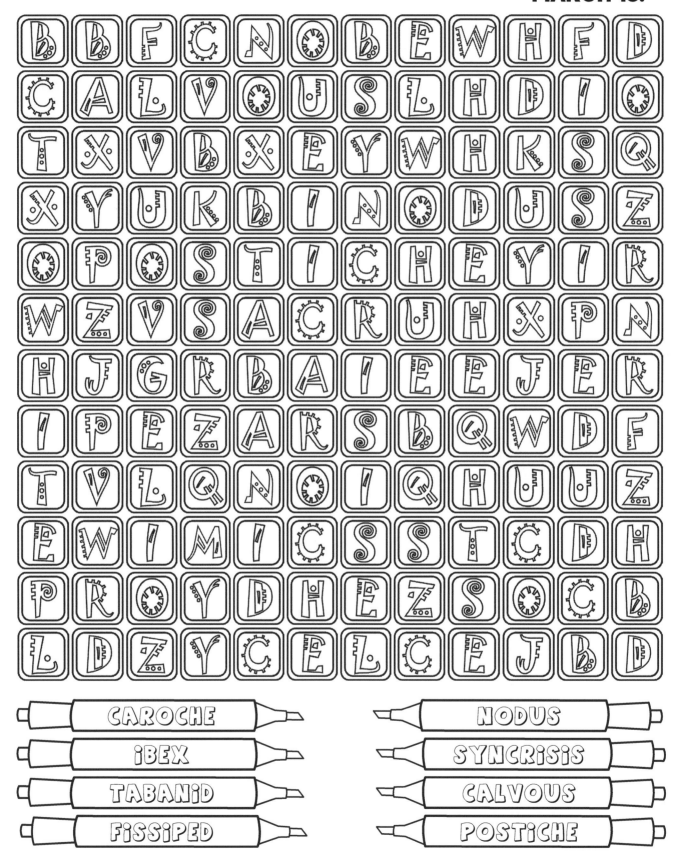

CAROCHE

iBEX

TABANiD

FiSSiPED

NODUS

SYNCRiSiS

CALVOUS

POSTiCHE

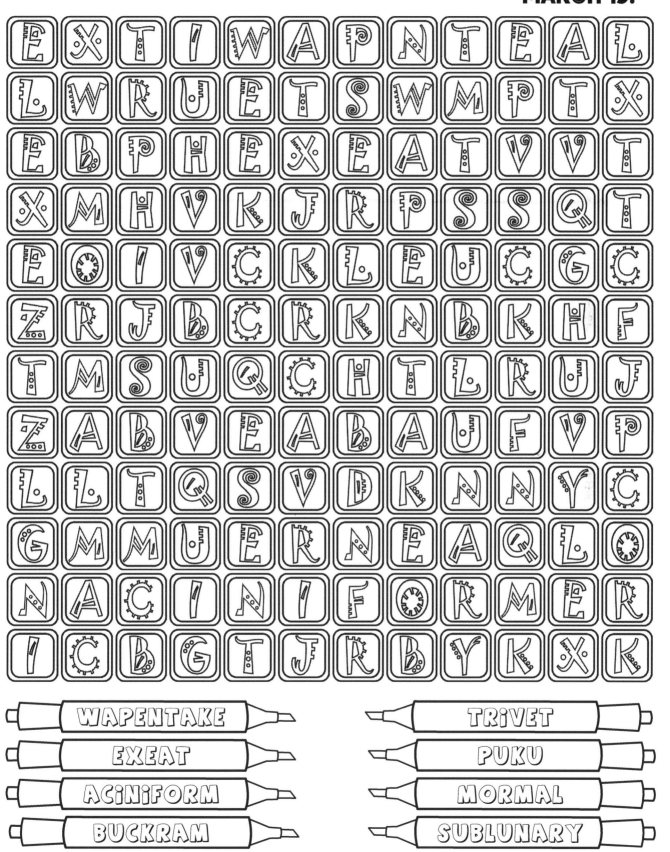

WAPENTAKE   TRIVET

EXEAT   PUKU

ACINIFORM   MORMAL

BUCKRAM   SUBLUNARY

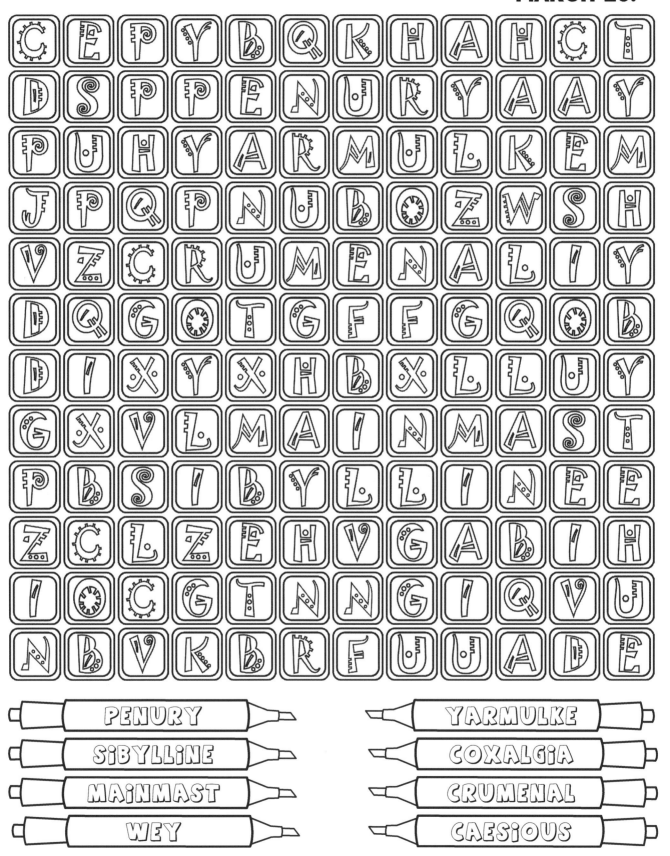

PENURY

SIBYLLINE

MAINMAST

WEY

YARMULKE

COXALGIA

CRUMENAL

CAESIOUS

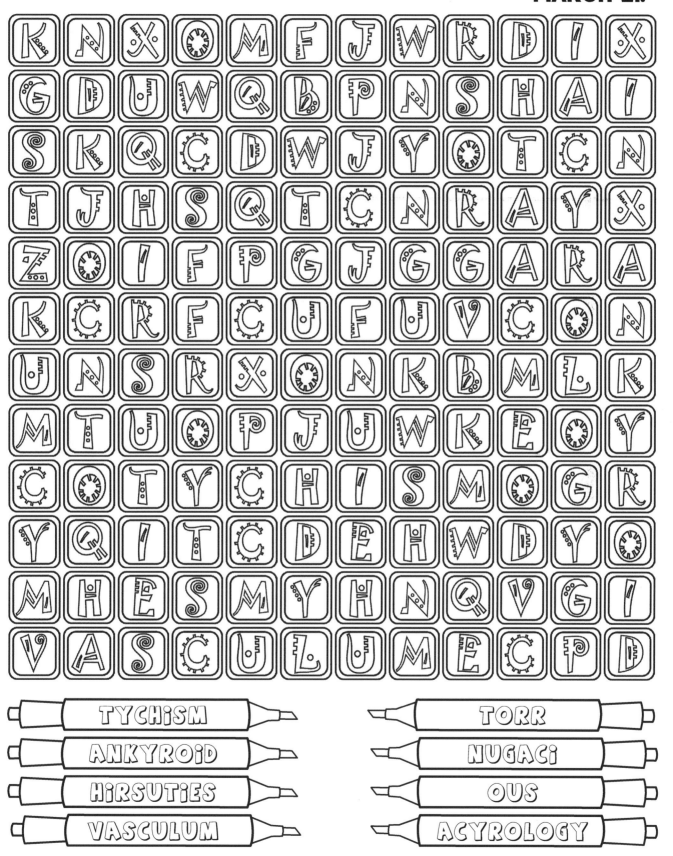

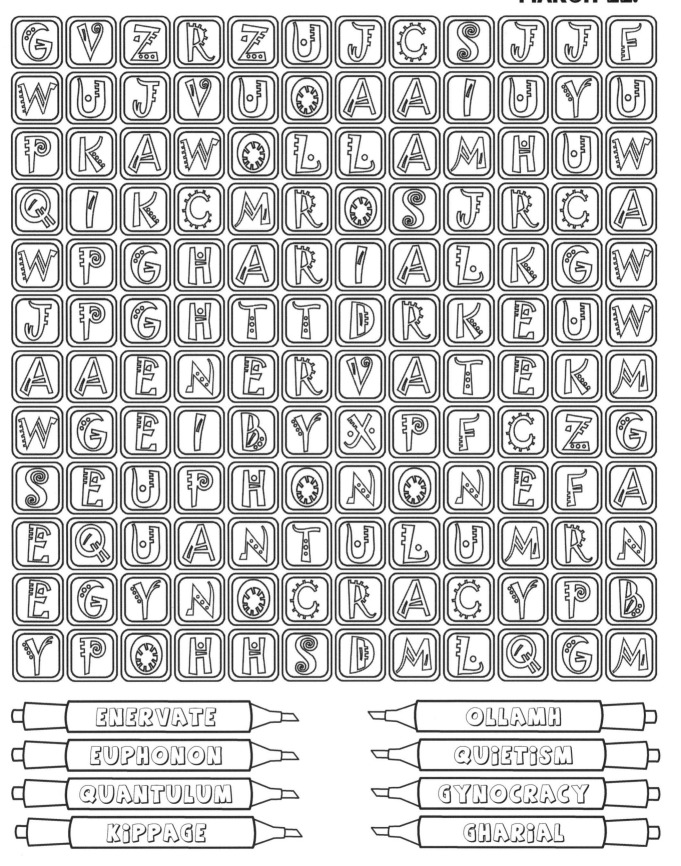

ENERVATE

EUPHONON

QUANTULUM

KIPPAGE

OLLAMH

QUIETISM

GYNOCRACY

GHARIAL

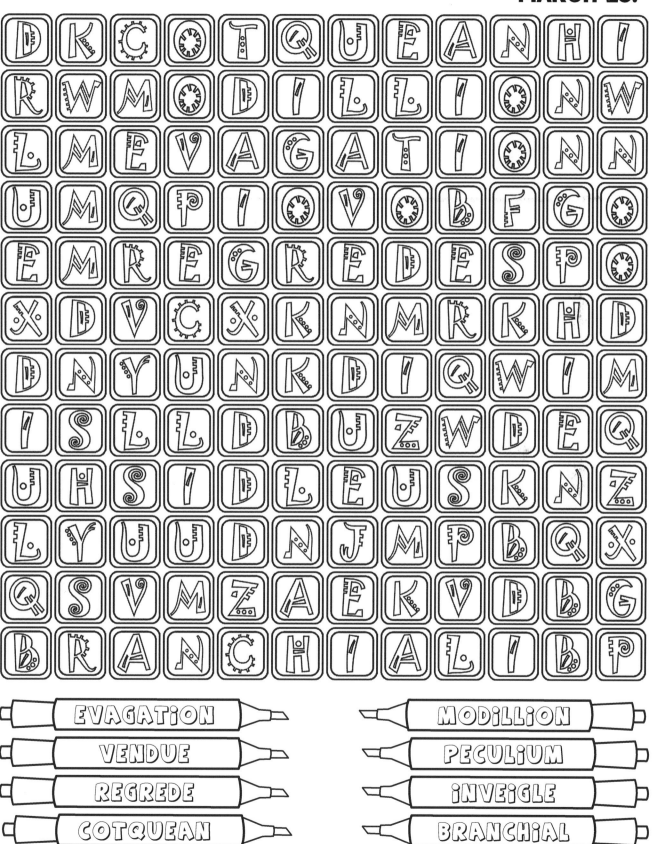

EVAGATION
VENDUE
REGREDE
COTQUEAN

MODILLION
PECULIUM
INVEIGLE
BRANCHIAL

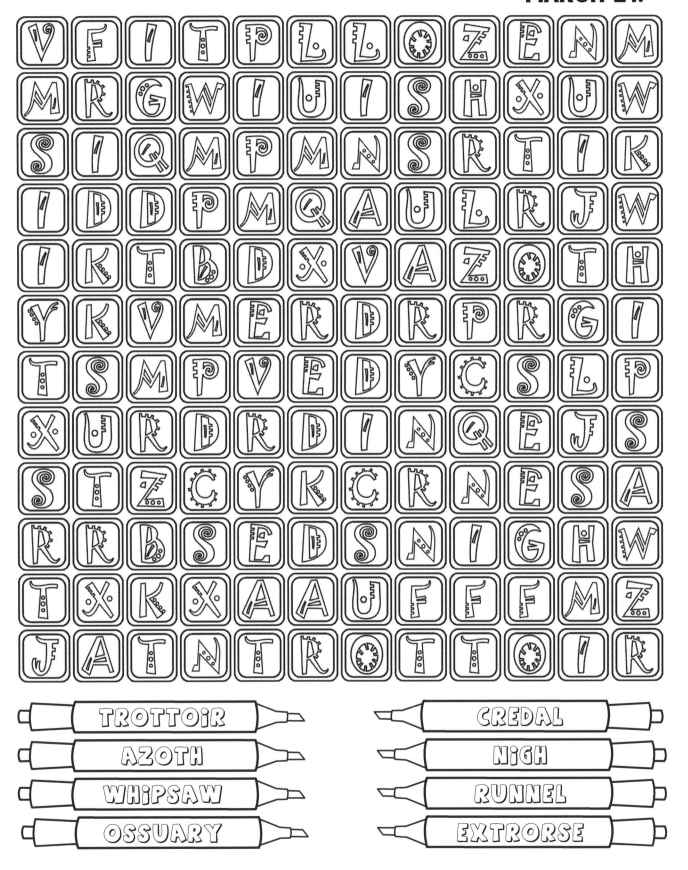

TROTTOIR

AZOTH

WHIPSAW

OSSUARY

CREDAL

NIGH

RUNNEL

EXTRORSE

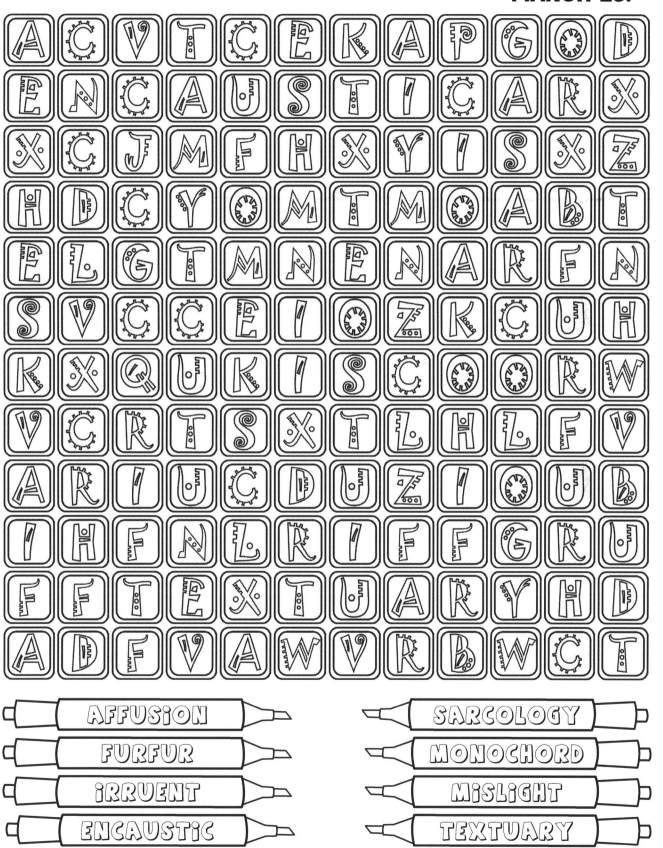

AFFUSION

FURFUR

IRRUENT

ENCAUSTIC

SARCOLOGY

MONOCHORD

MISLIGHT

TEXTUARY

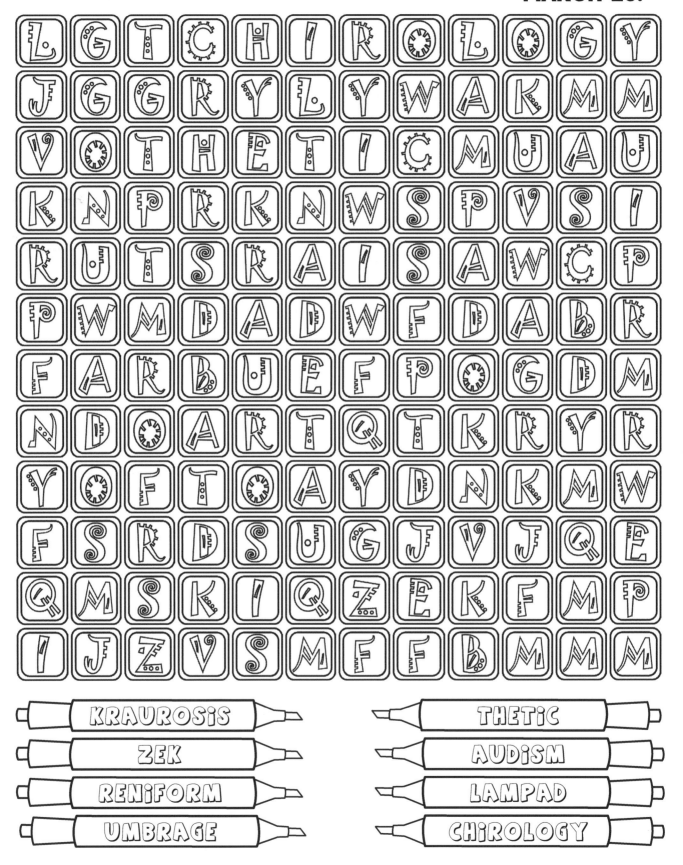

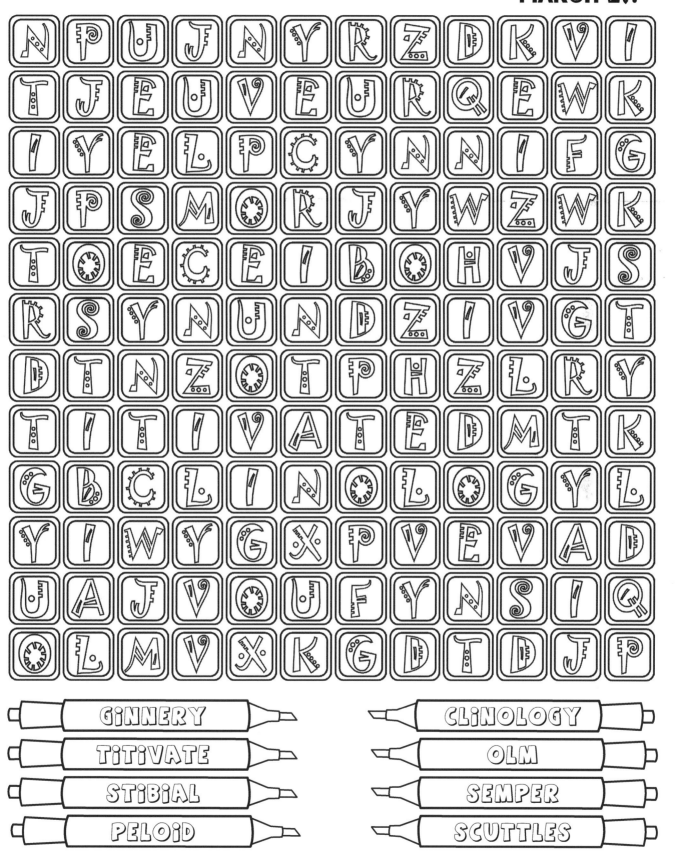

GINNERY

TITIVATE

STIBIAL

PELOID

CLINOLOGY

OLM

SEMPER

SCUTTLES

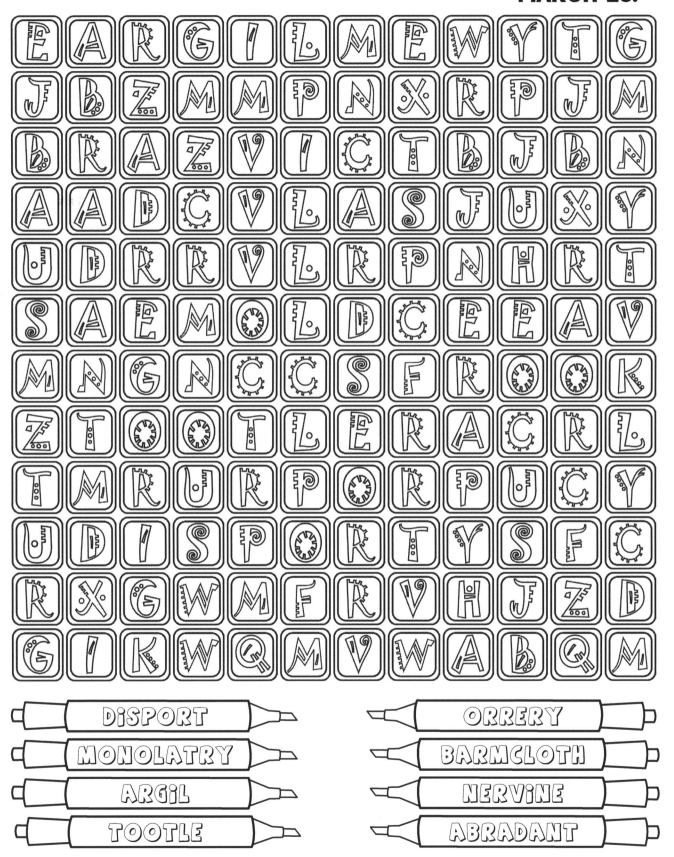

DISPORT

MONOLATRY

ARGIL

TOOTLE

ORRERY

BARMCLOTH

NERVINE

ABRADANT

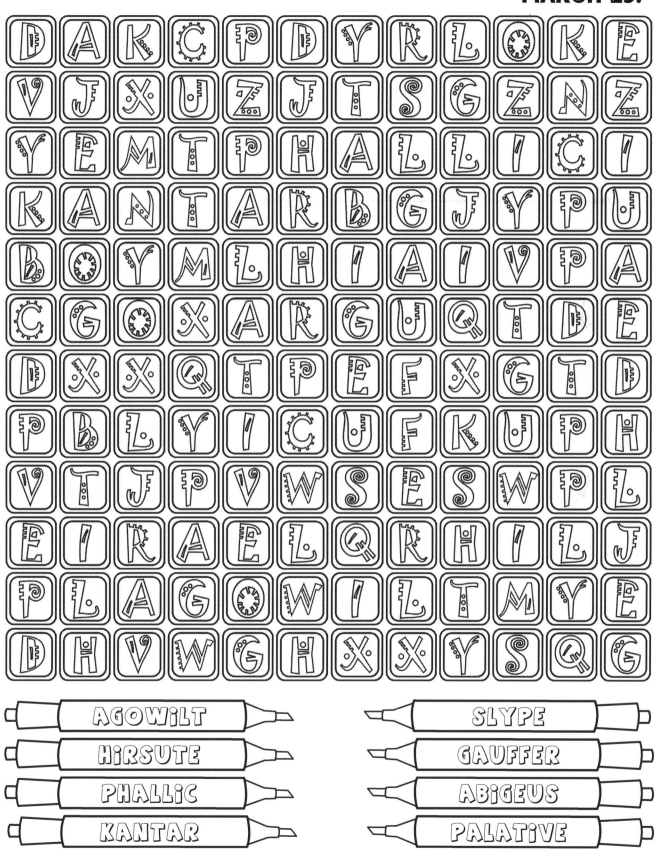

AGOWILT

HIRSUTE

PHALLIC

KANTAR

SLYPE

GAUFFER

ABIGEUS

PALATIVE

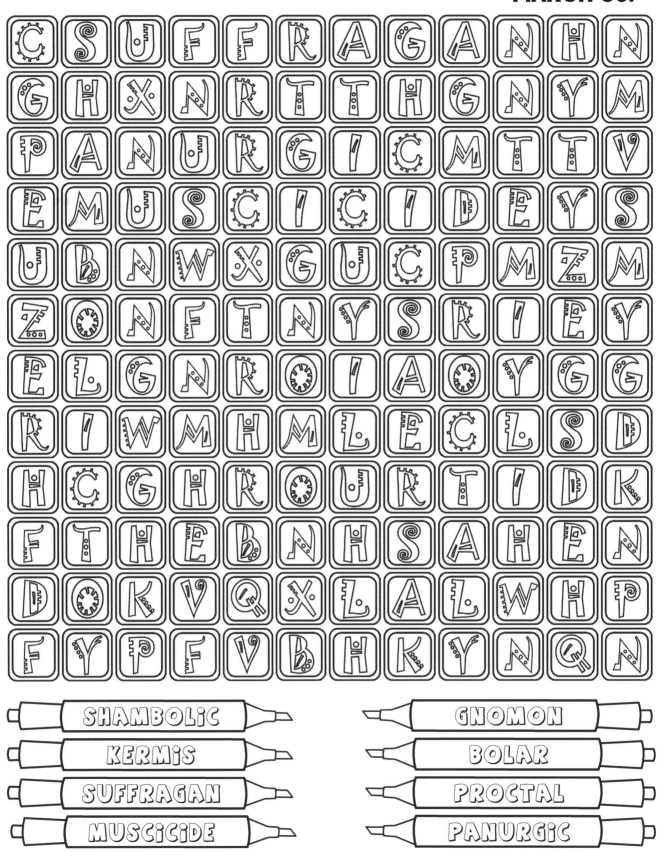

SHAMBOLIC
KERMIS
SUFFRAGAN
MUSCICIDE
GNOMON
BOLAR
PROCTAL
PANURGIC

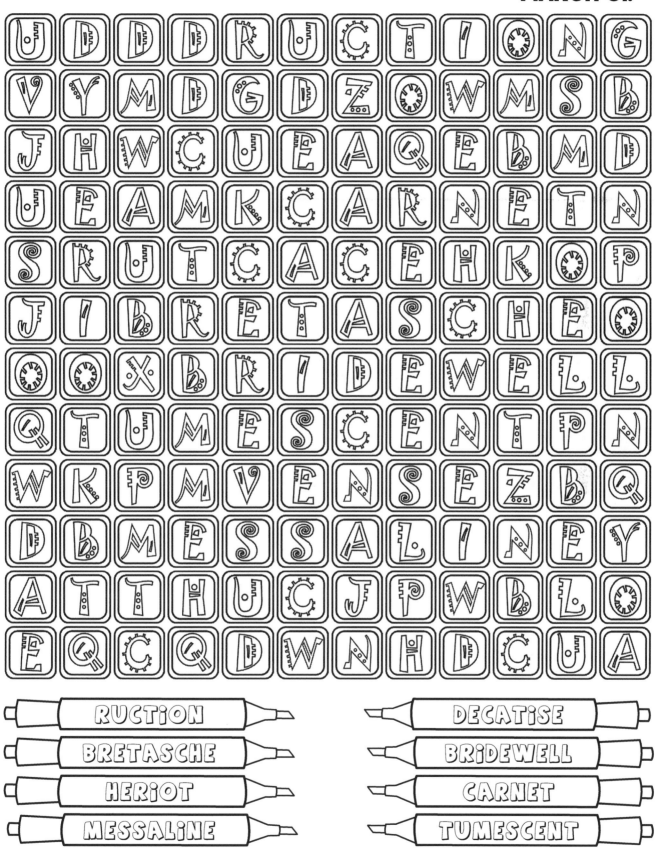

RUCTION

DECATISE

BRETASCHE

BRIDEWELL

HERIOT

CARNET

MESSALINE

TUMESCENT

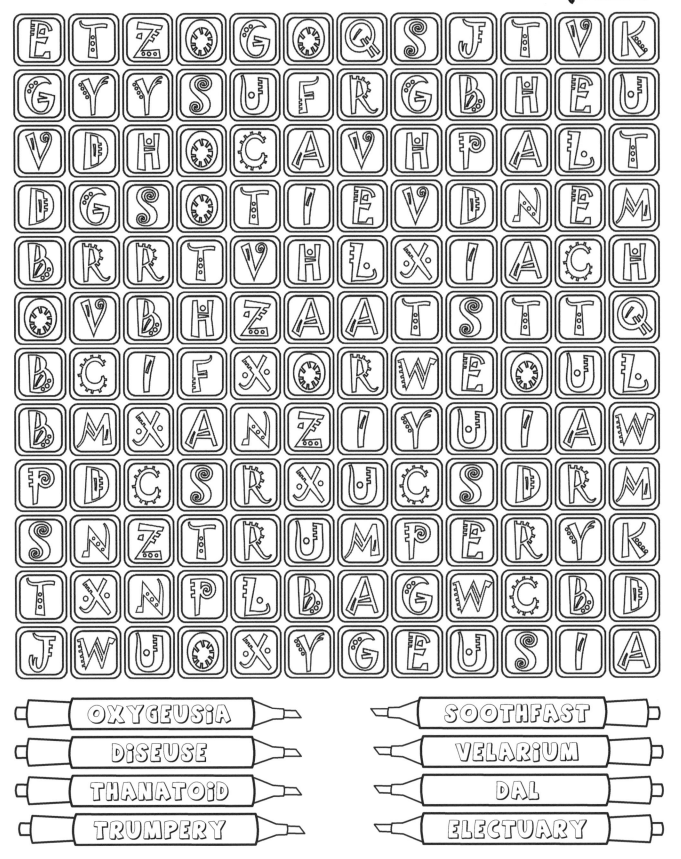

OXYGEUSIA

DISEUSE

THANATOID

TRUMPERY

SOOTHFAST

VELARIUM

DAL

ELECTUARY

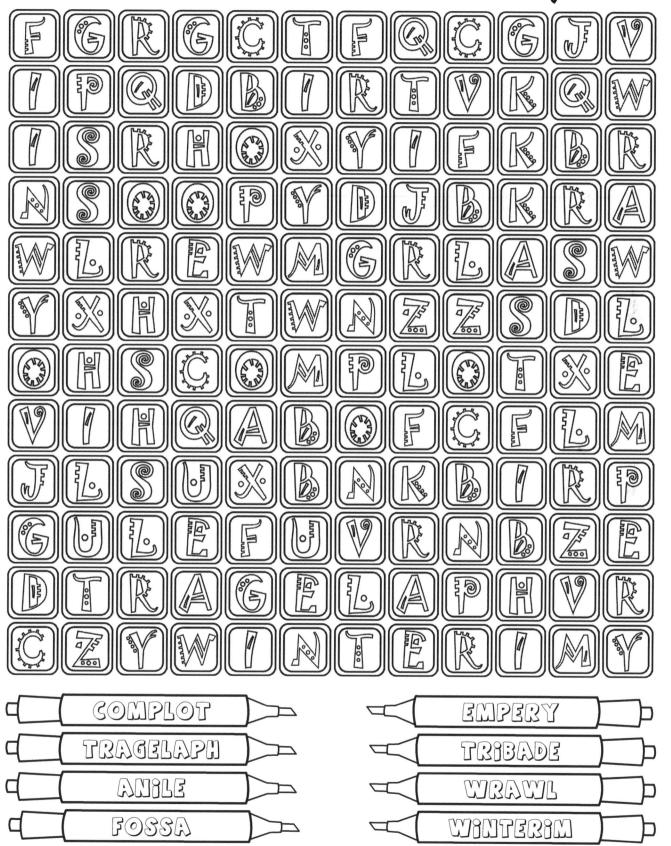

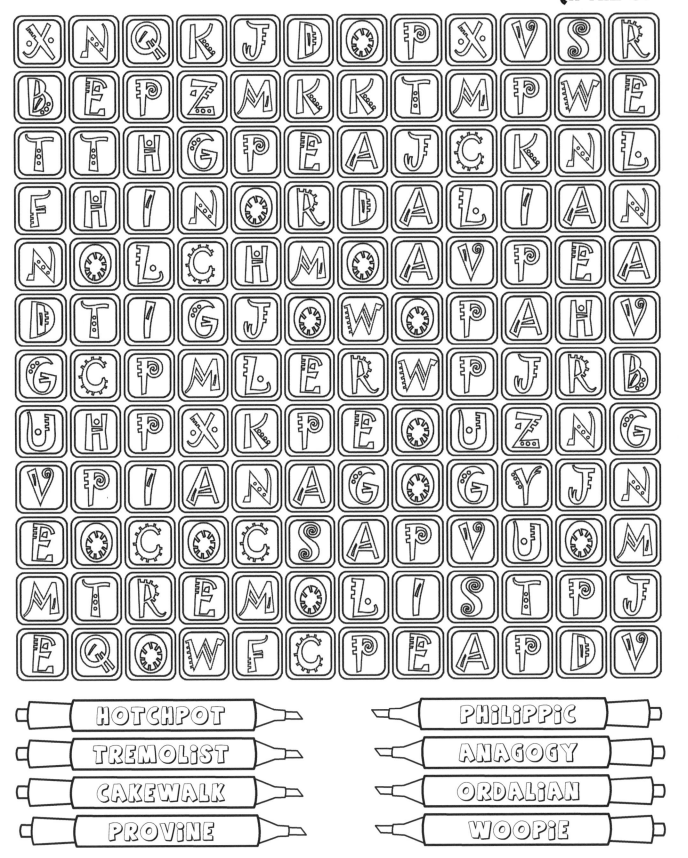

HOTCHPOT

TREMOLIST

CAKEWALK

PROVINE

PHILIPPIC

ANAGOGY

ORDALIAN

WOOPIE

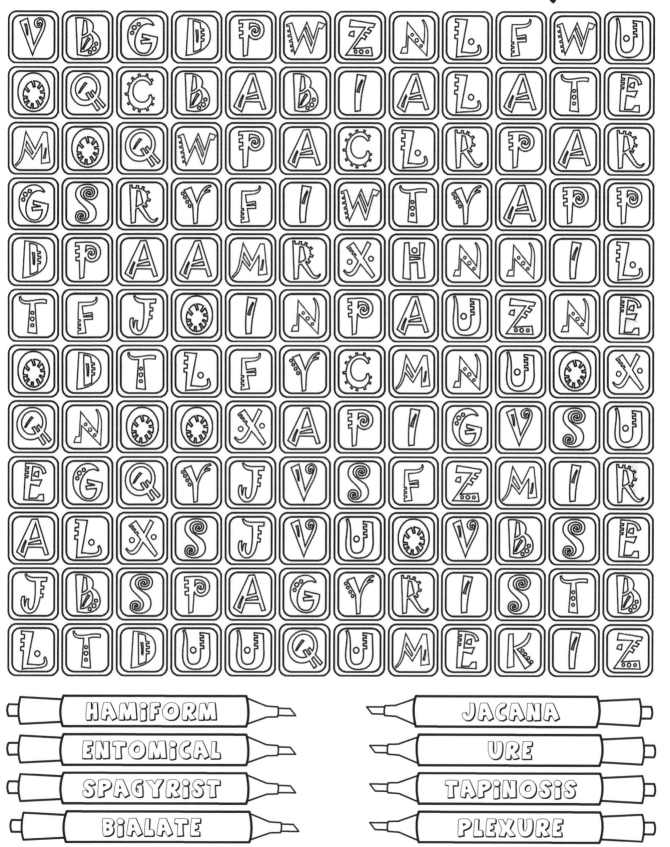

HAMIFORM

ENTOMICAL

SPAGYRIST

BIALATE

JACANA

URE

TAPINOSIS

PLEXURE

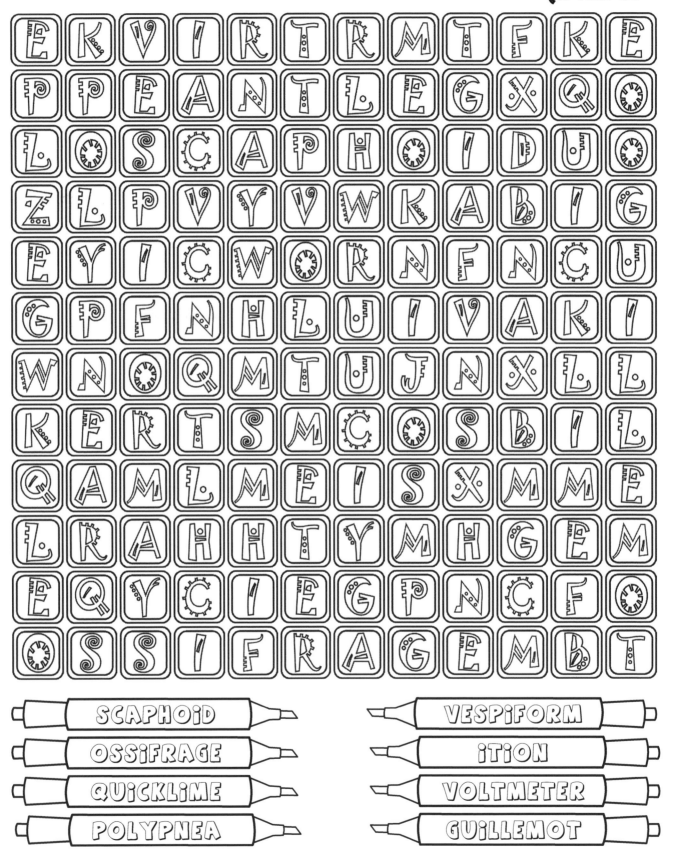

SCAPHOID

OSSIFRAGE

QUICKLIME

POLYPNEA

VESPIFORM

ITION

VOLTMETER

GUILLEMOT

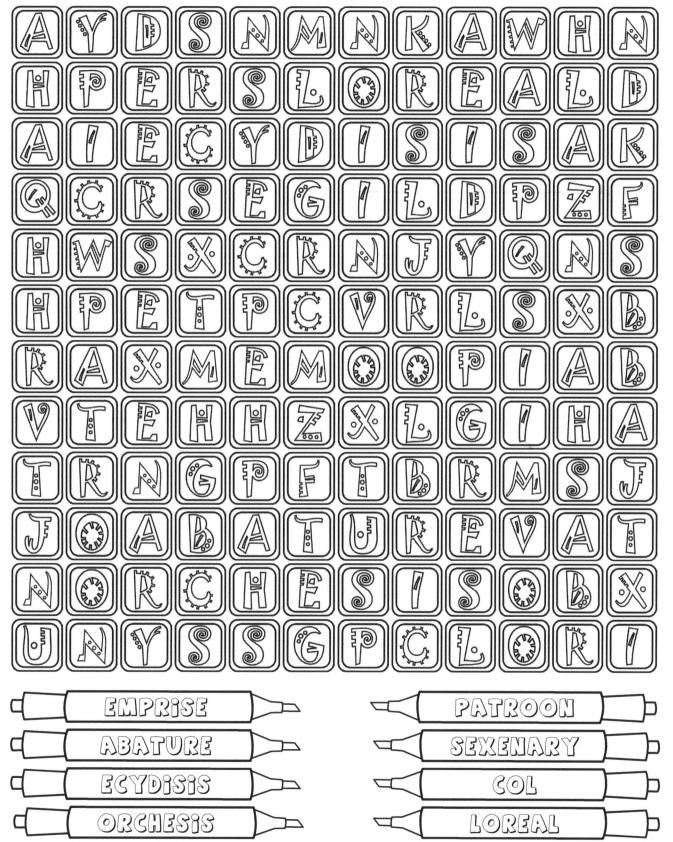

EMPRISE
ABATURE
ECYDISIS
ORCHESIS

PATROON
SEXENARY
COL
LOREAL

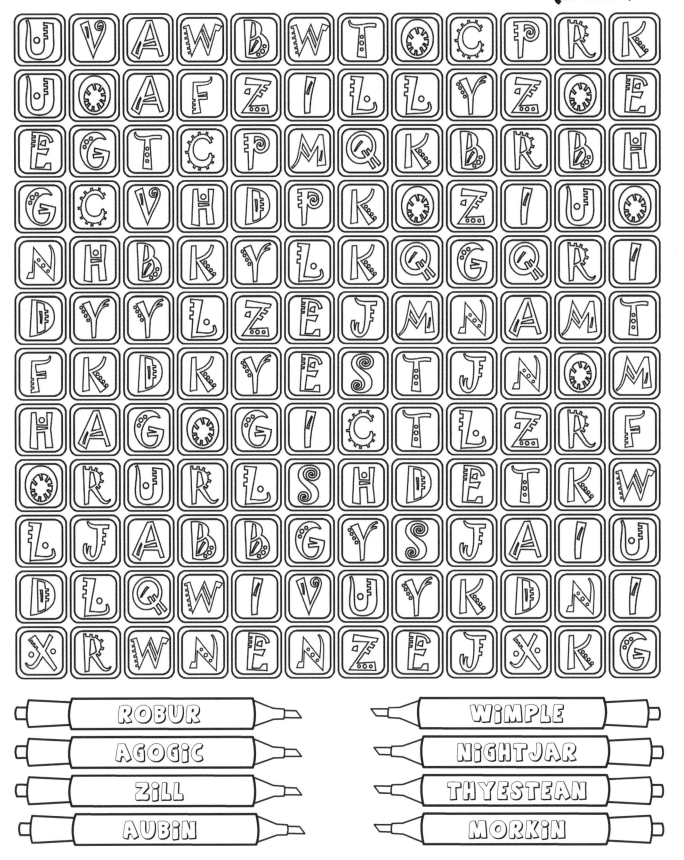

ROBUR

AGOGIC

ZILL

AUBIN

WIMPLE

NIGHTJAR

THYESTEAN

MORKIN

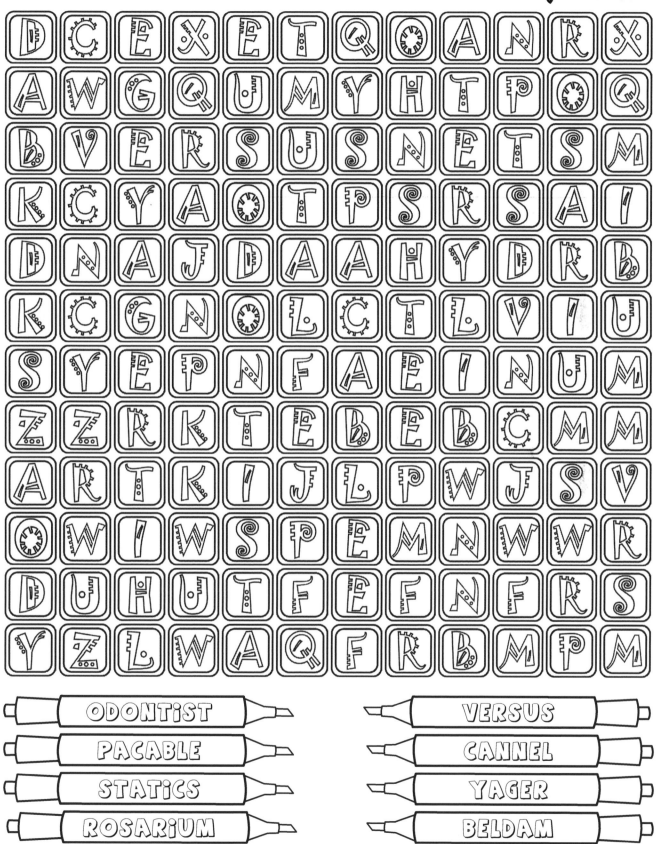

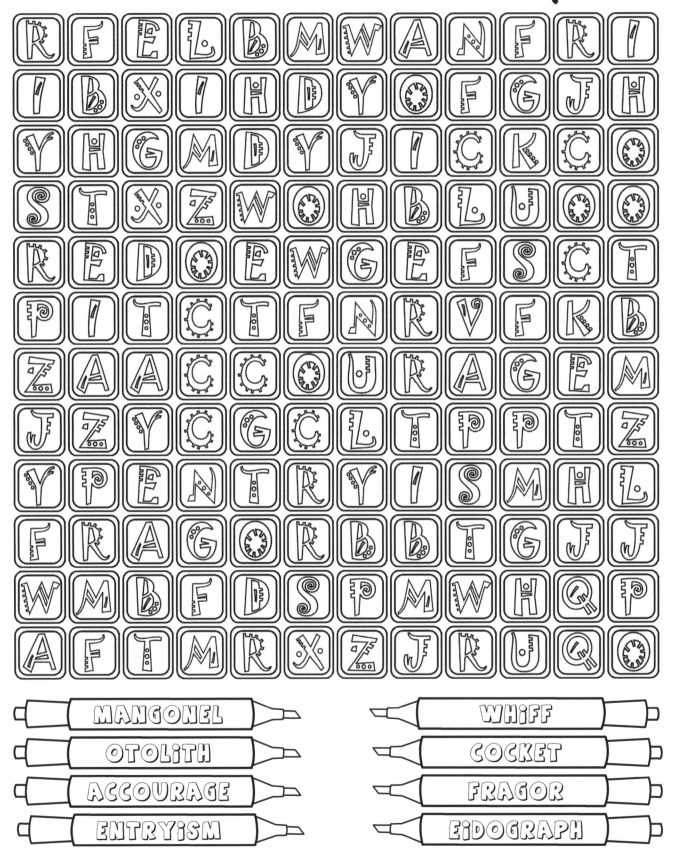

MANGONEL

OTOLITH

ACCOURAGE

ENTRYISM

WHIFF

COCKET

FRAGOR

EIDOGRAPH

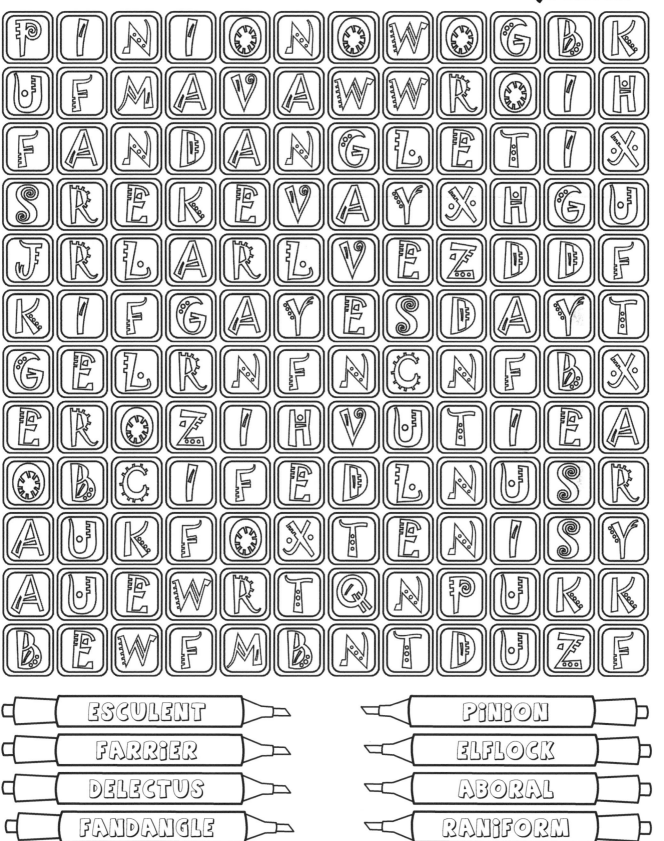

P	I	N	I	O	N	O	W	O	G	B	K
U	F	M	A	V	A	W	W	R	O	I	H
F	A	N	D	A	N	G	L	E	T	I	X
S	R	E	K	E	V	A	Y	X	H	G	U
J	R	Z	A	R	Z	V	E	Z	D	D	F
K	I	F	G	A	Y	E	S	D	A	Y	T
G	E	Z	R	N	F	N	C	N	F	B	X
E	R	Z	Z	I	H	V	U	T	I	E	A
O	B	C	I	F	E	D	Z	N	U	S	R
A	U	K	F	O	X	T	E	N	I	S	Y
A	U	E	W	R	T	Q	N	P	U	K	K
B	E	W	F	M	B	N	T	D	U	Z	F

ESCULENT

FARRIER

DELECTUS

FANDANGLE

PINION

ELFLOCK

ABORAL

RANIFORM

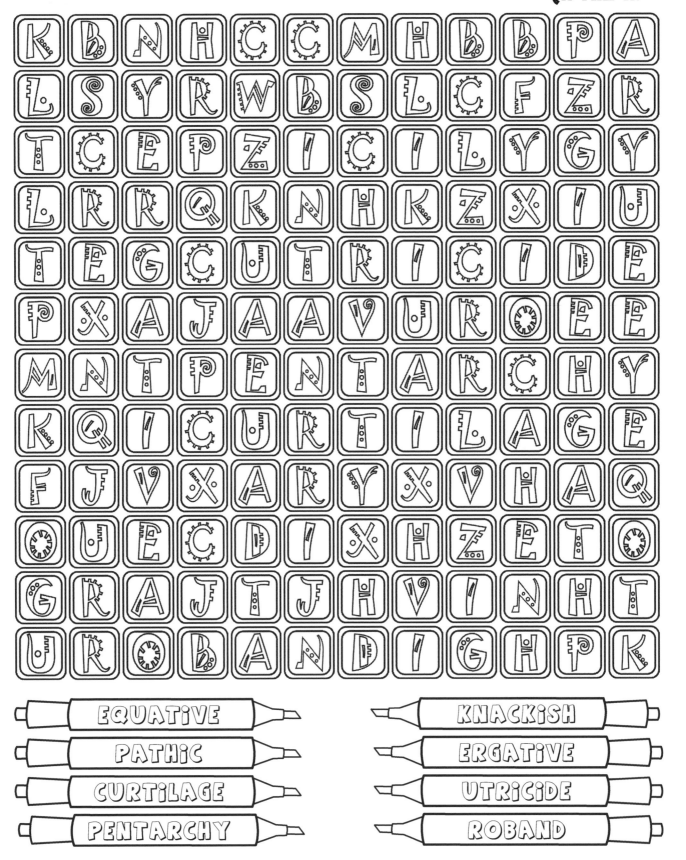

EQUATIVE

PATHIC

CURTILAGE

PENTARCHY

KNACKISH

ERGATIVE

UTRICIDE

ROBAND

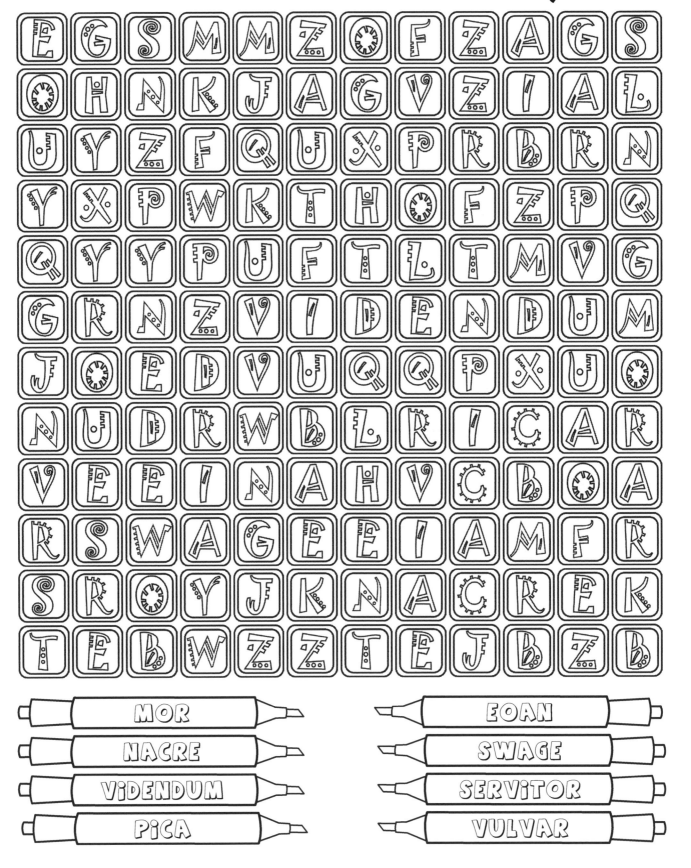

MOR

NACRE

VIDENDUM

PICA

EOAN

SWAGE

SERVITOR

VULVAR

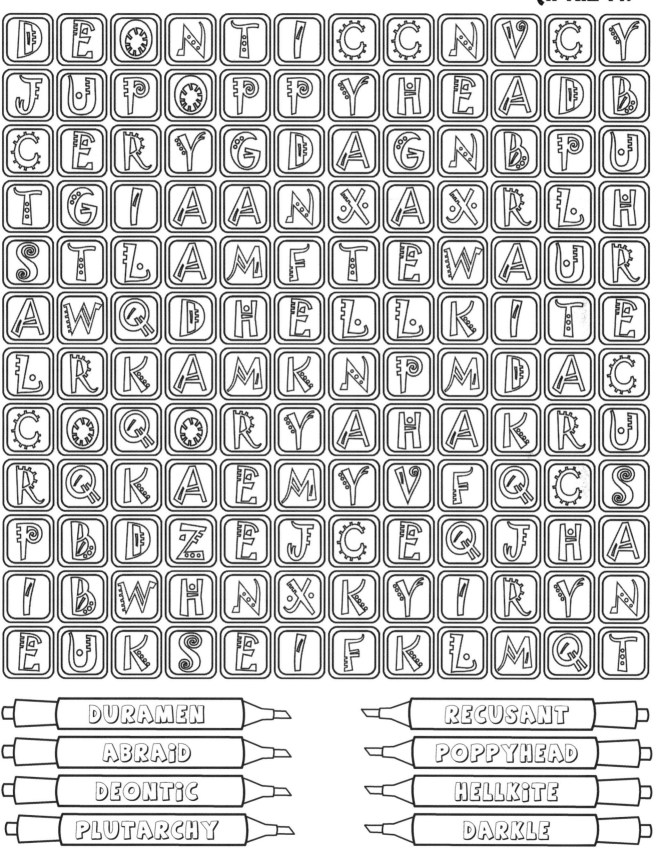

DURAMEN

ABRAID

DEONTIC

PLUTARCHY

RECUSANT

POPPYHEAD

HELLKITE

DARKLE

APRIL 15:

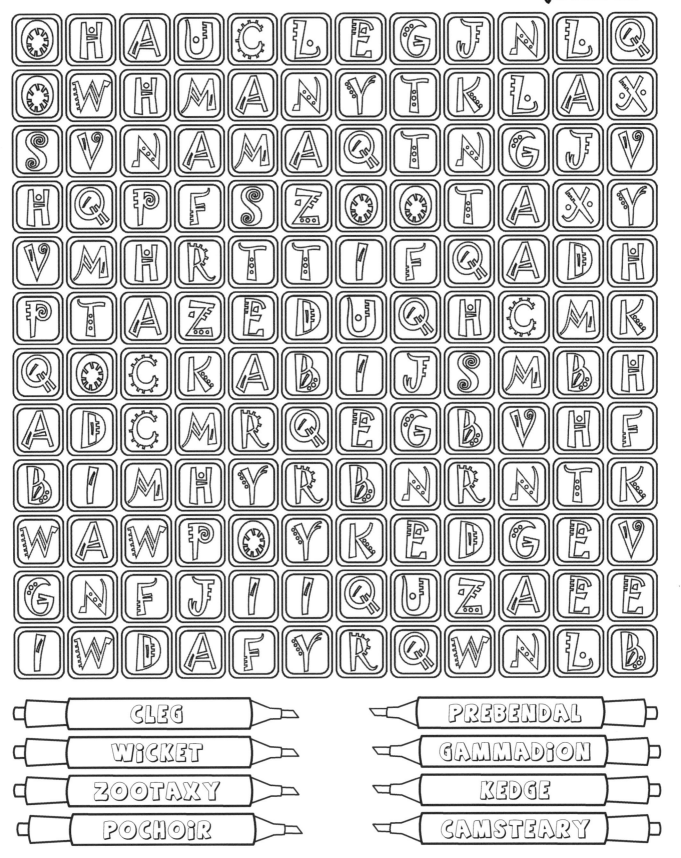

CLEG

WICKET

ZOOTAXY

POCHOIR

PREBENDAL

GAMMADION

KEDGE

CAMSTEARY

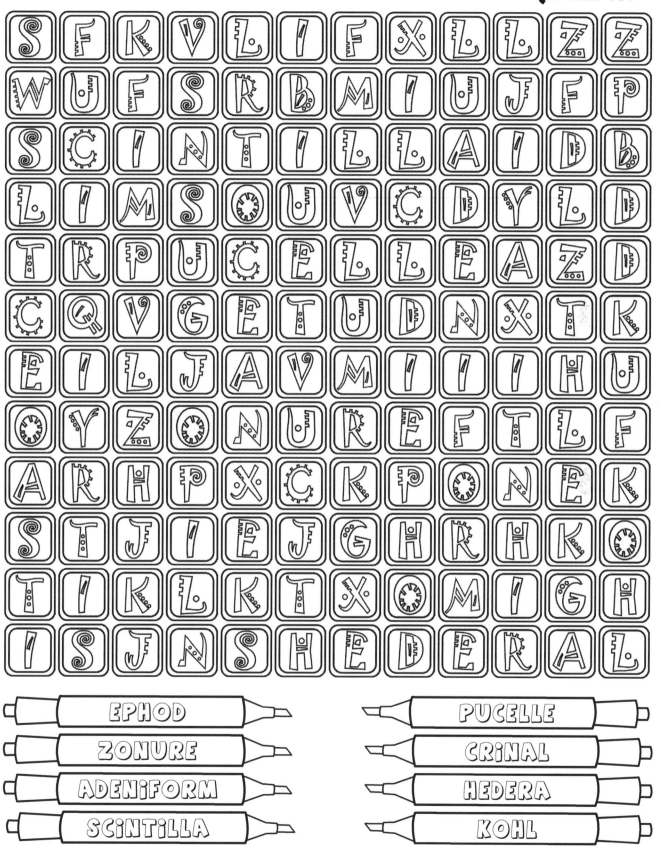

EPHOD

ZONURE

ADENIFORM

SCINTILLA

PUCELLE

CRINAL

HEDERA

KOHL

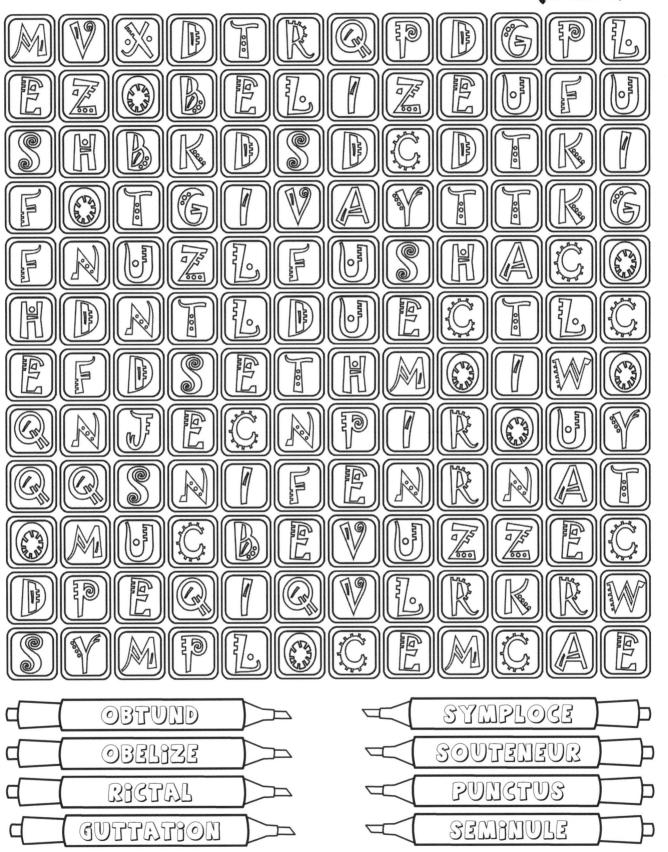

OBTUND

OBELIZE

RICTAL

GUTTATION

SYMPLOCE

SOUTENEUR

PUNCTUS

SEMINULE

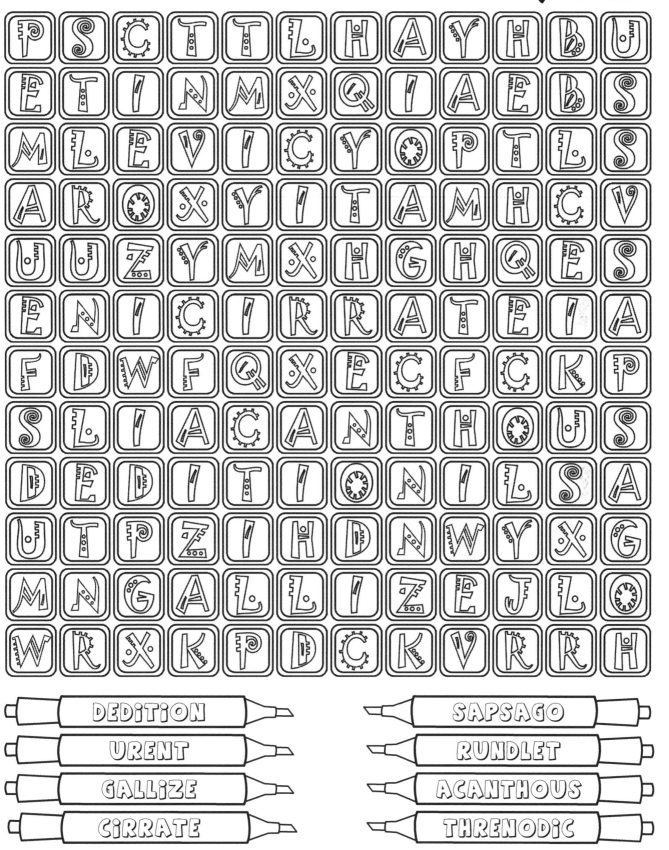

DEDITION

URENT

GALLIZE

CIRRATE

SAPSAGO

RUNDLET

ACANTHOUS

THRENODIC

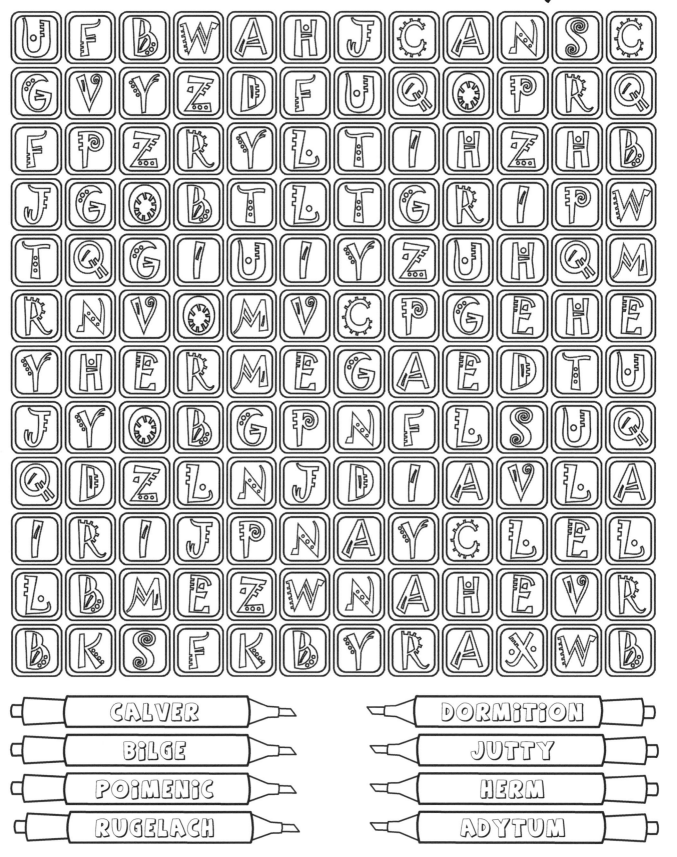

CALVER

BILGE

POIMENIC

RUGELACH

DORMITION

JUTTY

HERM

ADYTUM

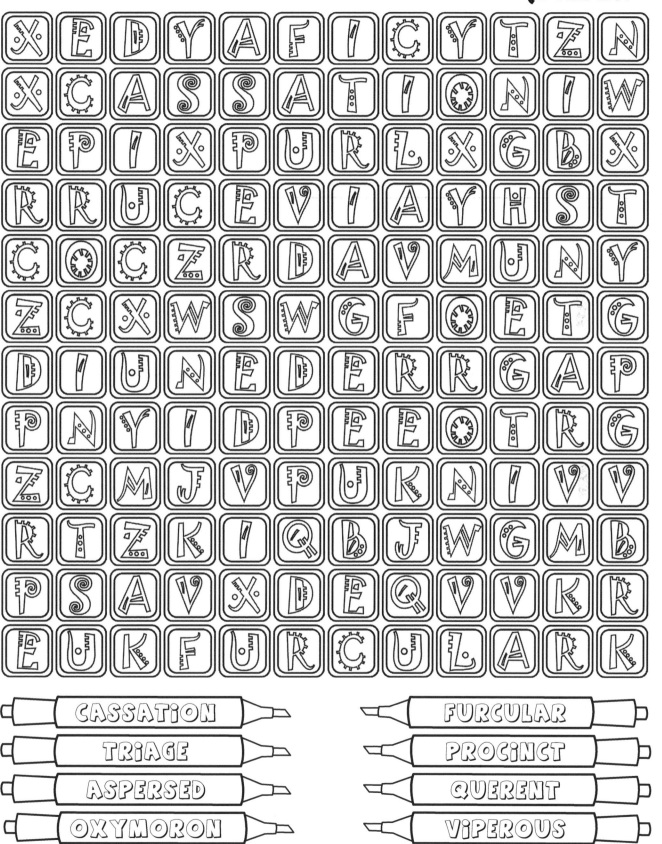

CASSATION

TRIAGE

ASPERSED

OXYMORON

FURCULAR

PROCINCT

QUERENT

VIPEROUS

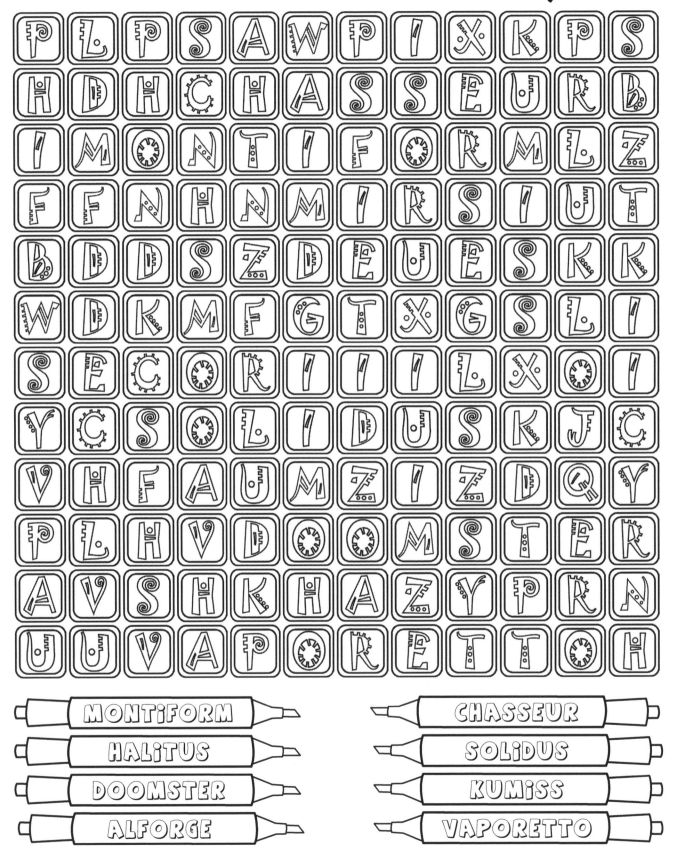

MONTIFORM

HALITUS

DOOMSTER

ALFORGE

CHASSEUR

SOLIDUS

KUMISS

VAPORETTO

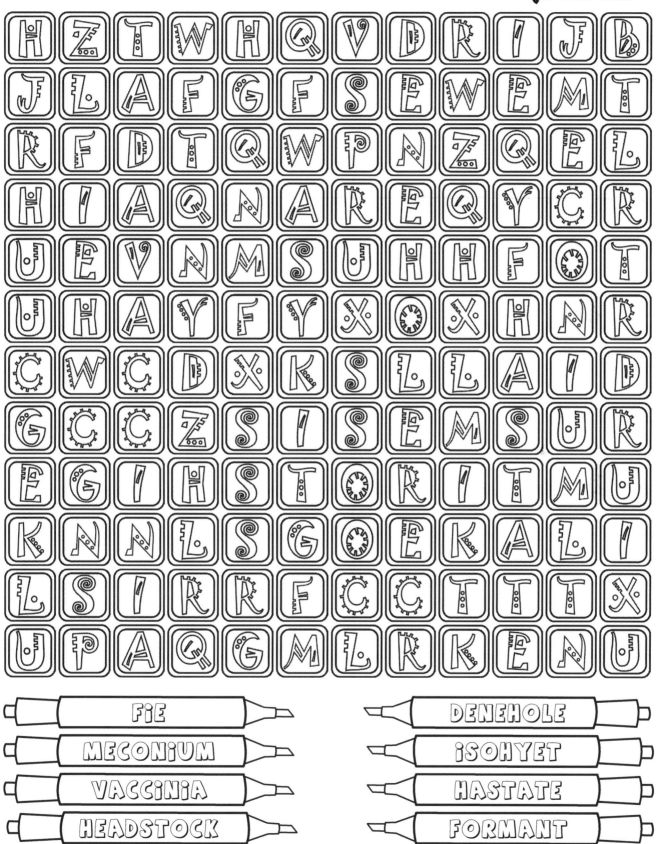

FIE

MECONIUM

VACCINIA

HEADSTOCK

DENEHOLE

ISOHYET

HASTATE

FORMANT

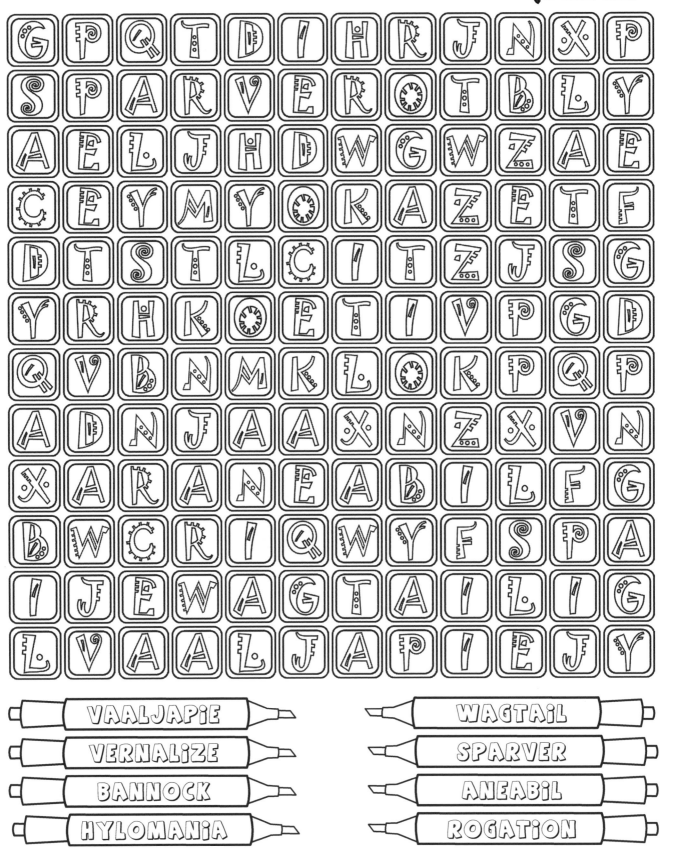

VAALJAPIE

VERNALIZE

BANNOCK

HYLOMANIA

WAGTAIL

SPARVER

ANEABIL

ROGATION

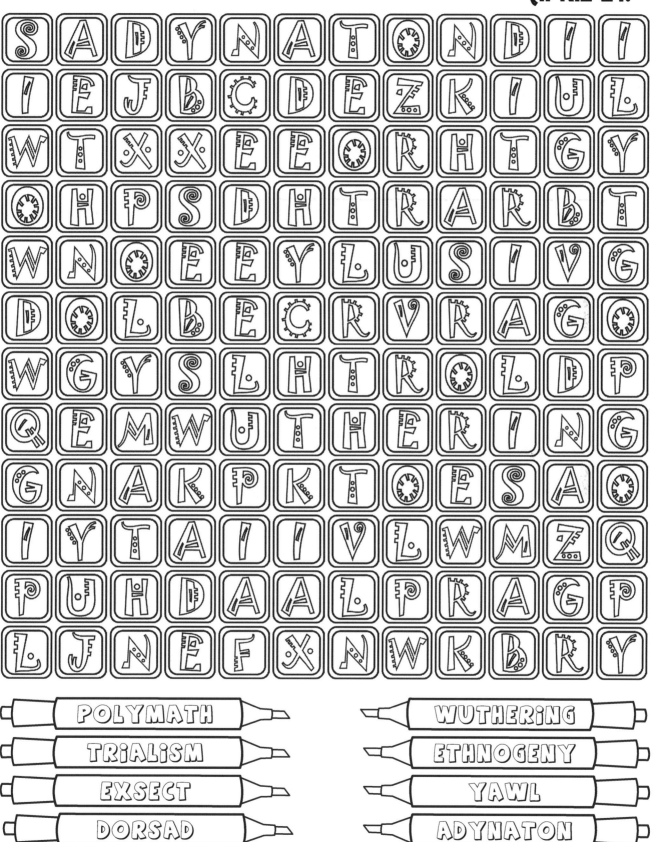

POLYMATH

TRIALISM

EXSECT

DORSAD

WUTHERING

ETHNOGENY

YAWL

ADYNATON

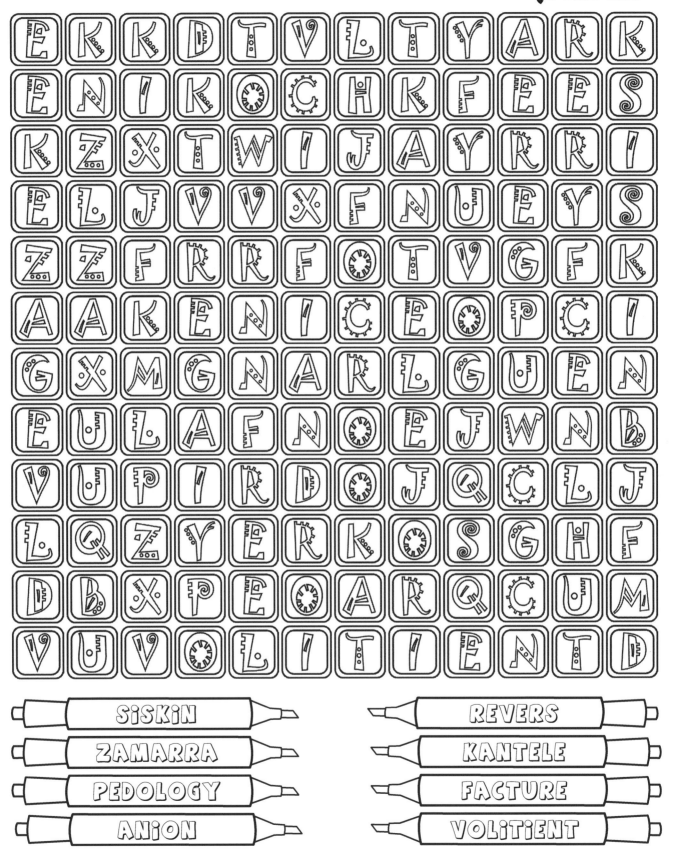

SISKIN

ZAMARRA

PEDOLOGY

ANION

REVERS

KANTELE

FACTURE

VOLITIENT

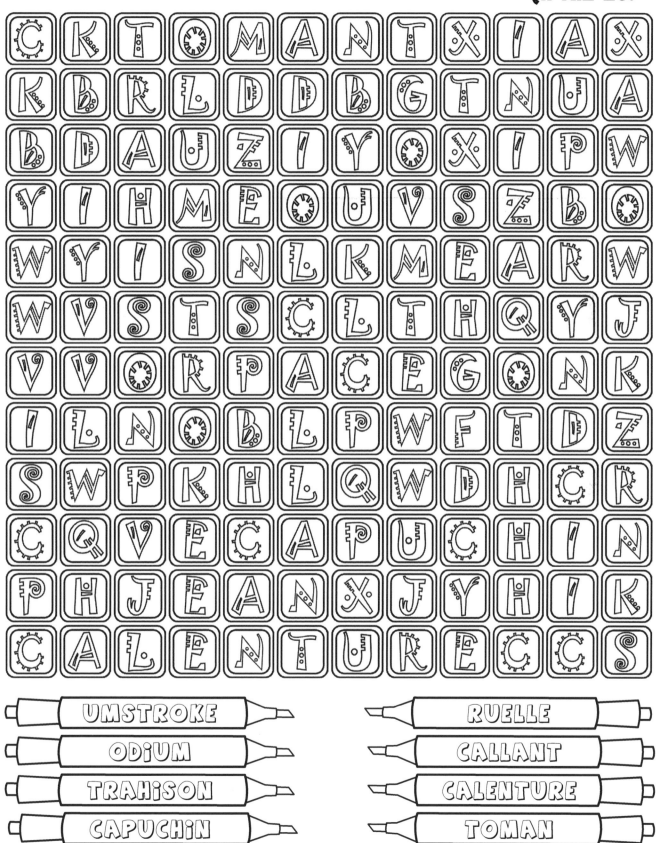

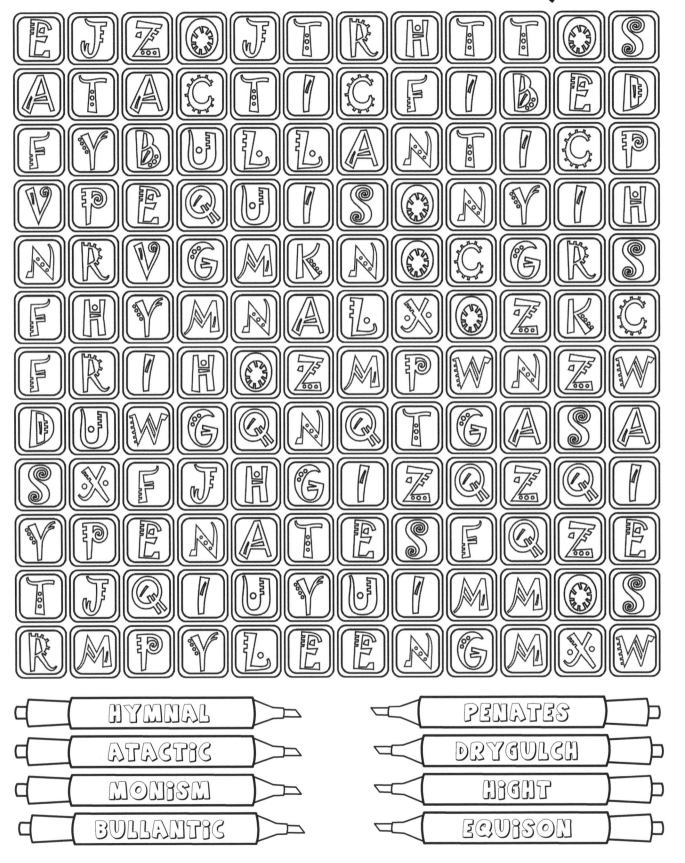

HYMNAL

ATACTIC

MONISM

BULLANTIC

PENATES

DRYGULCH

HIGHT

EQUISON

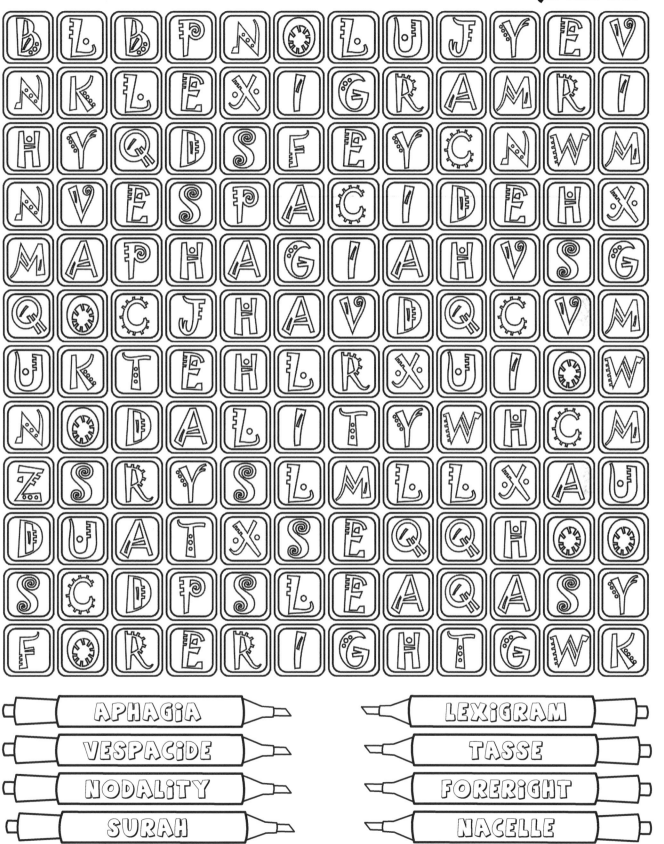

APHAGIA

VESPACIDE

NODALITY

SURAH

LEXIGRAM

TASSE

FORERIGHT

NACELLE

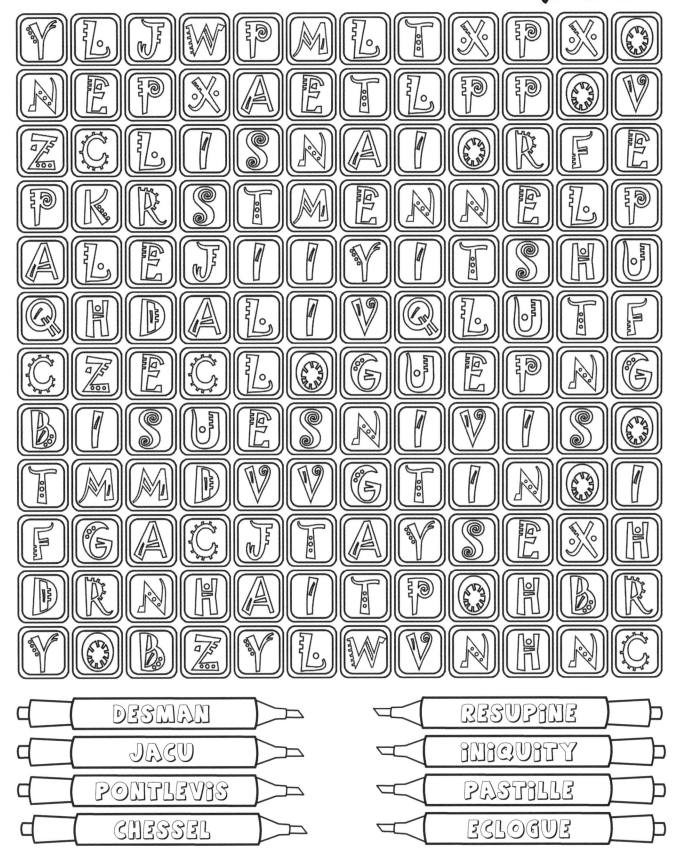

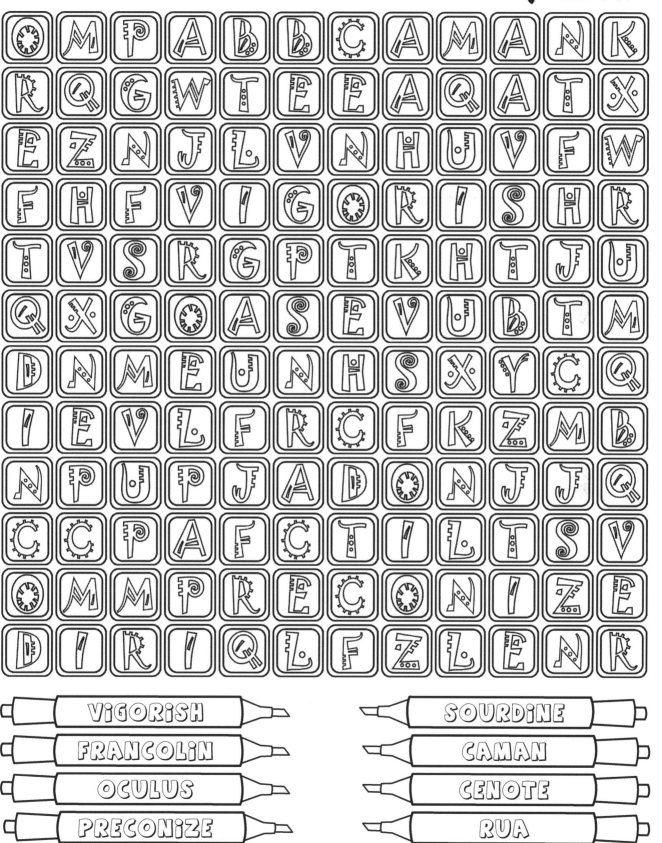

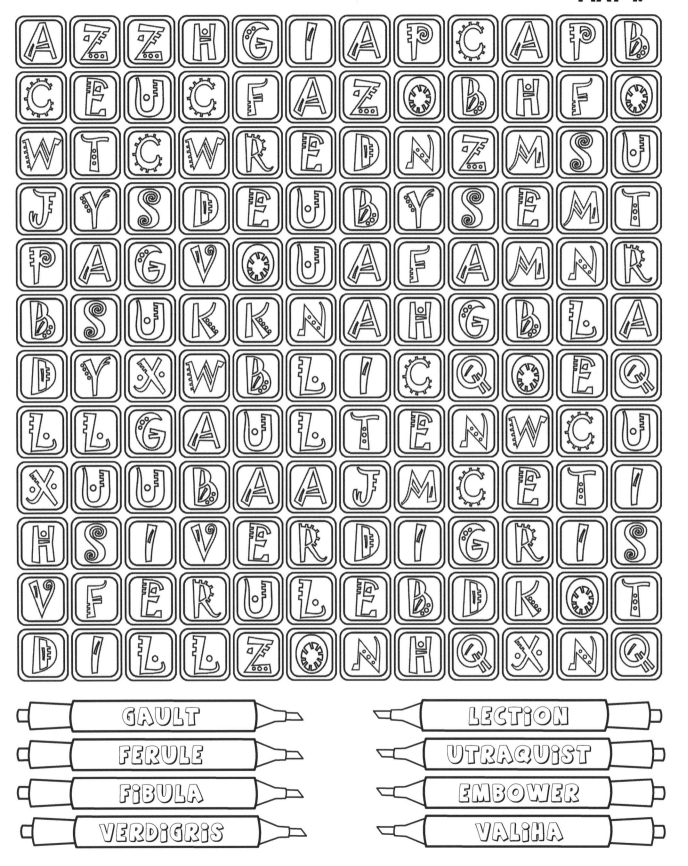

GAULT

FERULE

FIBULA

VERDIGRIS

LECTION

UTRAQUIST

EMBOWER

VALIHA

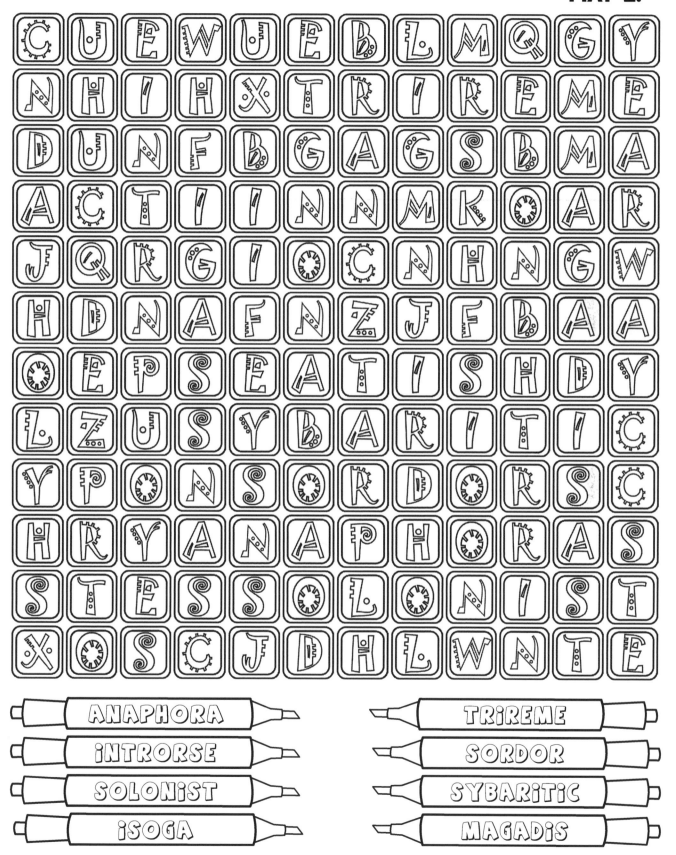

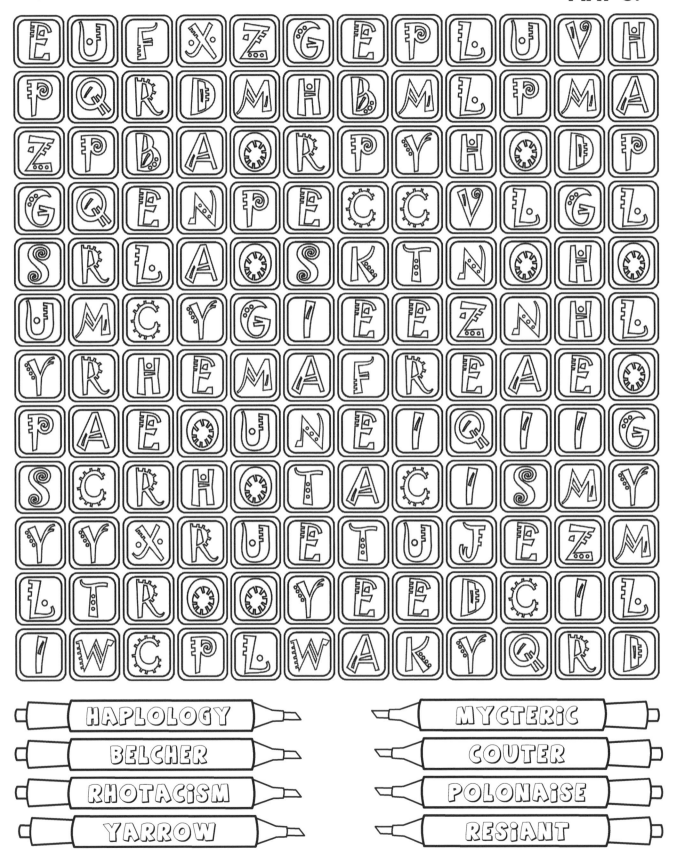

HAPLOLOGY

BELCHER

RHOTACISM

YARROW

MYCTERIC

COUTER

POLONAISE

RESIANT

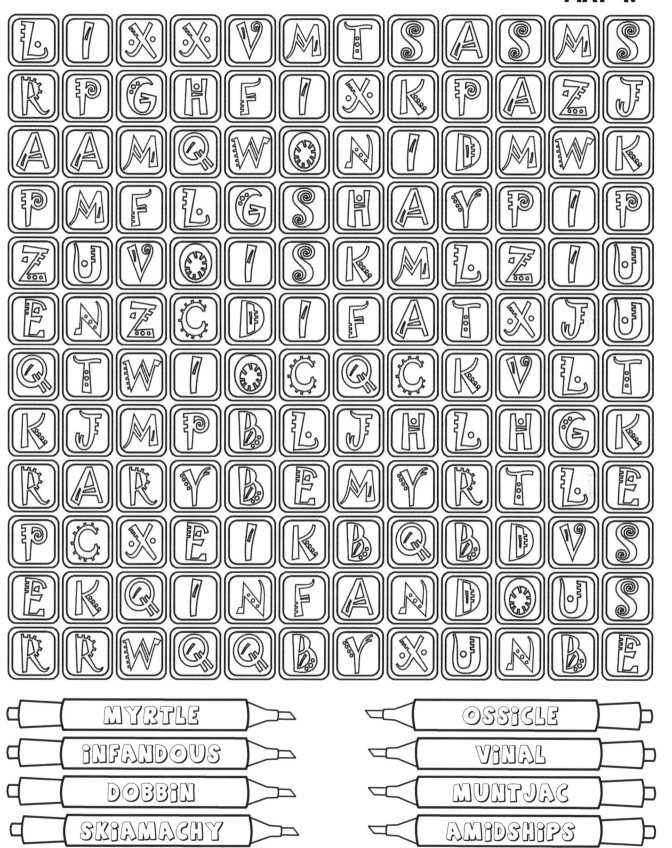

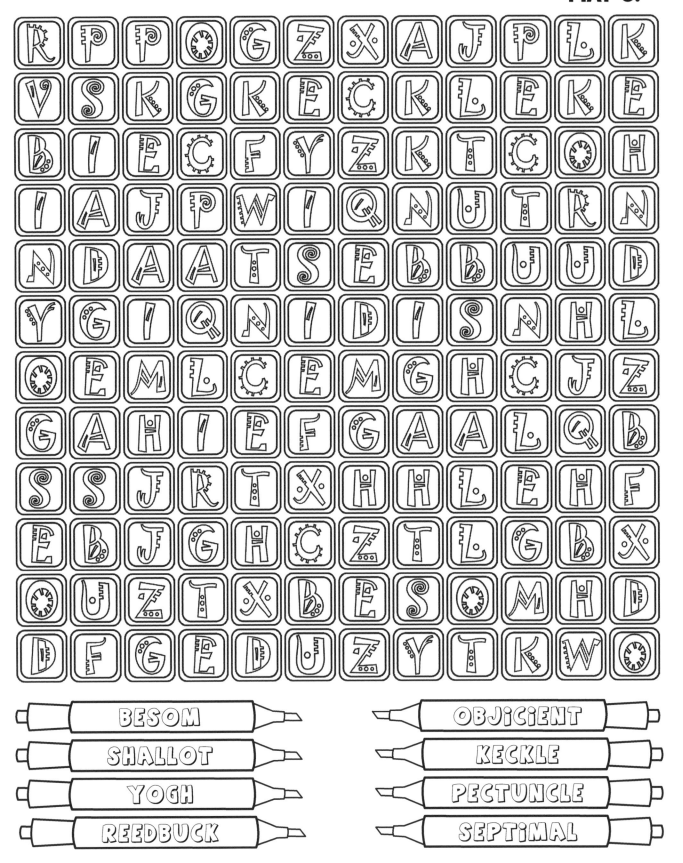

BESOM

SHALLOT

YOGH

REEDBUCK

OBJICIENT

KECKLE

PECTUNCLE

SEPTIMAL

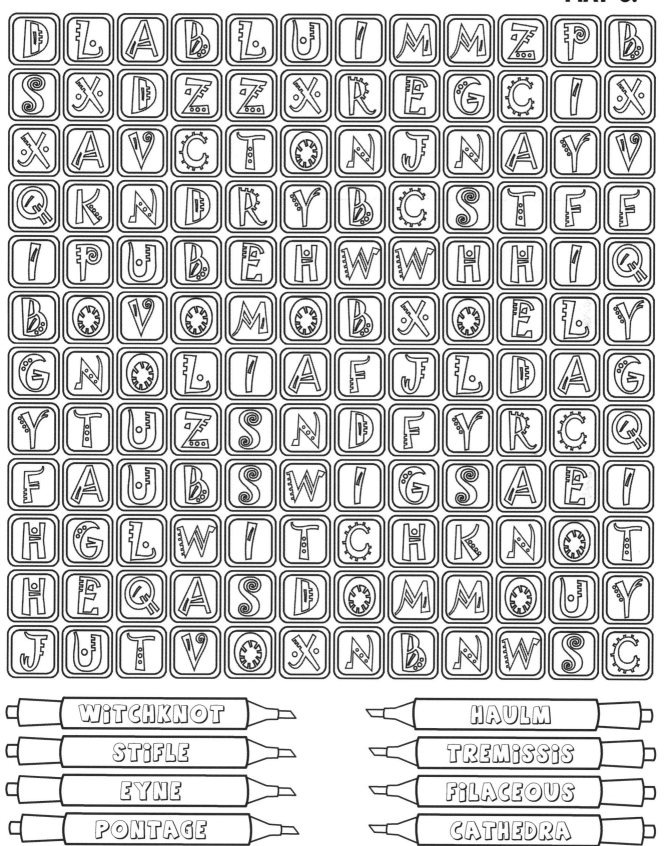

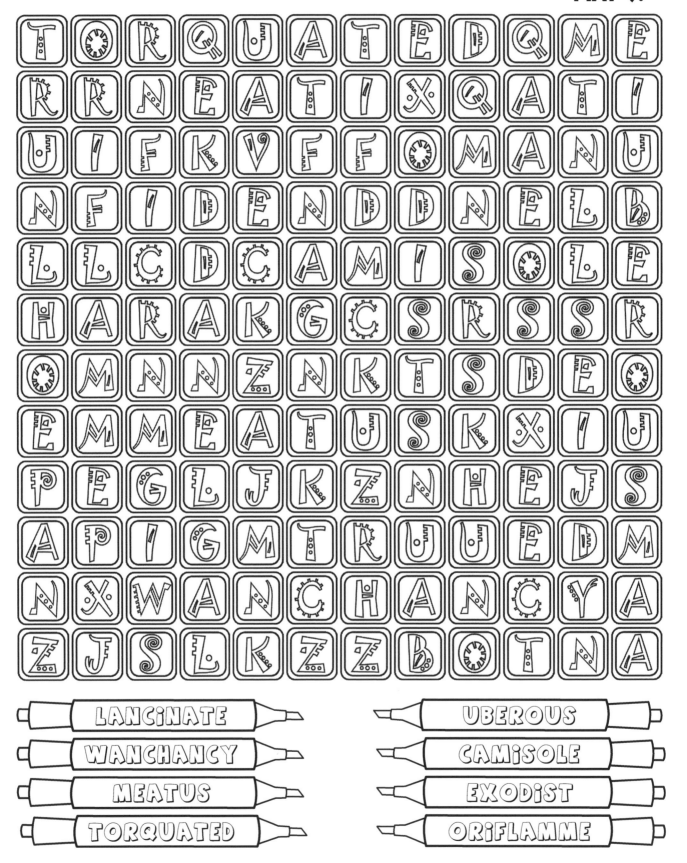

LANCINATE

WANCHANCY

MEATUS

TORQUATED

UBEROUS

CAMISOLE

EXODIST

ORIFLAMME

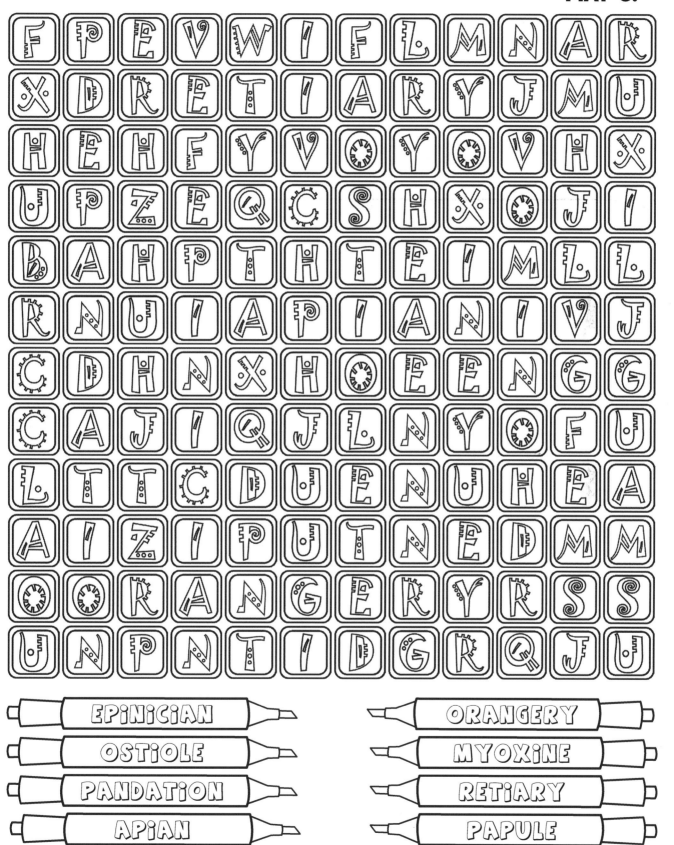

EPINICIAN
OSTIOLE
PANDATION
APIAN
ORANGERY
MYOXINE
RETIARY
PAPULE

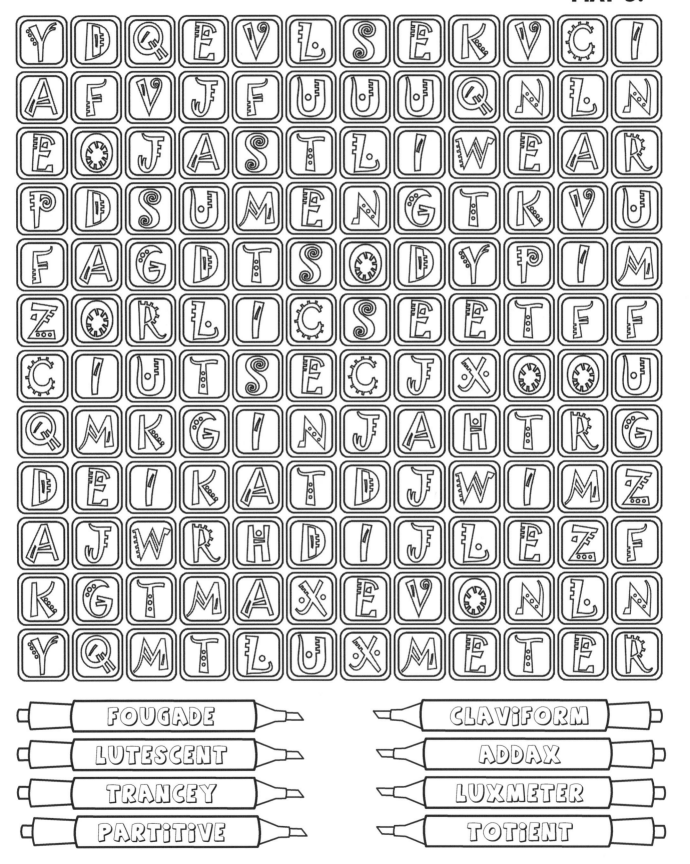

FOUGADE

LUTESCENT

TRANCEY

PARTITIVE

CLAVIFORM

ADDAX

LUXMETER

TOTIENT

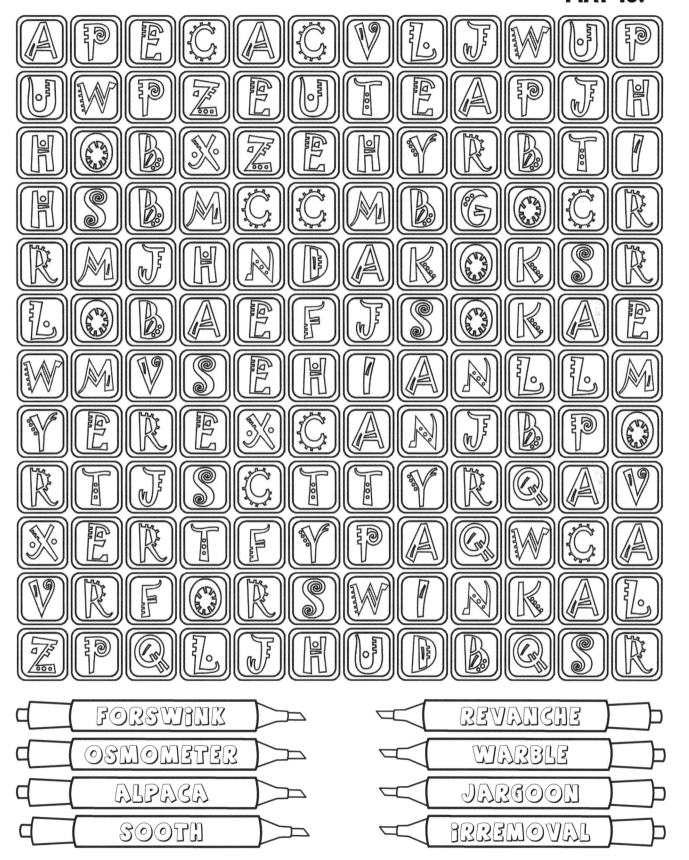

FORSWINK

OSMOMETER

ALPACA

SOOTH

REVANCHE

WARBLE

JARGOON

IRREMOVAL

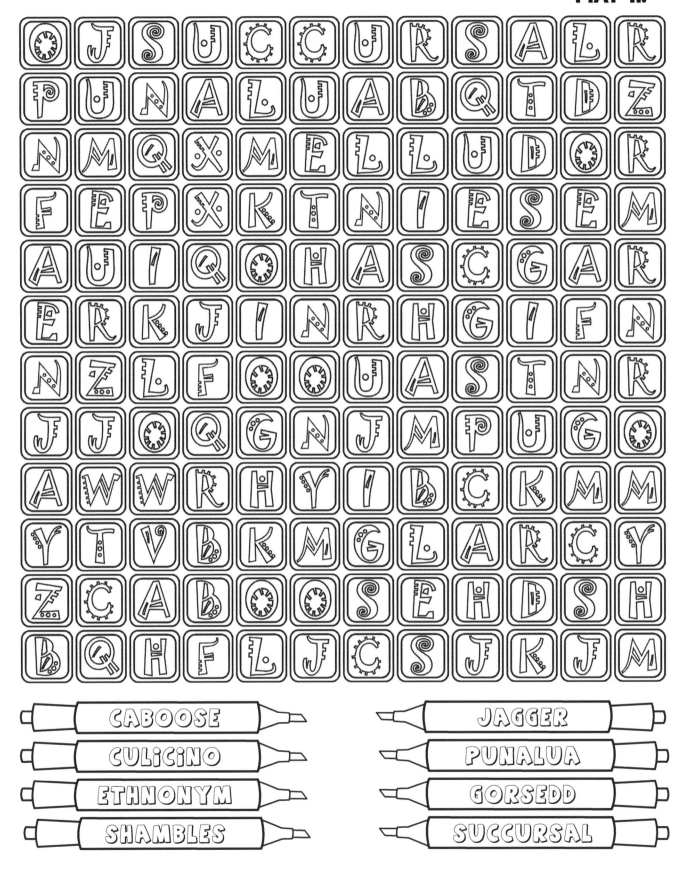

CABOOSE

JAGGER

CULICINO

PUNALUA

ETHNONYM

GORSEDD

SHAMBLES

SUCCURSAL

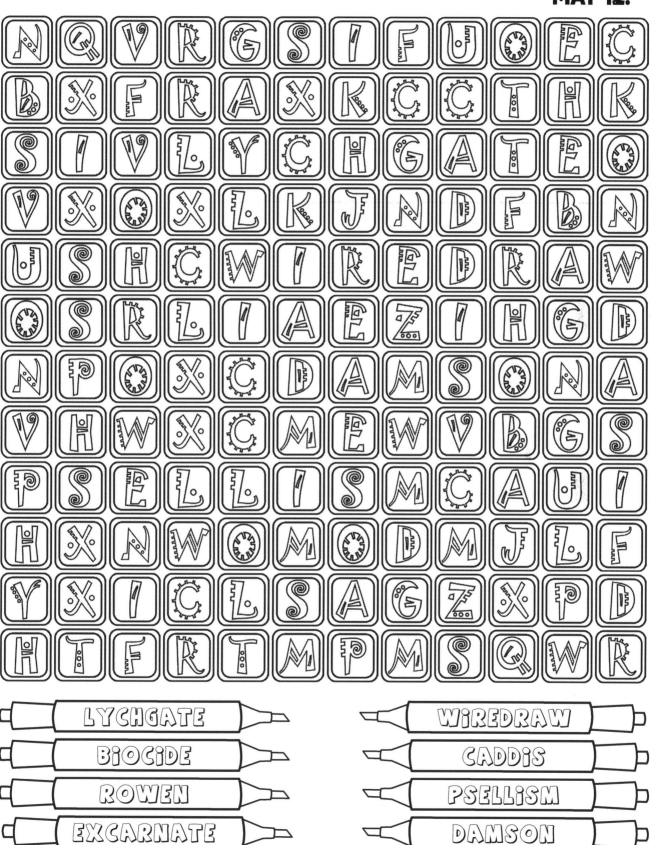

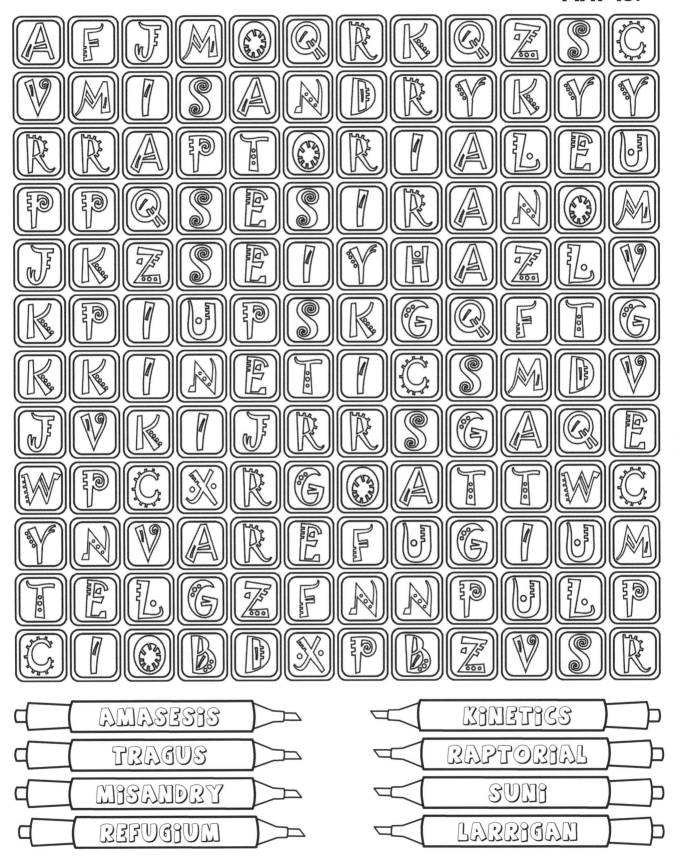

AMASESIS

TRAGUS

MISANDRY

REFUGIUM

KINETICS

RAPTORIAL

SUNI

LARRIGAN

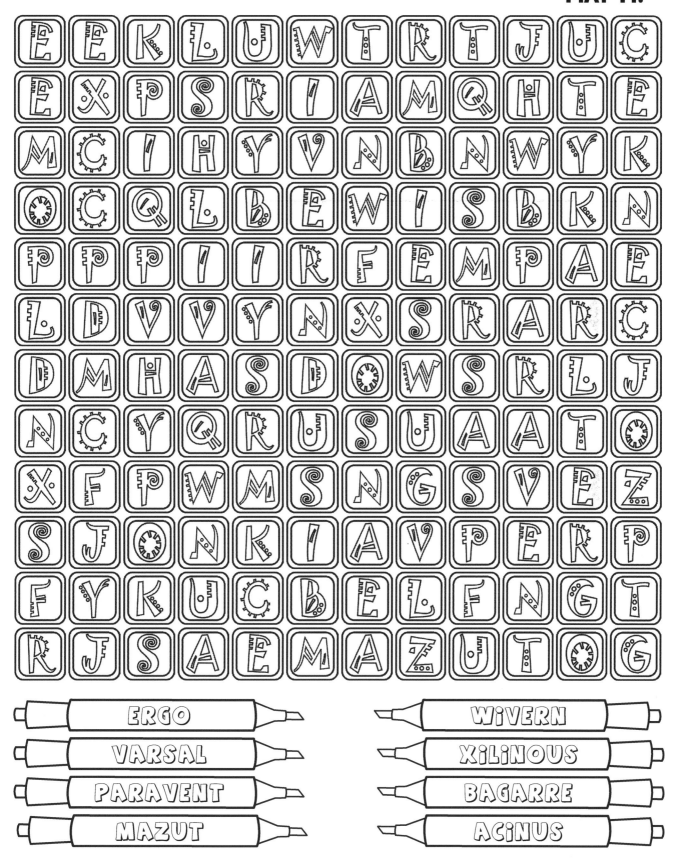

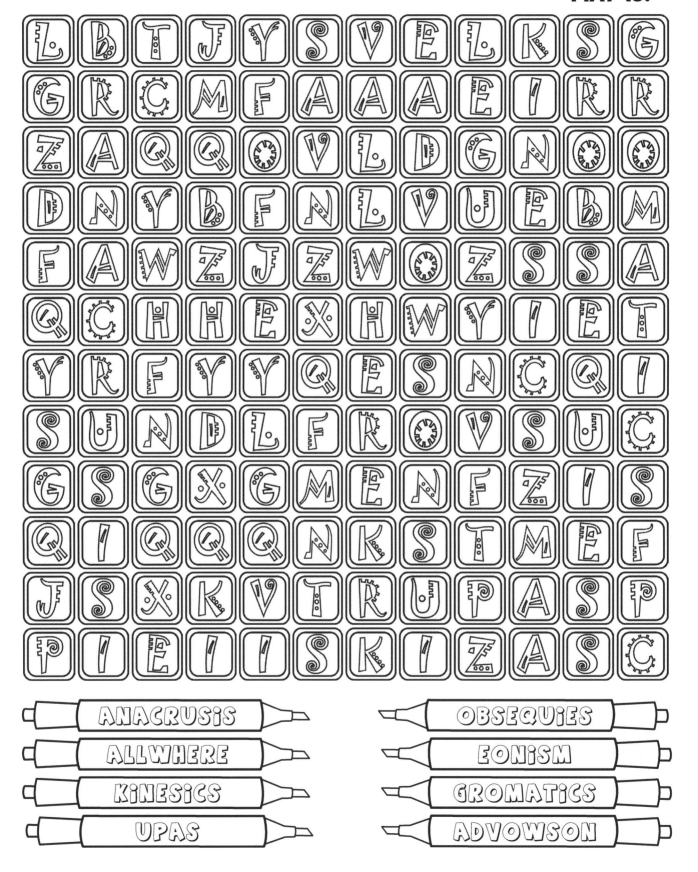

ANACRUSIS

ALLWHERE

KINESICS

UPAS

OBSEQUIES

EONISM

GROMATICS

ADVOWSON

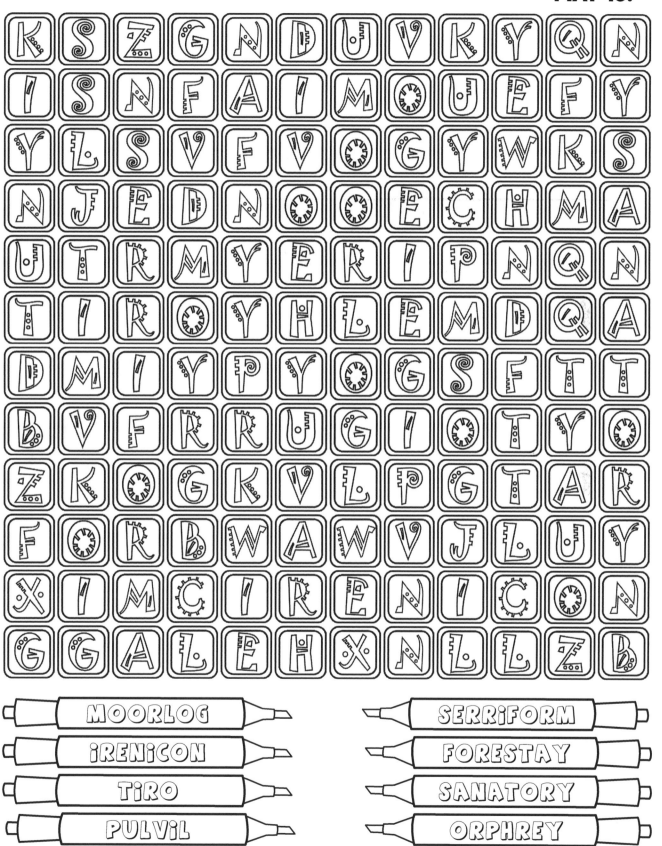

MOORLOG

SERRiFORM

iRENiCON

FORESTAY

TiRO

SANATORY

PULViL

ORPHREY

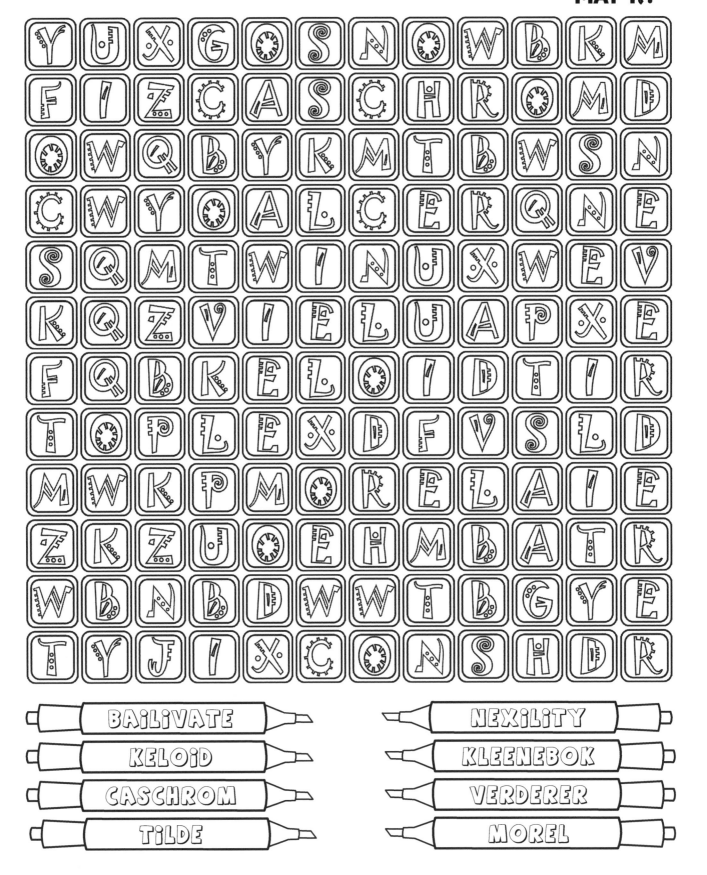

BAILIVATE

KELOID

CASCHROM

TILDE

NEXILITY

KLEENEBOK

VERDERER

MOREL

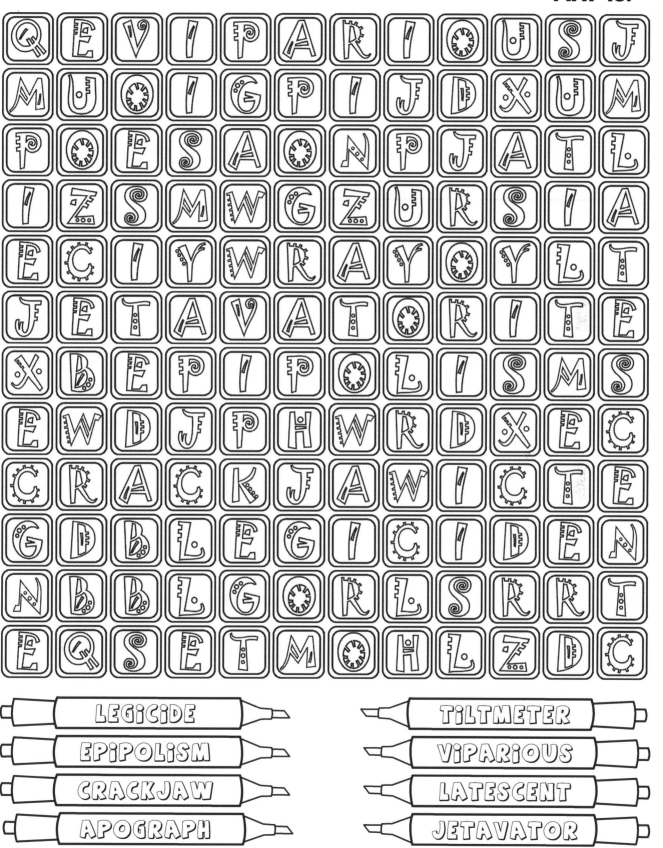

LEGICIDE

EPIPOLISM

CRACKJAW

APOGRAPH

TILTMETER

VIPARIOUS

LATESCENT

JETAVATOR

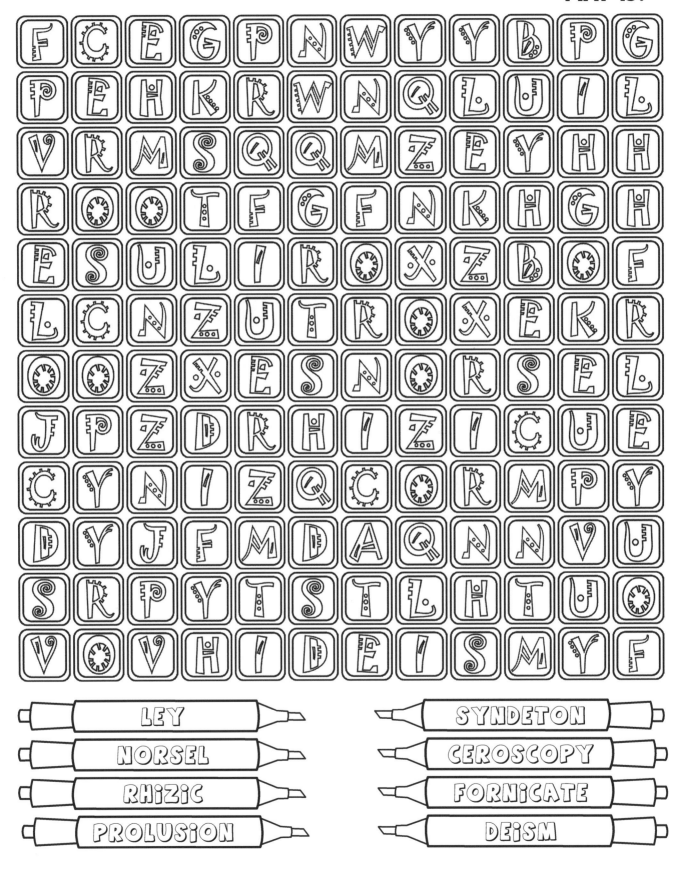

LEY

NORSEL

RHIZIC

PROLUSION

SYNDETON

CEROSCOPY

FORNICATE

DEISM

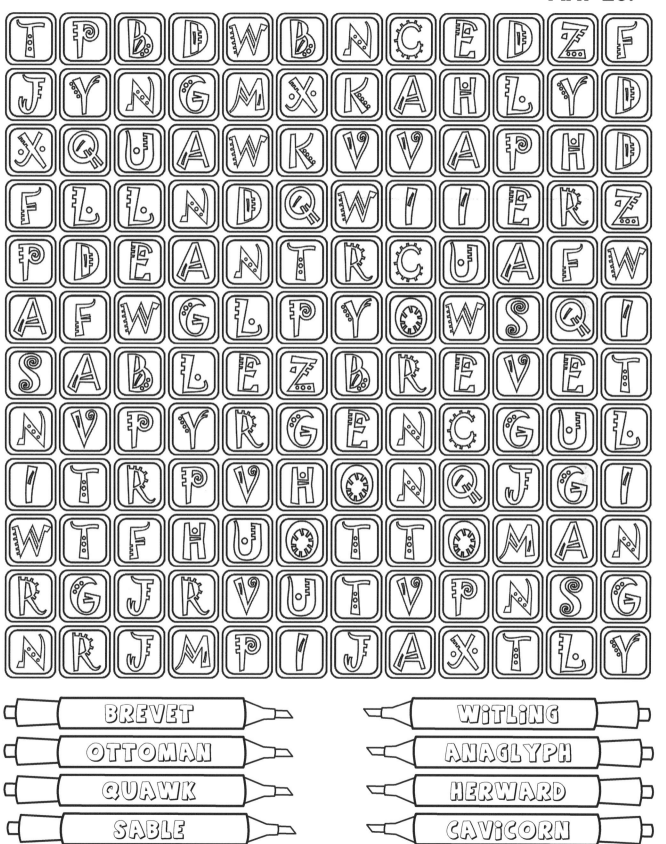

BREVET

OTTOMAN

QUAWK

SABLE

WITLING

ANAGLYPH

HERWARD

CAVICORN

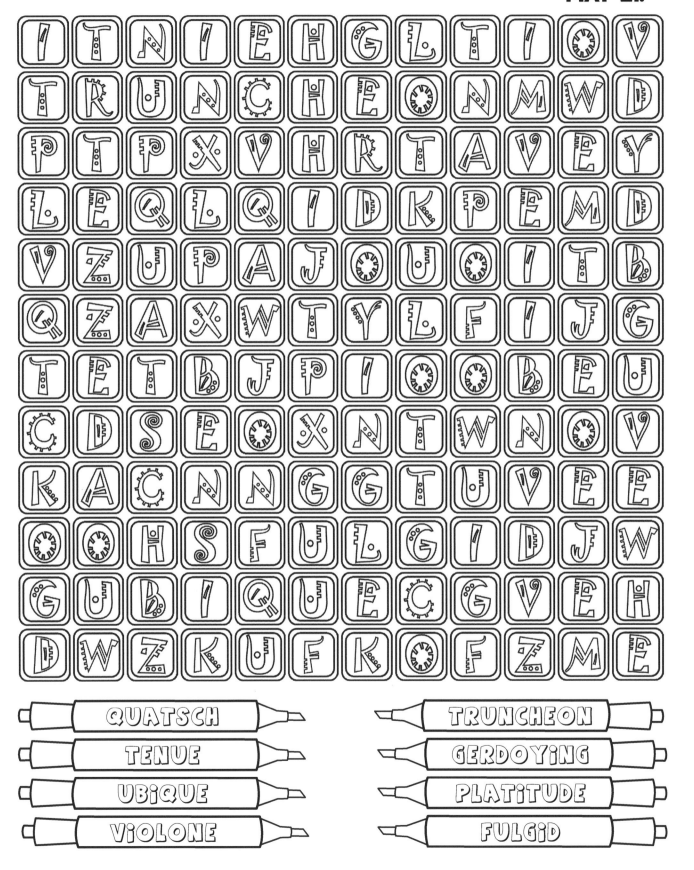

QUATSCH

TENUE

UBIQUE

VIOLONE

TRUNCHEON

GERDOYING

PLATITUDE

FULGID

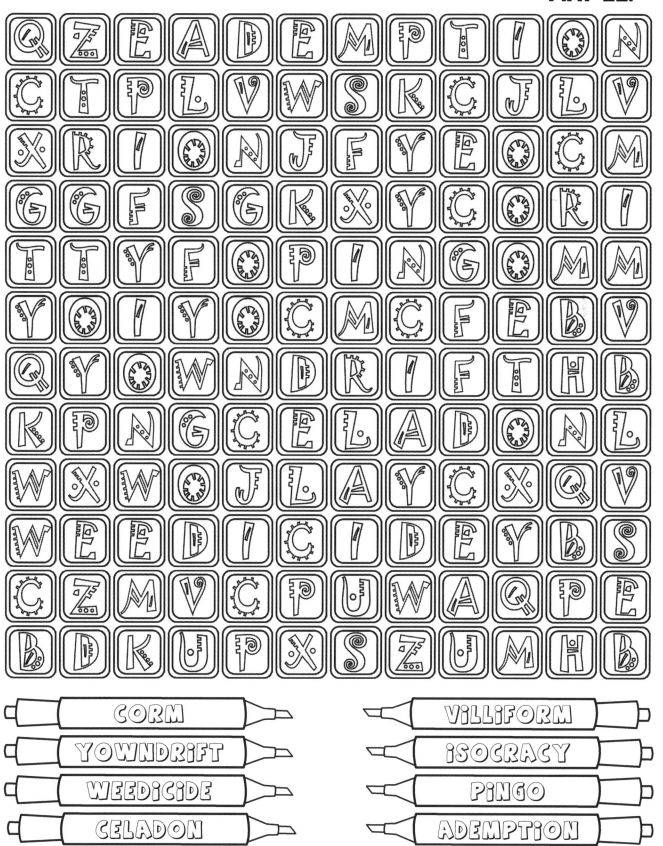

QZEADEMPTION
CTPLVWSKCJLV
XRION JFYEOCM
GGFSGKXYCRI
TTYFOPINGOMM
YOIYCMCFEBV
QYOWNDRIFTHB
KPNGCELADONLZ
WXWOJLAYCXQV
WEEDICIDEYBS
CZMVCPUWAQPE
BDKUPXSZUMHB

CORM
YOWNDRIFT
WEEDICIDE
CELADON

VILLIFORM
ISOCRACY
PINGO
ADEMPTION

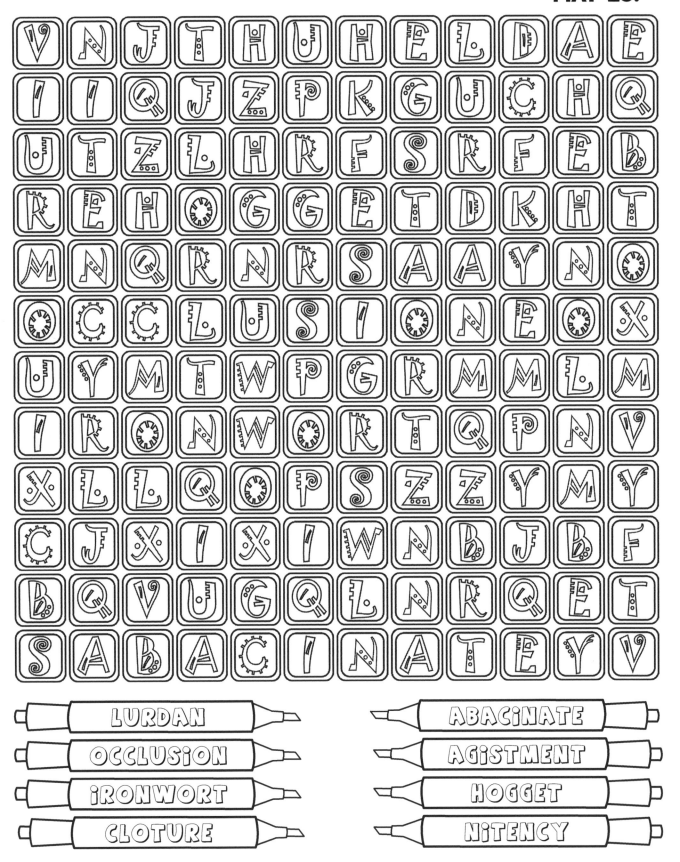

LURDAN

OCCLUSION

IRONWORT

CLOTURE

ABACINATE

AGISTMENT

HOGGET

NITENCY

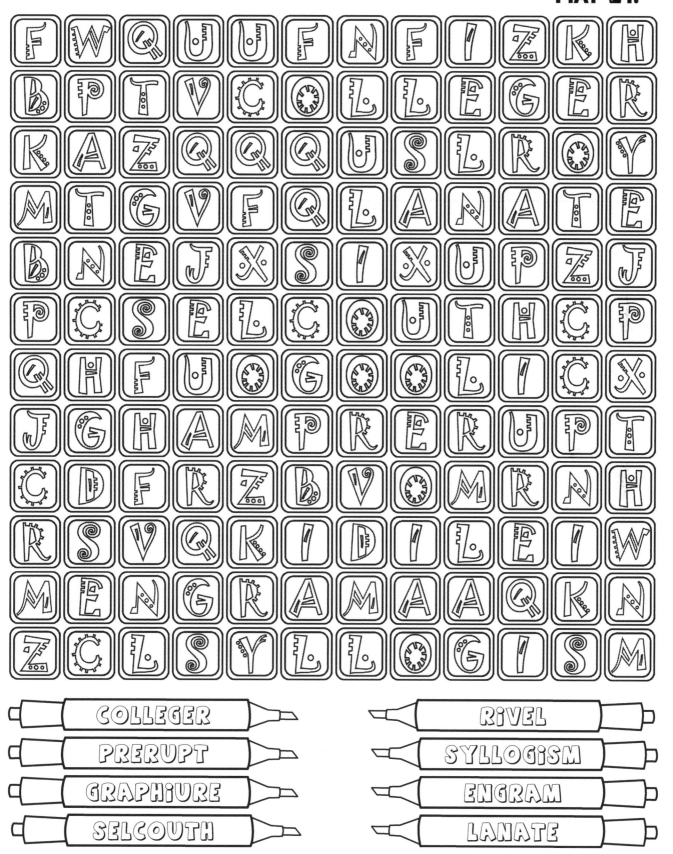

COLLEGER

PRERUPT

GRAPHIURE

SELCOUTH

RIVEL

SYLLOGISM

ENGRAM

LANATE

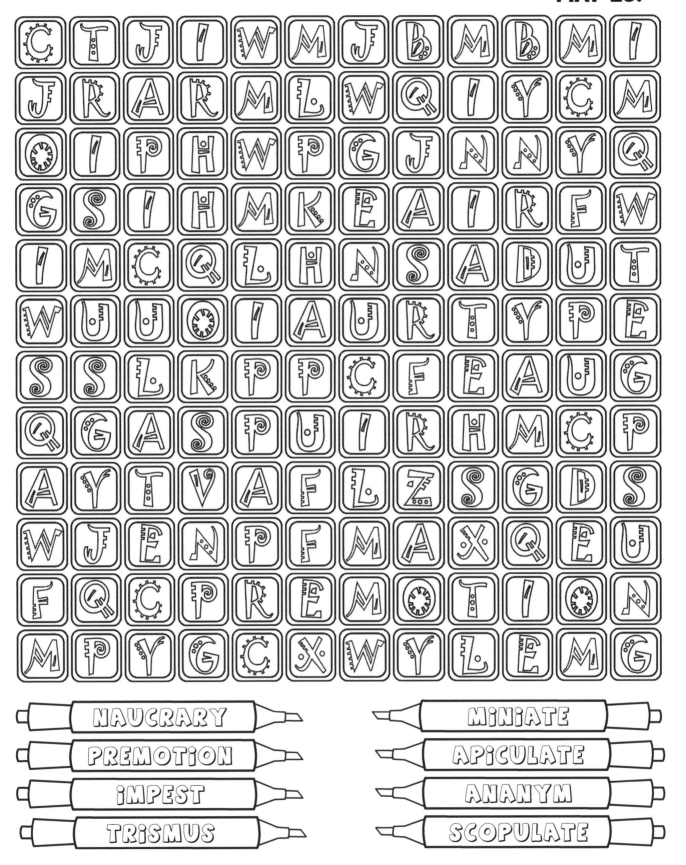

NAUCRARY

PREMOTION

IMPEST

TRISMUS

MINIATE

APICULATE

ANANYM

SCOPULATE

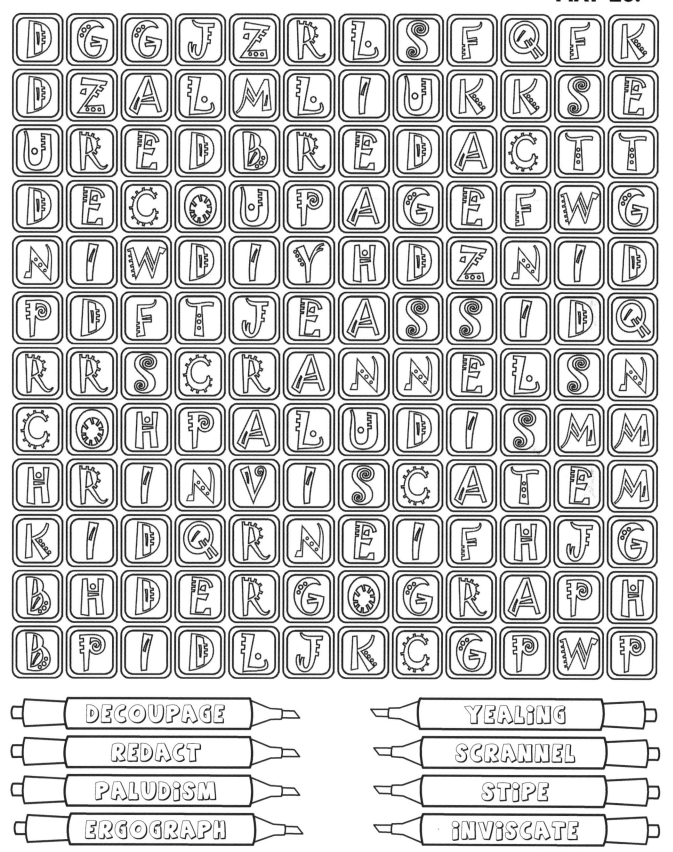

DECOUPAGE

REDACT

PALUDISM

ERGOGRAPH

YEALING

SCRANNEL

STIPE

INVISCATE

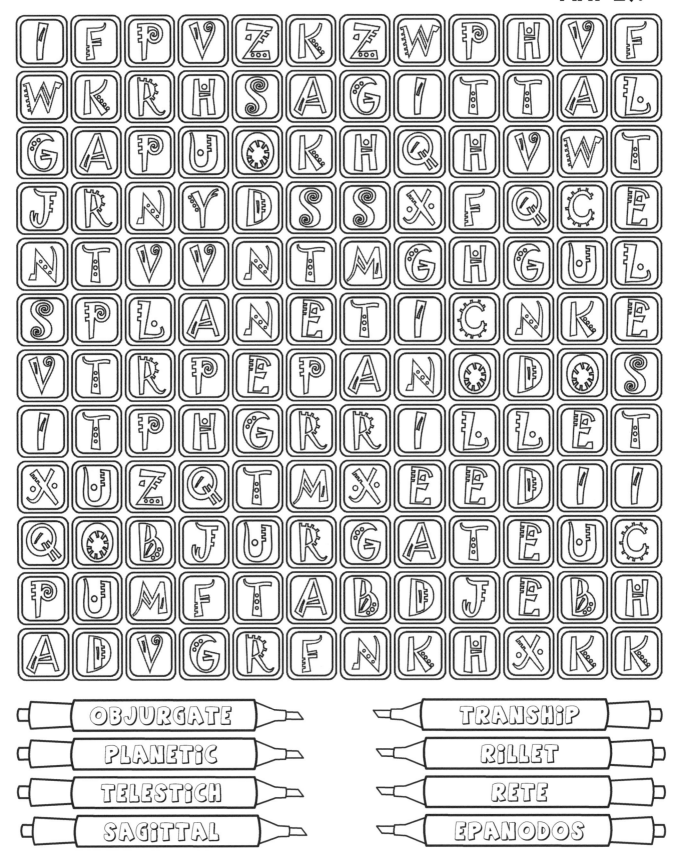

OBJURGATE

PLANETIC

TELESTICH

SAGITTAL

TRANSHIP

RILLET

RETE

EPANODOS

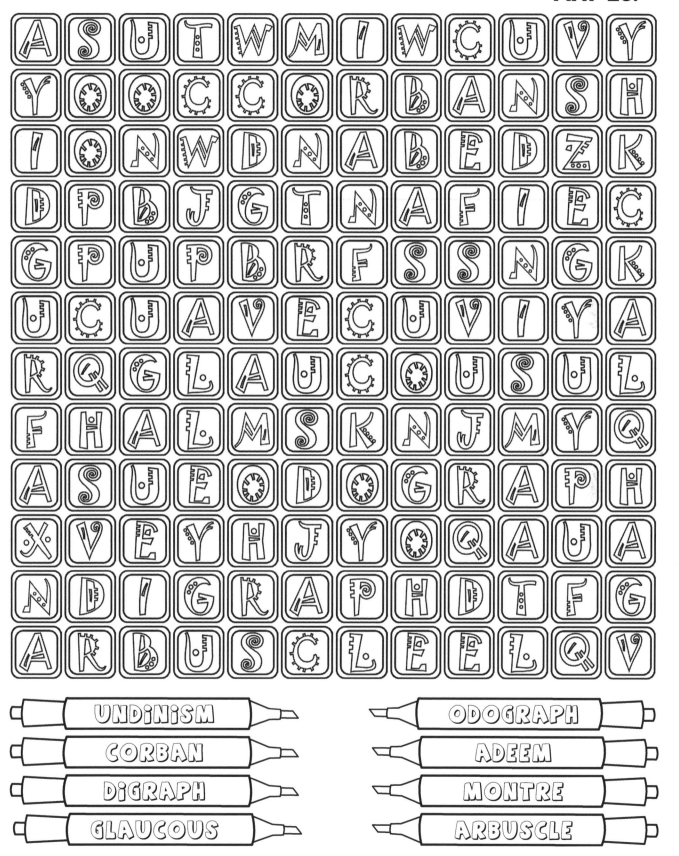

UNDINISM

CORBAN

DIGRAPH

GLAUCOUS

ODOGRAPH

ADEEM

MONTRE

ARBUSCLE

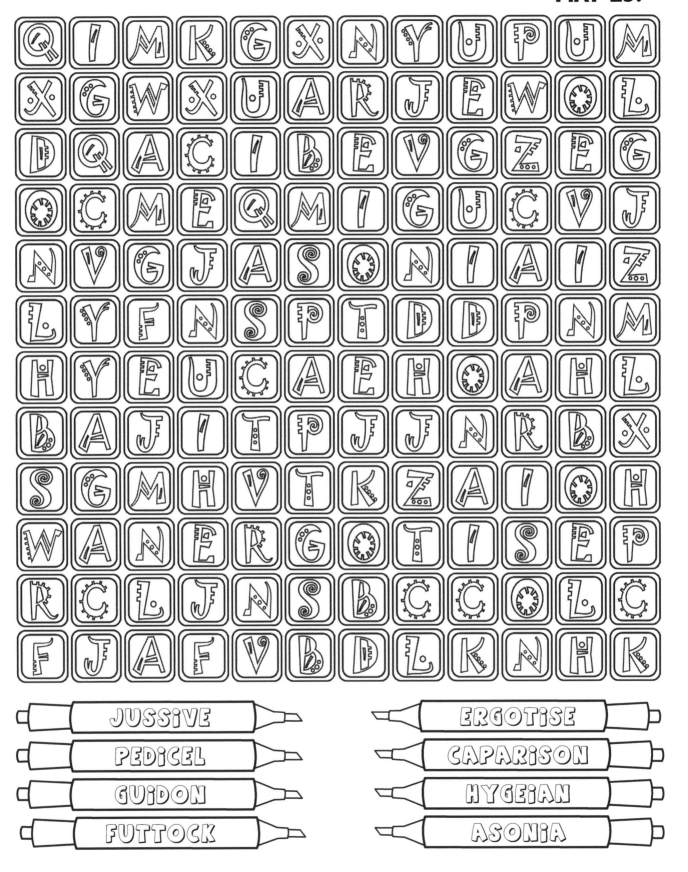

JUSSIVE

PEDICEL

GUIDON

FUTTOCK

ERGOTISE

CAPARISON

HYGEIAN

ASONIA

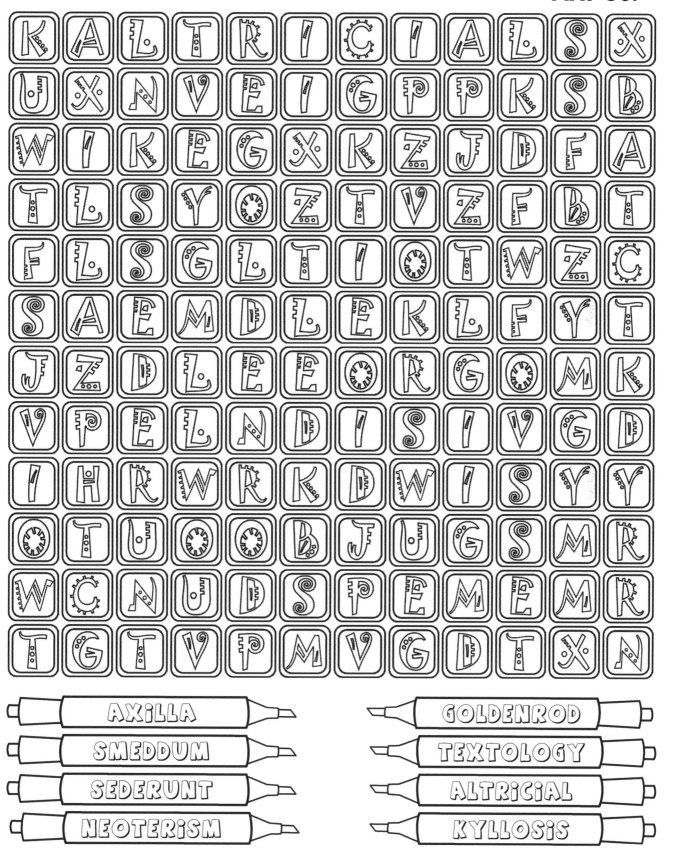

AXILLA

SMEDDUM

SEDERUNT

NEOTERISM

GOLDENROD

TEXTOLOGY

ALTRICIAL

KYLLOSIS

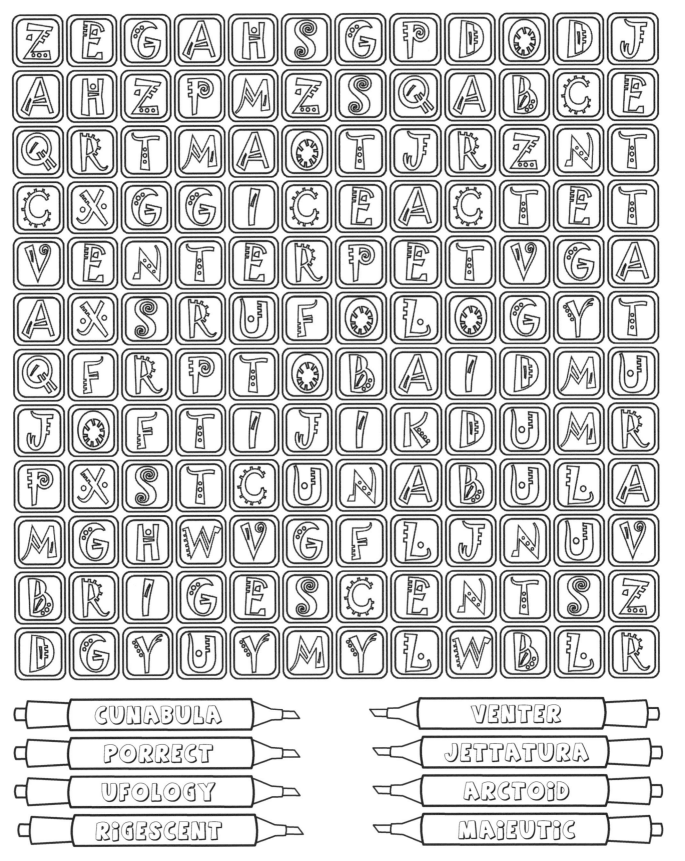

CUNABULA

PORRECT

UFOLOGY

RIGESCENT

VENTER

JETTATURA

ARCTOID

MAIEUTIC

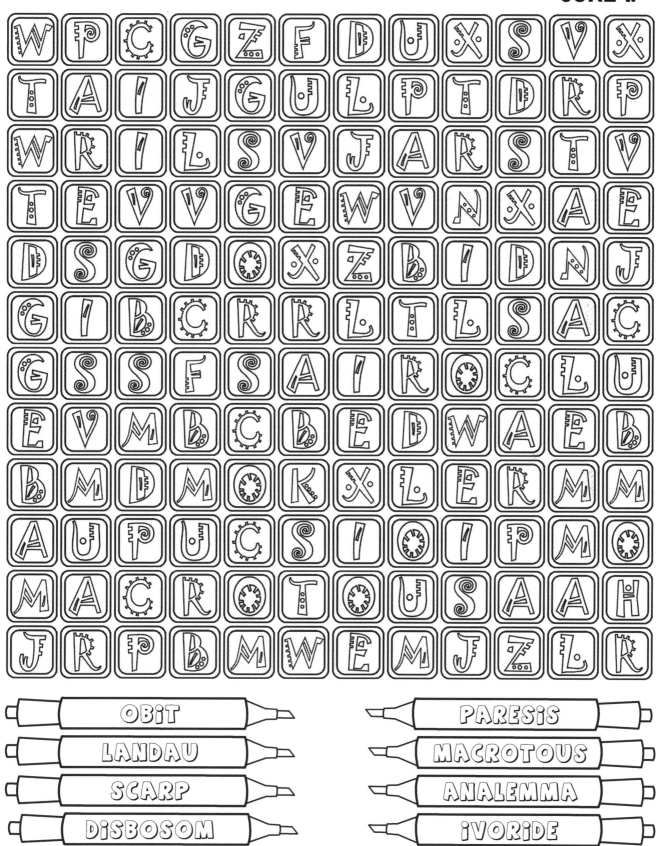

OBIT

LANDAU

SCARP

DISBOSOM

PARESIS

MACROTOUS

ANALEMMA

IVORIDE

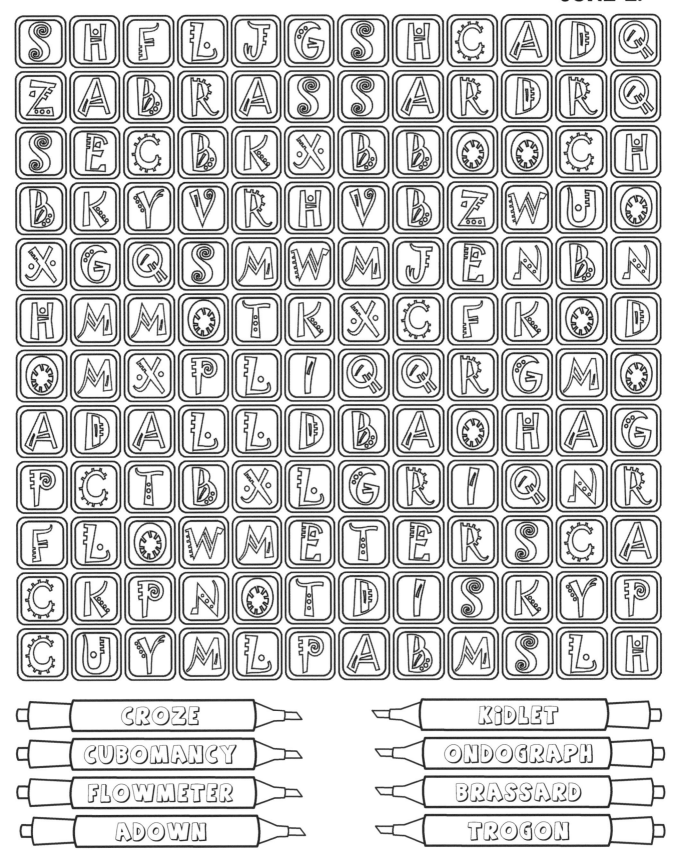

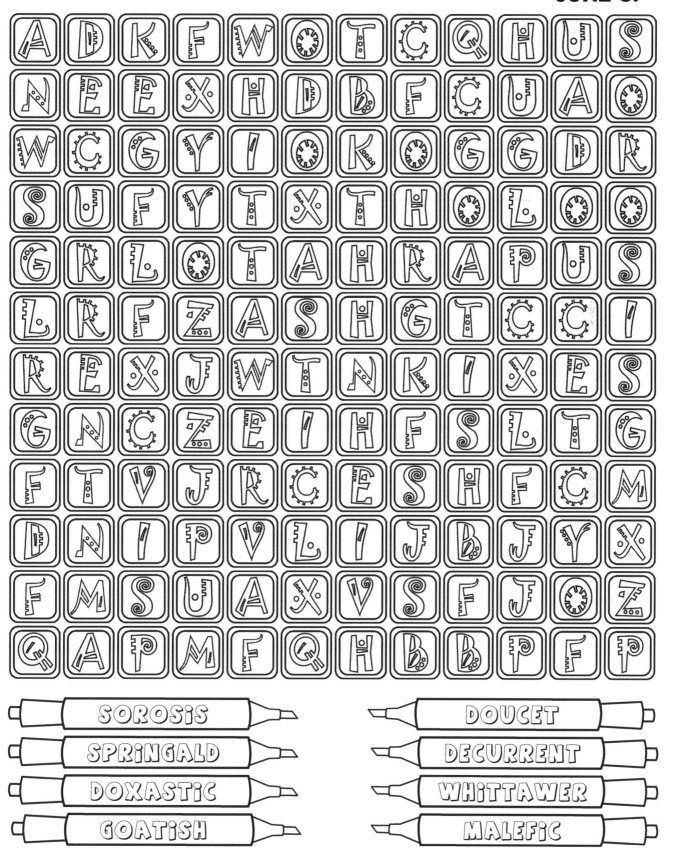

SOROSIS

SPRINGALD

DOXASTIC

GOATISH

DOUCET

DECURRENT

WHITTAWER

MALEFIC

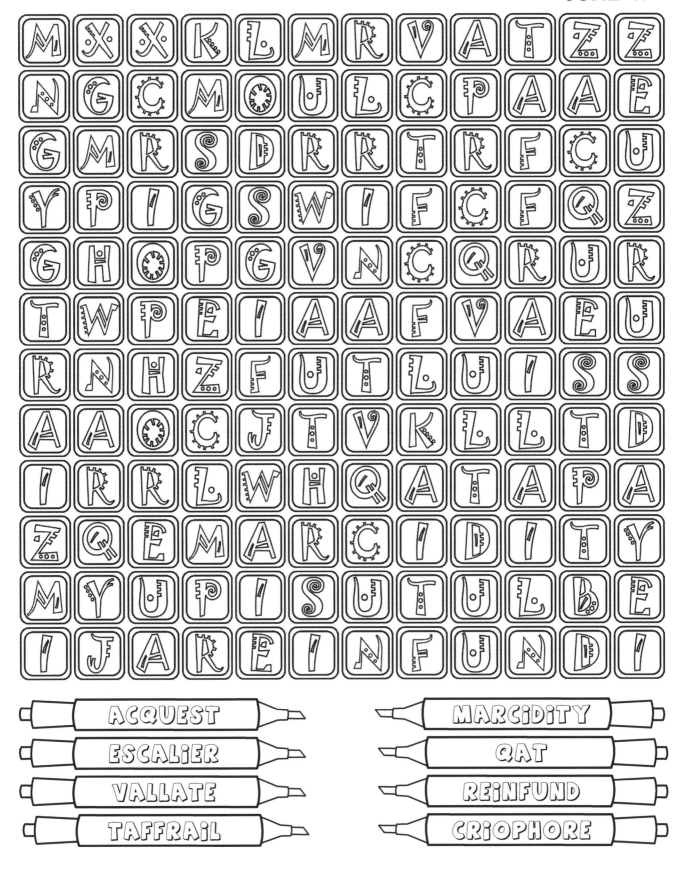

ACQUEST

ESCALIER

VALLATE

TAFFRAIL

MARCIDITY

QAT

REINFUND

CRIOPHORE

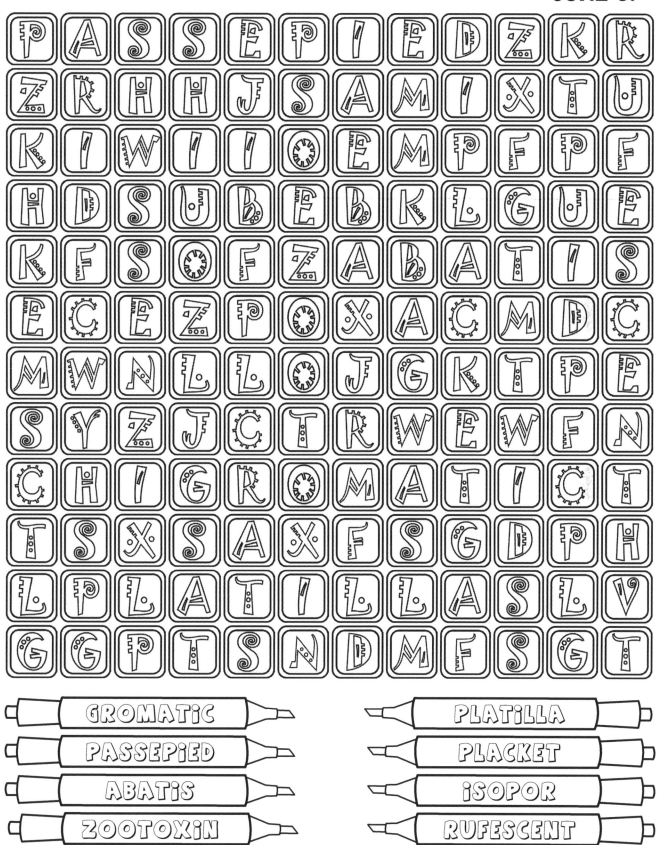

GROMATIC

PASSEPIED

ABATIS

ZOOTOXIN

PLATILLA

PLACKET

ISOPOR

RUFESCENT

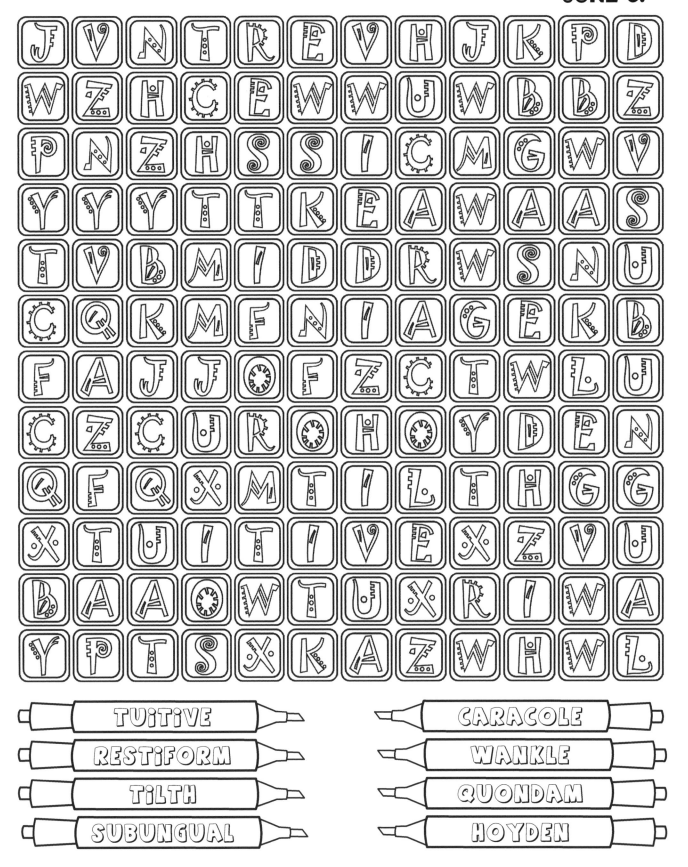

TUITIVE

CARACOLE

RESTIFORM

WANKLE

TILTH

QUONDAM

SUBUNGUAL

HOYDEN

RUBESCENT

TERRET

LOCELLUS

FLEAM

BELAY

METHYSIS

VILLUS

COIGN

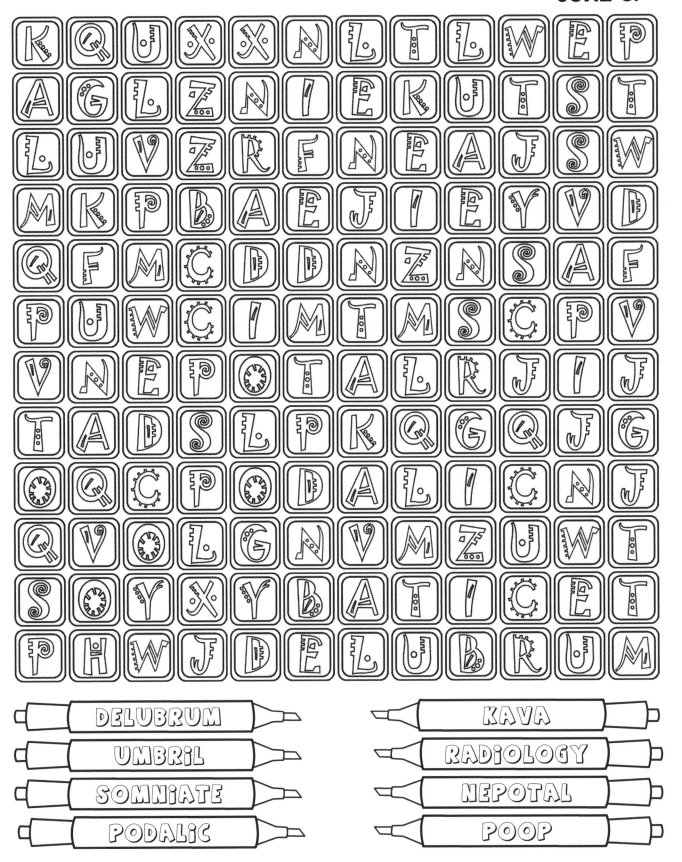

DELUBRUM

UMBRIL

SOMNIATE

PODALIC

KAVA

RADIOLOGY

NEPOTAL

POOP

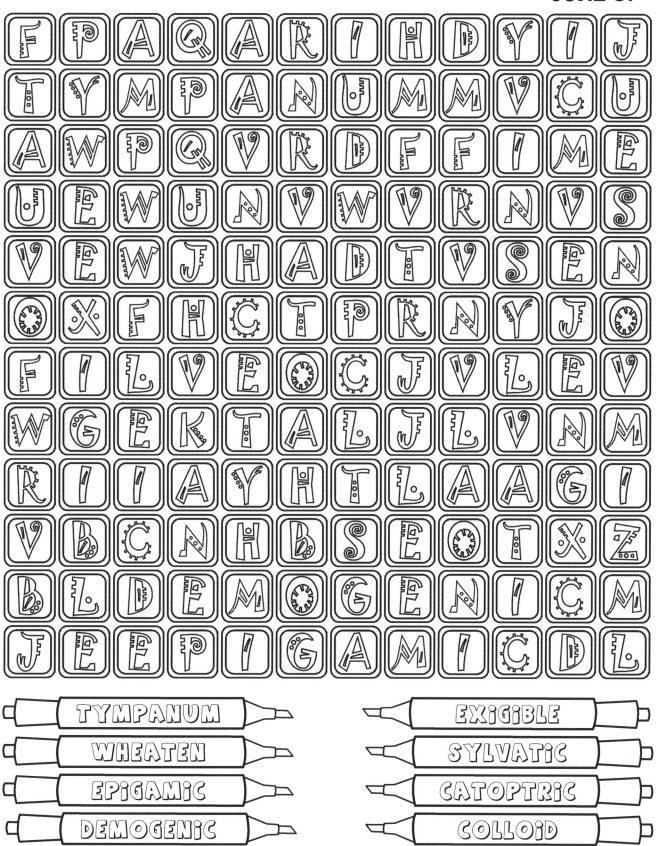

TYMPANUM

WHEATEN

EPIGAMIC

DEMOGENIC

EXIGIBLE

SYLVATIC

CATOPTRIC

COLLOID

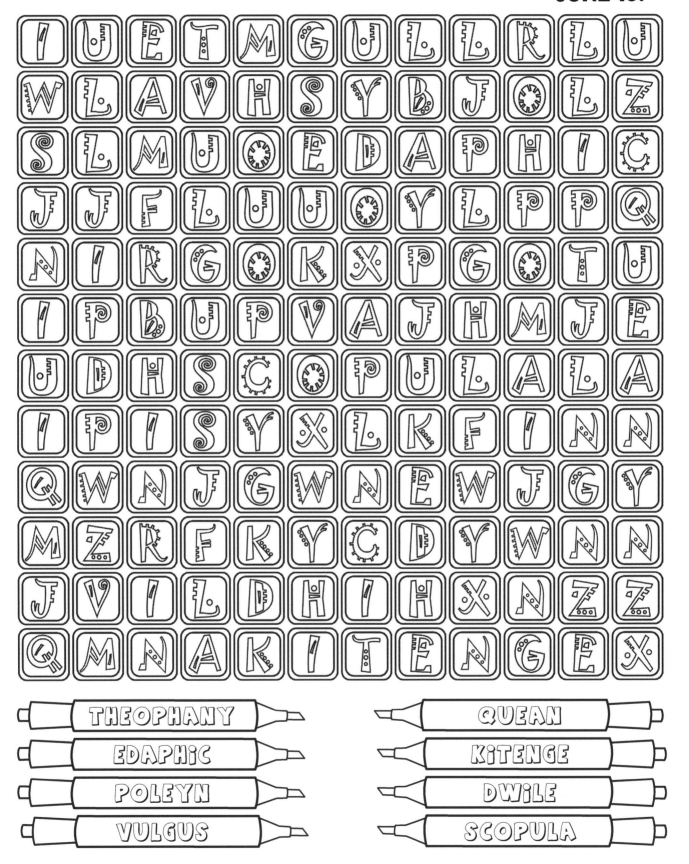

THEOPHANY

EDAPHIC

POLEYN

VULGUS

QUEAN

KITENGE

DWILE

SCOPULA

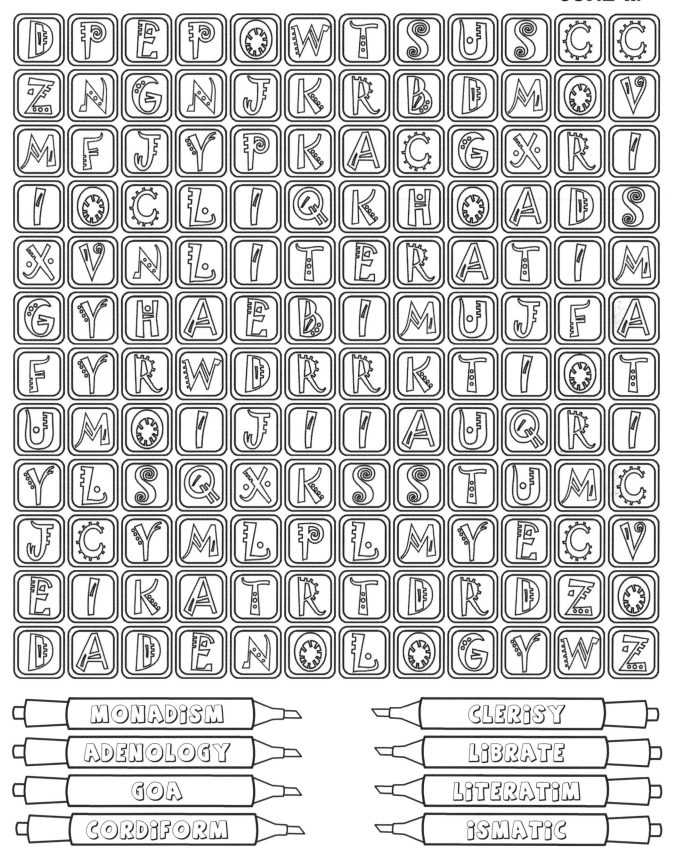

MONADISM

ADENOLOGY

GOA

CORDIFORM

CLERISY

LIBRATE

LITERATIM

ISMATIC

JUNE 12:

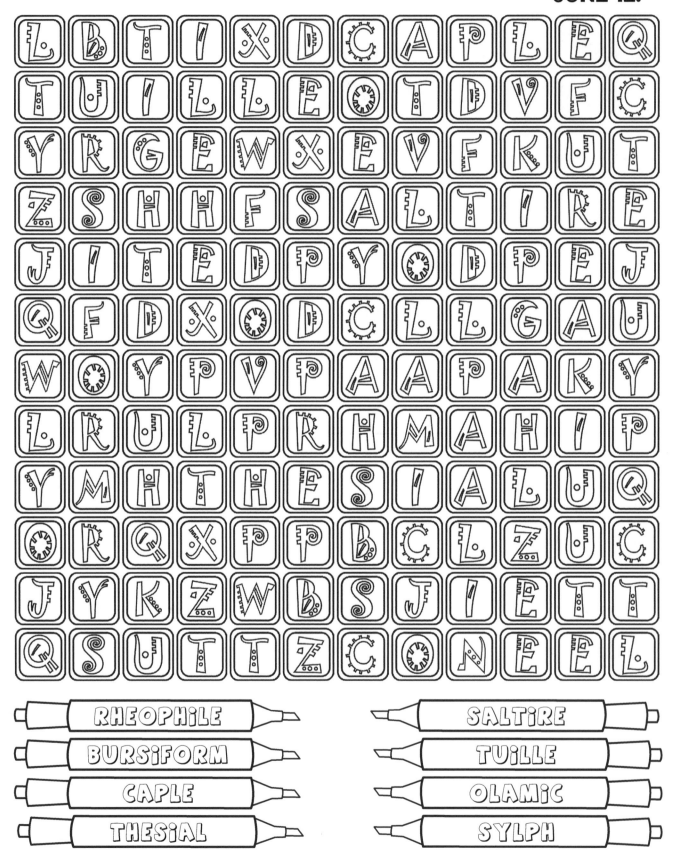

RHEOPHILE

BURSIFORM

CAPLE

THESIAL

SALTIRE

TUILLE

OLAMIC

SYLPH

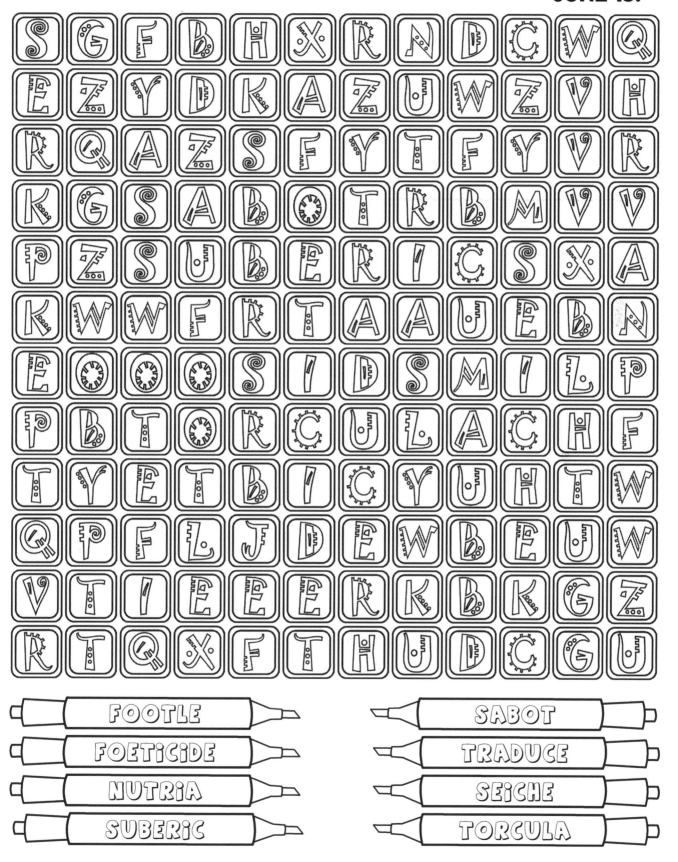

FOOTLE

FOETICIDE

NUTRIA

SUBERIC

SABOT

TRADUCE

SEICHE

TORCULA

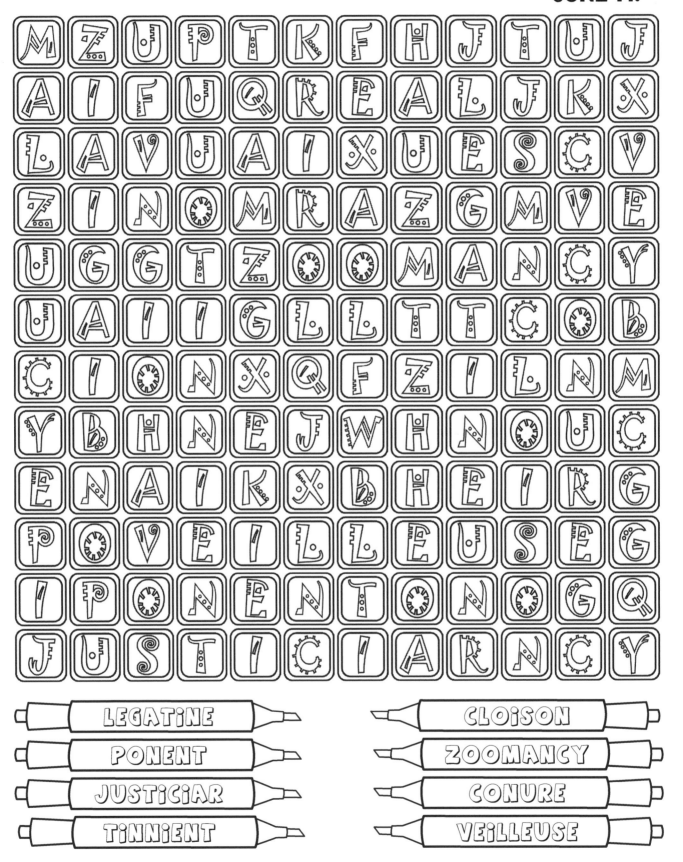

LEGATINE
PONENT
JUSTICIAR
TINNIENT

CLOISON
ZOOMANCY
CONURE
VEILLEUSE

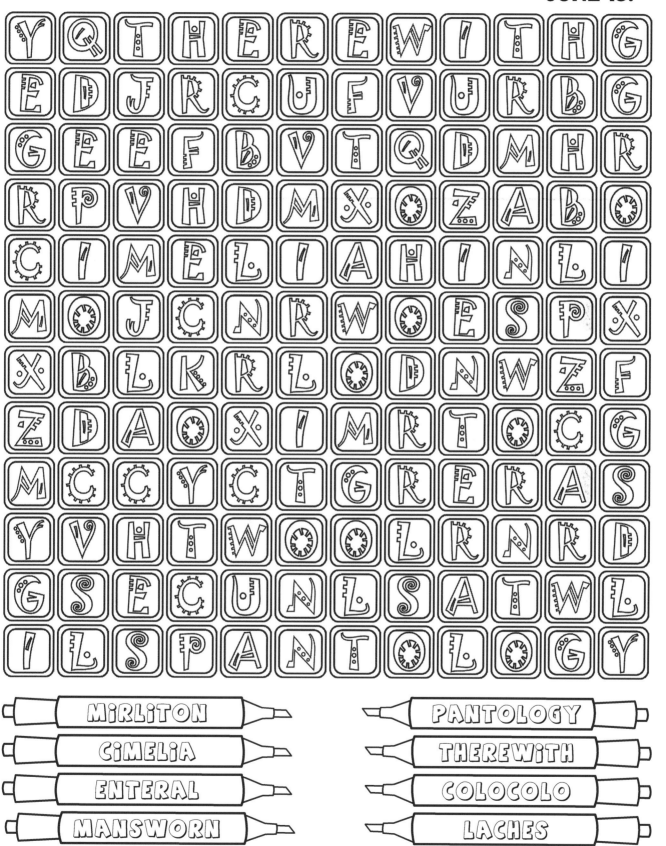

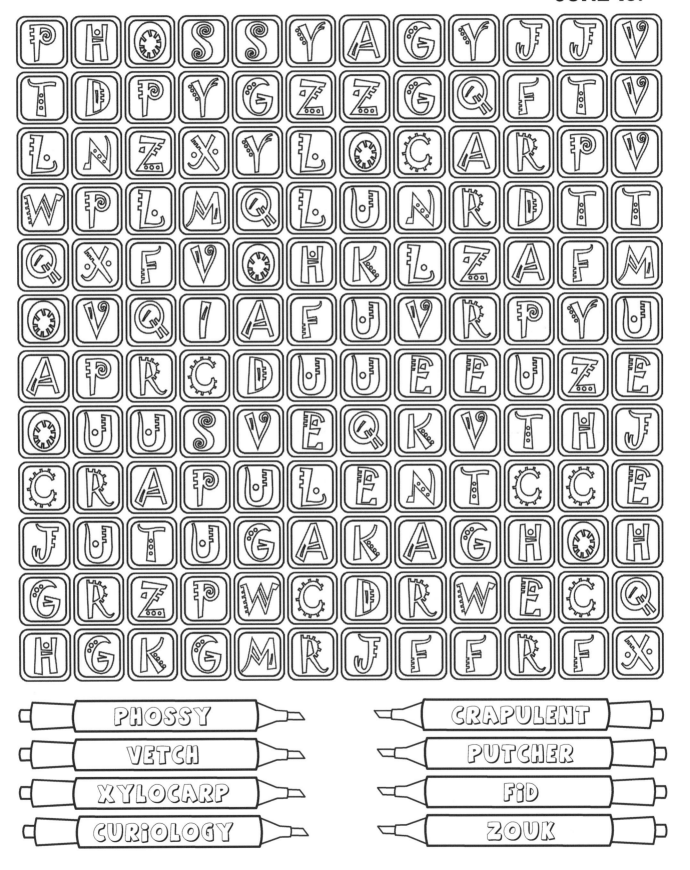

PHOSSY

VETCH

XYLOCARP

CURIOLOGY

CRAPULENT

PUTCHER

FID

ZOUK

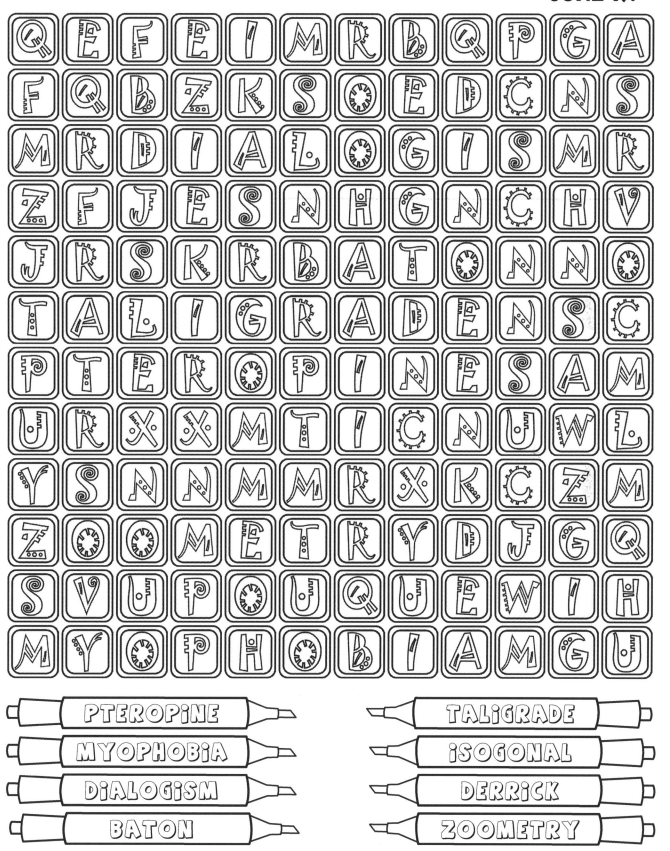

PTEROPINE

MYOPHOBIA

DIALOGISM

BATON

TALIGRADE

ISOGONAL

DERRICK

ZOOMETRY

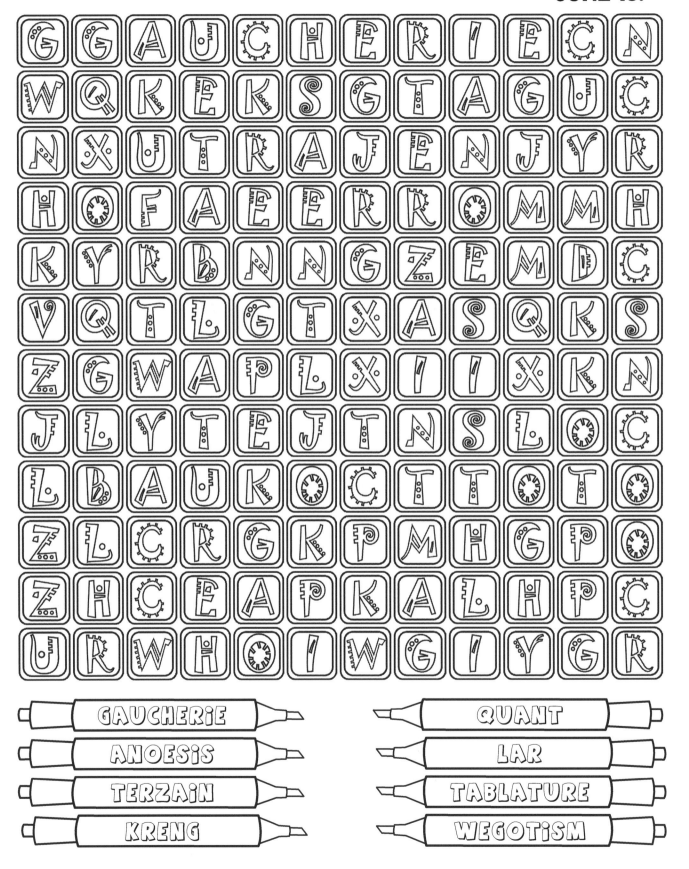

GAUCHERIE

ANOESIS

TERZAIN

KRENG

QUANT

LAR

TABLATURE

WEGOTISM

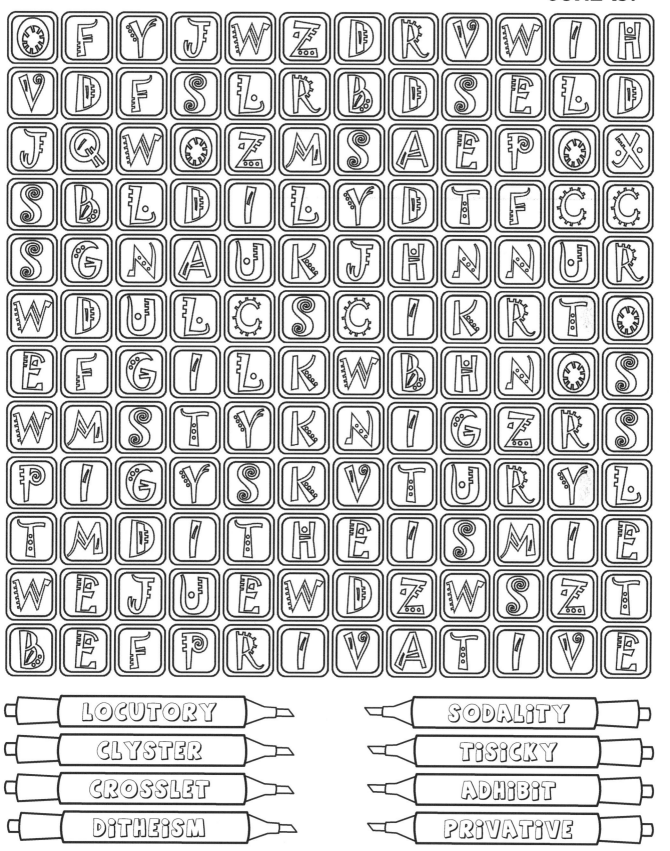

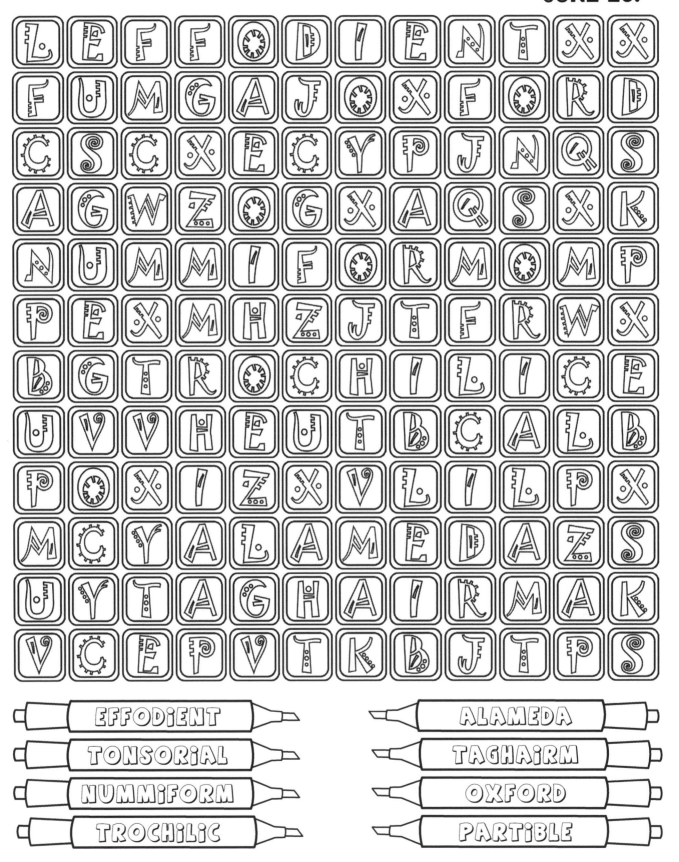

EFFODIENT

TONSORIAL

NUMMIFORM

TROCHILIC

ALAMEDA

TAGHAIRM

OXFORD

PARTIBLE

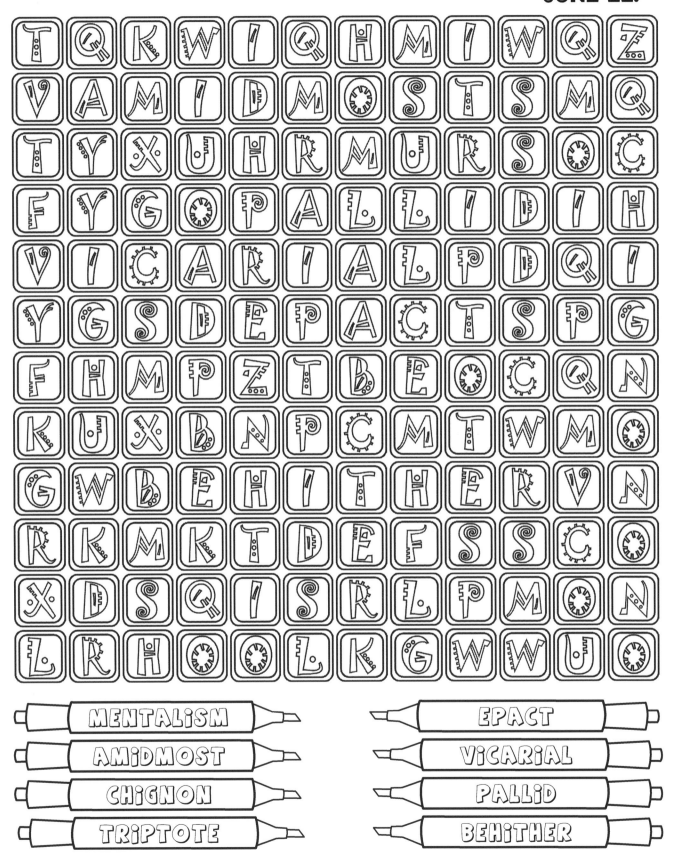

MENTALISM   EPACT

AMIDMOST   VICARIAL

CHIGNON   PALLID

TRIPTOTE   BEHITHER

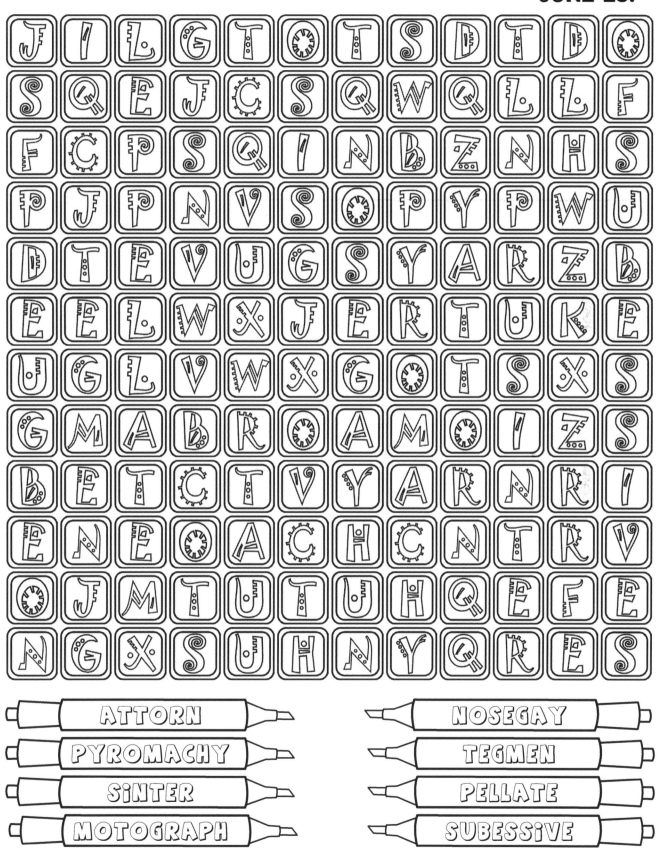

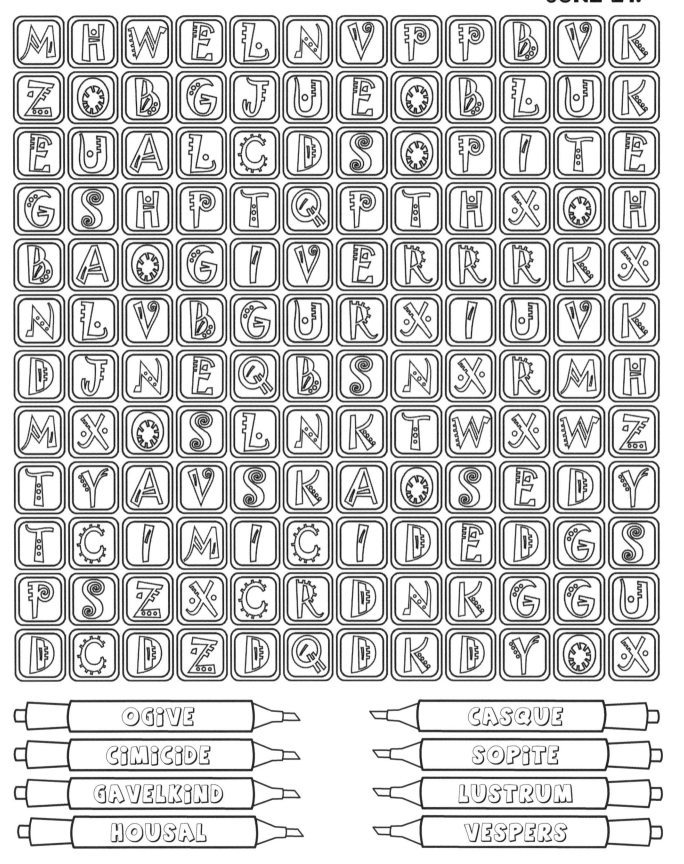

OGIVE

CIMICIDE

GAVELKIND

HOUSAL

CASQUE

SOPITE

LUSTRUM

VESPERS

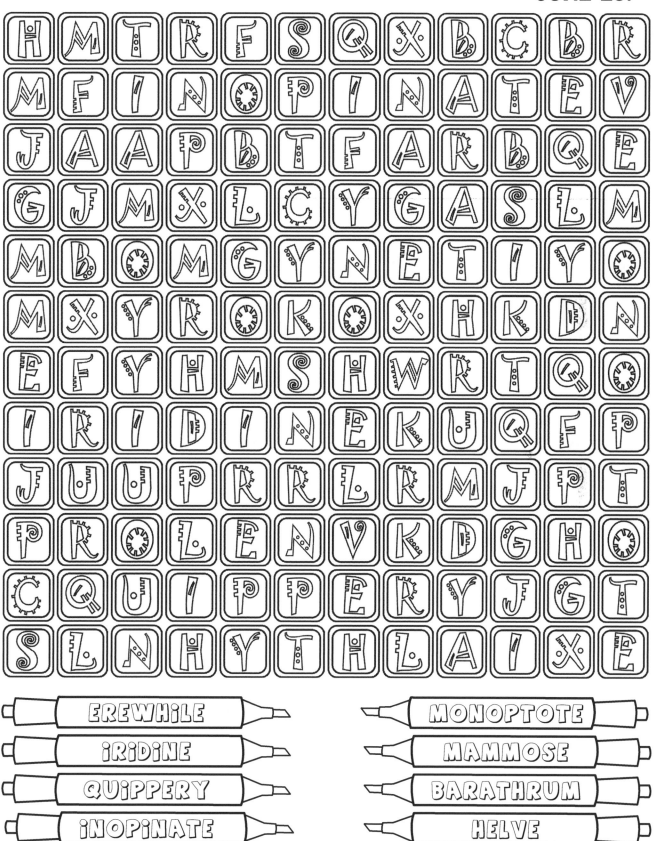

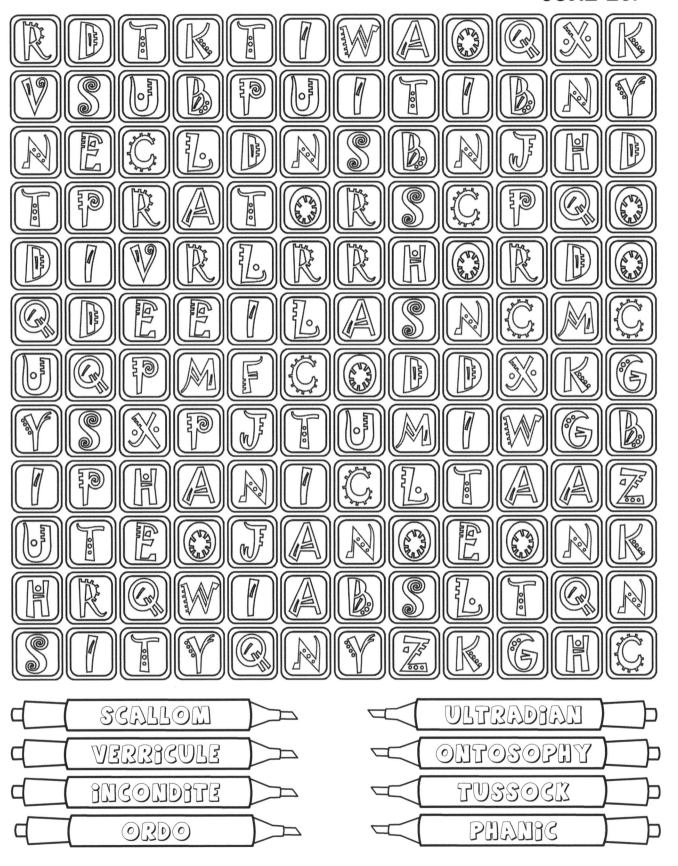

SCALLOM

VERRICULE

INCONDITE

ORDO

ULTRADIAN

ONTOSOPHY

TUSSOCK

PHANIC

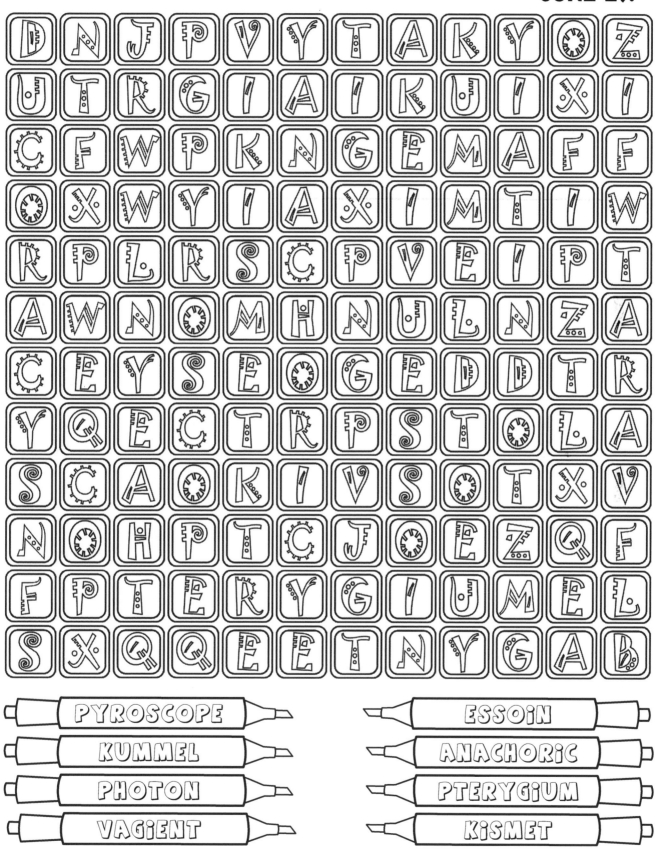

PYROSCOPE
KUMMEL
PHOTON
VAGIENT

ESSOIN
ANACHORIC
PTERYGIUM
KISMET

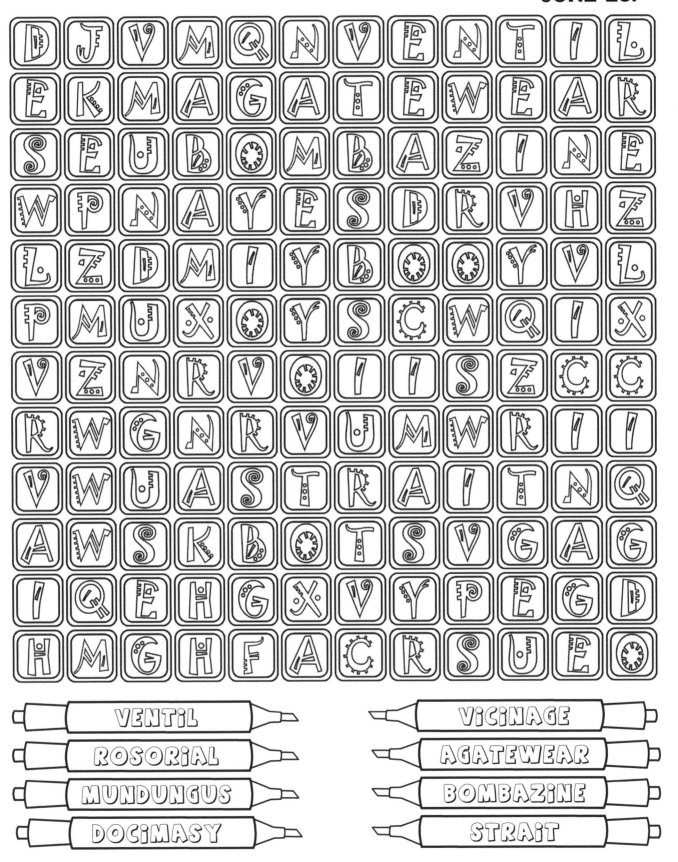

VENTIL

VICINAGE

ROSORIAL

AGATEWEAR

MUNDUNGUS

BOMBAZINE

DOCIMASY

STRAIT

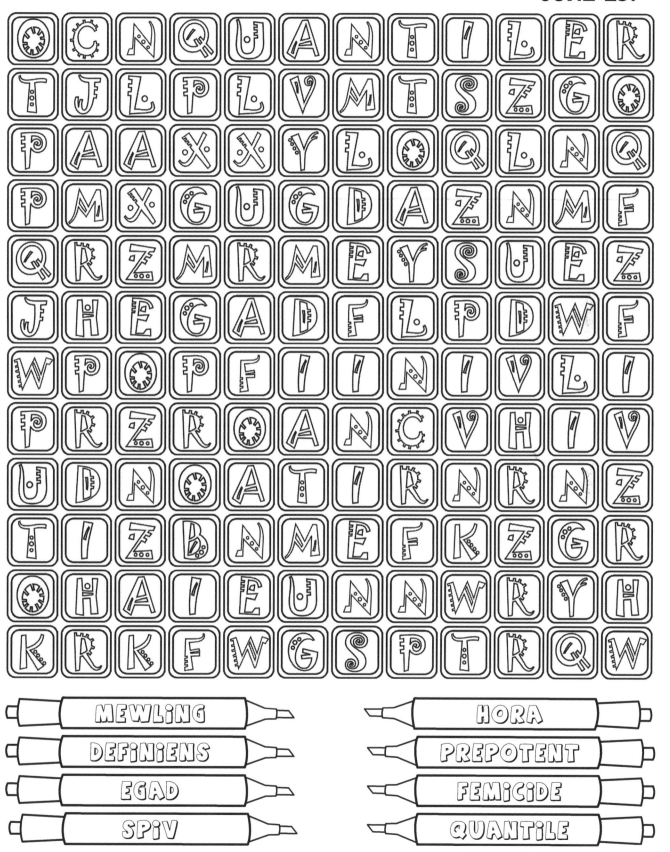

MEWLING

DEFINIENS

EGAD

SPIV

HORA

PREPOTENT

FEMICIDE

QUANTILE

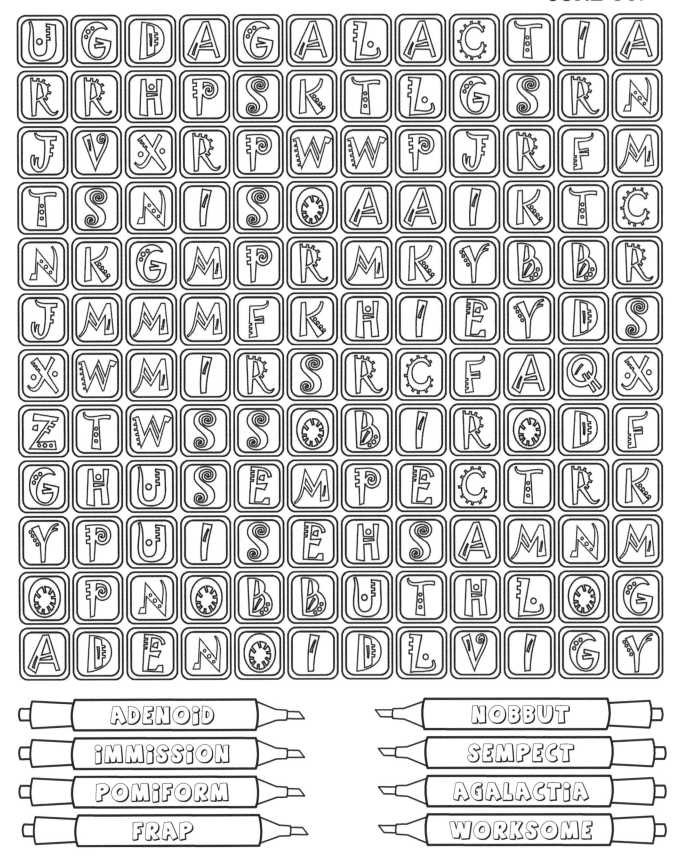

ADENOID

IMMISSION

POMIFORM

FRAP

NOBBUT

SEMPECT

AGALACTIA

WORKSOME

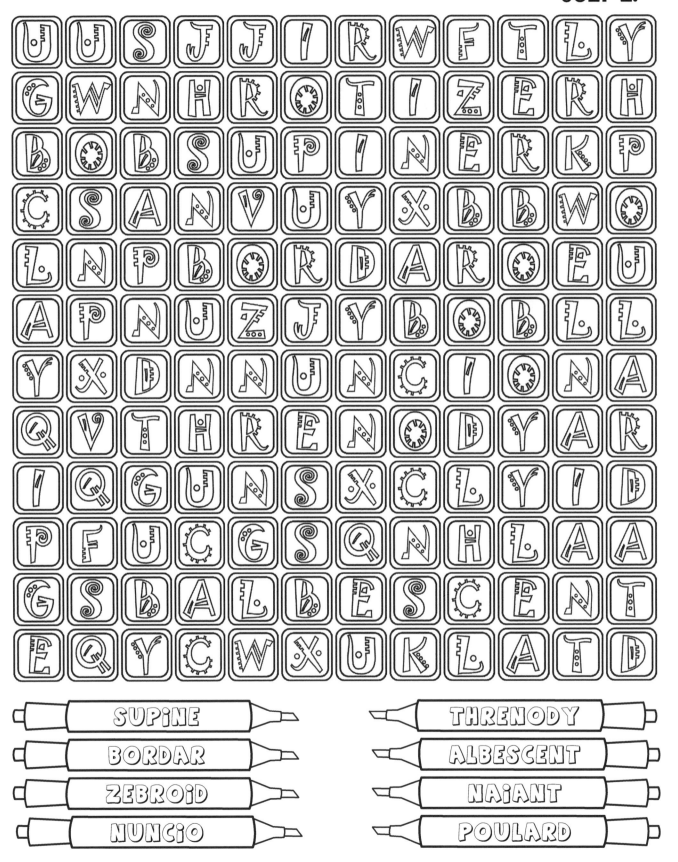

SUPINE

BORDAR

ZEBROID

NUNCIO

THRENODY

ALBESCENT

NAIANT

POULARD

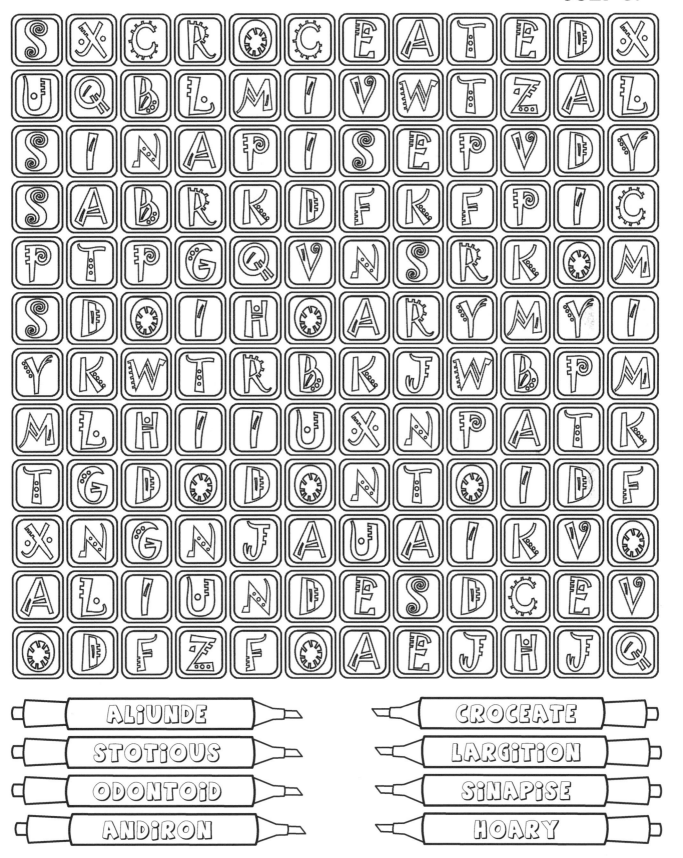

ALIUNDE

STOTIOUS

ODONTOID

ANDIRON

CROCEATE

LARGITION

SINAPISE

HOARY

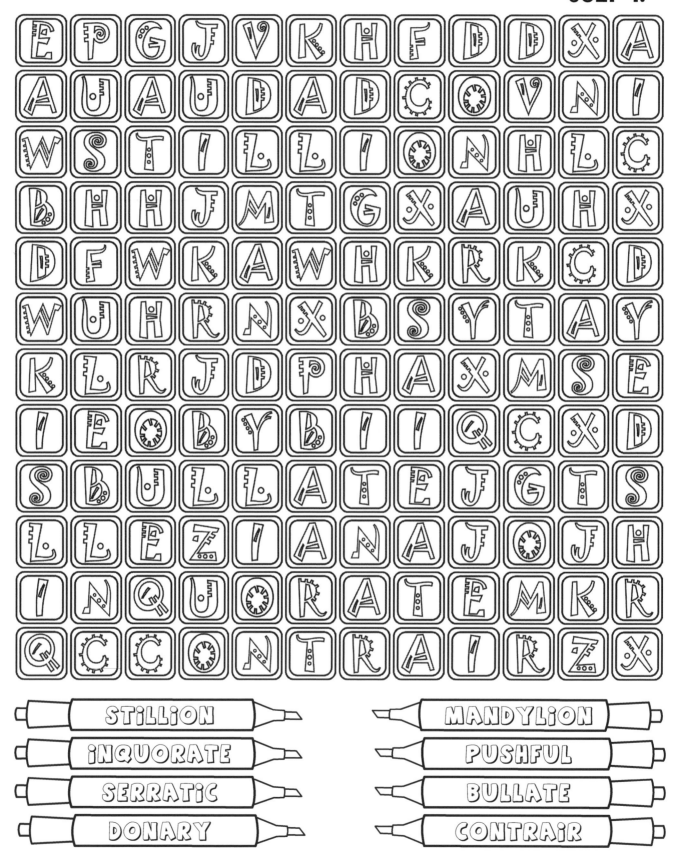

STILLION

INQUORATE

SERRATIC

DONARY

MANDYLION

PUSHFUL

BULLATE

CONTRAIR

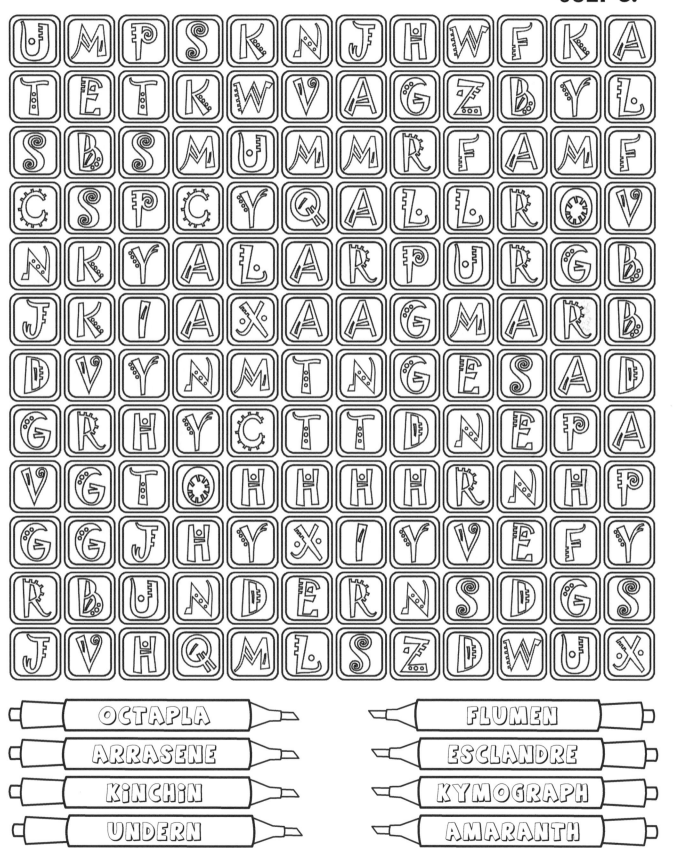

OCTAPLA

ARRASENE

KINCHIN

UNDERN

FLUMEN

ESCLANDRE

KYMOGRAPH

AMARANTH

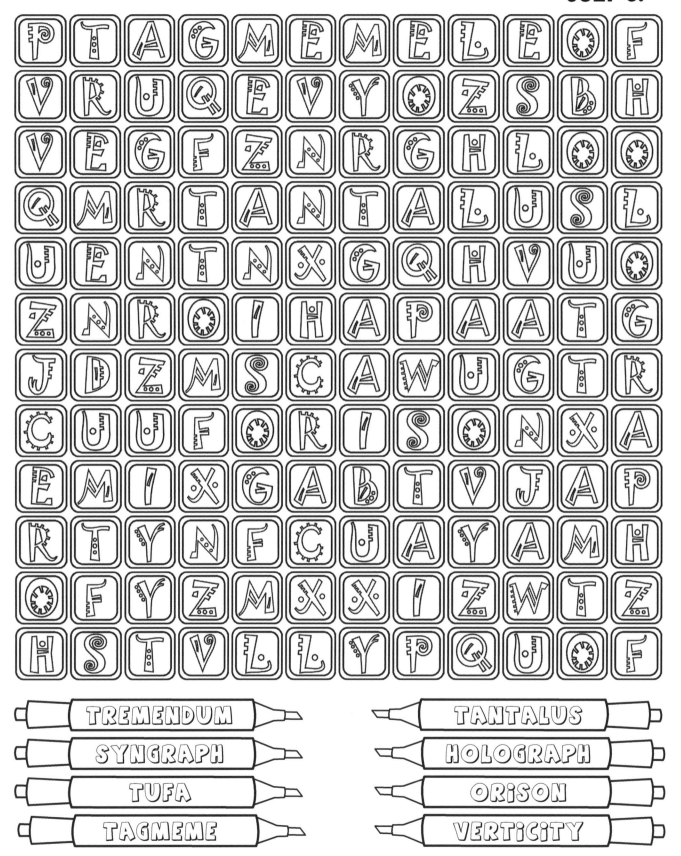

TREMENDUM

SYNGRAPH

TUFA

TAGMEME

TANTALUS

HOLOGRAPH

ORISON

VERTICITY

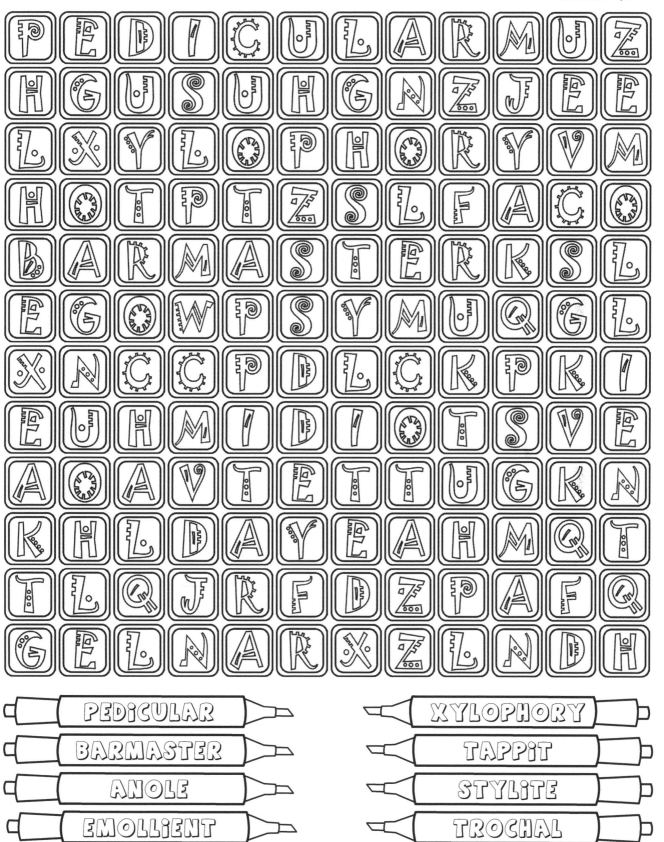

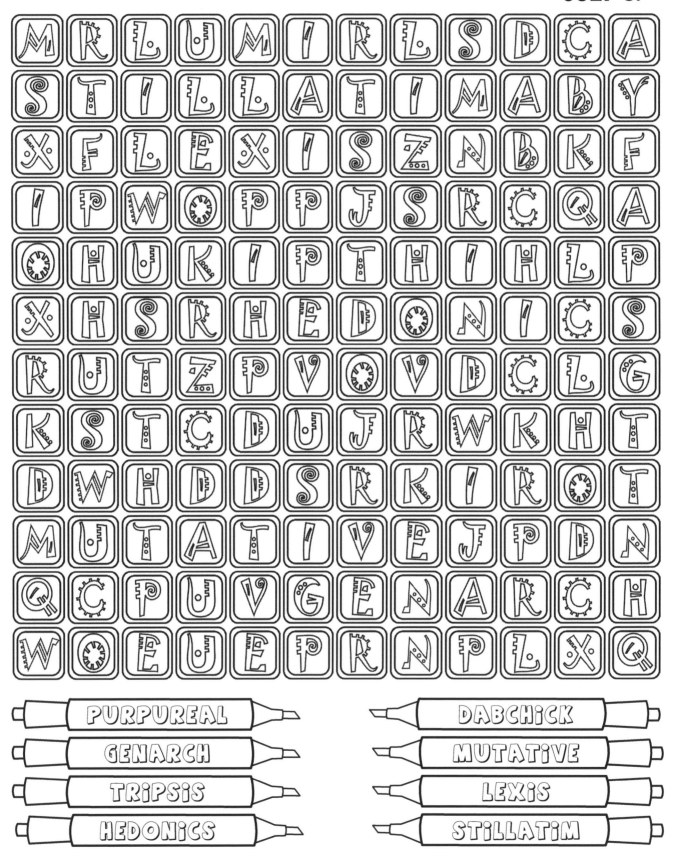

PURPUREAL

GENARCH

TRIPSIS

HEDONICS

DABCHICK

MUTATIVE

LEXIS

STILLATIM

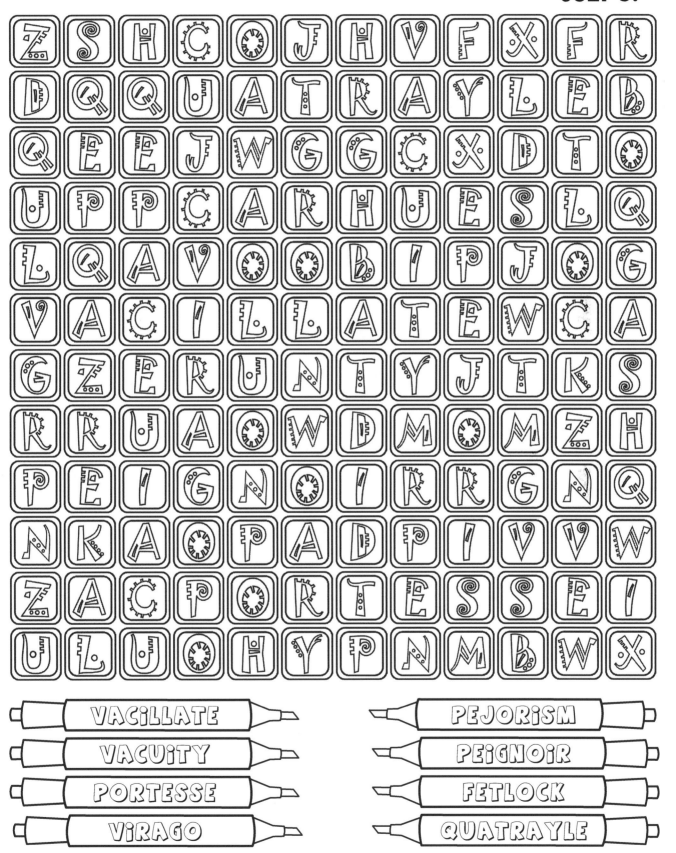

VACILLATE

VACUITY

PORTESSE

VIRAGO

PEJORISM

PEIGNOIR

FETLOCK

QUATRAYLE

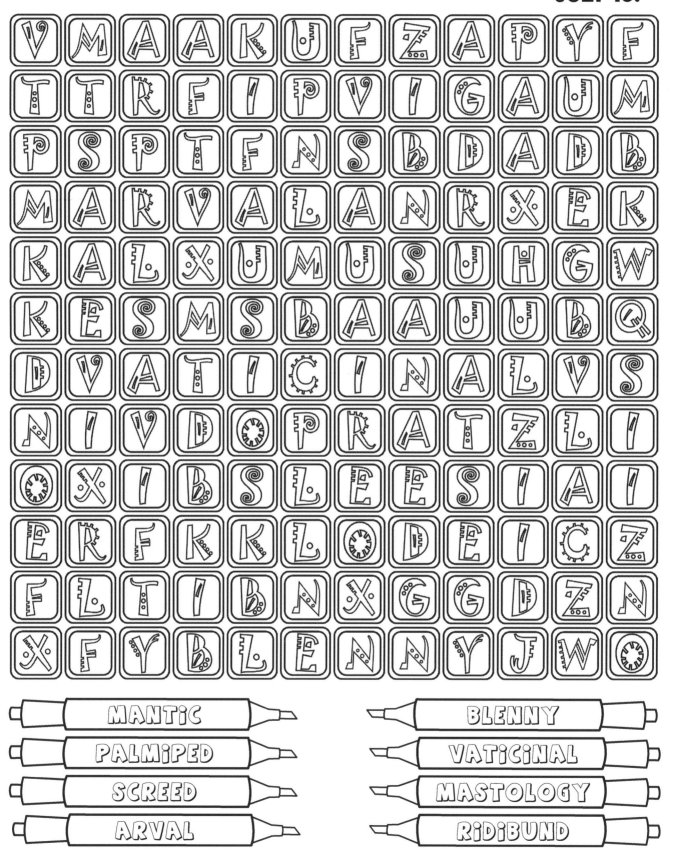

MANTIC

PALMIPED

SCREED

ARVAL

BLENNY

VATICINAL

MASTOLOGY

RIDIBUND

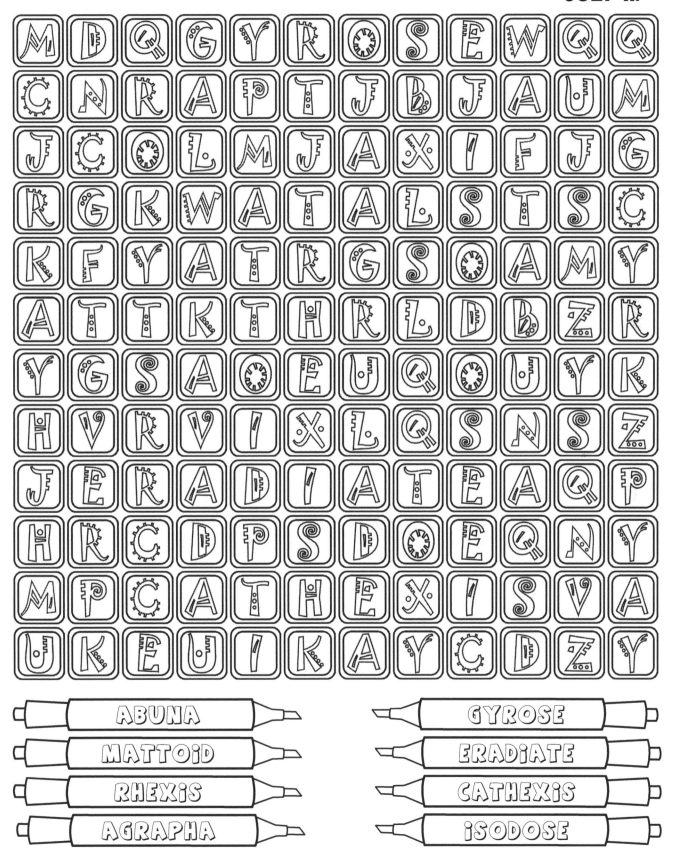

ABUNA

MATTOID

RHEXIS

AGRAPHA

GYROSE

ERADIATE

CATHEXIS

ISODOSE

OCTOTHORP

BEADSMAN

AMRITA

VINOLENT

SUBTEND

FUSAIN

VERBID

ZOOGRAPHY

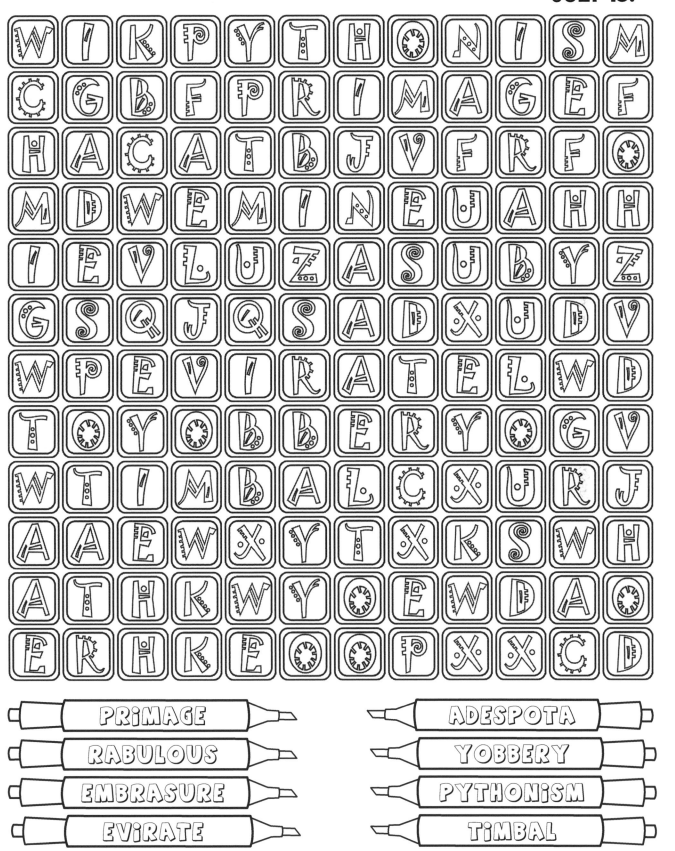

PRIMAGE

RABULOUS

EMBRASURE

EVIRATE

ADESPOTA

YOBBERY

PYTHONISM

TIMBAL

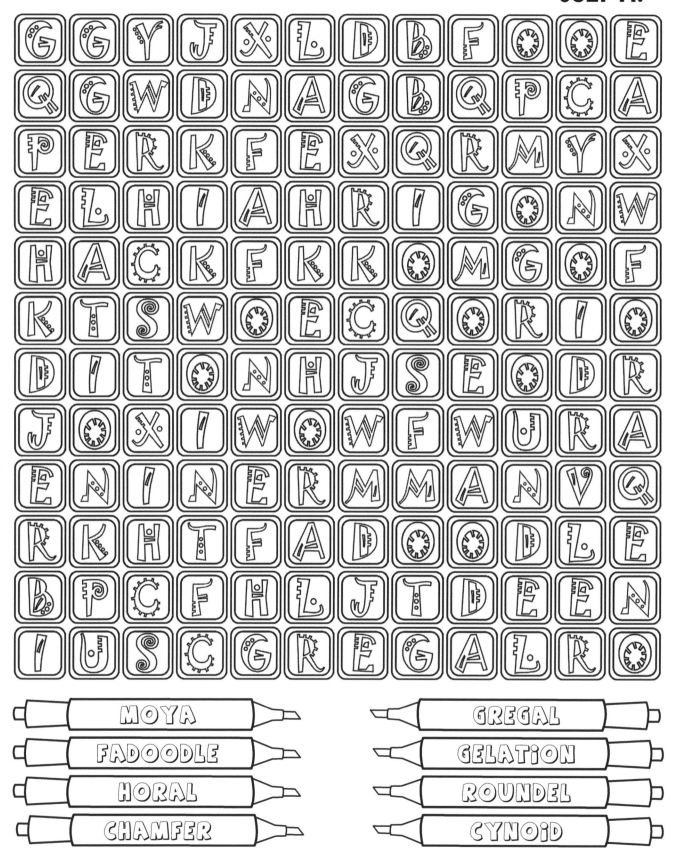

MOYA

FADOODLE

HORAL

CHAMFER

GREGAL

GELATION

ROUNDEL

CYNOID

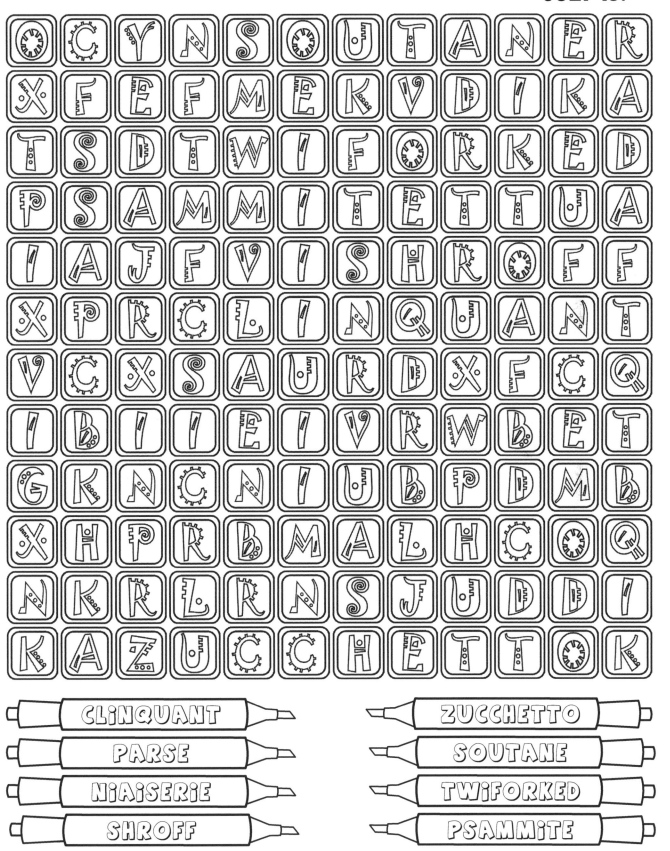

CLINQUANT

PARSE

NIAISERIE

SHROFF

ZUCCHETTO

SOUTANE

TWIFORKED

PSAMMITE

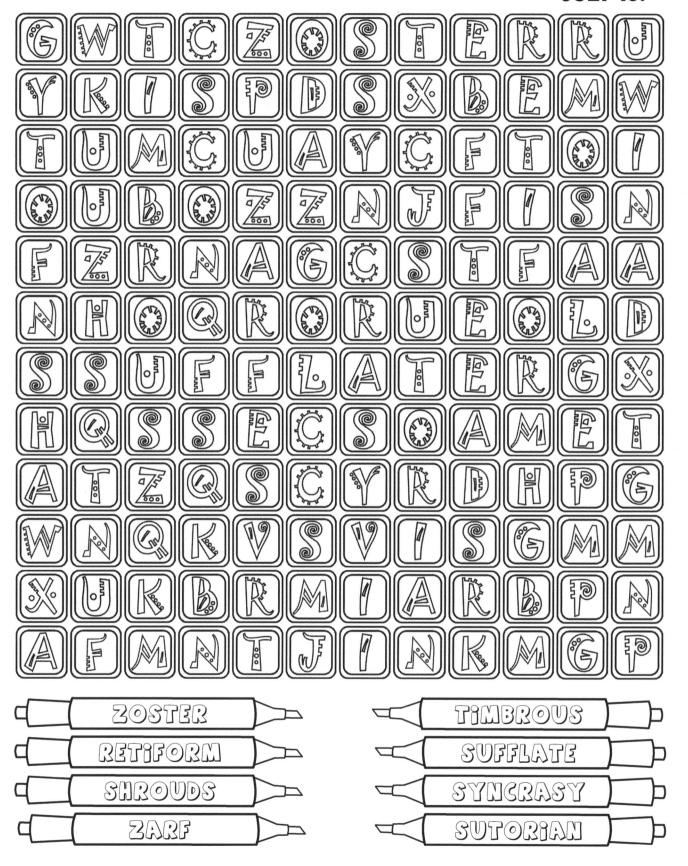

ZOSTER
RETIFORM
SHROUDS
ZARF

TIMBROUS
SUFFLATE
SYNCRASY
SUTORIAN

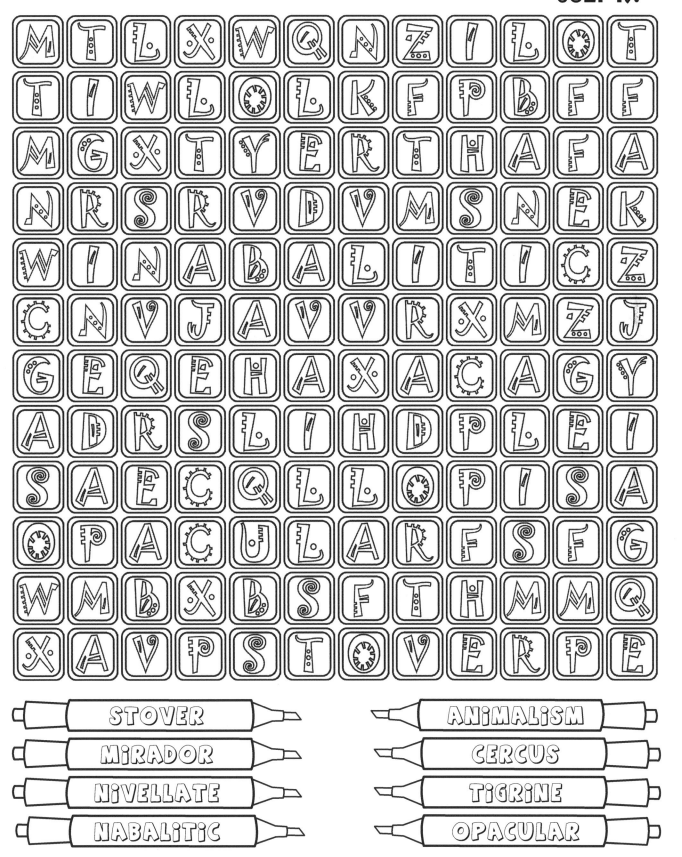

STOVER

MIRADOR

NIVELLATE

NABALITIC

ANIMALISM

CERCUS

TIGRINE

OPACULAR

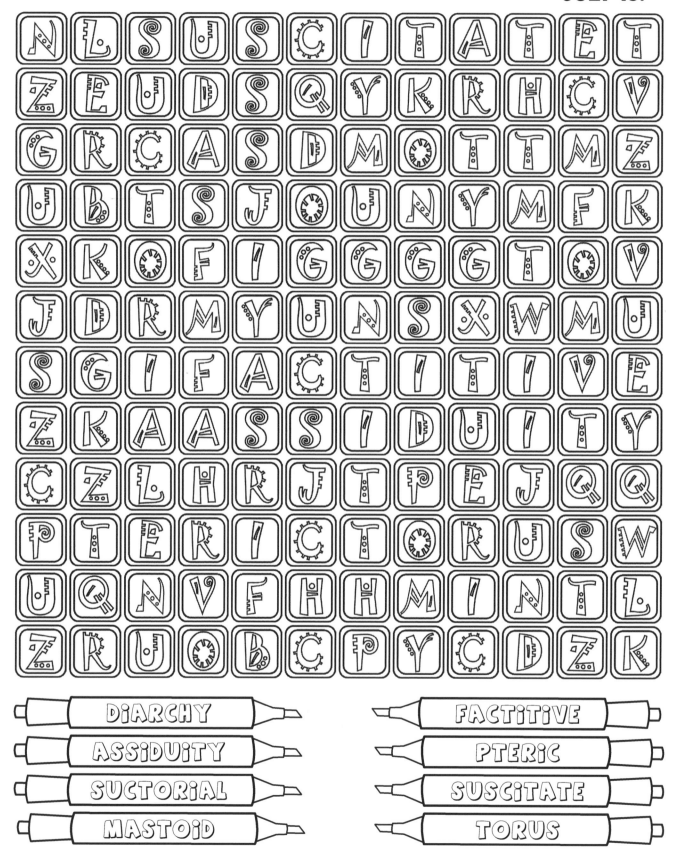

DIARCHY

ASSIDUITY

SUCTORIAL

MASTOID

FACTITIVE

PTERIC

SUSCITATE

TORUS

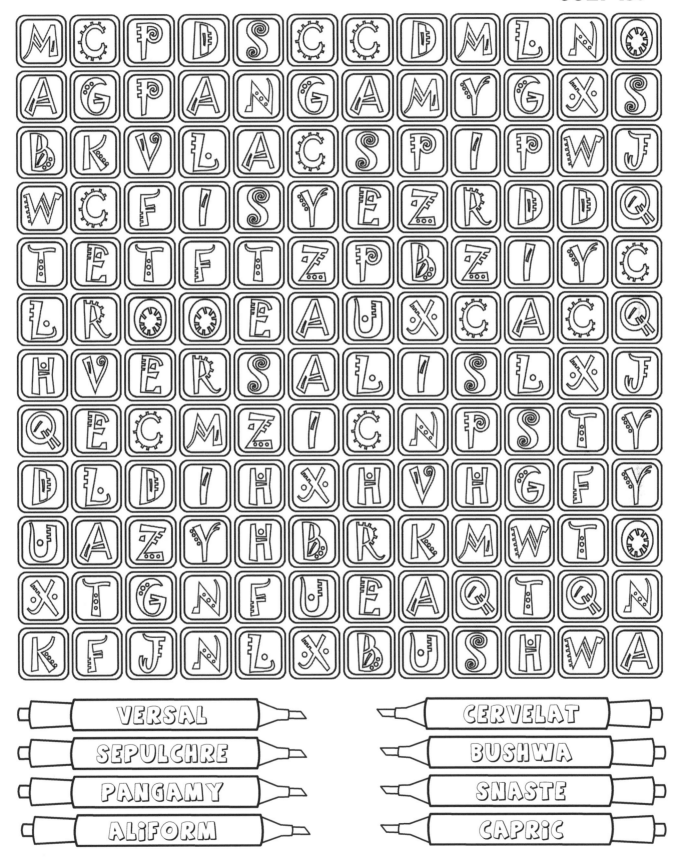

VERSAL

SEPULCHRE

PANGAMY

ALIFORM

CERVELAT

BUSHWA

SNASTE

CAPRIC

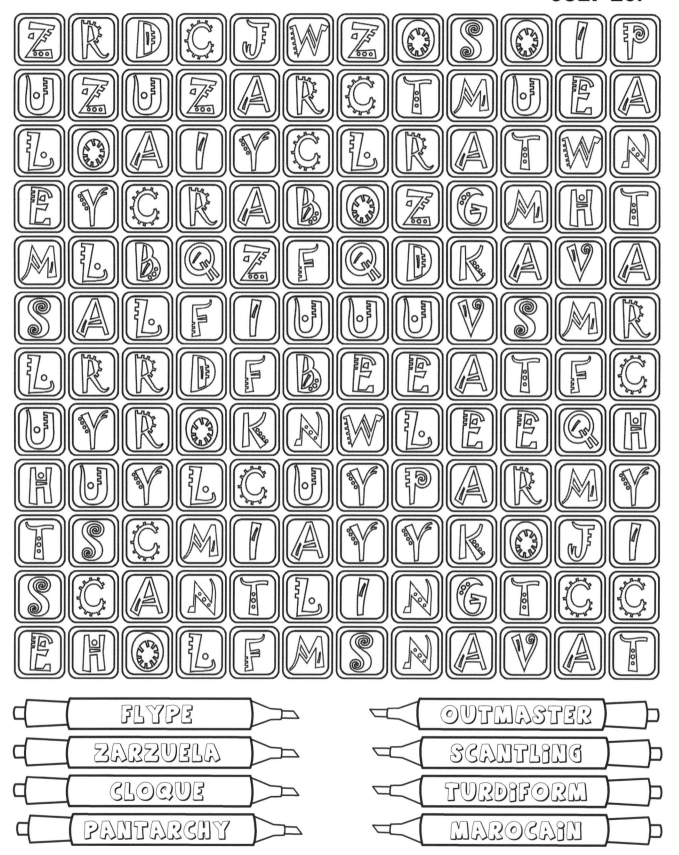

FLYPE

ZARZUELA

CLOQUE

PANTARCHY

OUTMASTER

SCANTLING

TURDIFORM

MAROCAIN

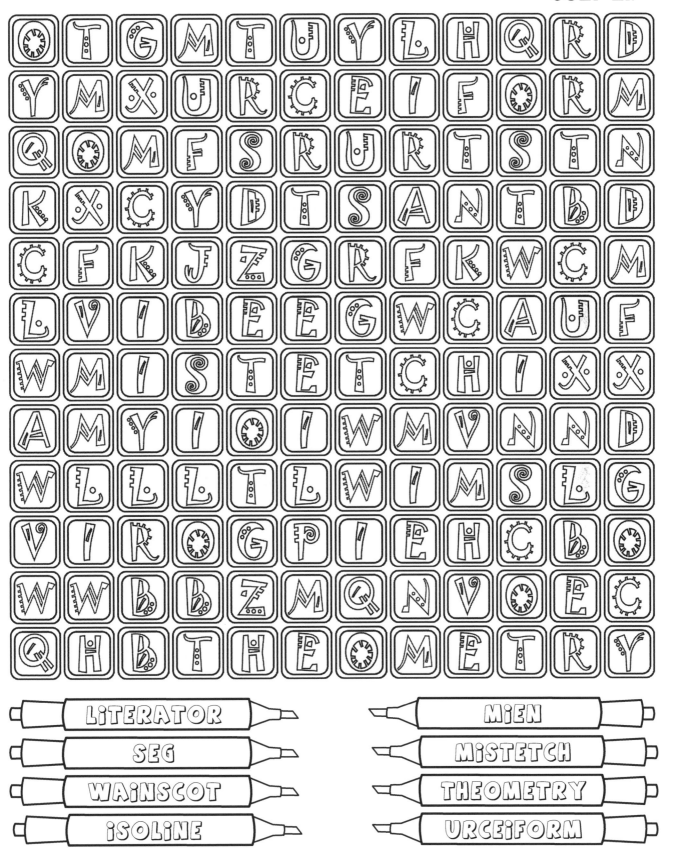

LITERATOR

SEG

WAINSCOT

ISOLINE

MIEN

MISTETCH

THEOMETRY

URCEIFORM

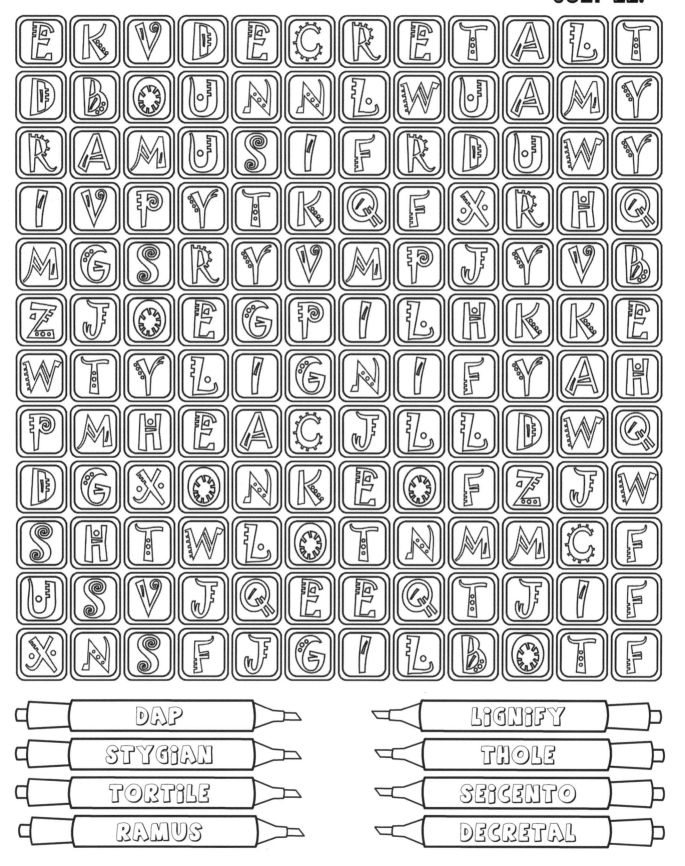

DAP

STYGIAN

TORTILE

RAMUS

LIGNIFY

THOLE

SEICENTO

DECRETAL

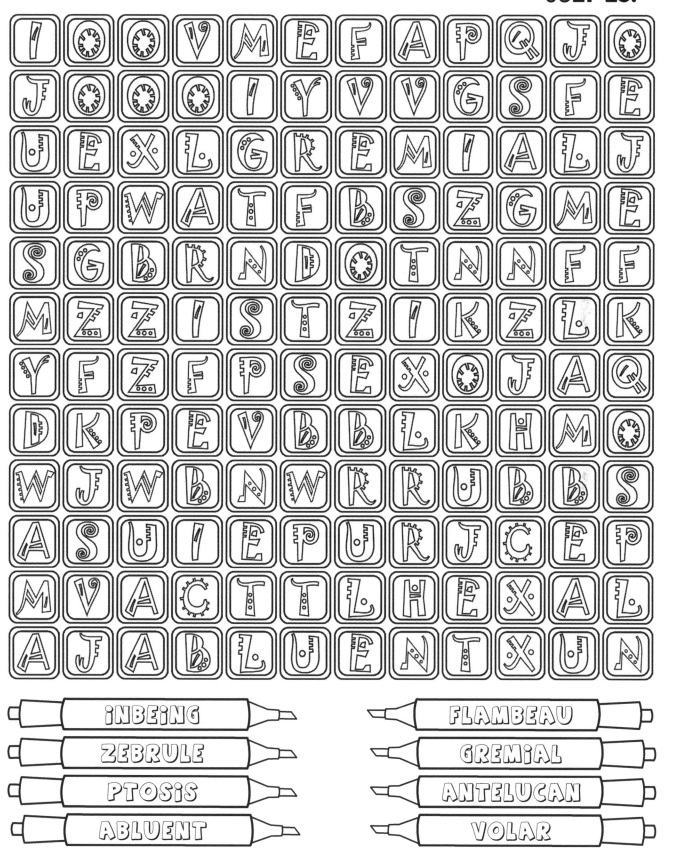

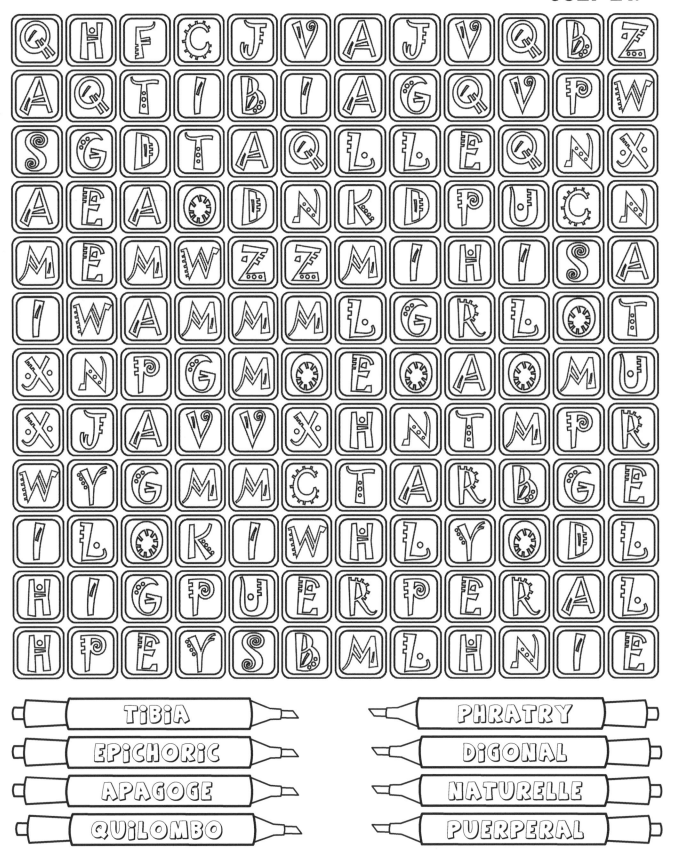

TIBIA

EPICHORIC

APAGOGE

QUILOMBO

PHRATRY

DIGONAL

NATURELLE

PUERPERAL

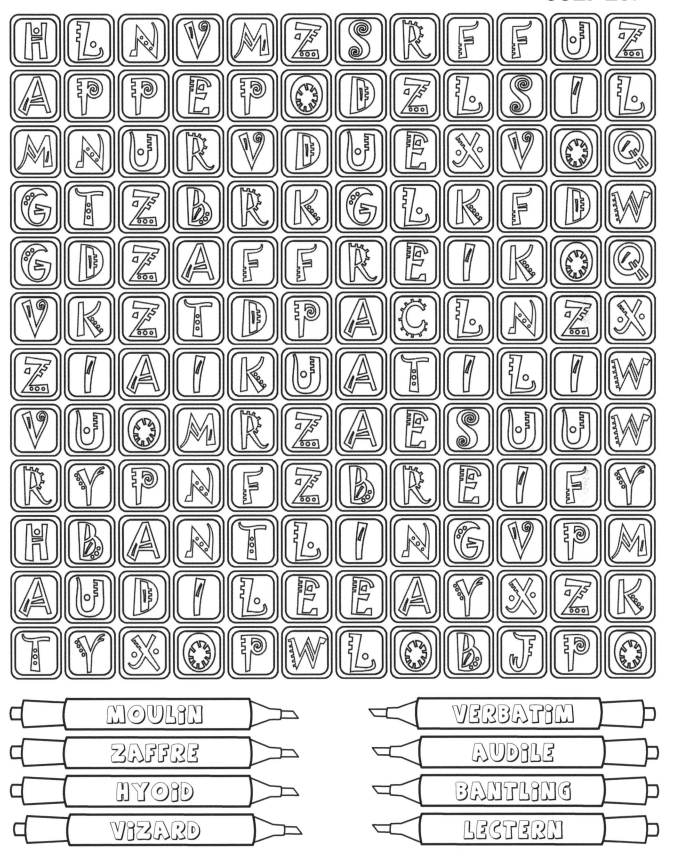

MOULIN

ZAFFRE

HYOID

VIZARD

VERBATIM

AUDILE

BANTLING

LECTERN

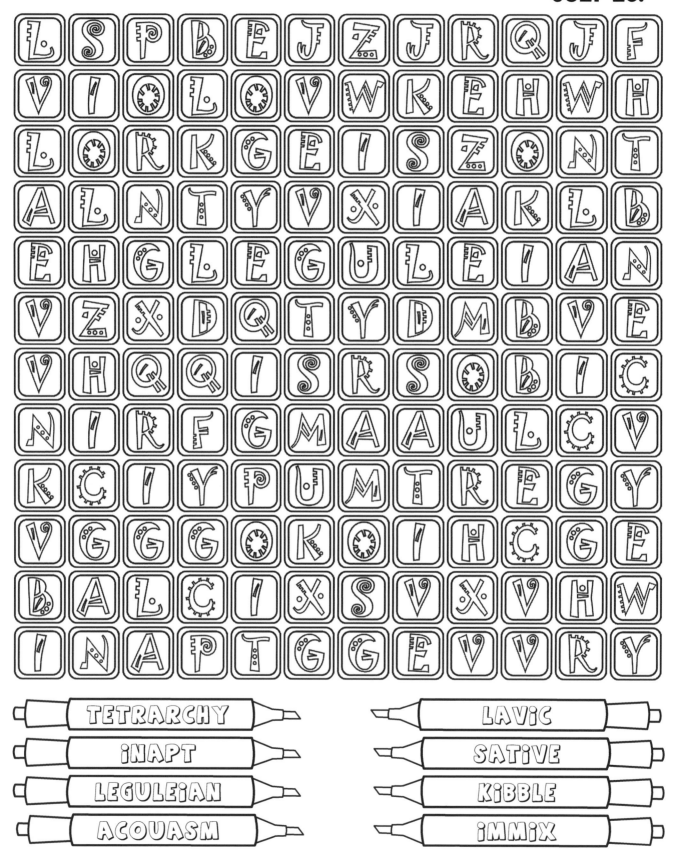

TETRARCHY

INAPT

LEGULEIAN

ACOUASM

LAVIC

SATIVE

KIBBLE

IMMIX

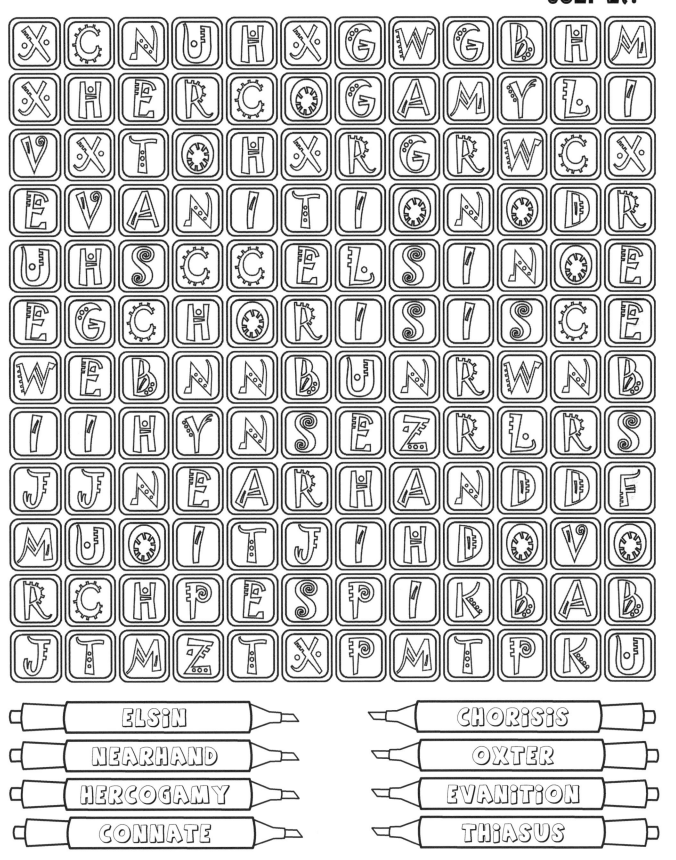

ELSIN

NEARHAND

HERCOGAMY

CONNATE

CHORISIS

OXTER

EVANITION

THIASUS

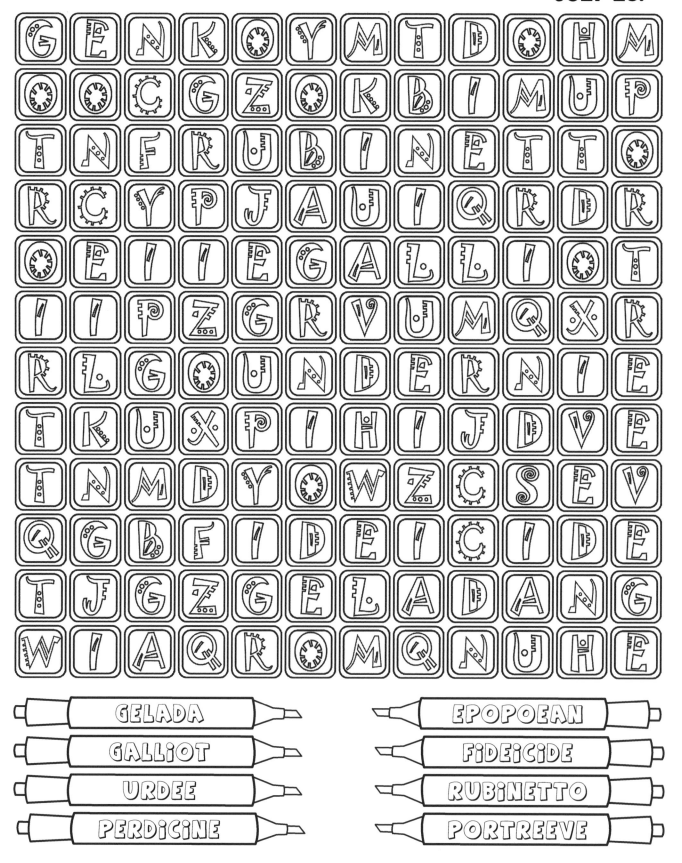

GELADA

GALLIOT

URDEE

PERDICINE

EPOPOEAN

FIDEICIDE

RUBINETTO

PORTREEVE

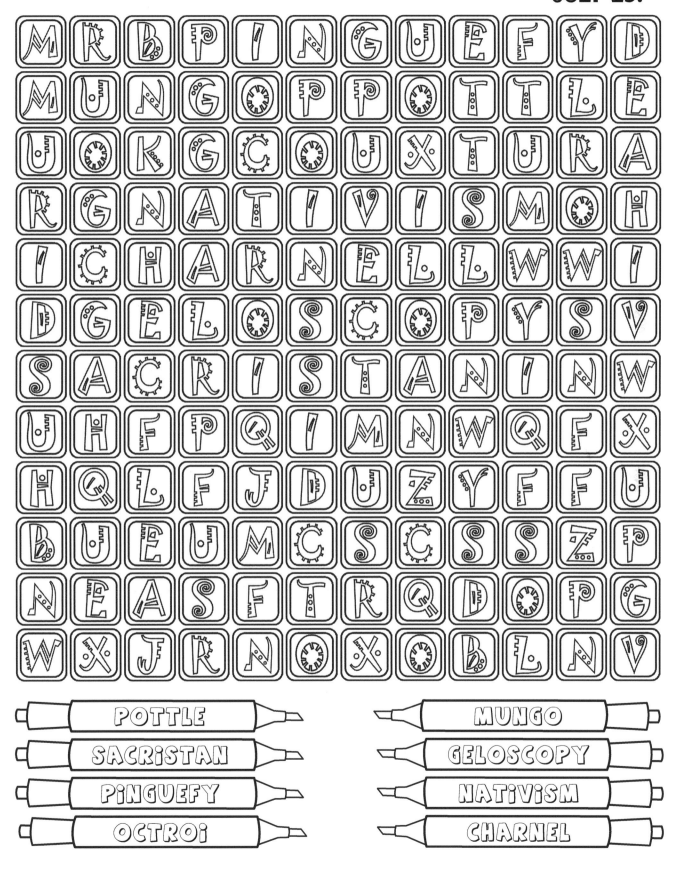

POTTLE

SACRISTAN

PINGUEFY

OCTROI

MUNGO

GELOSCOPY

NATIVISM

CHARNEL

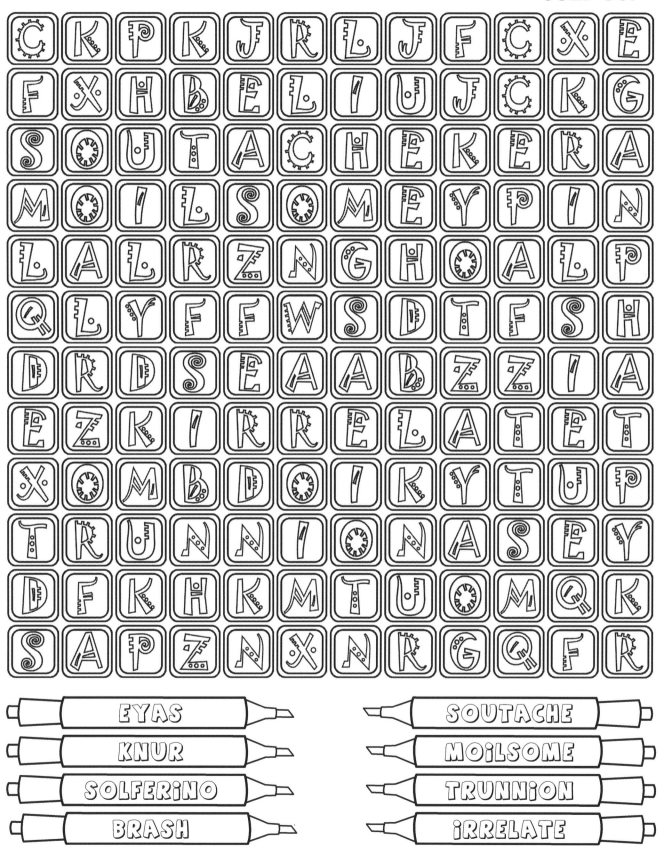

EYAS

KNUR

SOLFERINO

BRASH

SOUTACHE

MOILSOME

TRUNNION

IRRELATE

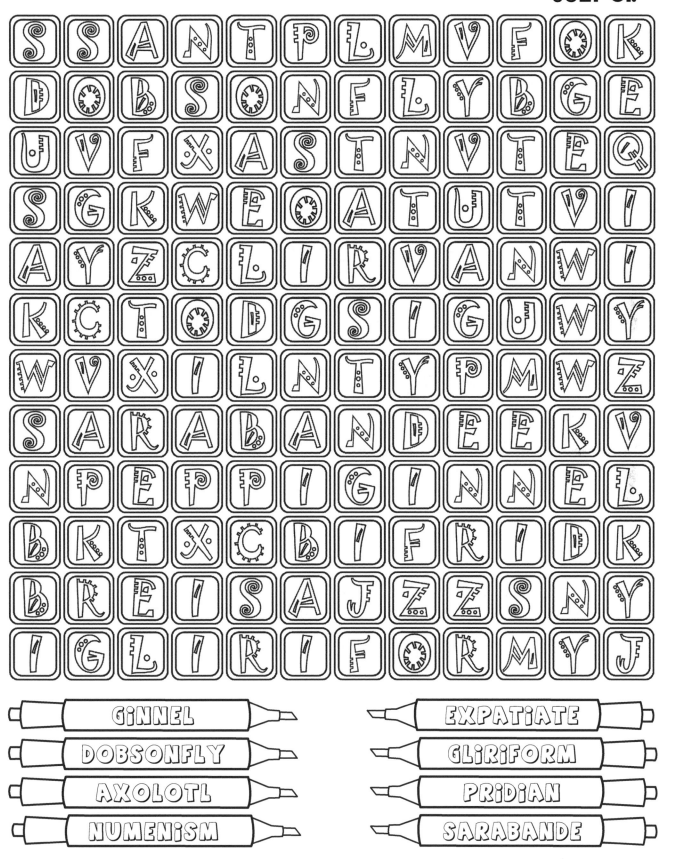

GINNEL

DOBSONFLY

AXOLOTL

NUMENISM

EXPATIATE

GLIRIFORM

PRIDIAN

SARABANDE

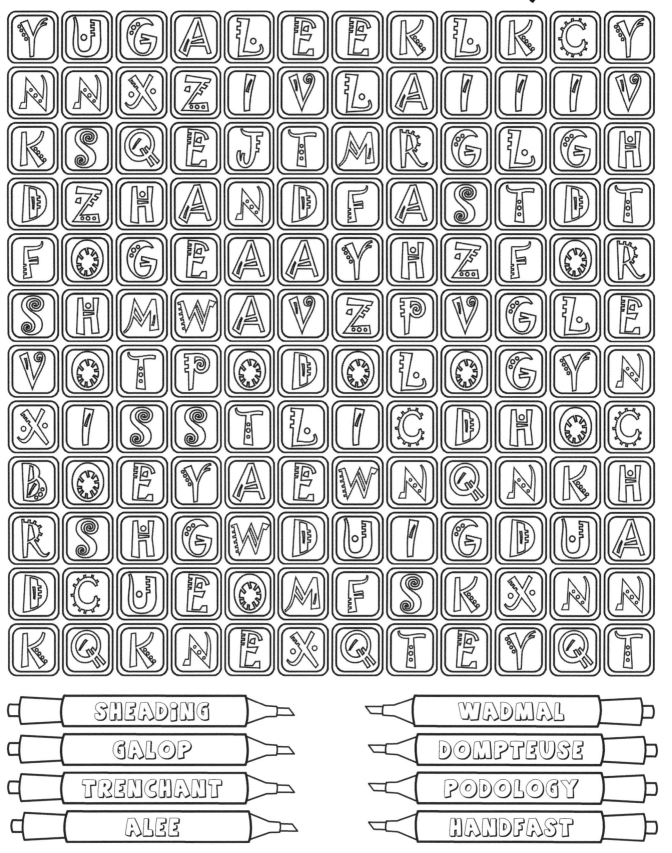

SHEADING

GALOP

TRENCHANT

ALEE

WADMAL

DOMPTEUSE

PODOLOGY

HANDFAST

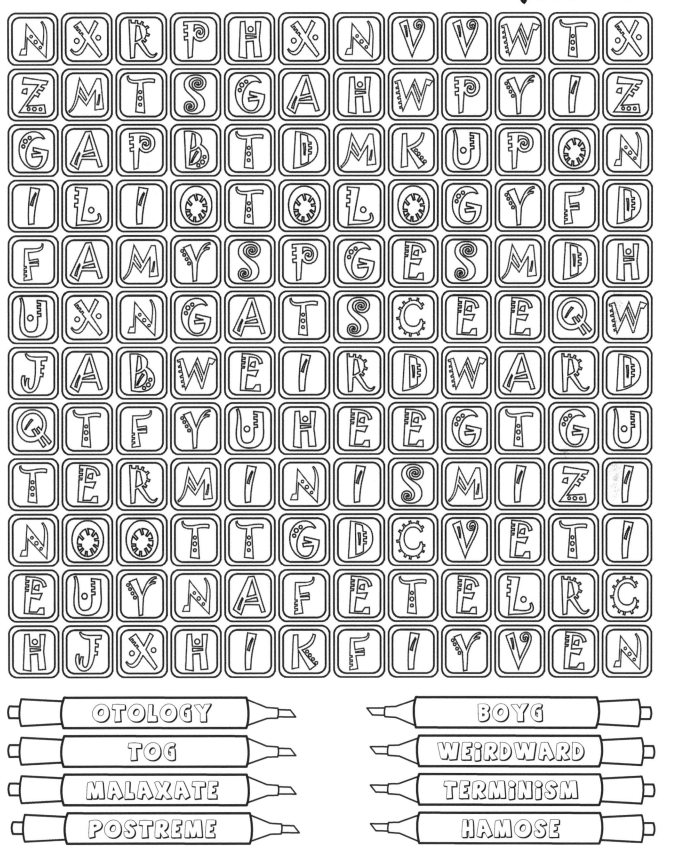

OTOLOGY

TOG

MALAXATE

POSTREME

BOYG

WEIRDWARD

TERMINISM

HAMOSE

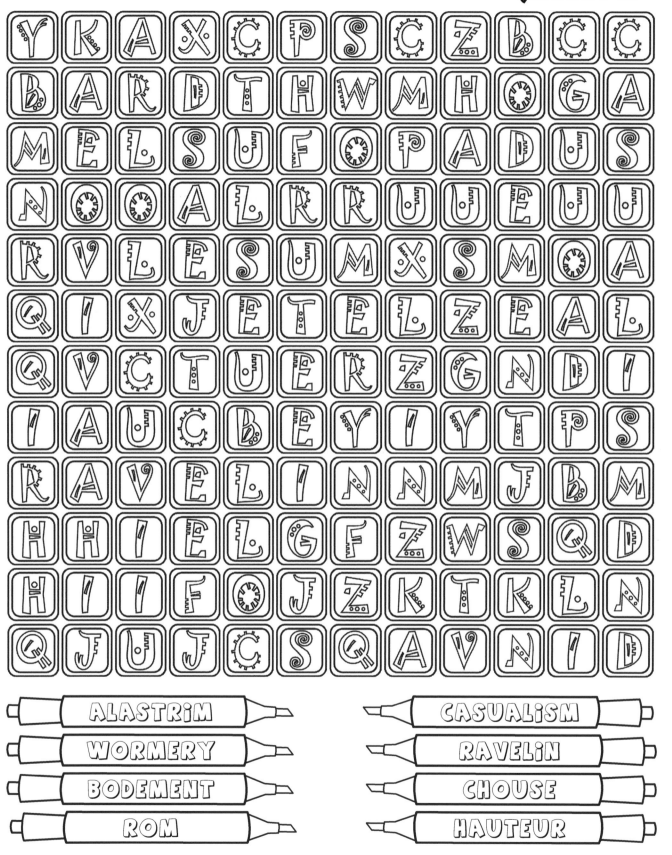

ALASTRIM

WORMERY

BODEMENT

ROM

CASUALISM

RAVELIN

CHOUSE

HAUTEUR

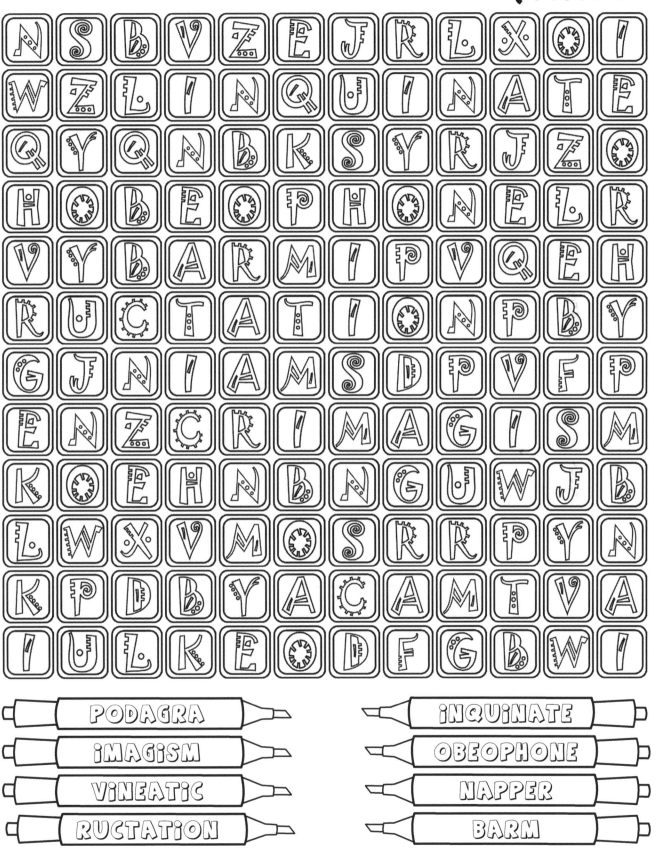

PODAGRA

IMAGISM

VINEATIC

RUCTATION

INQUINATE

OBEOPHONE

NAPPER

BARM

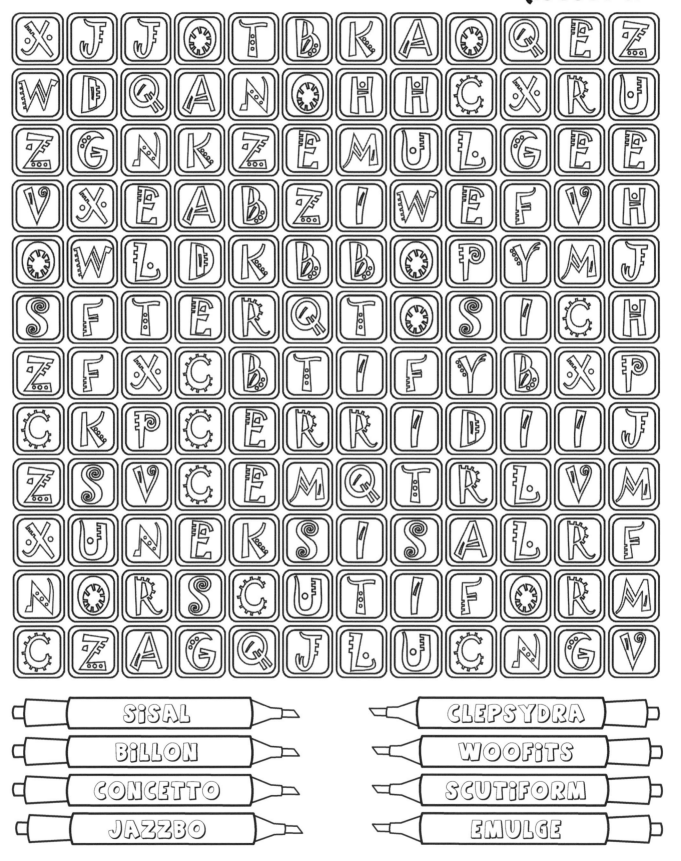

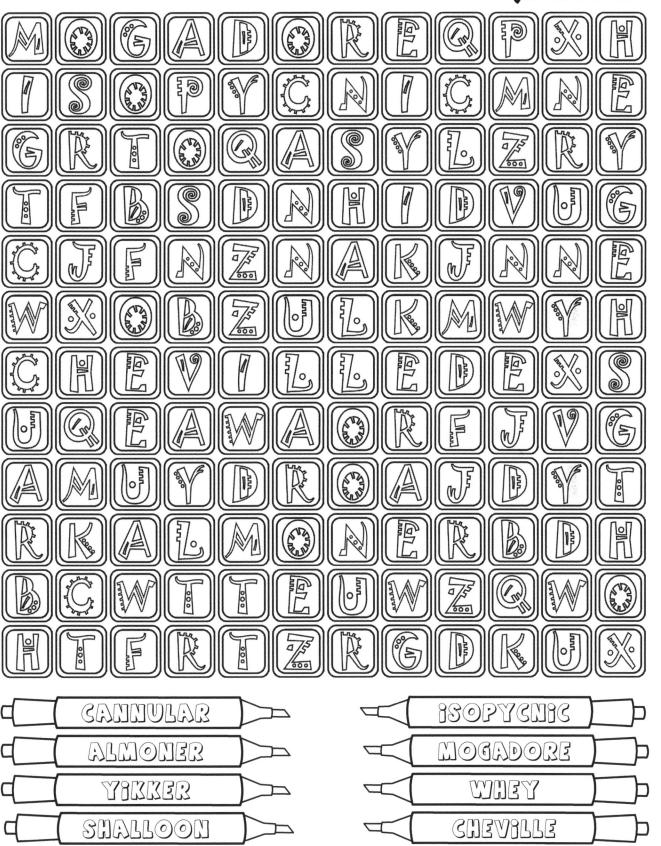

CANNULAR

ISOPYCNIC

ALMONER

MOGADORE

YIKKER

WHEY

SHALLOON

CHEVILLE

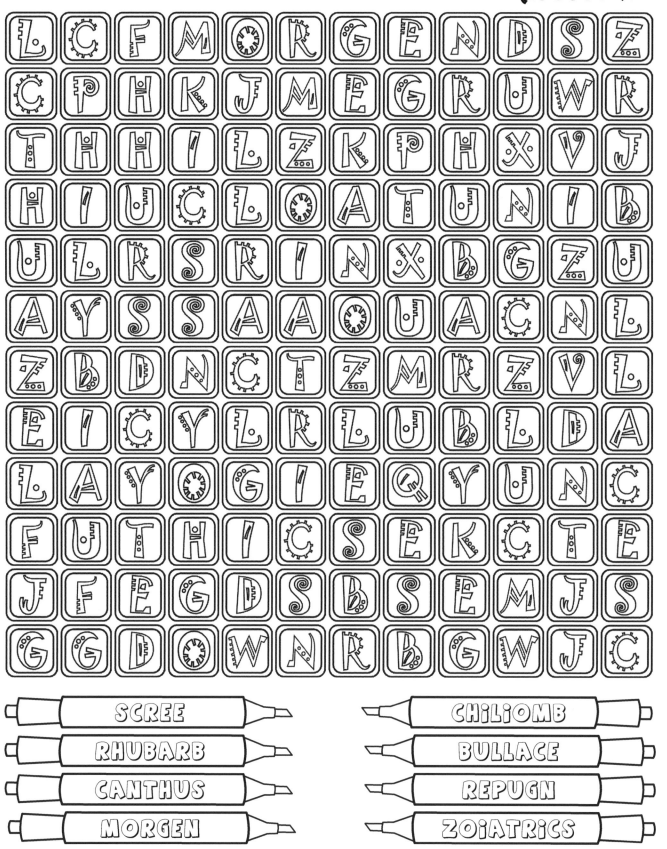

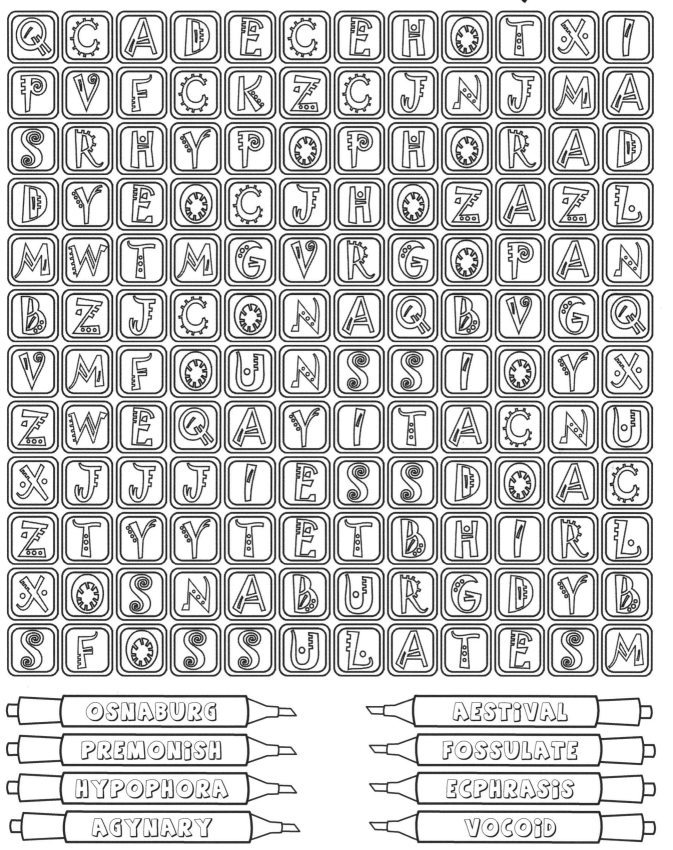

OSNABURG

PREMONISH

HYPOPHORA

AGYNARY

AESTIVAL

FOSSULATE

ECPHRASIS

VOCOID

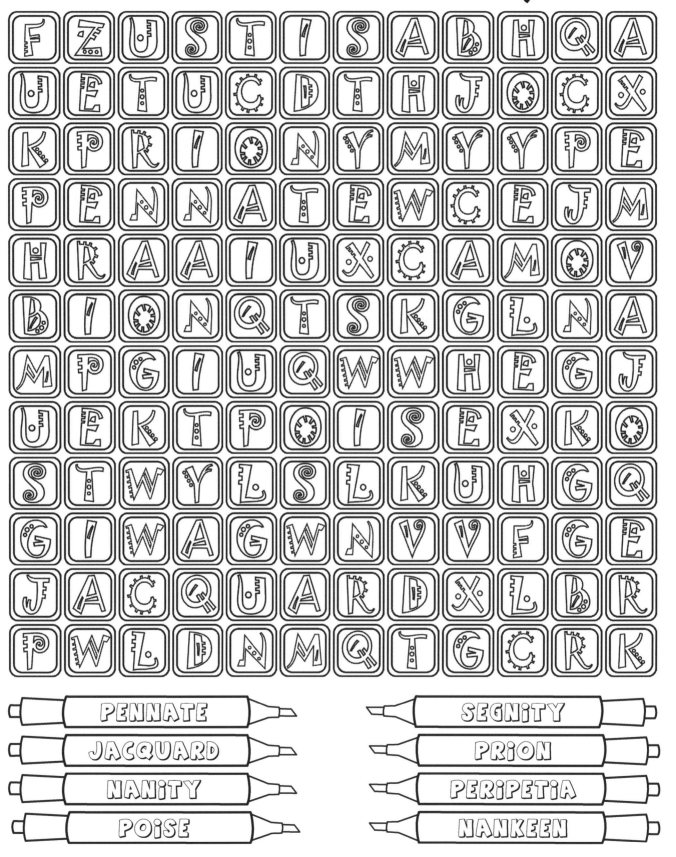

PENNATE

JACQUARD

NANITY

POISE

SEGNITY

PRION

PERIPETIA

NANKEEN

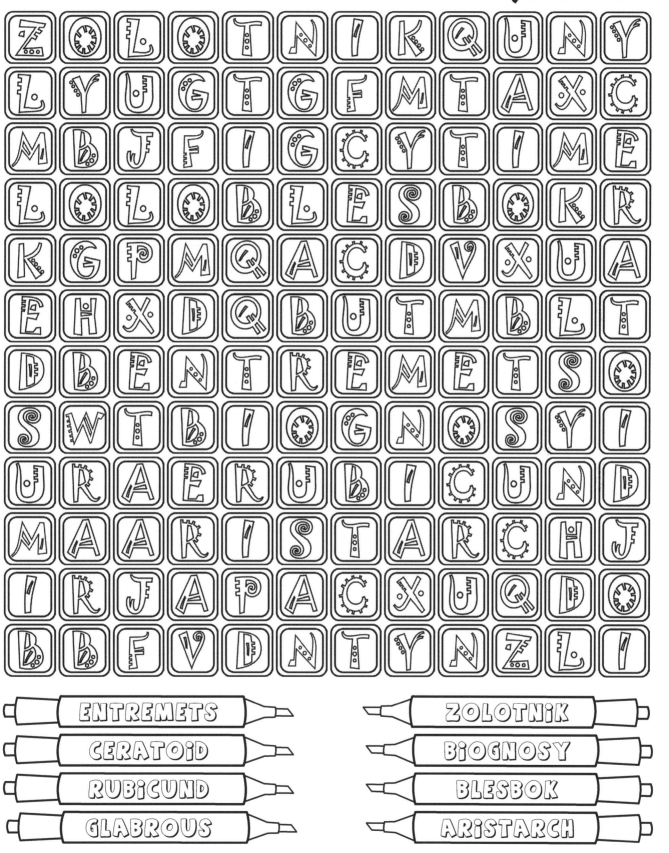

ENTREMETS

ZOLOTNIK

CERATOID

BIOGNOSY

RUBICUND

BLESBOK

GLABROUS

ARISTARCH

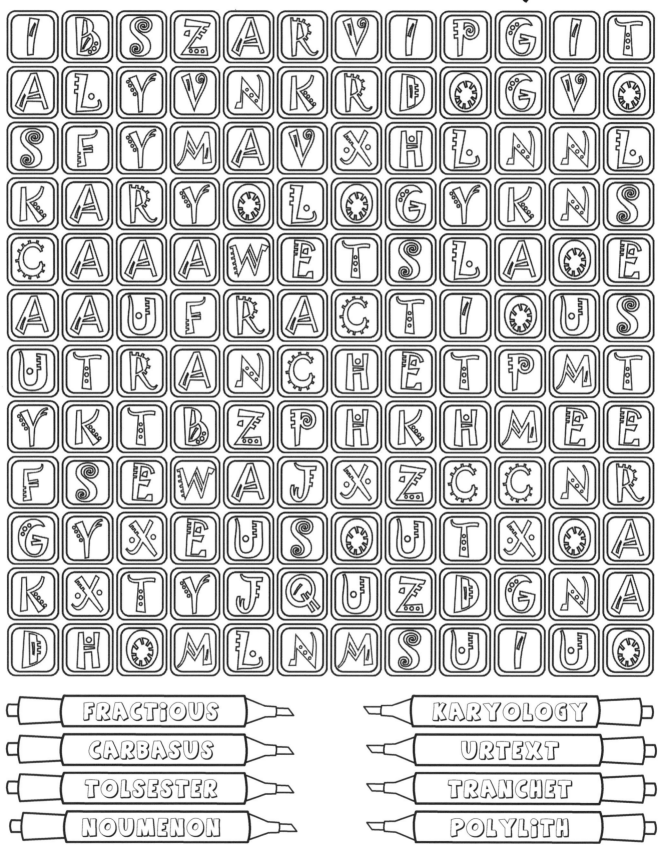

FRACTIOUS
CARBASUS
TOLSESTER
NOUMENON

KARYOLOGY
URTEXT
TRANCHET
POLYLITH

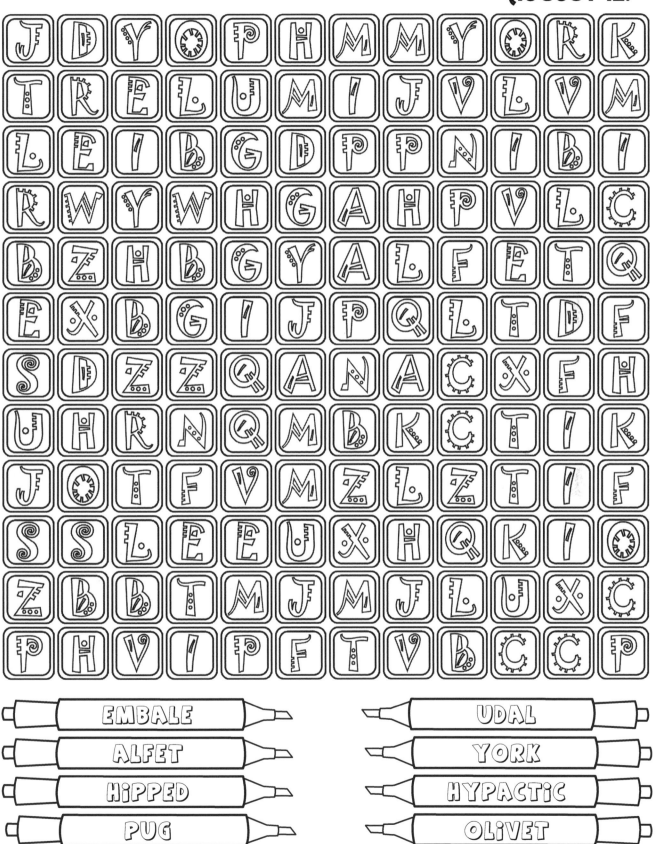

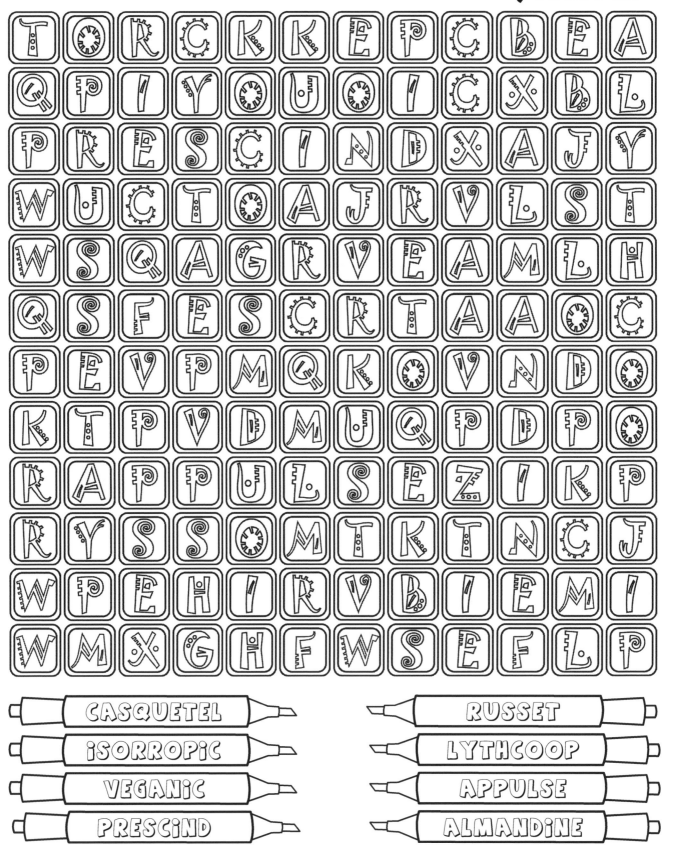

T O R C K K E P C B E A
Q P I Y O U O I C X B L
P R E S C I N D X A J Y
W U C T O A J R V L S T
W S Q A G R V E A M L H
Q S F E S C R T A A O C
P E V P M Q K O V N D O
K T P V D M U Q P D P O
R A P P U Z S E Z I K P
R Y S S O M T K T N C J
W P E H I R V B I E M I
W M X G H F W S E F L P

CASQUETEL   RUSSET

ISORROPIC   LYTHCOOP

VEGANIC   APPULSE

PRESCIND   ALMANDINE

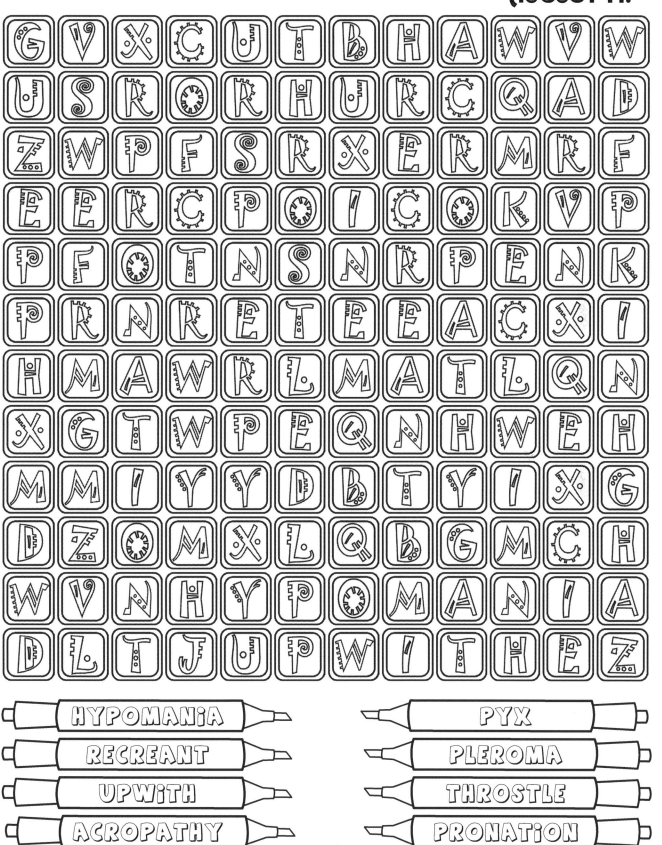

HYPOMANIA

RECREANT

UPWITH

ACROPATHY

PYX

PLEROMA

THROSTLE

PRONATION

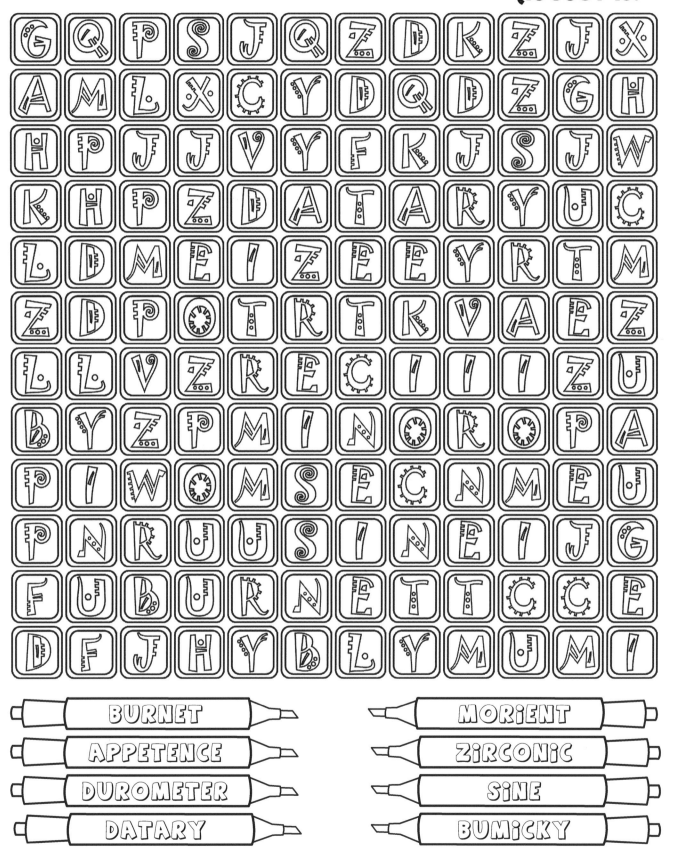

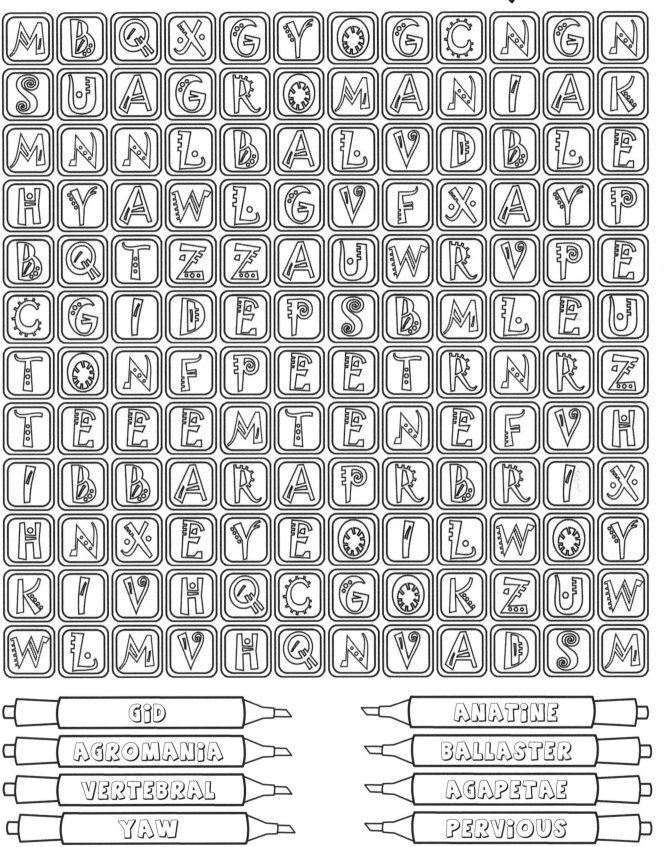

GID

AGROMANIA

VERTEBRAL

YAW

ANATINE

BALLASTER

AGAPETAE

PERVIOUS

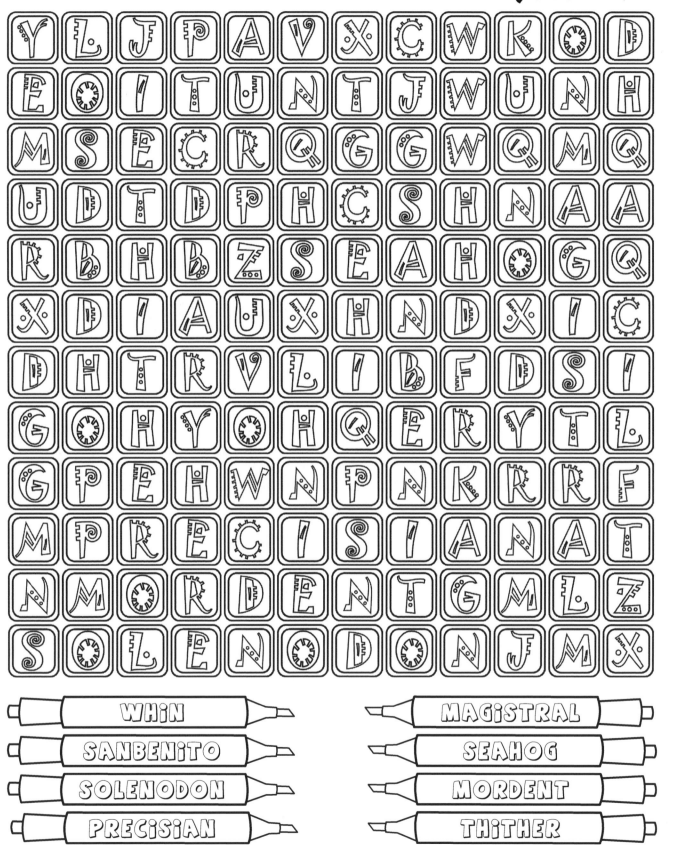

WHIN

SANBENITO

SOLENODON

PRECISIAN

MAGISTRAL

SEAHOG

MORDENT

THITHER

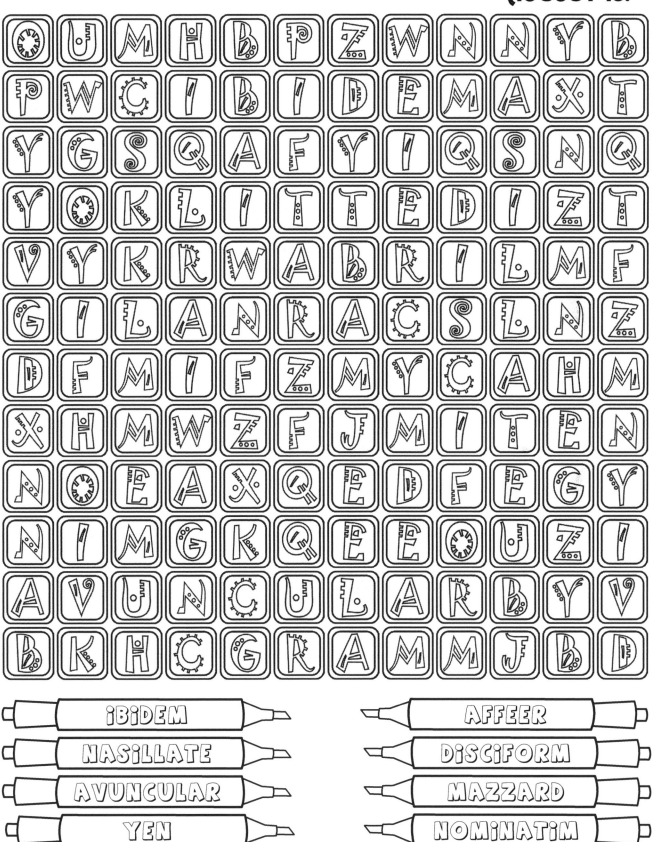

IBIDEM

NASILLATE

AVUNCULAR

YEN

AFFEER

DISCIFORM

MAZZARD

NOMINATIM

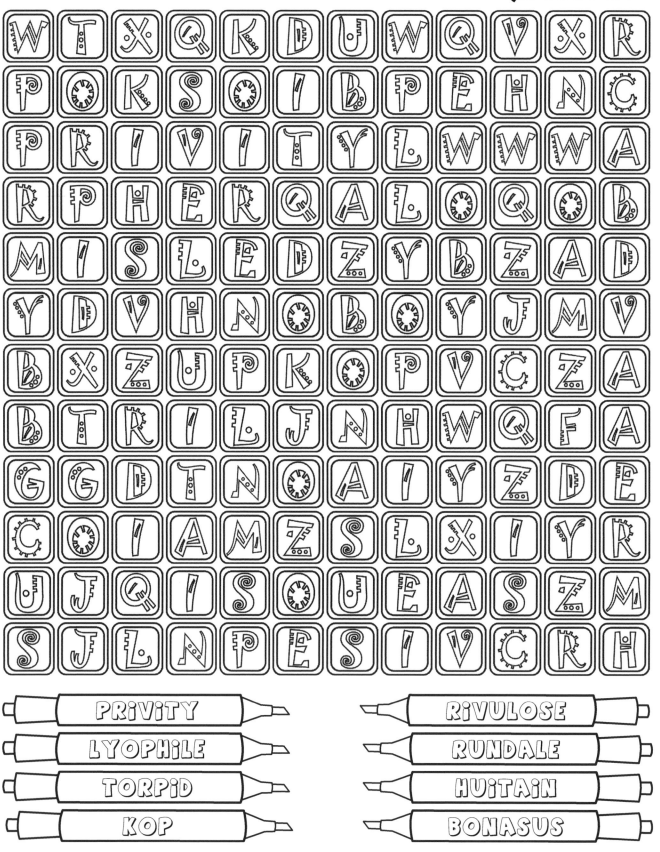

PRIVITY

LYOPHILE

TORPID

KOP

RIVULOSE

RUNDALE

HUITAIN

BONASUS

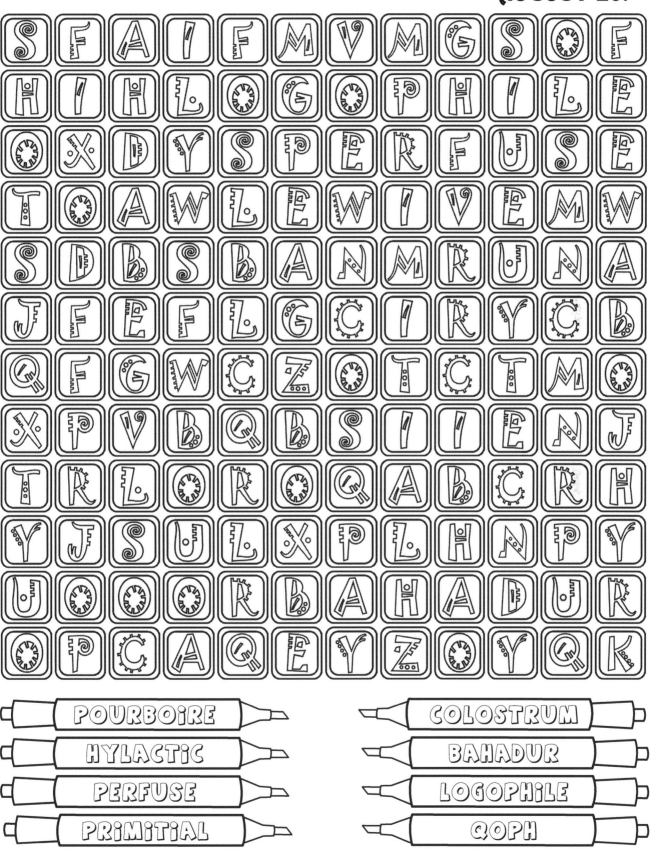

POURBOIRE

HYLACTIC

PERFUSE

PRIMITIAL

COLOSTRUM

BAHADUR

LOGOPHILE

QOPH

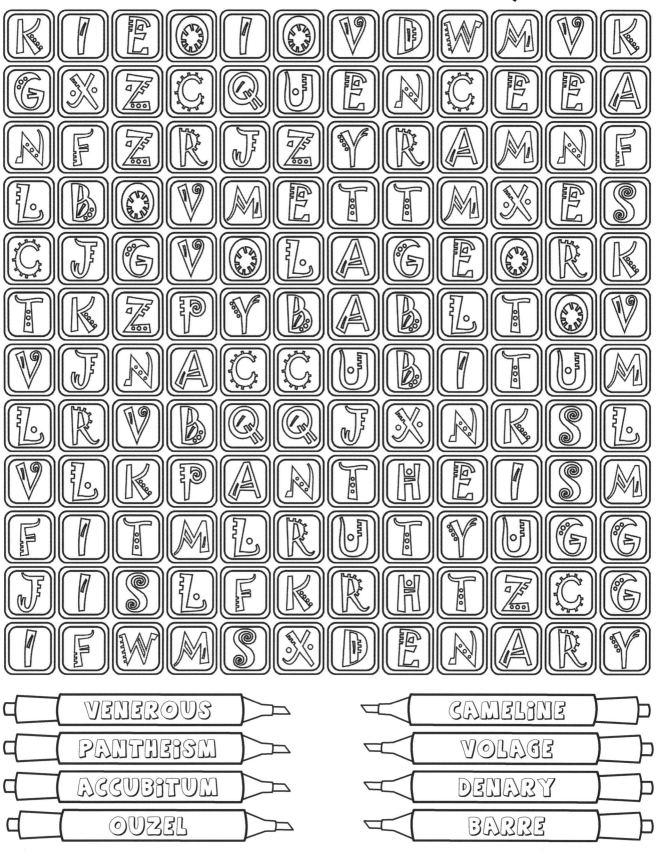

VENEROUS

PANTHEISM

ACCUBITUM

OUZEL

CAMELINE

VOLAGE

DENARY

BARRE

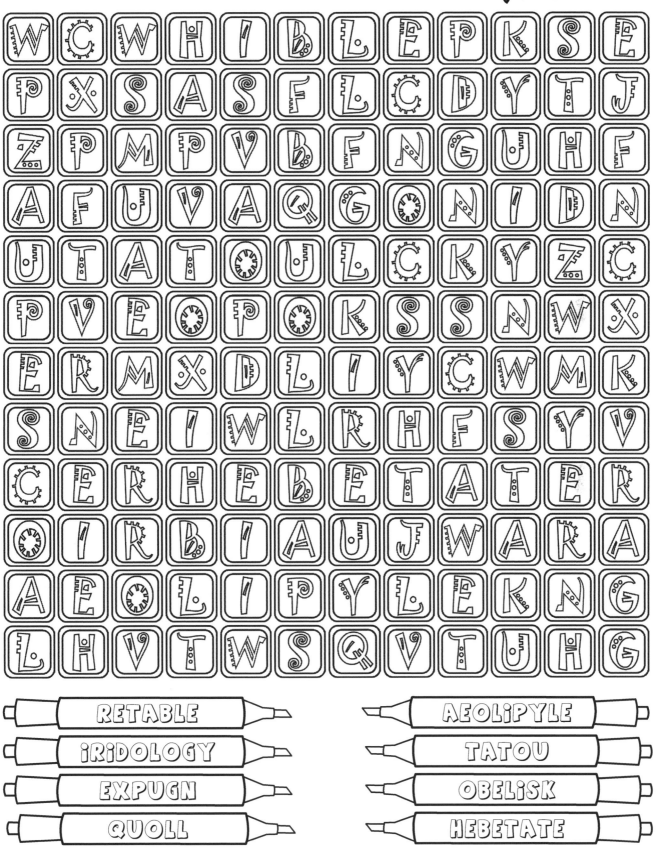

RETABLE
IRIDOLOGY
EXPUGN
QUOLL

AEOLIPYLE
TATOU
OBELISK
HEBETATE

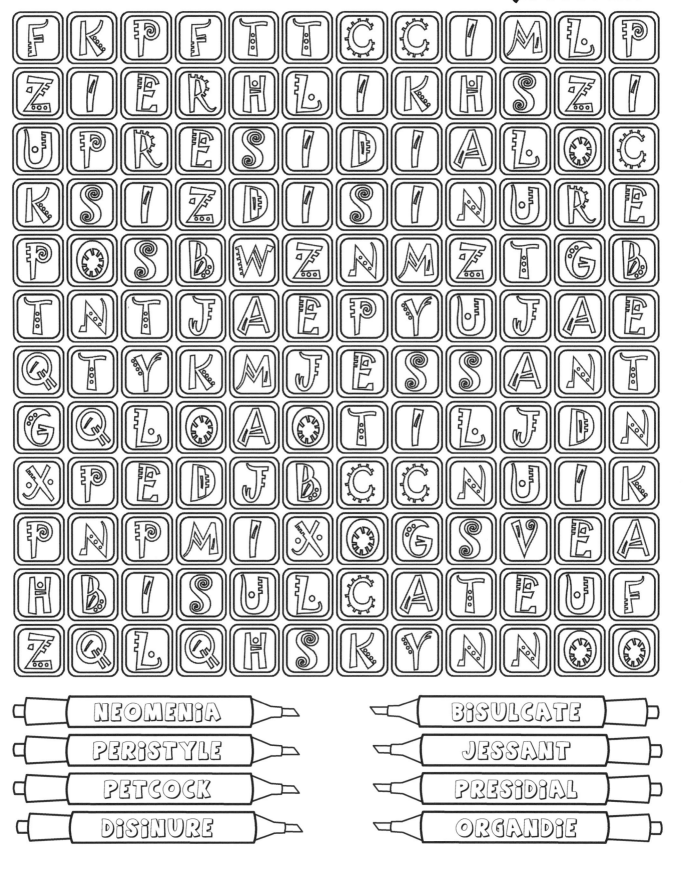

NEOMENIA

PERISTYLE

PETCOCK

DISINURE

BISULCATE

JESSANT

PRESIDIAL

ORGANDIE

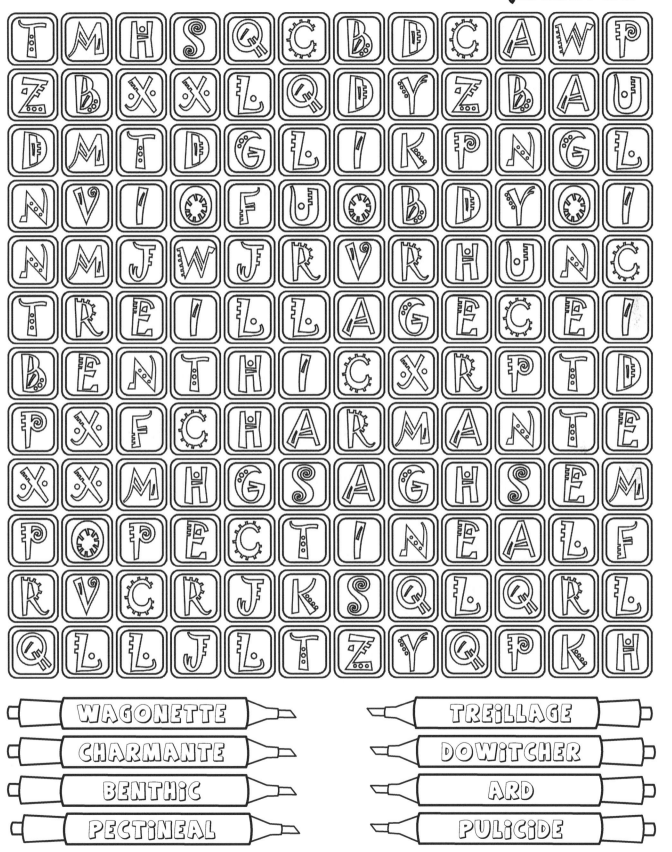

WAGONETTE

TREILLAGE

CHARMANTE

DOWITCHER

BENTHIC

ARD

PECTINEAL

PULICIDE

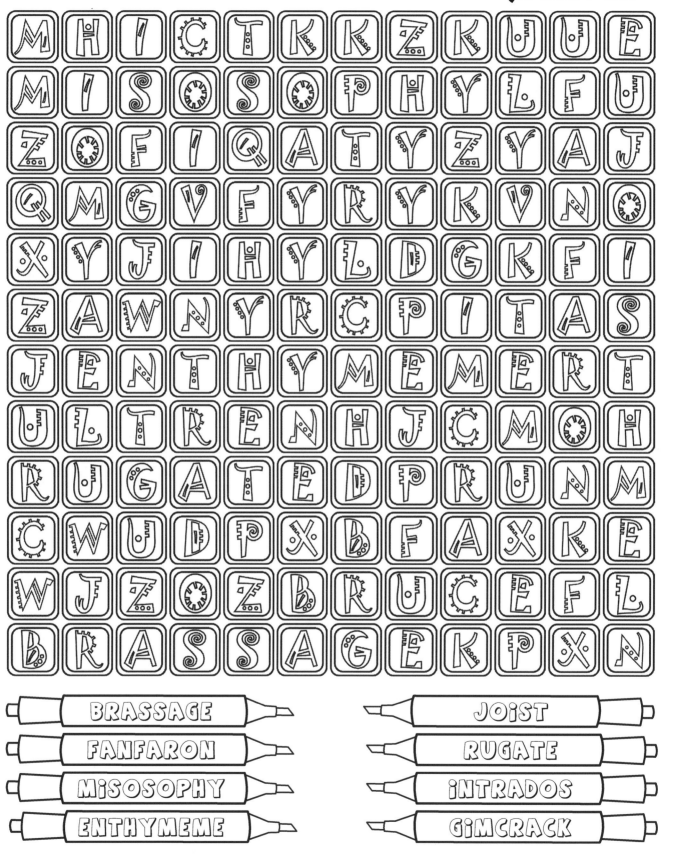

BRASSAGE

FANFARON

MISOSOPHY

ENTHYMEME

JOIST

RUGATE

INTRADOS

GIMCRACK

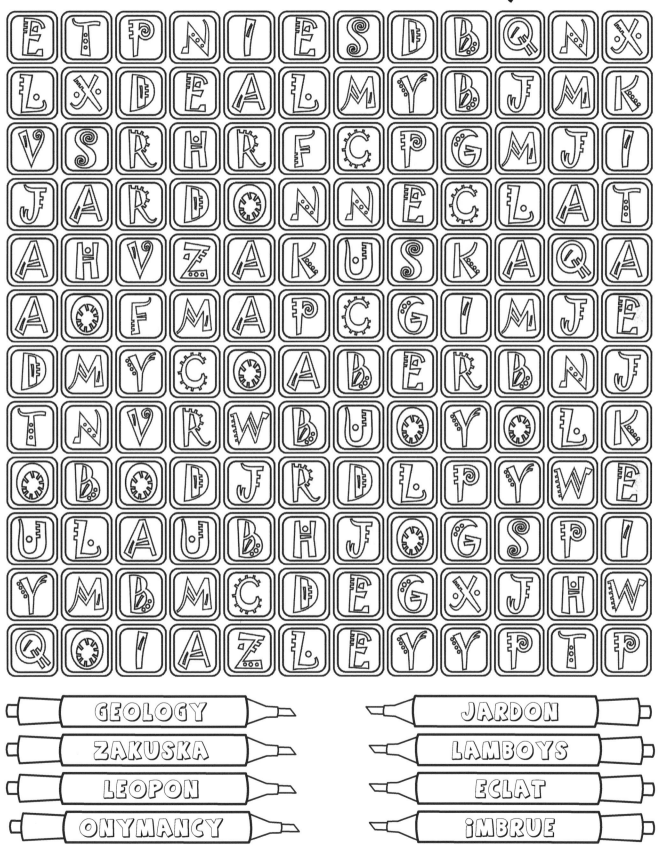

GEOLOGY

ZAKUSKA

LEOPON

ONYMANCY

JARDON

LAMBOYS

ECLAT

IMBRUE

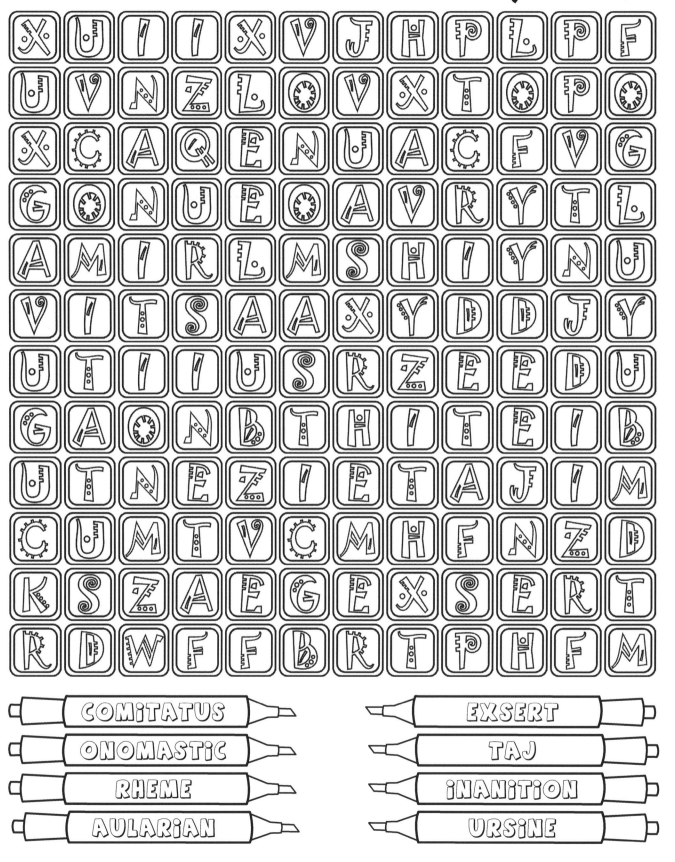

COMITATUS

ONOMASTIC

RHEME

AULARIAN

EXSERT

TAJ

INANITION

URSINE

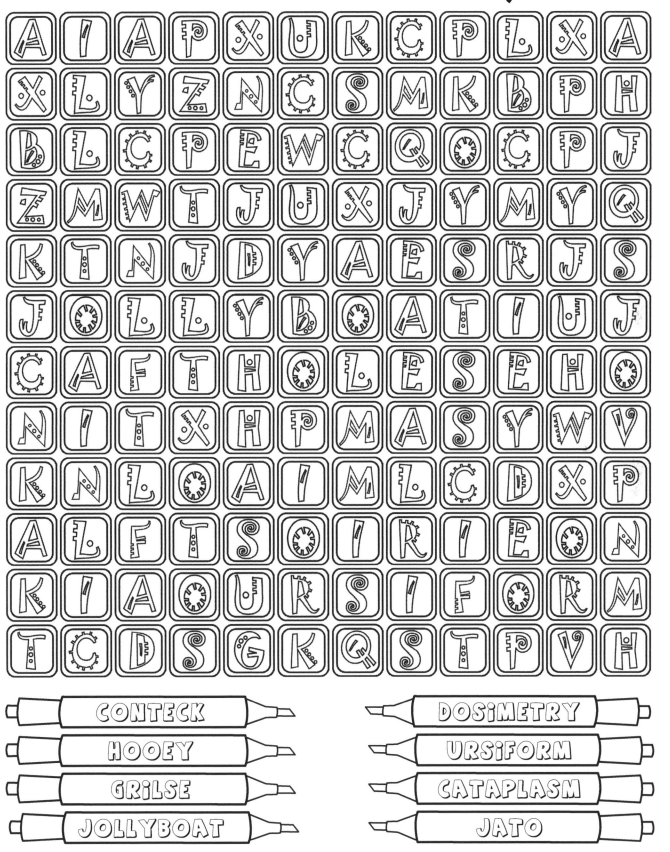

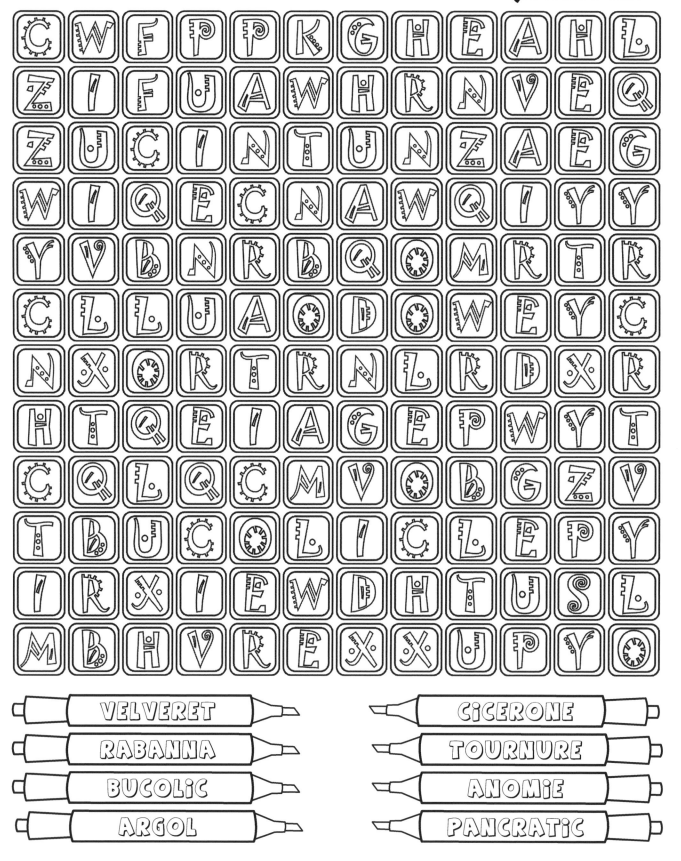

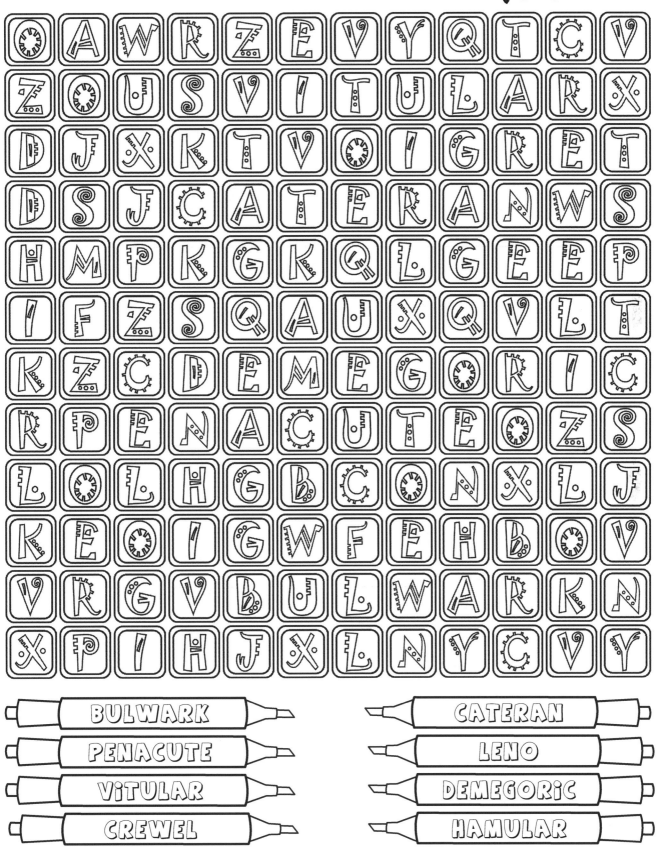

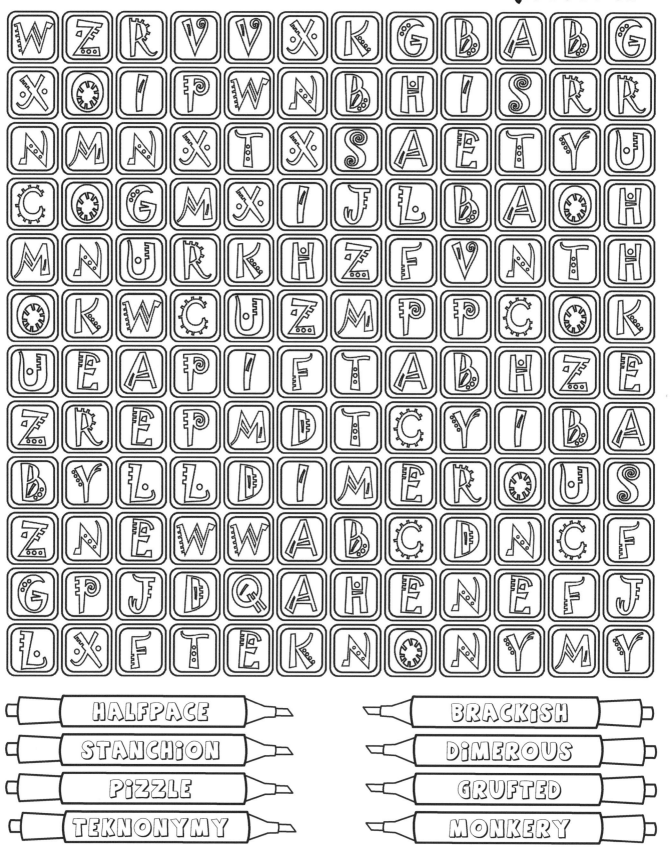

HALFPACE

STANCHION

PIZZLE

TEKNONYMY

BRACKISH

DIMEROUS

GRUFTED

MONKERY

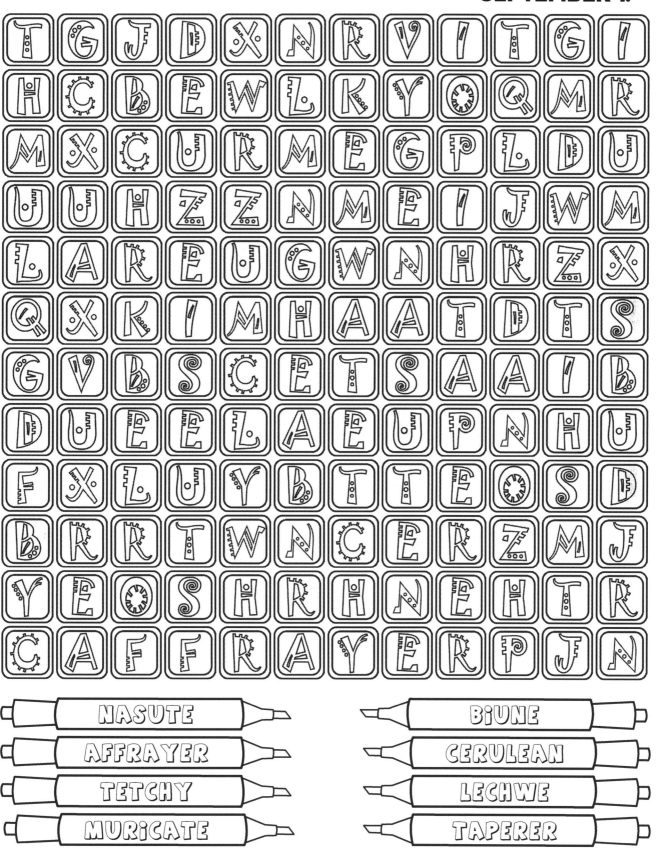

NASUTE

BIUNE

AFFRAYER

CERULEAN

TETCHY

LECHWE

MURICATE

TAPERER

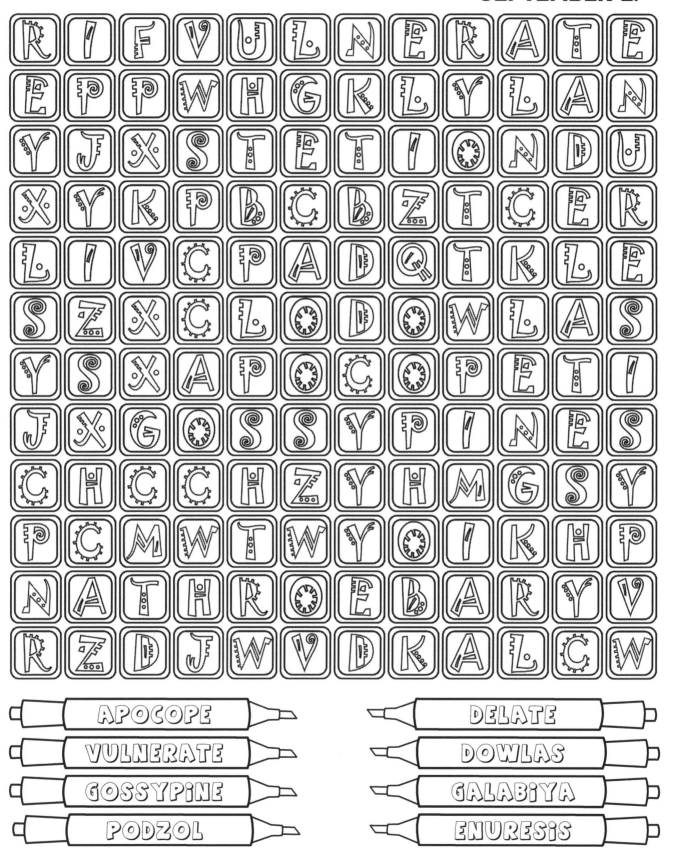

APOCOPE

VULNERATE

GOSSYPINE

PODZOL

DELATE

DOWLAS

GALABIYA

ENURESIS

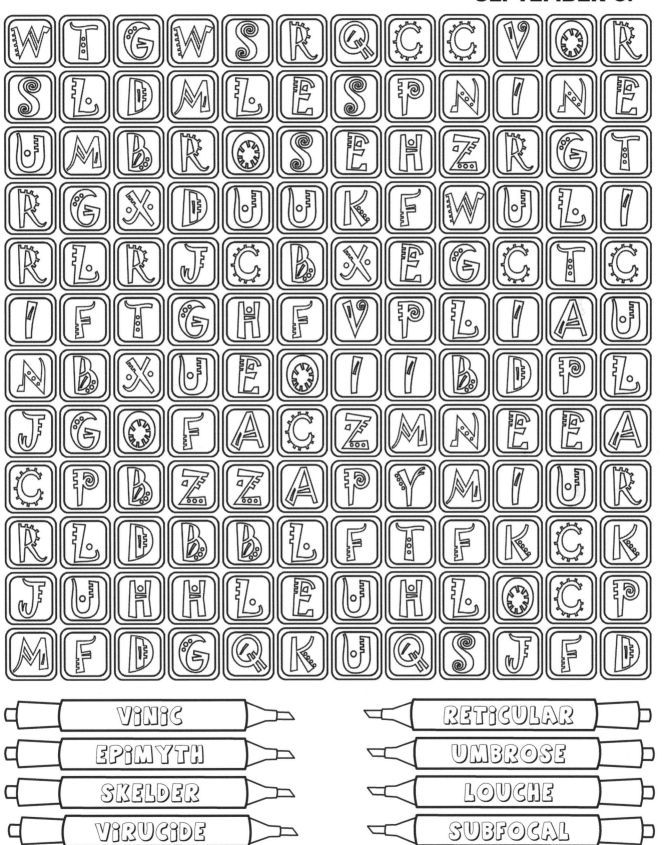

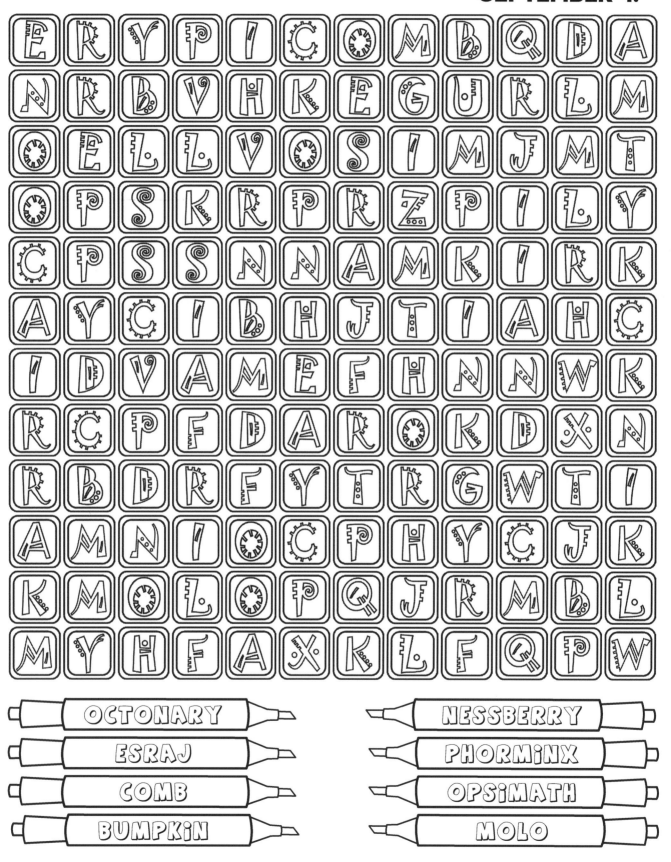

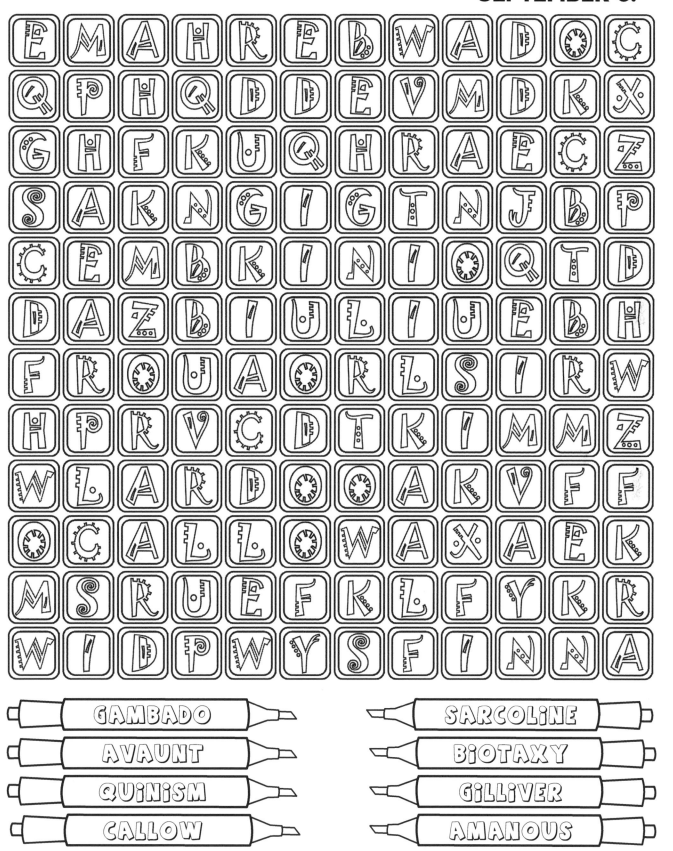

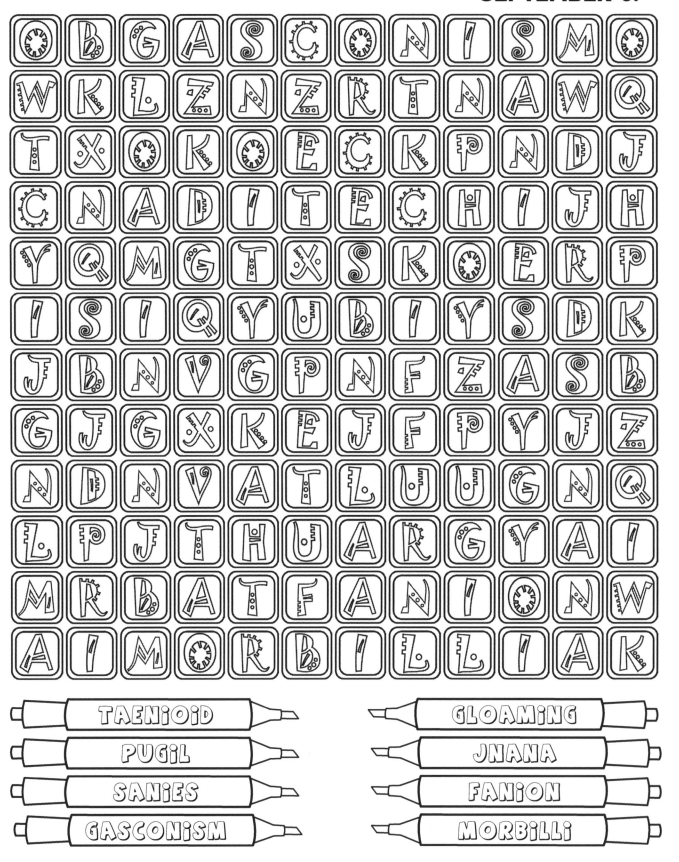

TAENIOID
PUGIL
SANIES
GASCONISM

GLOAMING
JNANA
FANION
MORBILLI

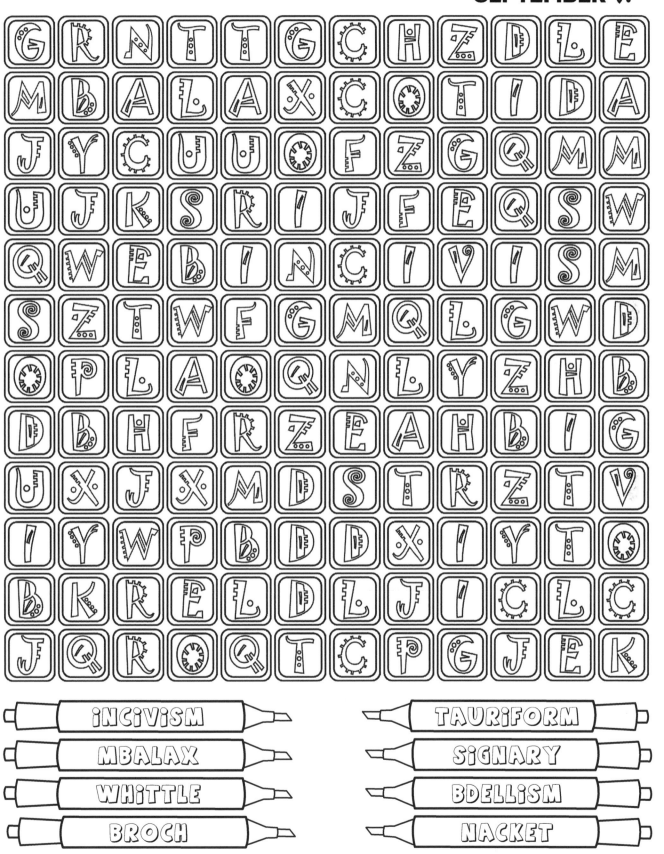

INCIVISM

MBALAX

WHITTLE

BROCH

TAURIFORM

SIGNARY

BDELLISM

NACKET

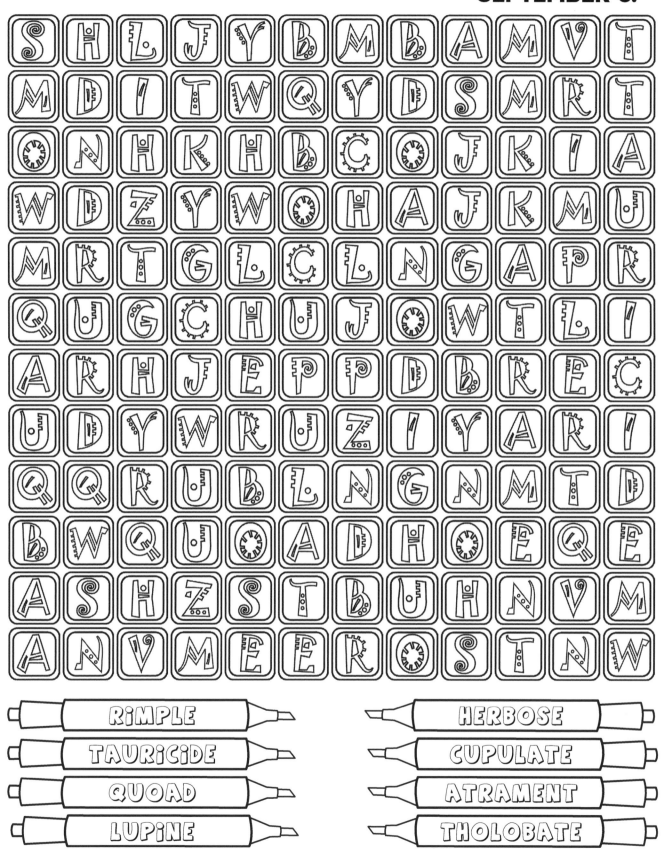

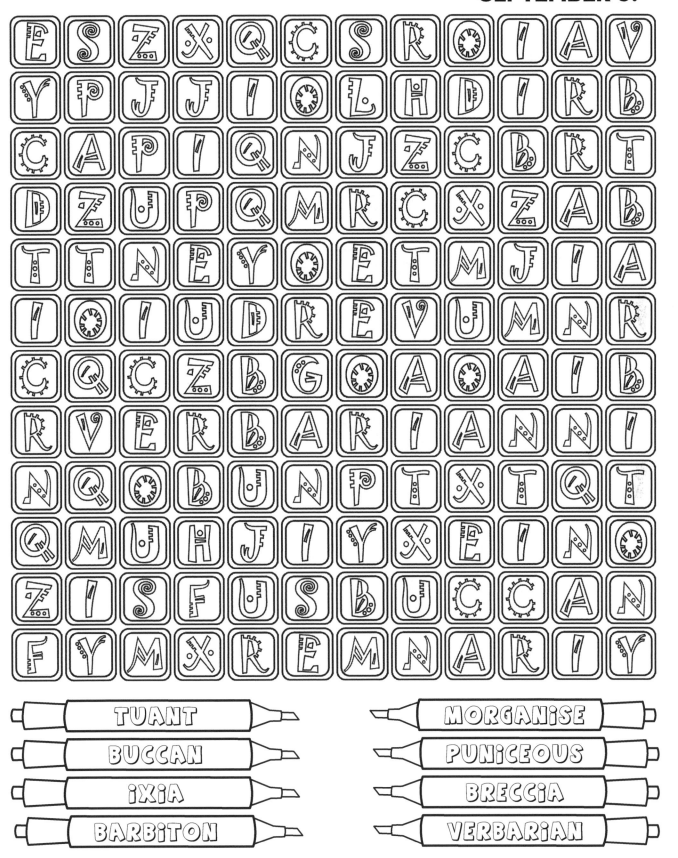

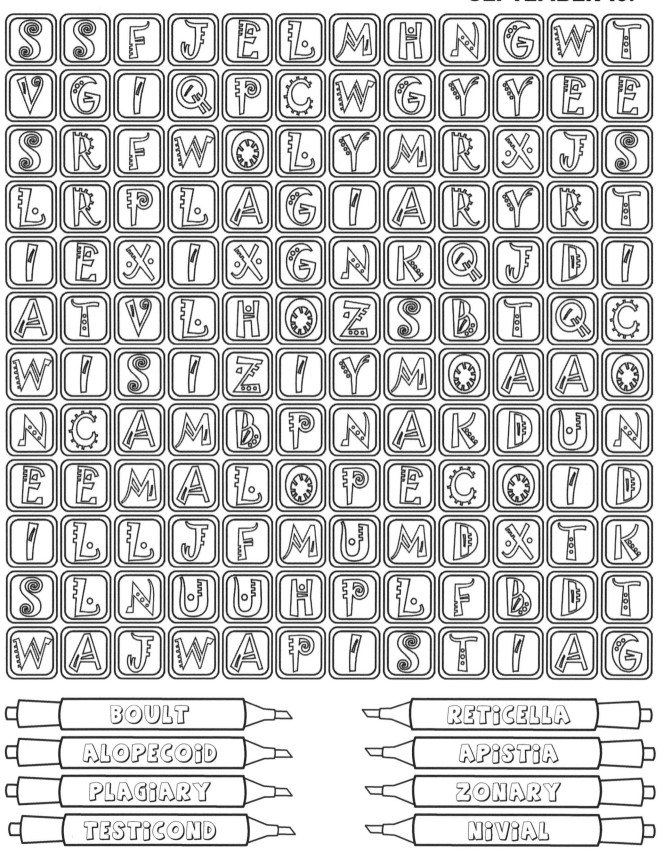

BOULT

ALOPECOID

PLAGIARY

TESTICOND

RETICELLA

APISTIA

ZONARY

NIVIAL

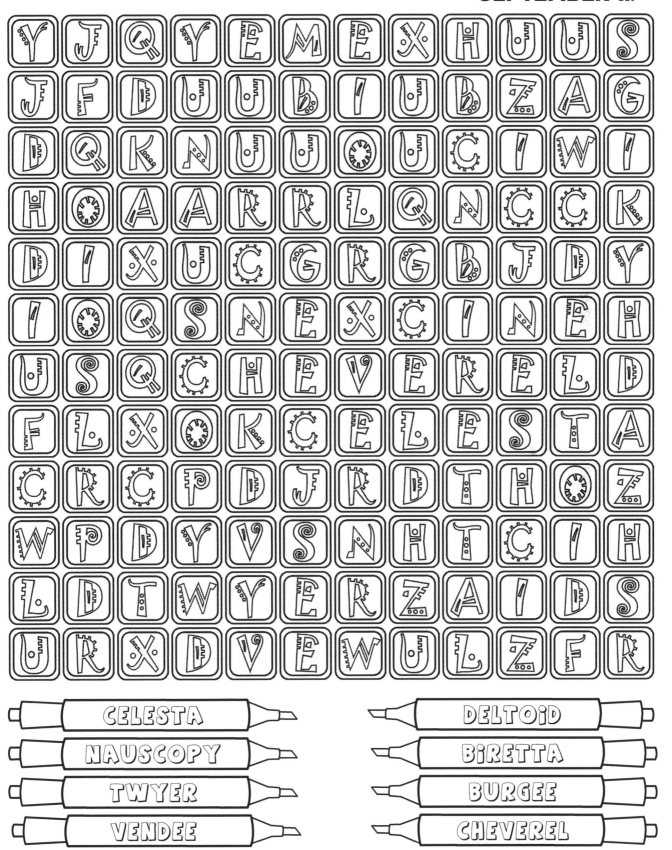

CELESTA

NAUSCOPY

TWYER

VENDEE

DELTOID

BIRETTA

BURGEE

CHEVEREL

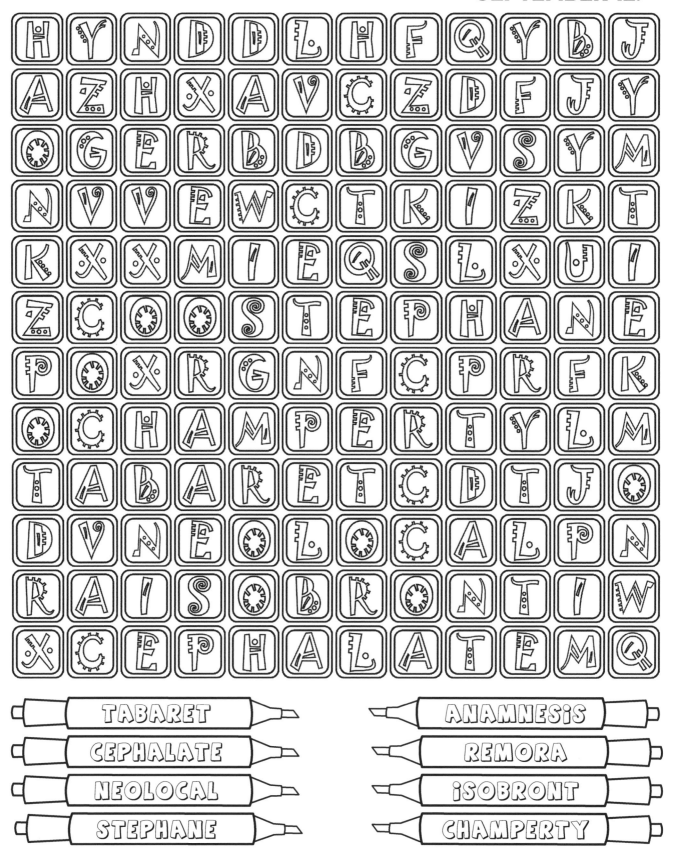

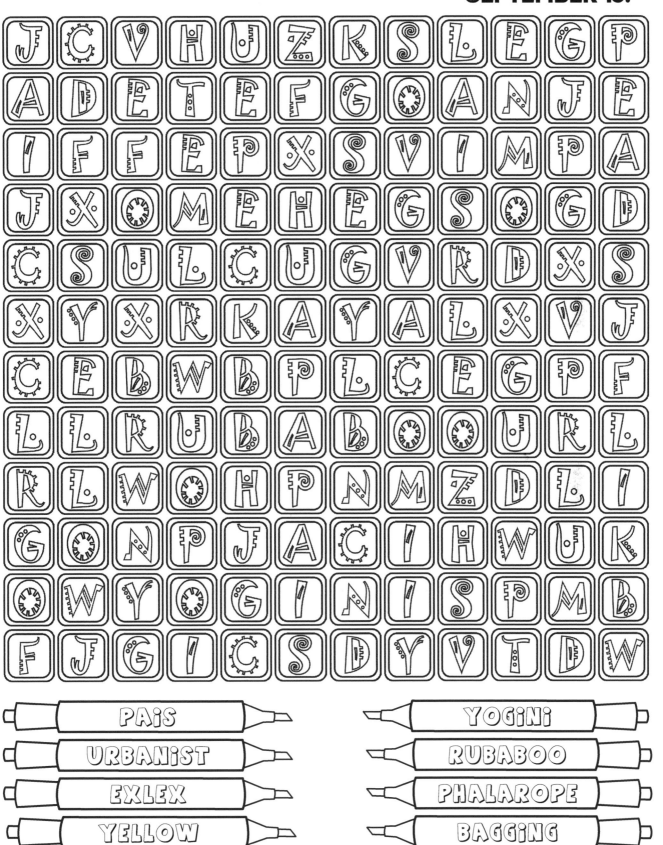

PAIS
URBANIST
EXLEX
YELLOW

YOGINI
RUBABOO
PHALAROPE
BAGGING

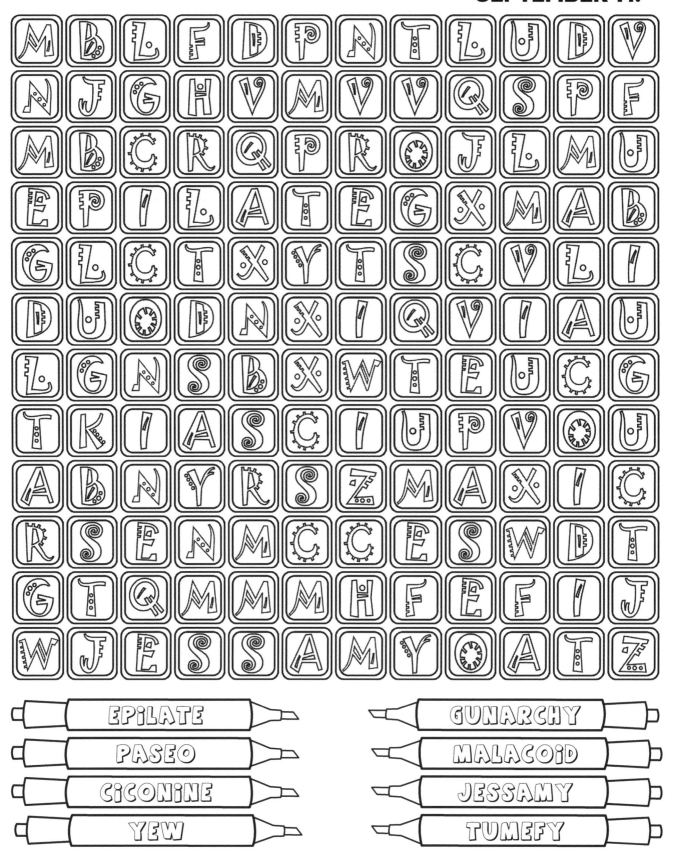

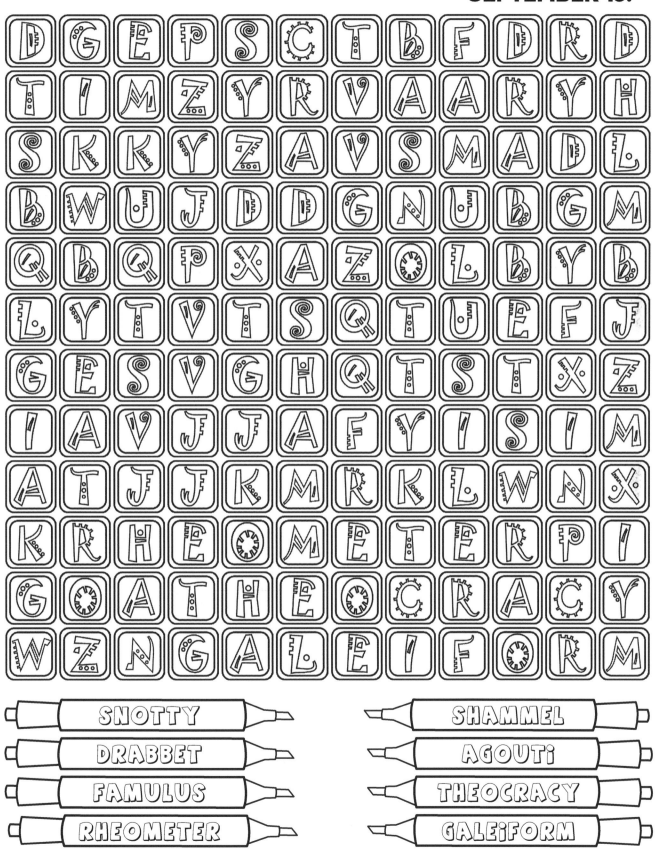

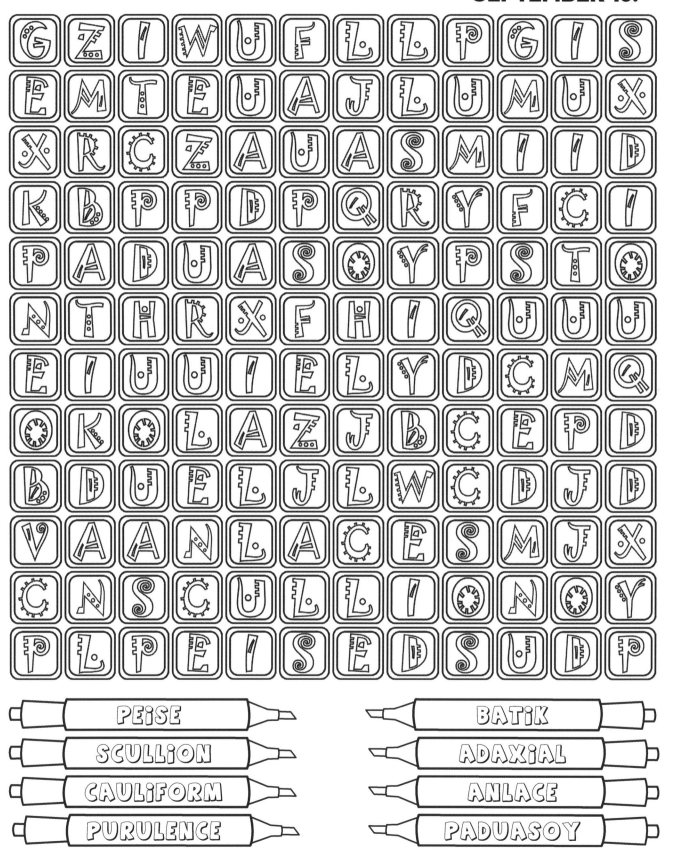

PEISE

SCULLION

CAULIFORM

PURULENCE

BATIK

ADAXIAL

ANLACE

PADUASOY

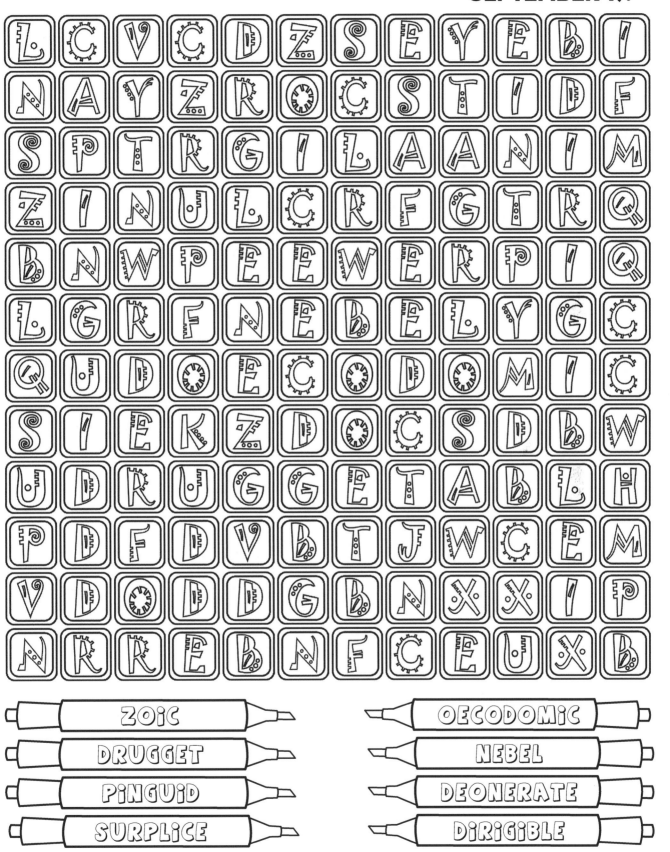

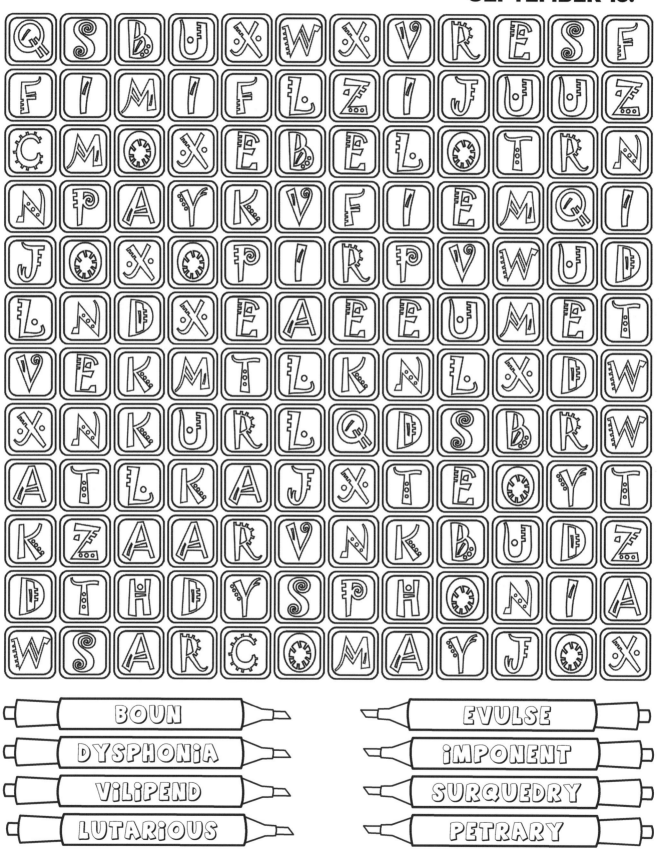

BOUN

DYSPHONIA

VILIPEND

LUTARIOUS

EVULSE

IMPONENT

SURQUEDRY

PETRARY

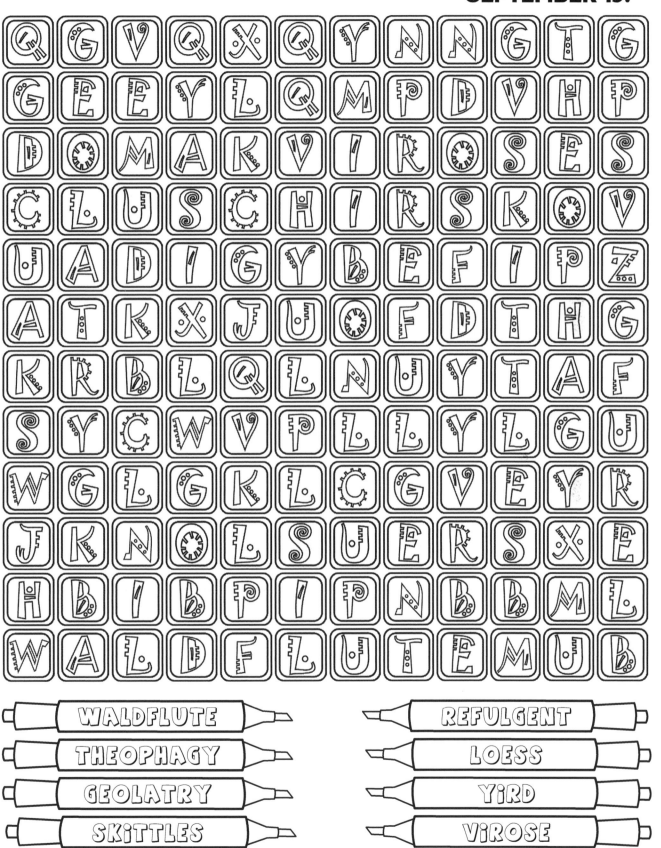

WALDFLUTE

THEOPHAGY

GEOLATRY

SKITTLES

REFULGENT

LOESS

YIRD

VIROSE

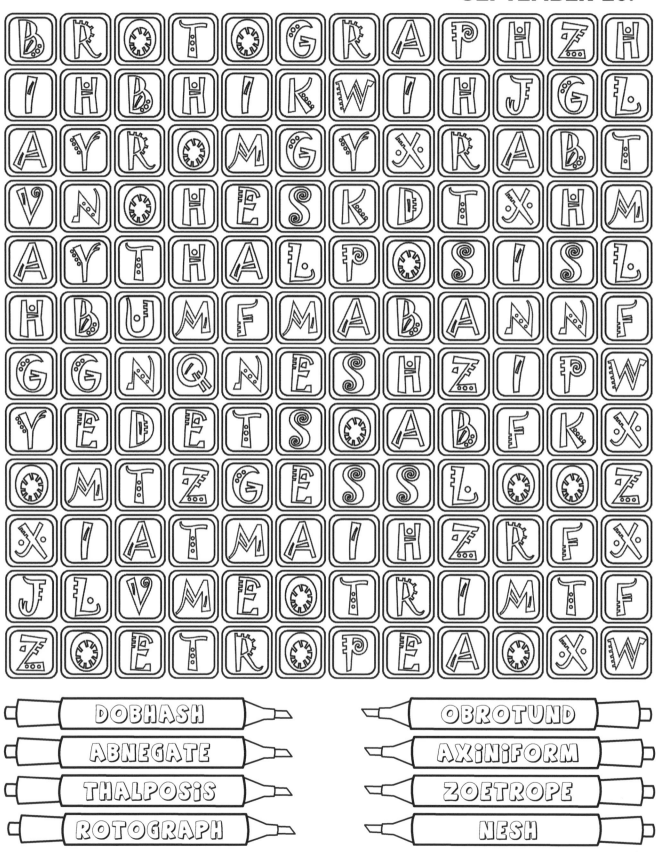

DOBHASH

ABNEGATE

THALPOSIS

ROTOGRAPH

OBROTUND

AXINIFORM

ZOETROPE

NESH

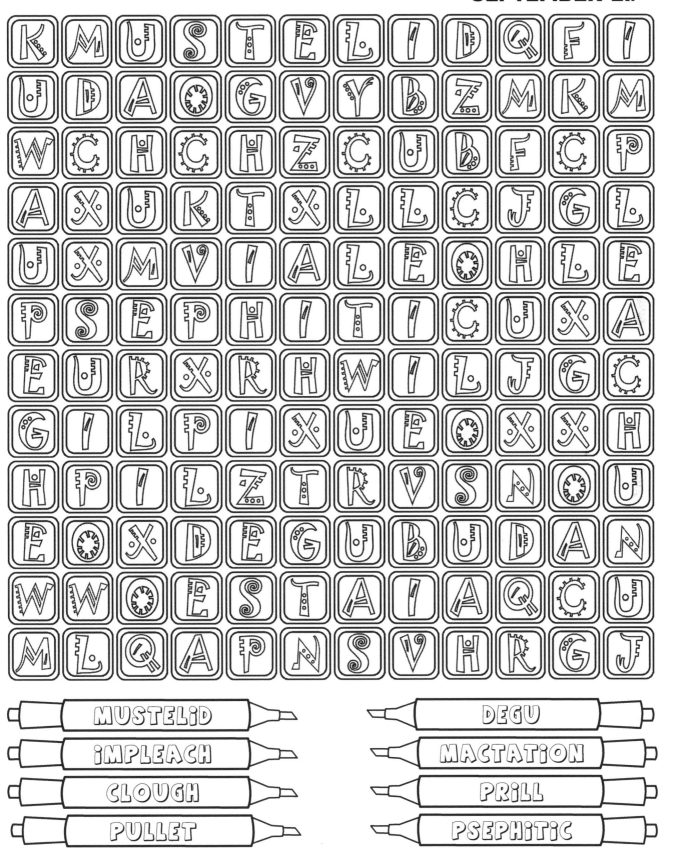

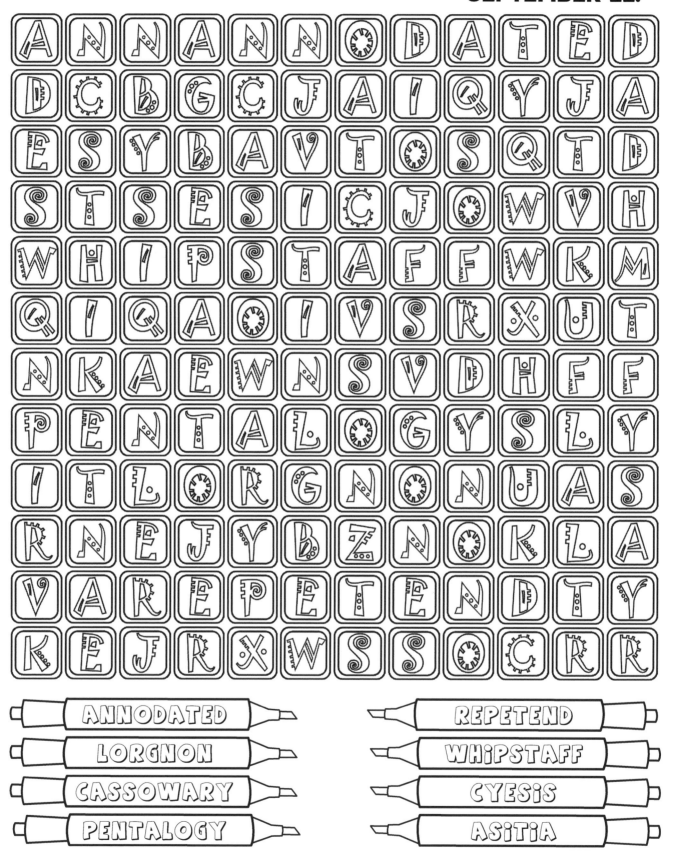

ANNODATED
LORGNON
CASSOWARY
PENTALOGY

REPETEND
WHIPSTAFF
CYESIS
ASITIA

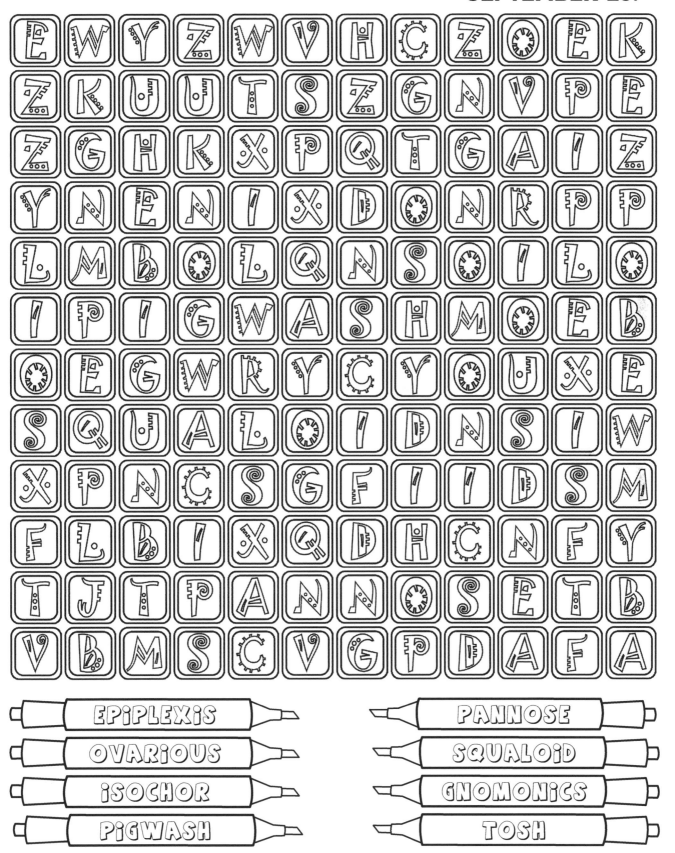

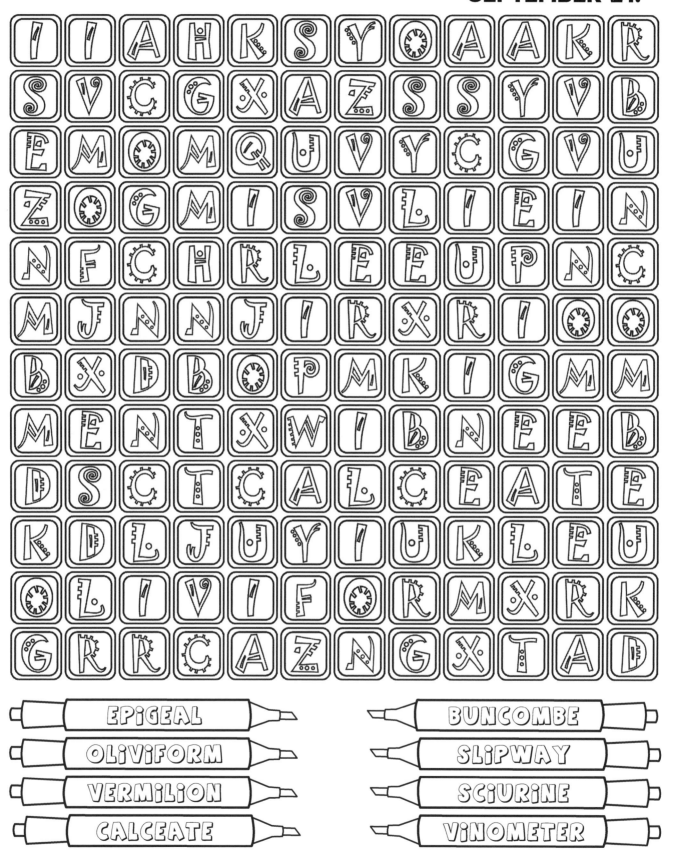

EPIGEAL

OLIVIFORM

VERMILION

CALCEATE

BUNCOMBE

SLIPWAY

SCIURINE

VINOMETER

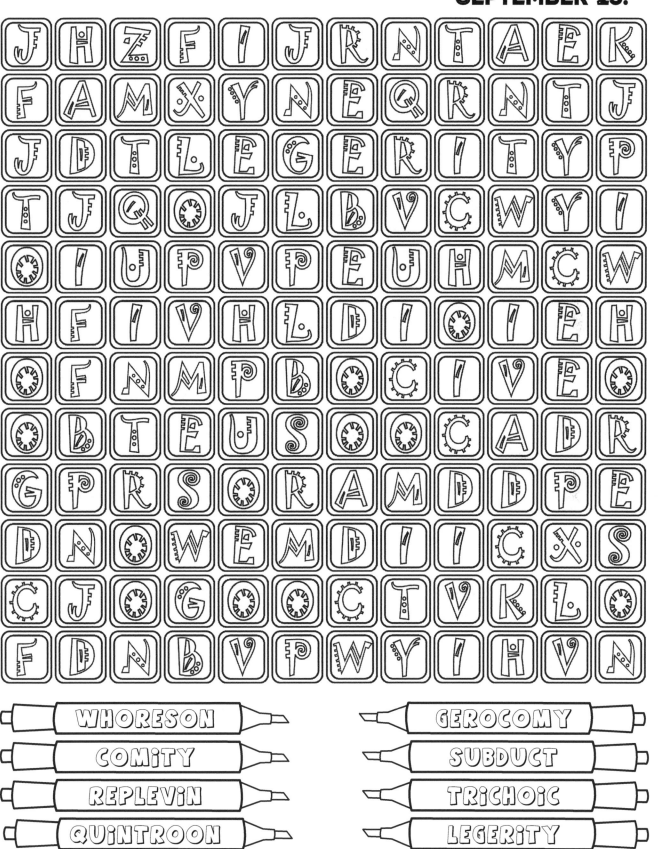

WHORESON

COMITY

REPLEVIN

QUINTROON

GEROCOMY

SUBDUCT

TRICHOIC

LEGERITY

SEPTEMBER 26:

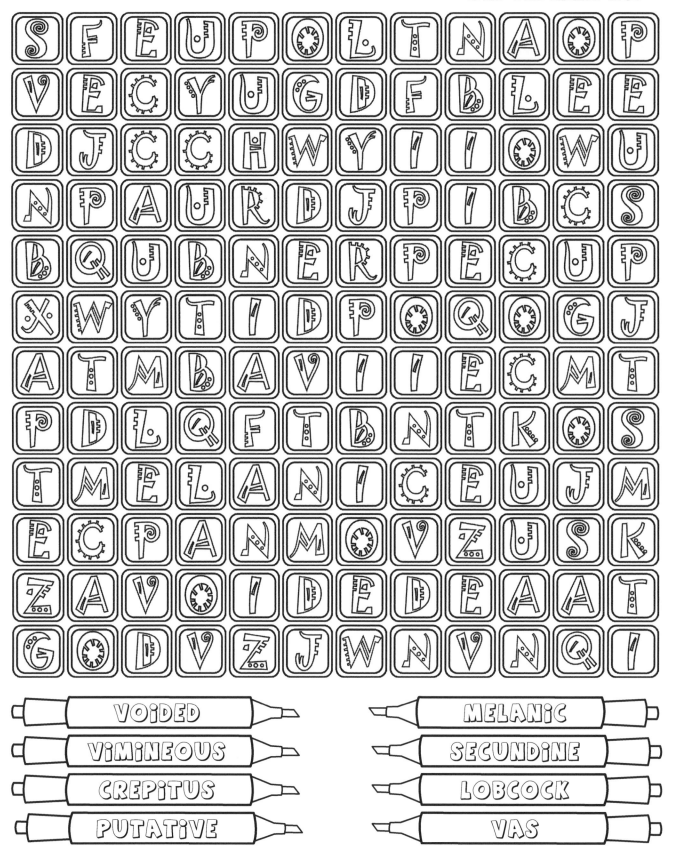

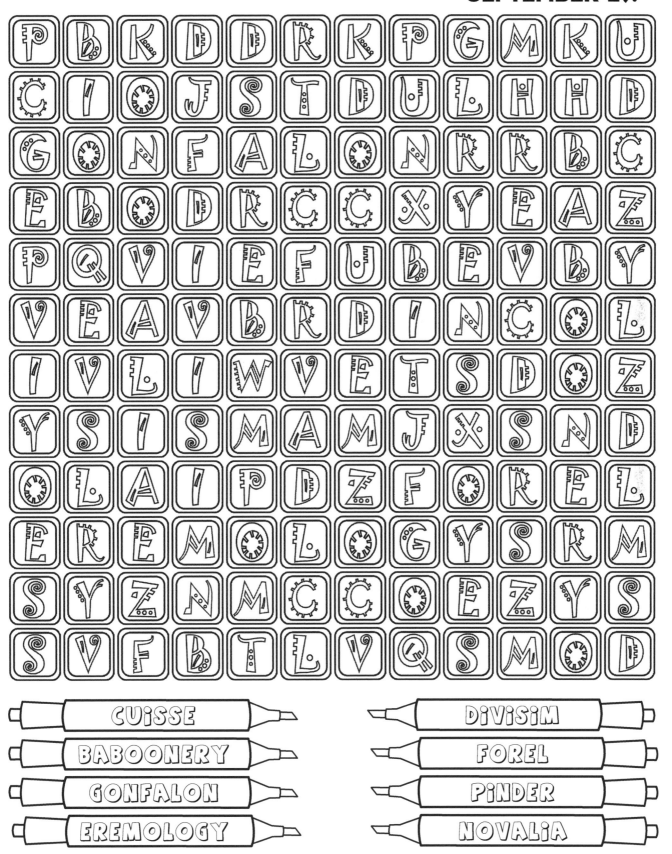

CUISSE

DIVISIM

BABOONERY

FOREL

GONFALON

PINDER

EREMOLOGY

NOVALIA

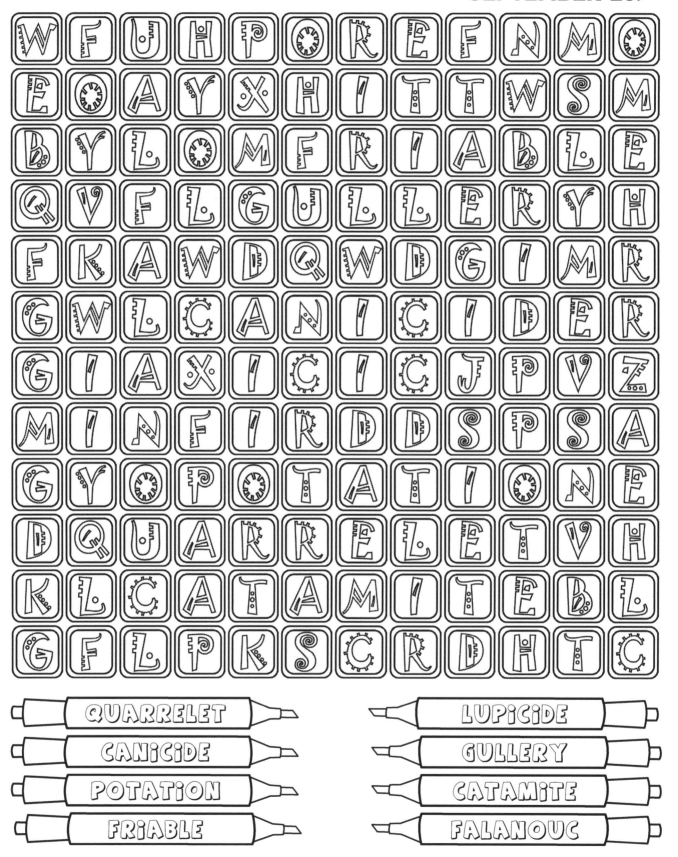

QUARRELET

CANICIDE

POTATION

FRIABLE

LUPICIDE

GULLERY

CATAMITE

FALANOUC

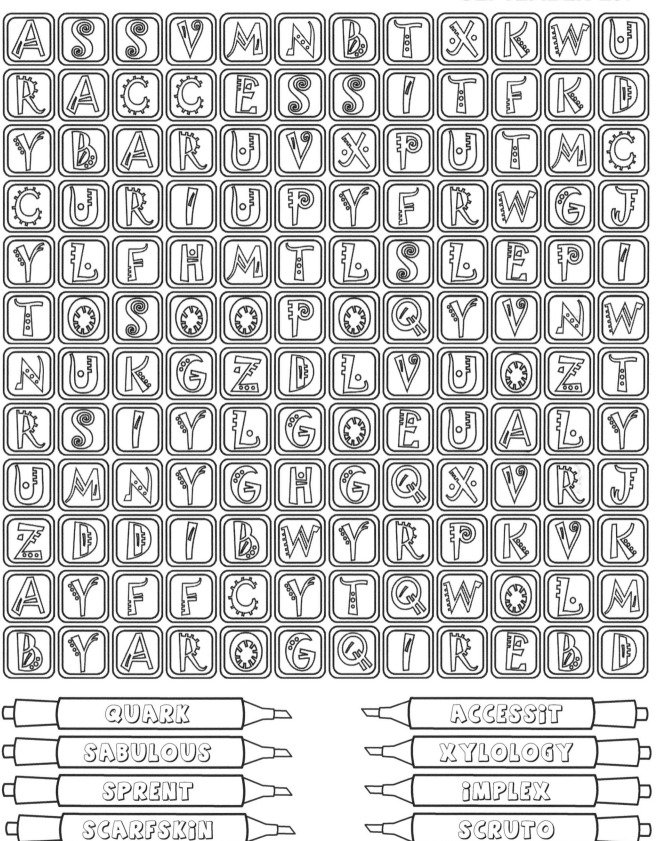

QUARK

SABULOUS

SPRENT

SCARFSKIN

ACCESSIT

XYLOLOGY

IMPLEX

SCRUTO

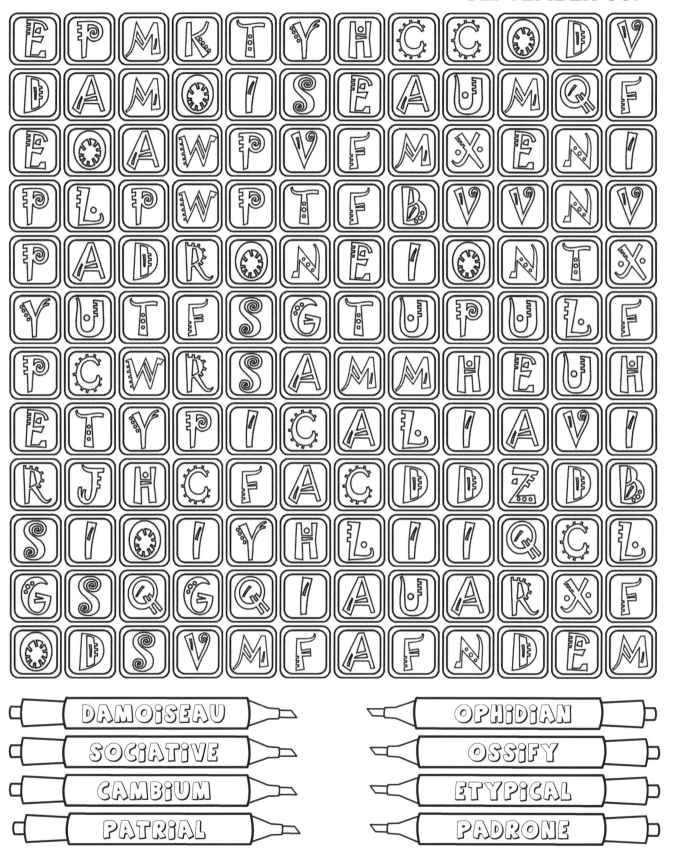

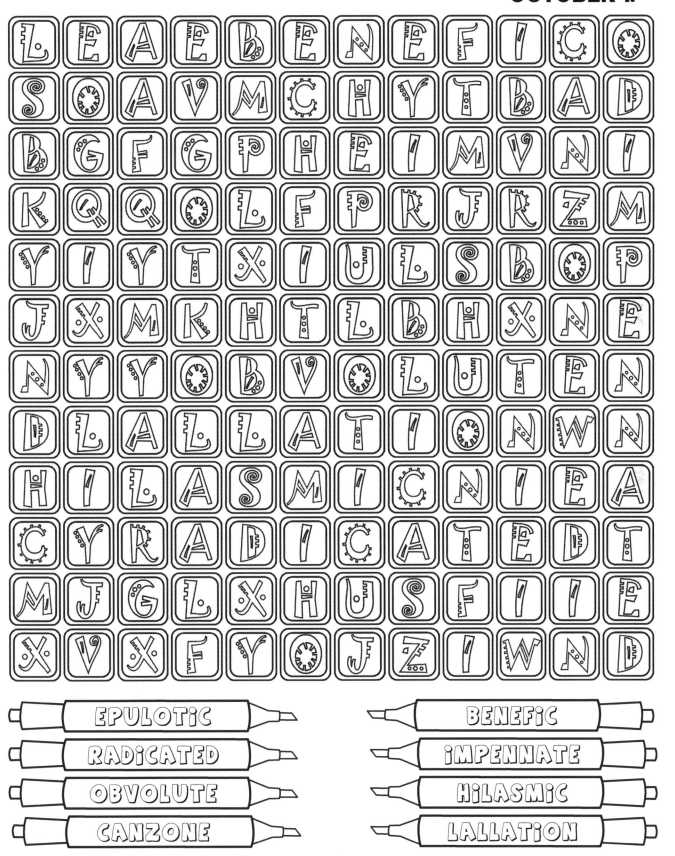

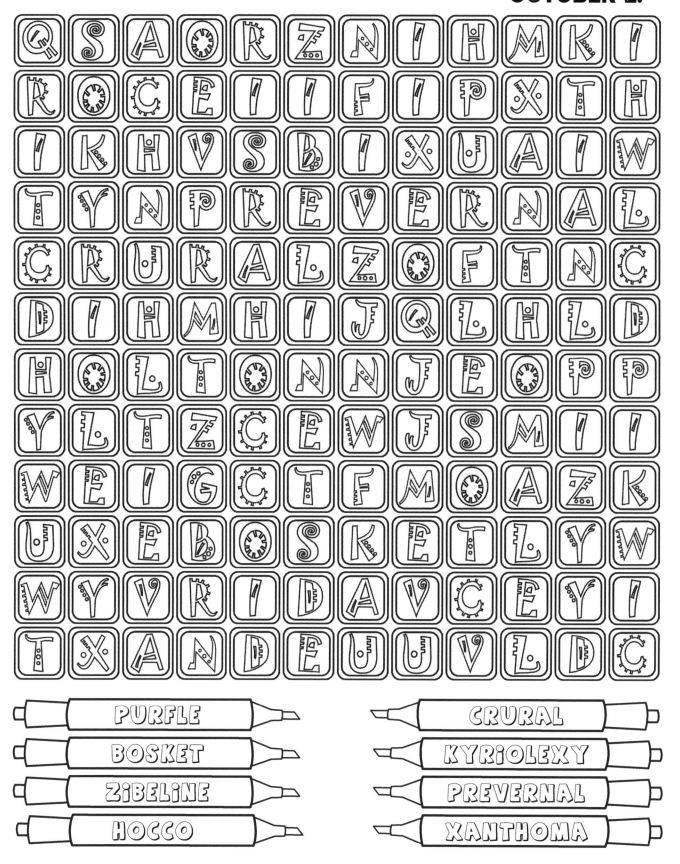

PURFLE

BOSKET

ZIBELINE

HOCCO

CRURAL

KYRIOLEXY

PREVERNAL

XANTHOMA

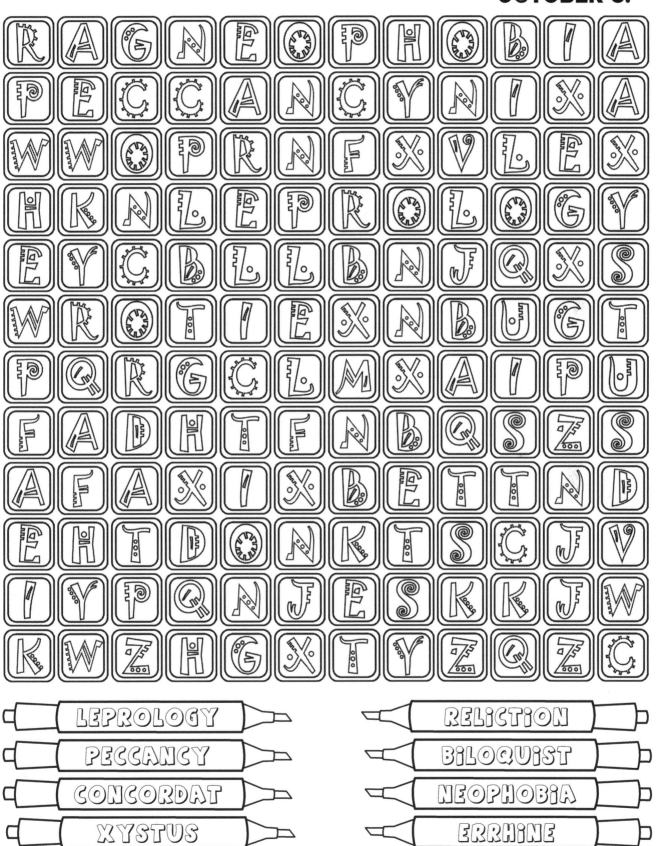

LEPROLOGY

PECCANCY

CONCORDAT

XYSTUS

RELICTION

BILOQUIST

NEOPHOBIA

ERRHINE

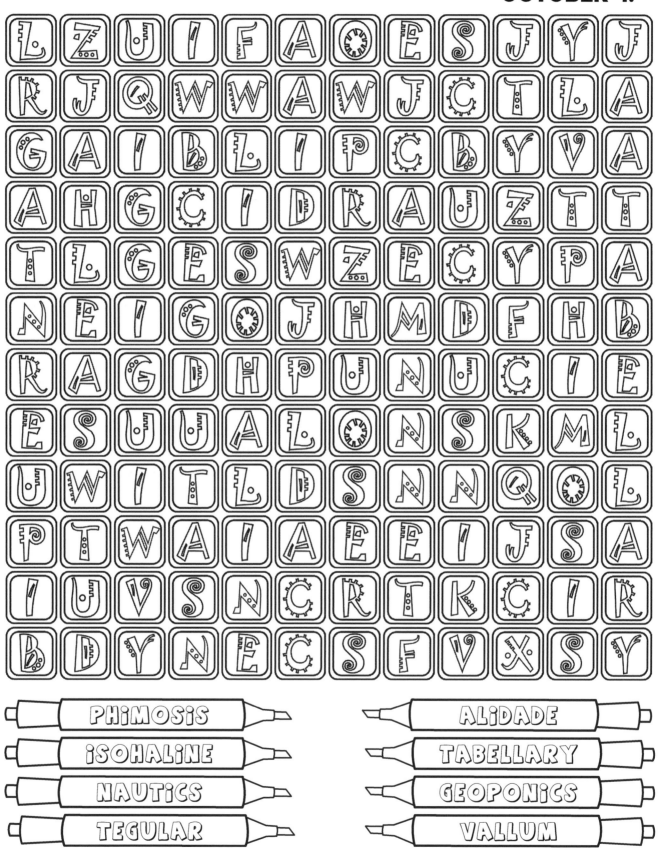

PHIMOSIS

ISOHALINE

NAUTICS

TEGULAR

ALIDADE

TABELLARY

GEOPONICS

VALLUM

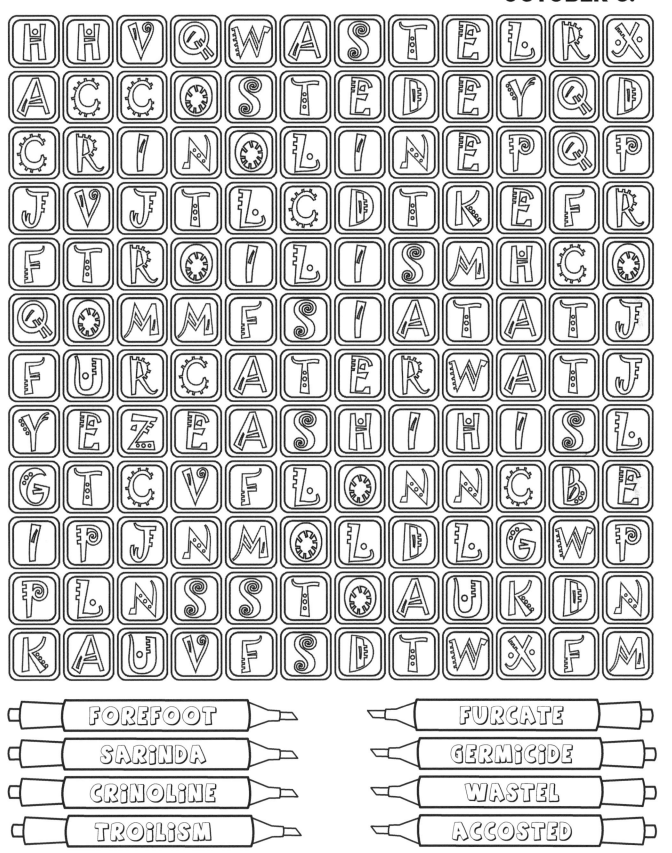

FOREFOOT   FURCATE
SARINDA   GERMICIDE
CRINOLINE   WASTEL
TROILISM   ACCOSTED

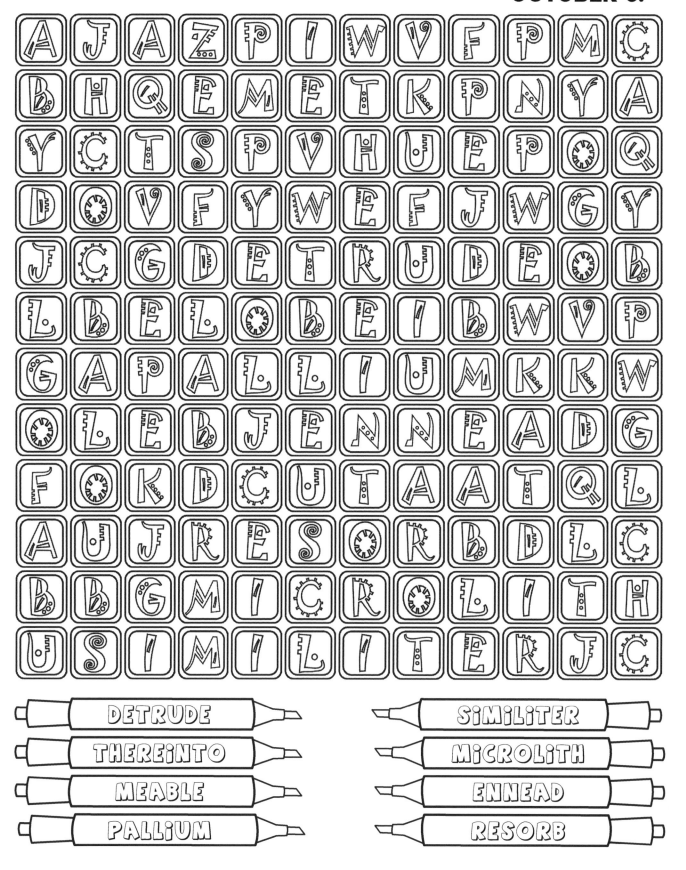

DETRUDE

THEREINTO

MEABLE

PALLIUM

SIMILITER

MICROLITH

ENNEAD

RESORB

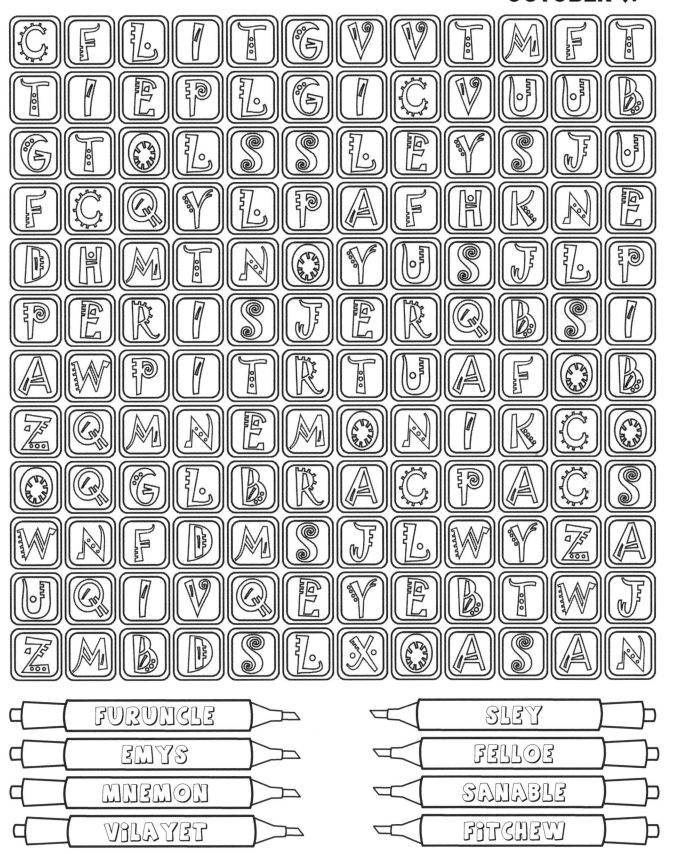

FURUNCLE

EMYS

MNEMON

VILAYET

SLEY

FELLOE

SANABLE

FITCHEW

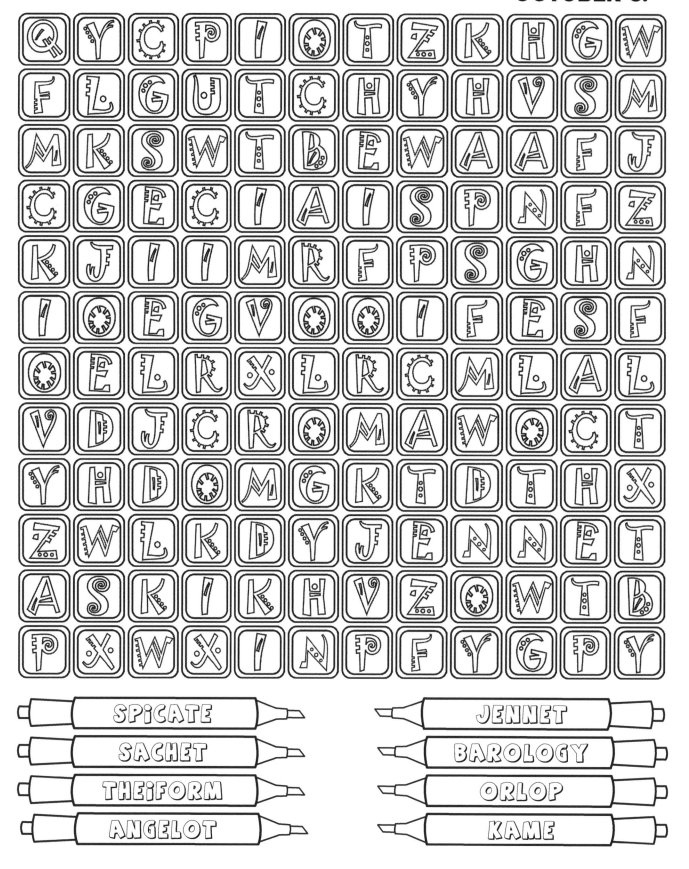

SPICATE

SACHET

THEIFORM

ANGELOT

JENNET

BAROLOGY

ORLOP

KAME

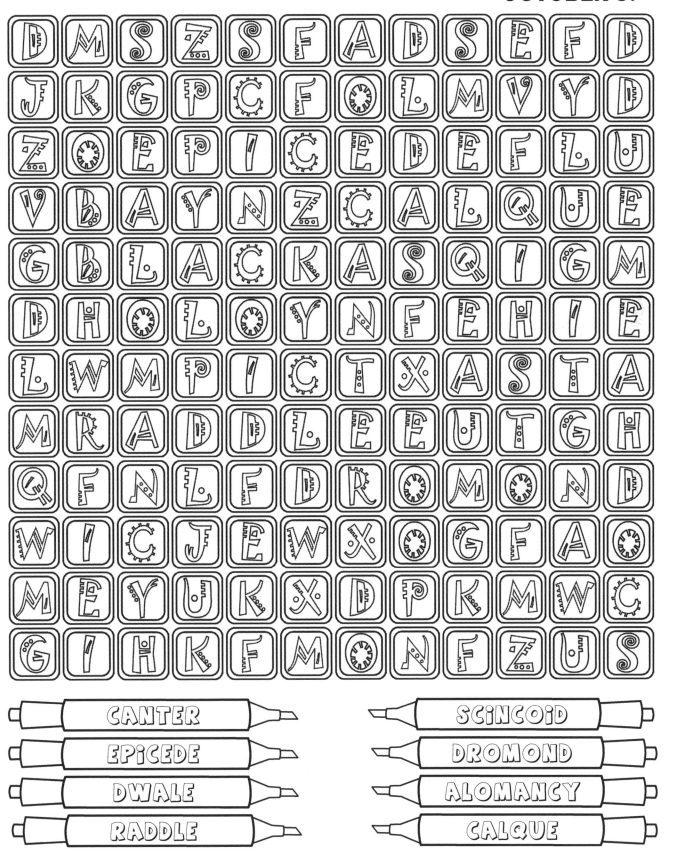

CANTER

EPICEDE

DWALE

RADDLE

SCINCOID

DROMOND

ALOMANCY

CALQUE

OCTOBER 10:

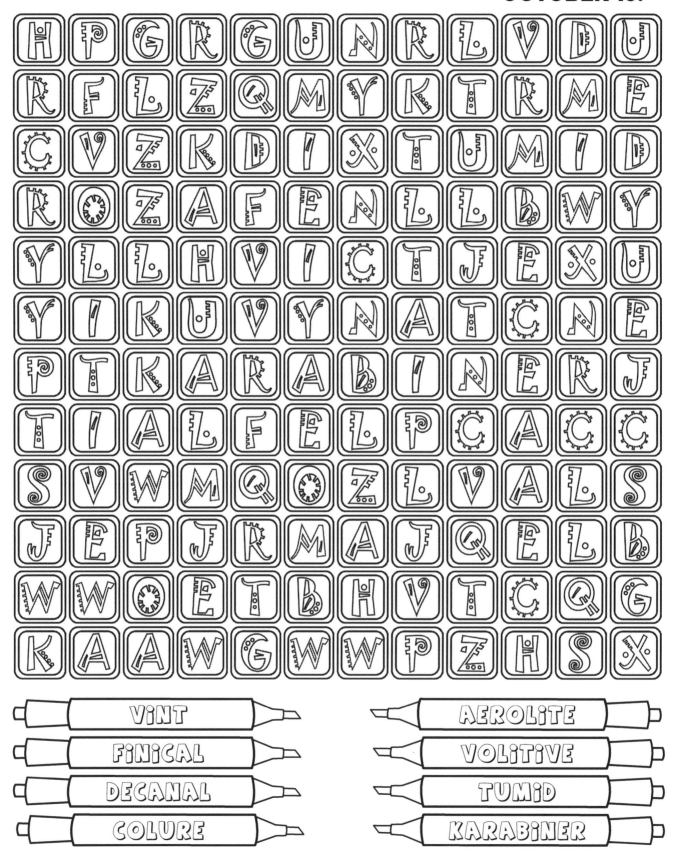

VINT

FINICAL

DECANAL

COLURE

AEROLITE

VOLITIVE

TUMID

KARABINER

OCTOBER 11:

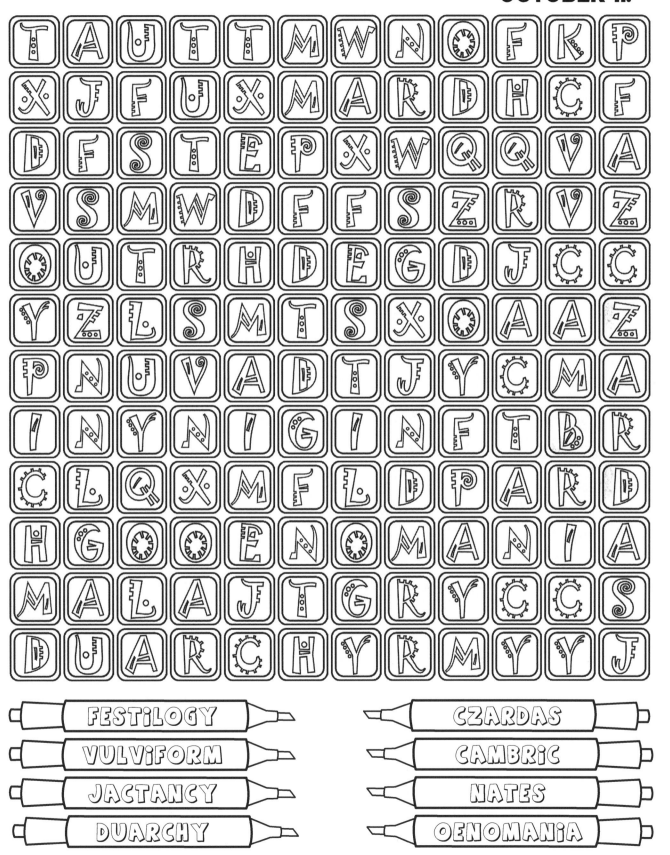

FESTILOGY

VULVIFORM

JACTANCY

DUARCHY

CZARDAS

CAMBRIC

NATES

OENOMANIA

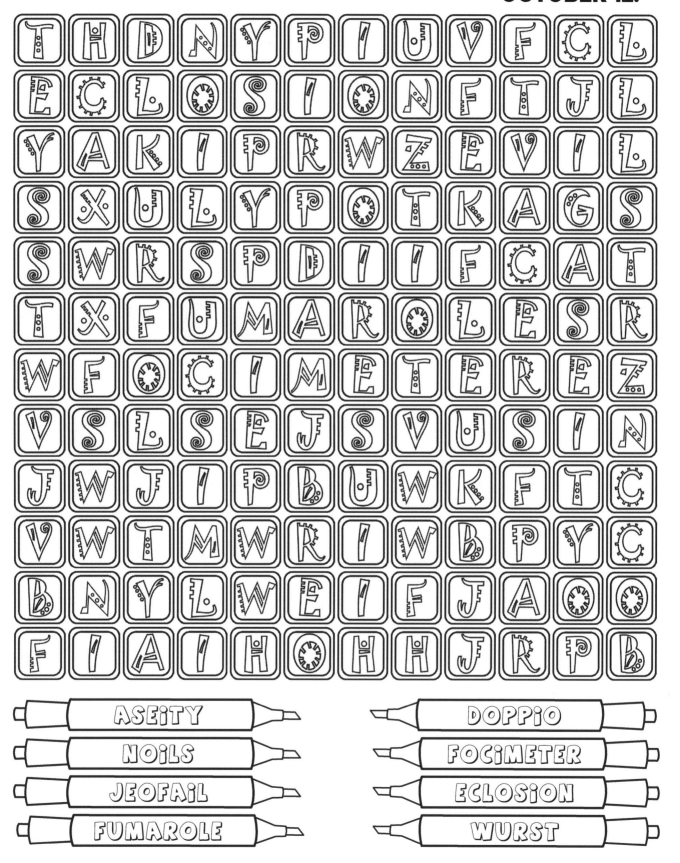

ASEITY

NOILS

JEOFAIL

FUMAROLE

DOPPIO

FOCIMETER

ECLOSION

WURST

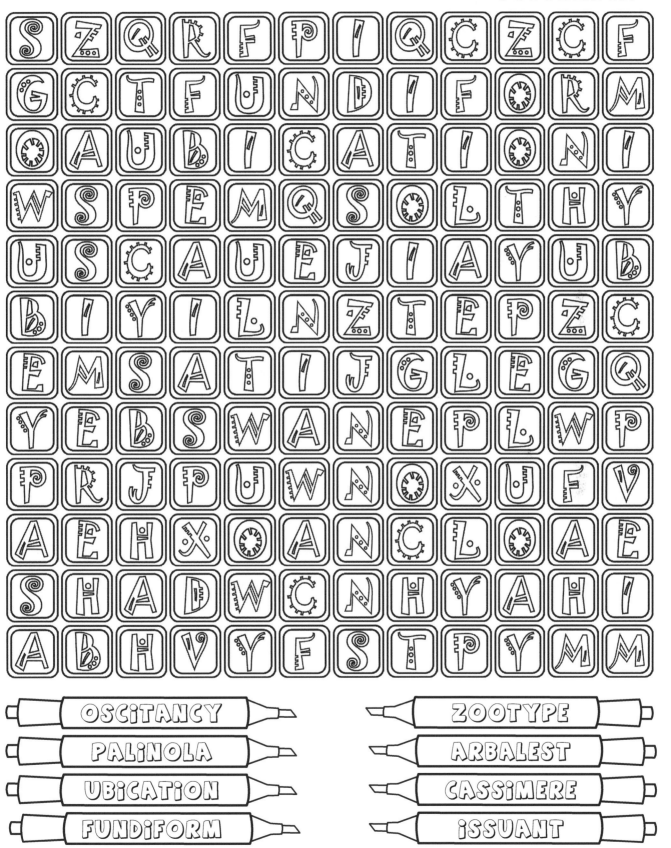

OSCITANCY

PALINOLA

UBICATION

FUNDIFORM

ZOOTYPE

ARBALEST

CASSIMERE

ISSUANT

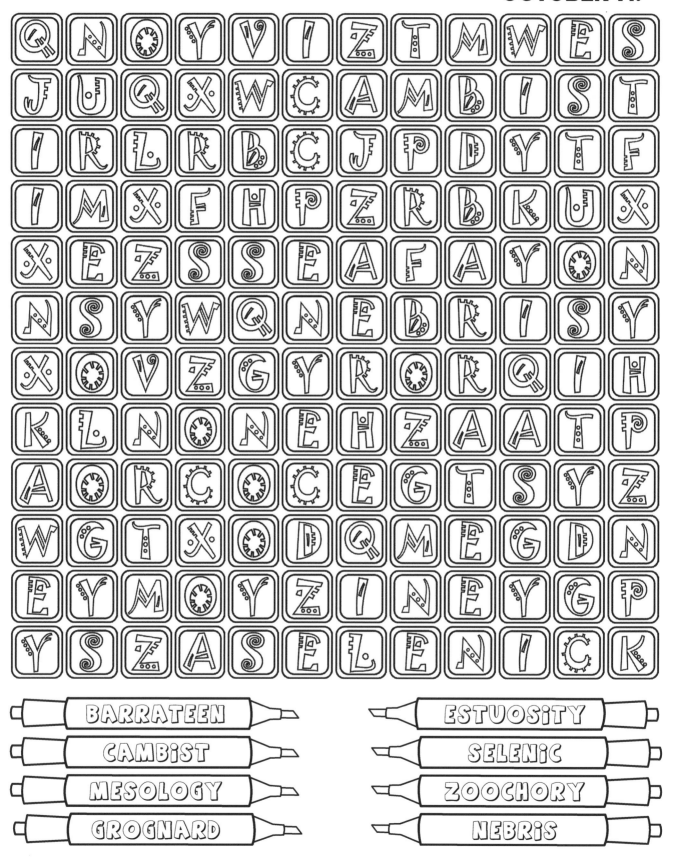

BARRATEEN

CAMBIST

MESOLOGY

GROGNARD

ESTUOSITY

SELENIC

ZOOCHORY

NEBRIS

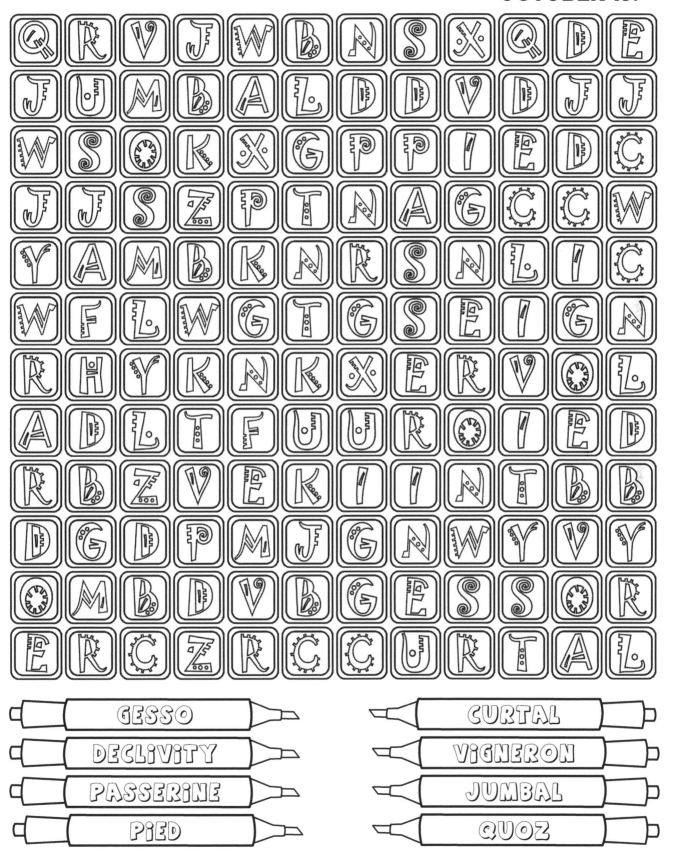

GESSO

DECLIVITY

PASSERINE

PIED

CURTAL

VIGNERON

JUMBAL

QUOZ

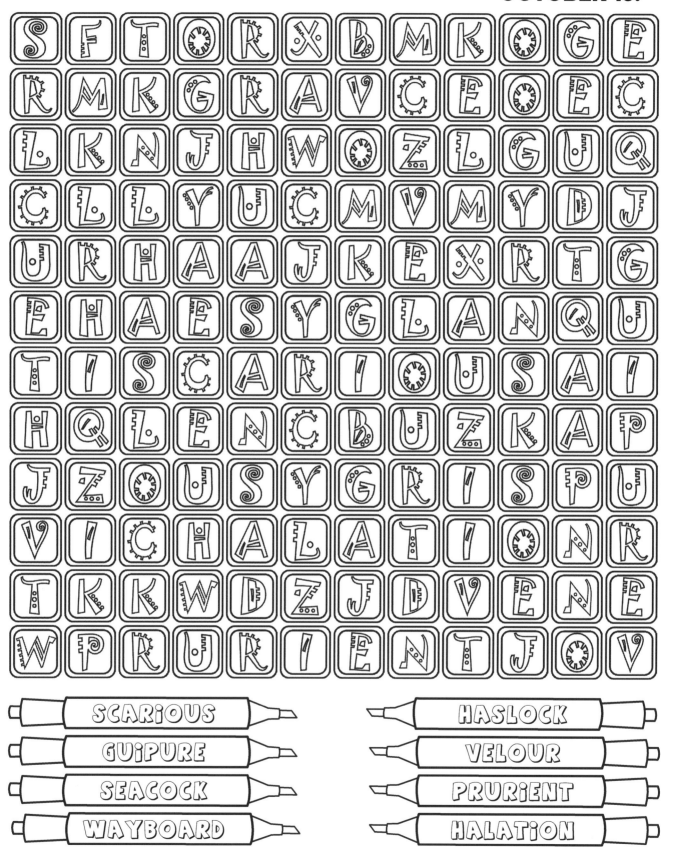

SCARIOUS

GUIPURE

SEACOCK

WAYBOARD

HASLOCK

VELOUR

PRURIENT

HALATION

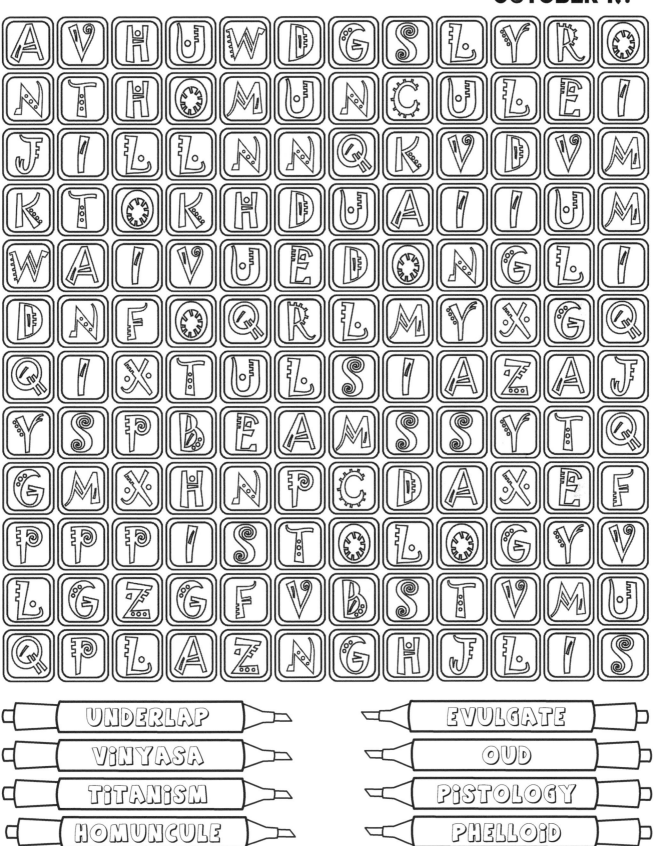

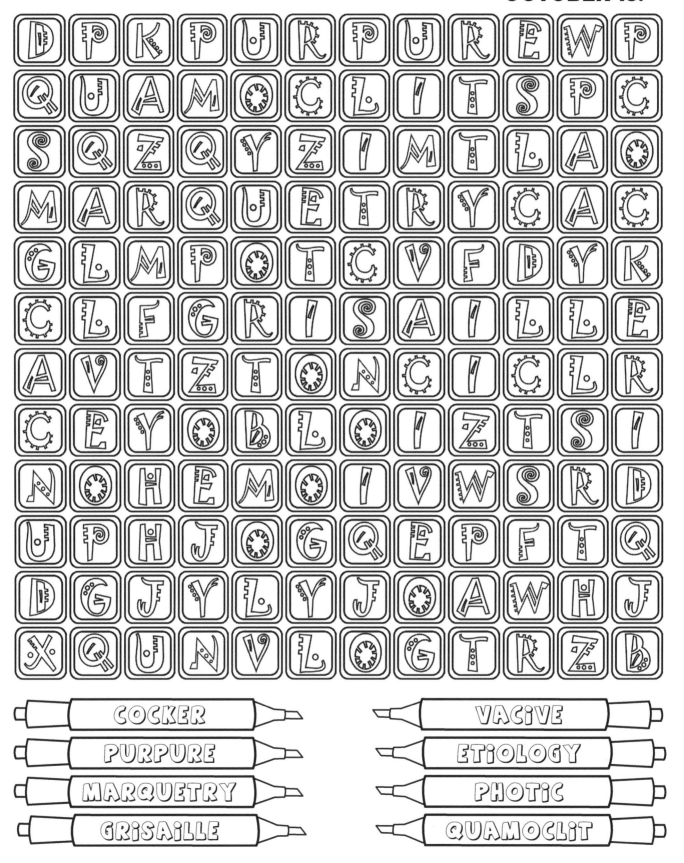

COCKER

PURPURE

MARQUETRY

GRISAILLE

VACIVE

ETIOLOGY

PHOTIC

QUAMOCLIT

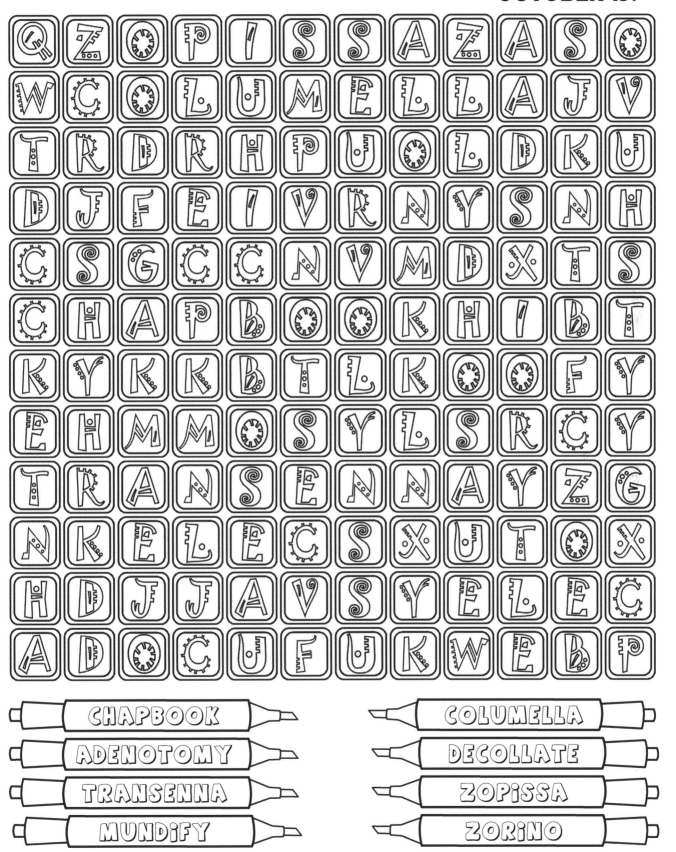

CHAPBOOK
ADENOTOMY
TRANSENNA
MUNDIFY

COLUMELLA
DECOLLATE
ZOPISSA
ZORINO

OCTOBER 20:

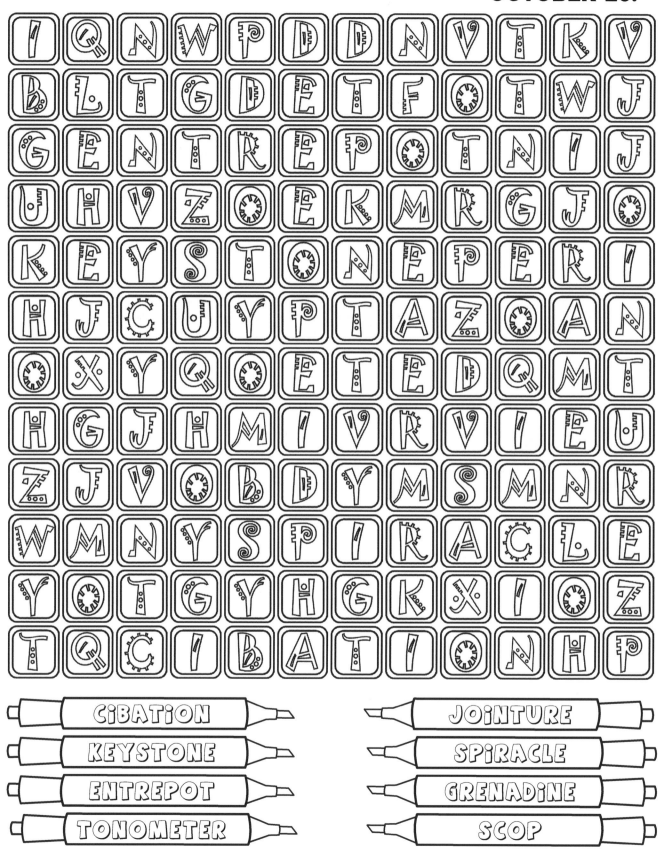

CIBATION
KEYSTONE
ENTREPOT
TONOMETER

JOINTURE
SPIRACLE
GRENADINE
SCOP

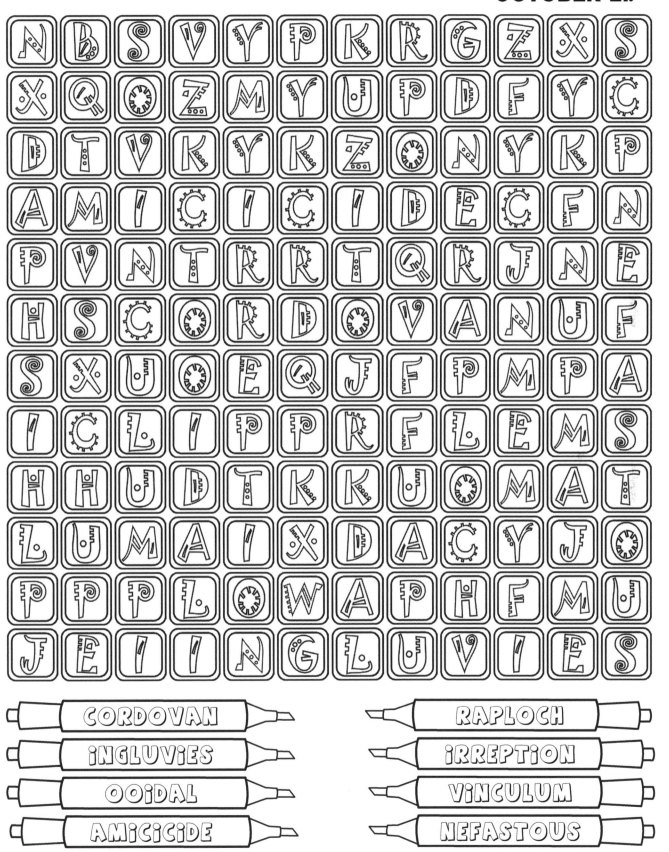

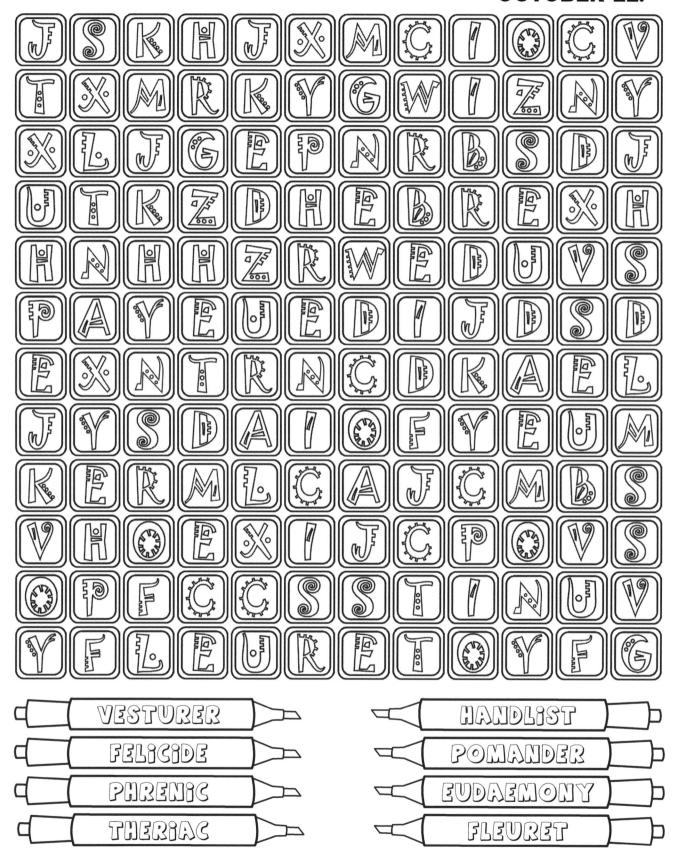

VESTURER

FELICIDE

PHRENIC

THERIAC

HANDLIST

POMANDER

EUDAEMONY

FLEURET

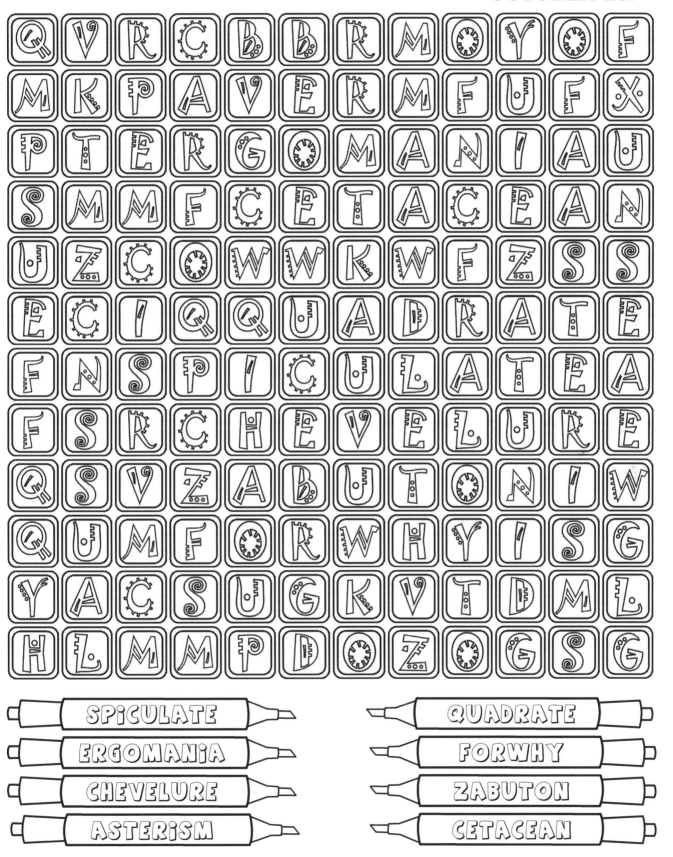

SPICULATE

ERGOMANIA

CHEVELURE

ASTERISM

QUADRATE

FORWHY

ZABUTON

CETACEAN

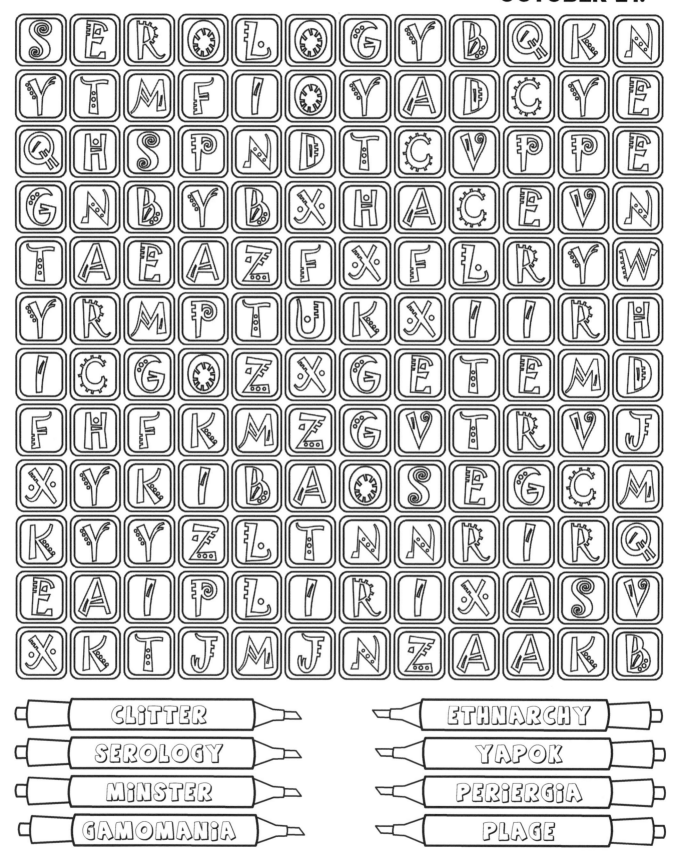

CLITTER

SEROLOGY

MINSTER

GAMOMANIA

ETHNARCHY

YAPOK

PERIERGIA

PLAGE

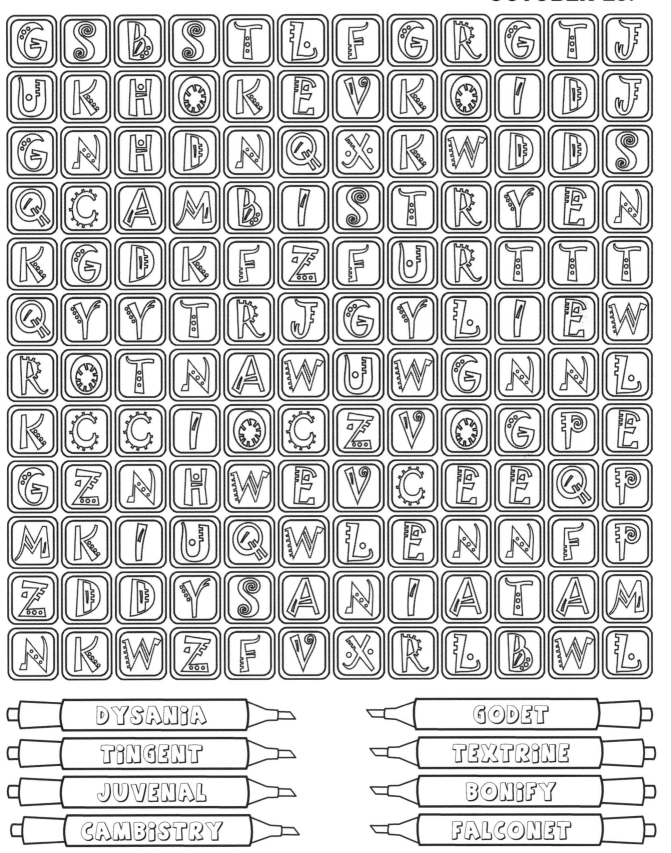

DYSANIA

TINGENT

JUVENAL

CAMBISTRY

GODET

TEXTRINE

BONIFY

FALCONET

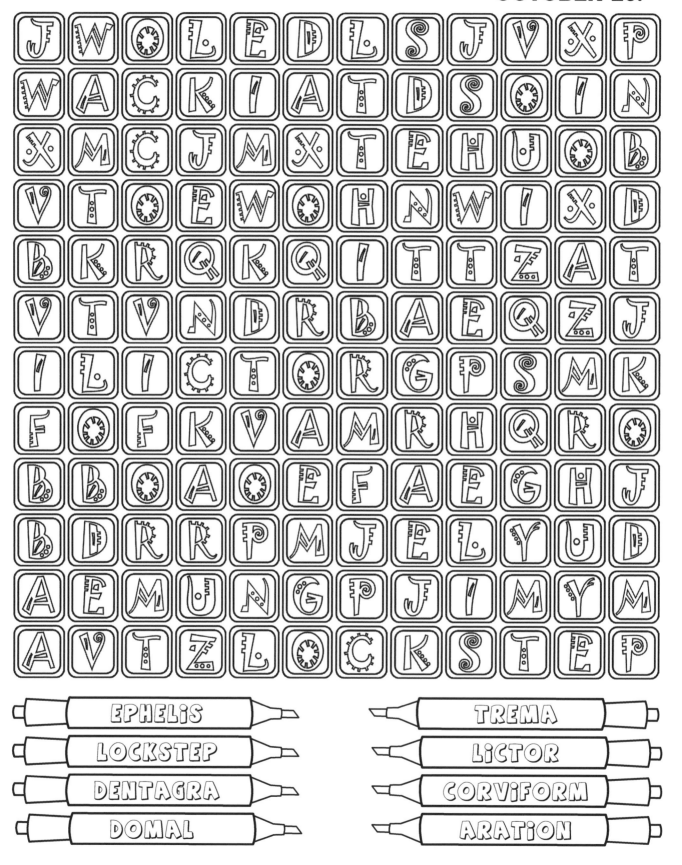

EPHELIS

LOCKSTEP

DENTAGRA

DOMAL

TREMA

LICTOR

CORVIFORM

ARATION

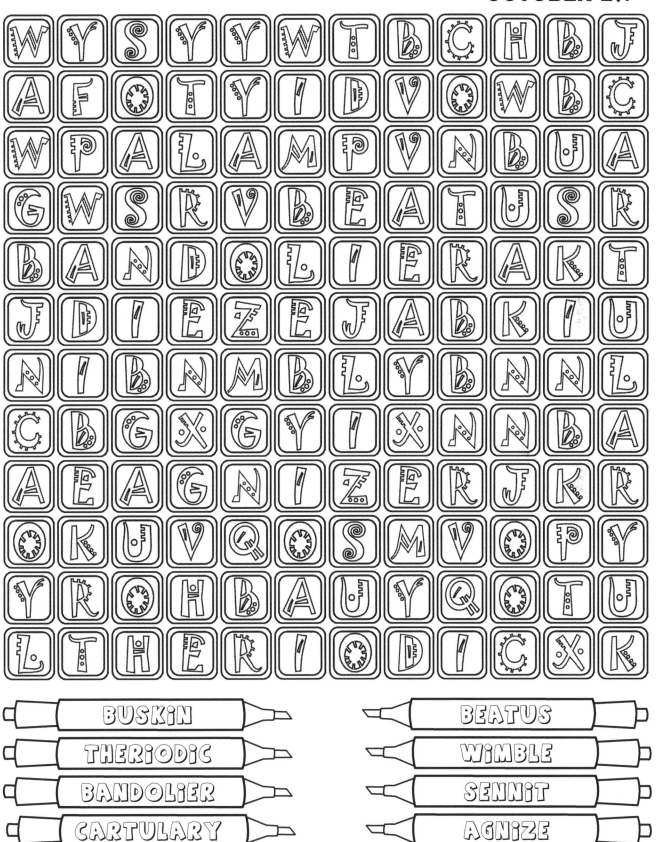

BUSKIN

THERIODIC

BANDOLIER

CARTULARY

BEATUS

WIMBLE

SENNIT

AGNIZE

COCKLOFT
ANTINOMY
ICTIC
GEORGIC

HECTOR
BATTOLOGY
RICTUS
ROLLICK

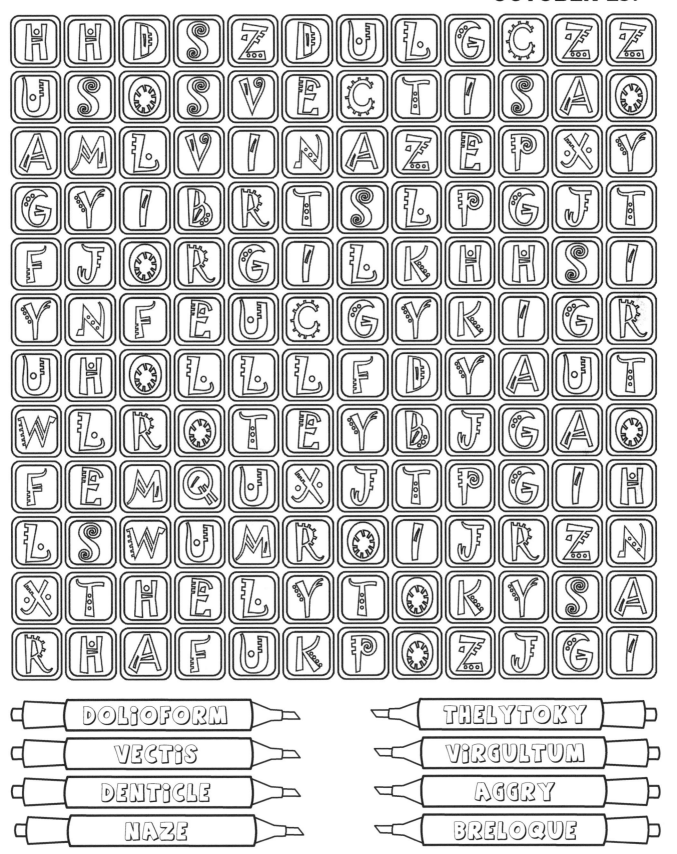

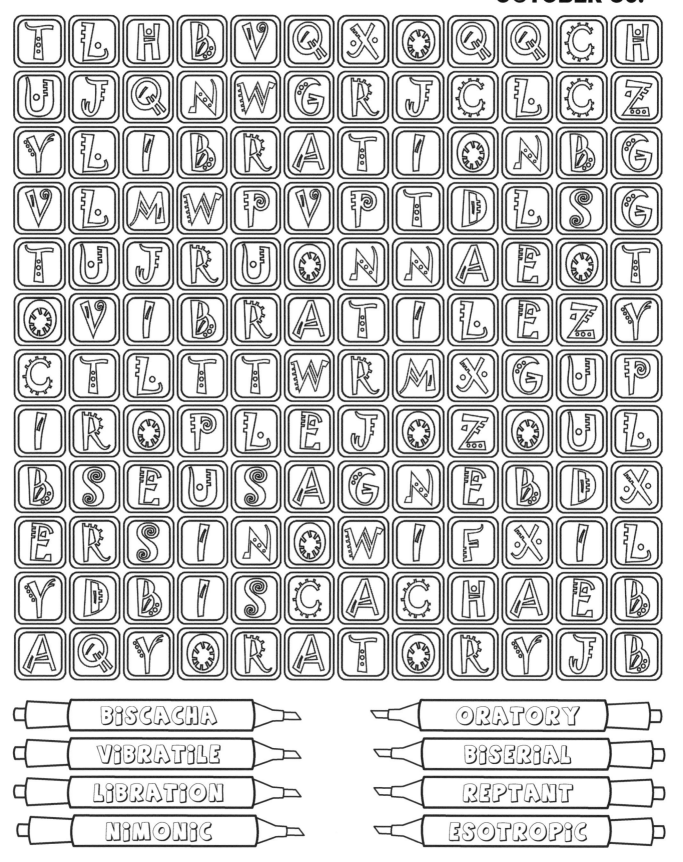

BISCACHA

VIBRATILE

LIBRATION

NIMONIC

ORATORY

BISERIAL

REPTANT

ESOTROPIC

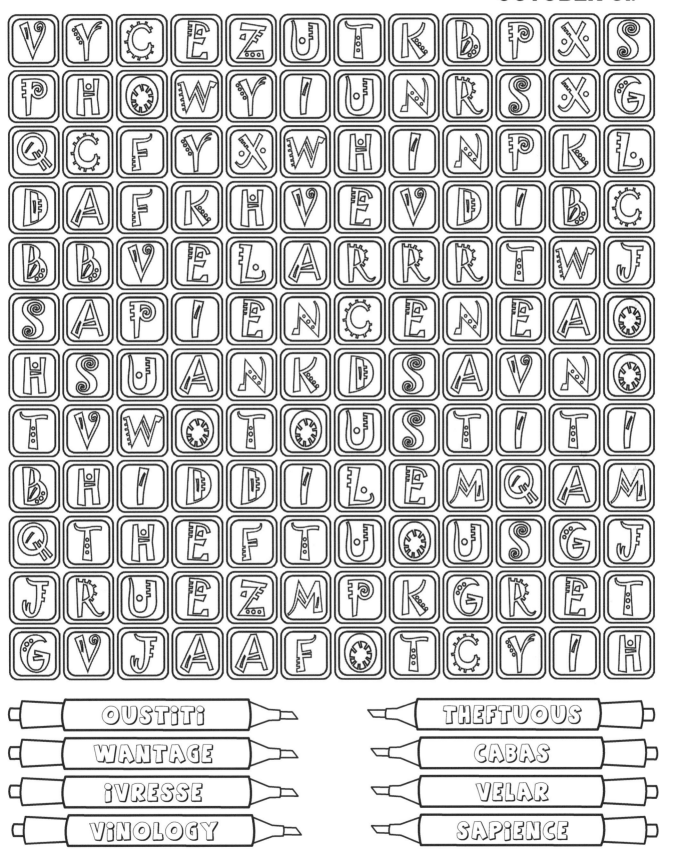

OUSTITI

THEFTUOUS

WANTAGE

CABAS

IVRESSE

VELAR

VINOLOGY

SAPIENCE

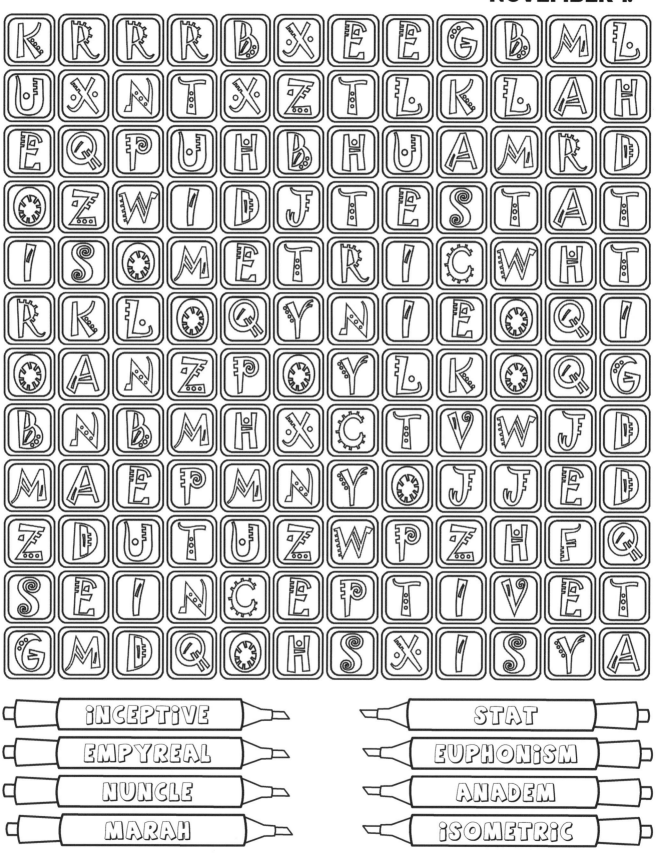

INCEPTIVE

EMPYREAL

NUNCLE

MARAH

STAT

EUPHONISM

ANADEM

ISOMETRIC

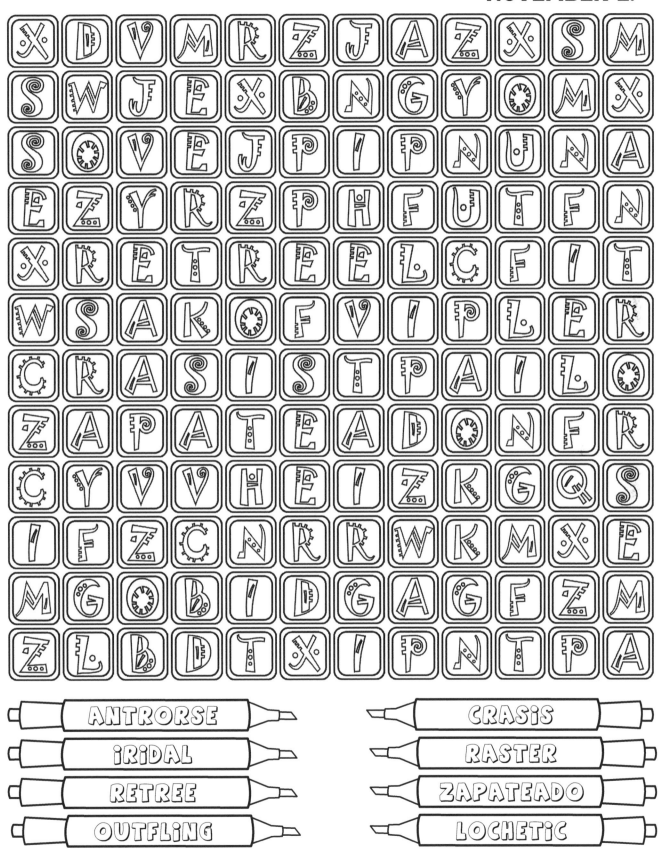

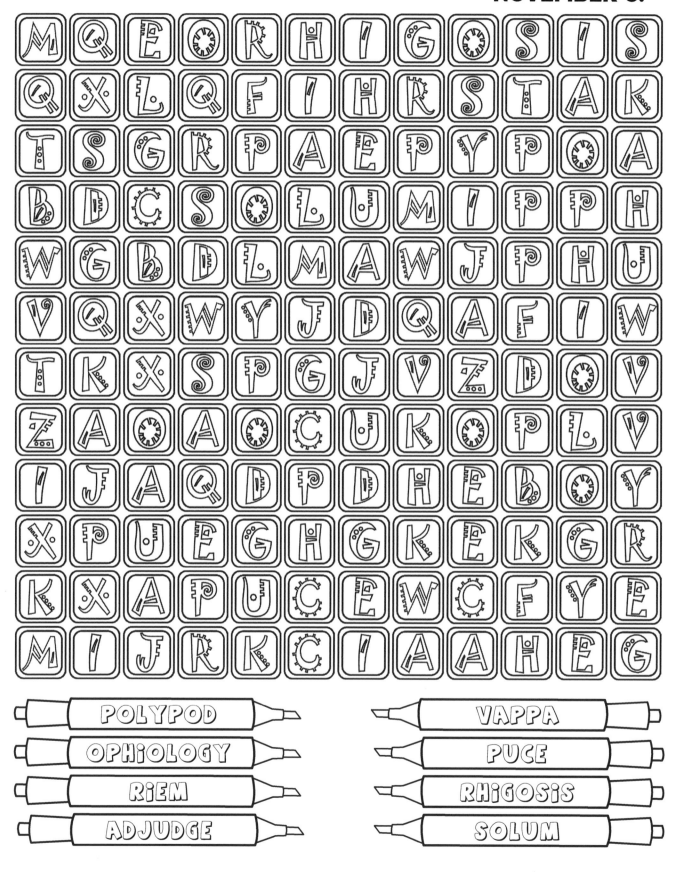

POLYPOD

OPHIOLOGY

RIEM

ADJUDGE

VAPPA

PUCE

RHIGOSIS

SOLUM

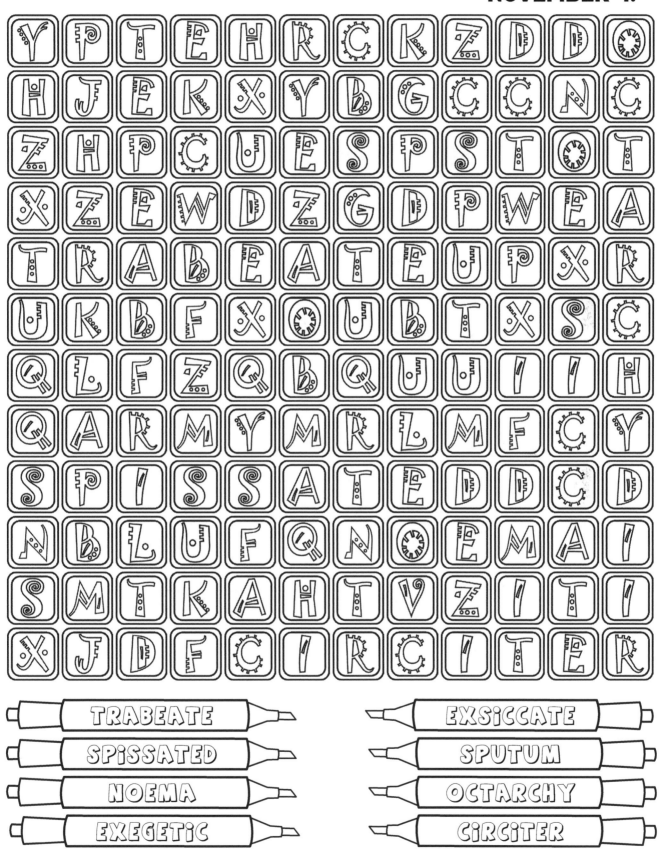

TRABEATE   EXSICCATE

SPISSATED   SPUTUM

NOEMA   OCTARCHY

EXEGETIC   CIRCITER

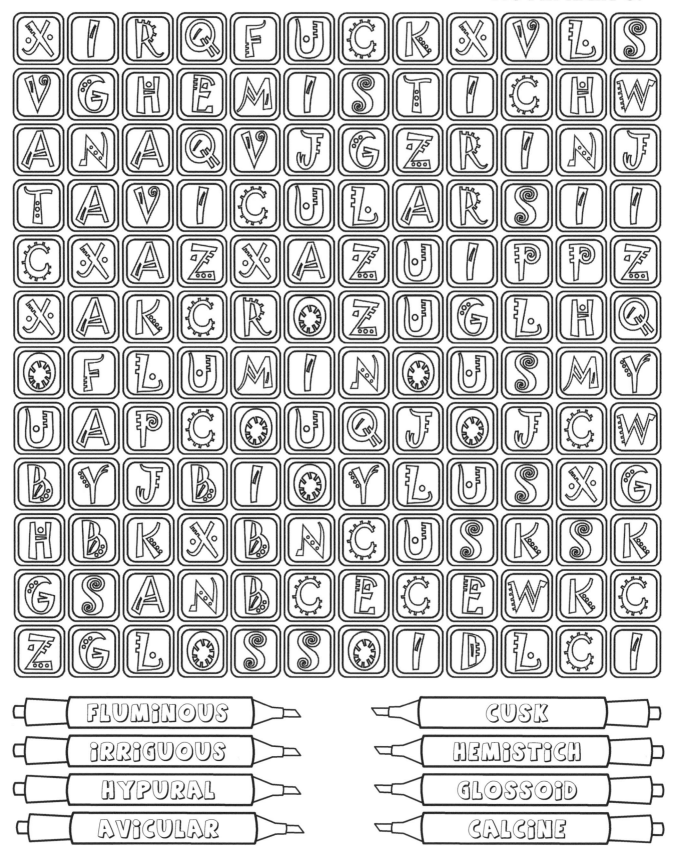

FLUMINOUS

IRRIGUOUS

HYPURAL

AVICULAR

CUSK

HEMISTICH

GLOSSOID

CALCINE

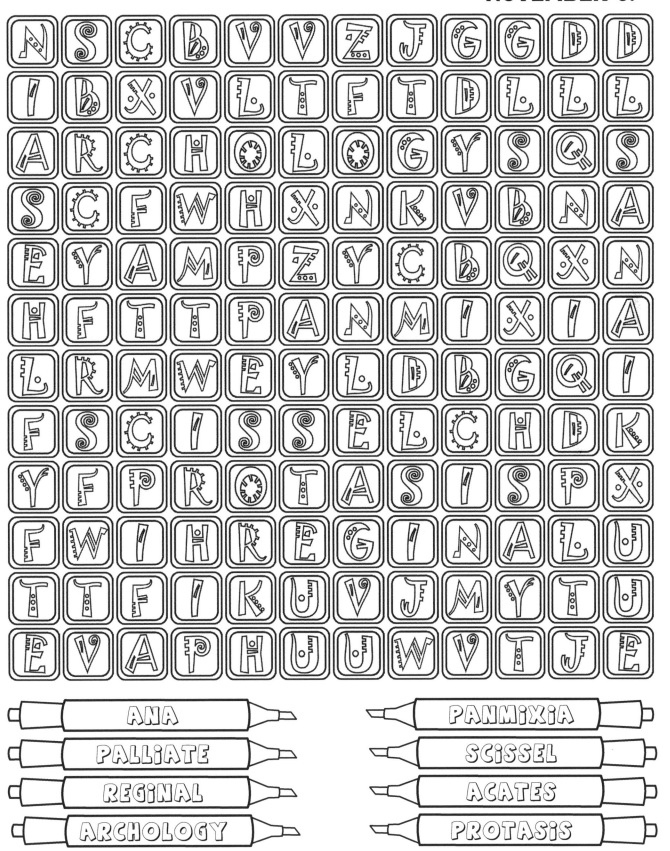

ANA

PALLIATE

REGINAL

ARCHOLOGY

PANMIXIA

SCISSEL

ACATES

PROTASIS

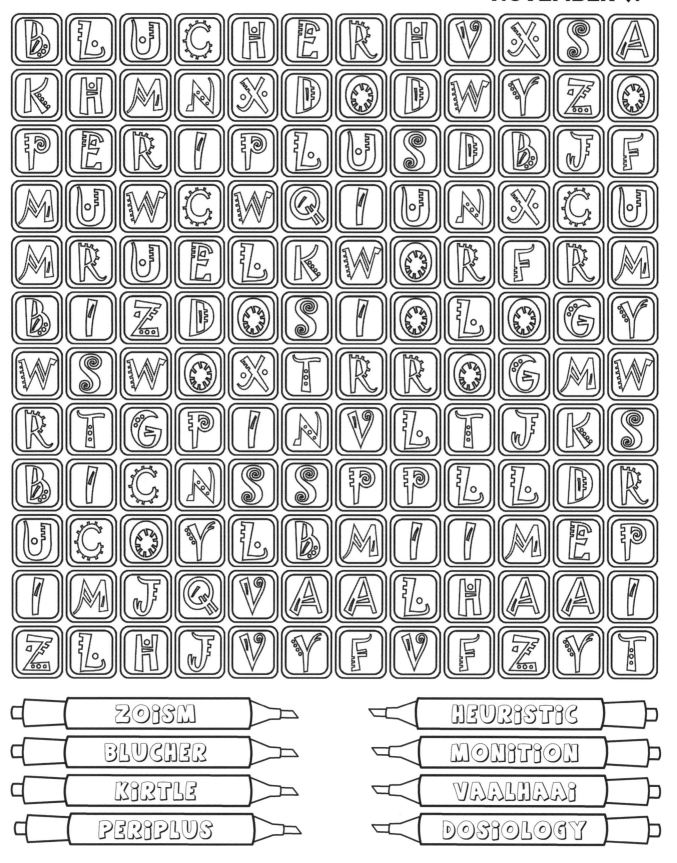

ZOISM

BLUCHER

KIRTLE

PERIPLUS

HEURISTIC

MONITION

VAALHAAI

DOSIOLOGY

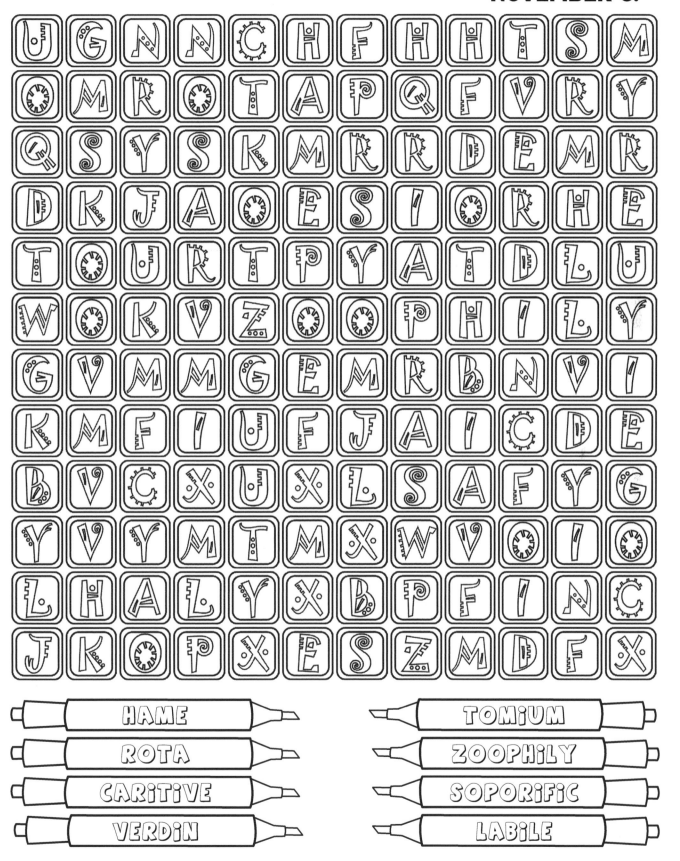

HAME
ROTA
CARITIVE
VERDIN

TOMIUM
ZOOPHILY
SOPORIFIC
LABILE

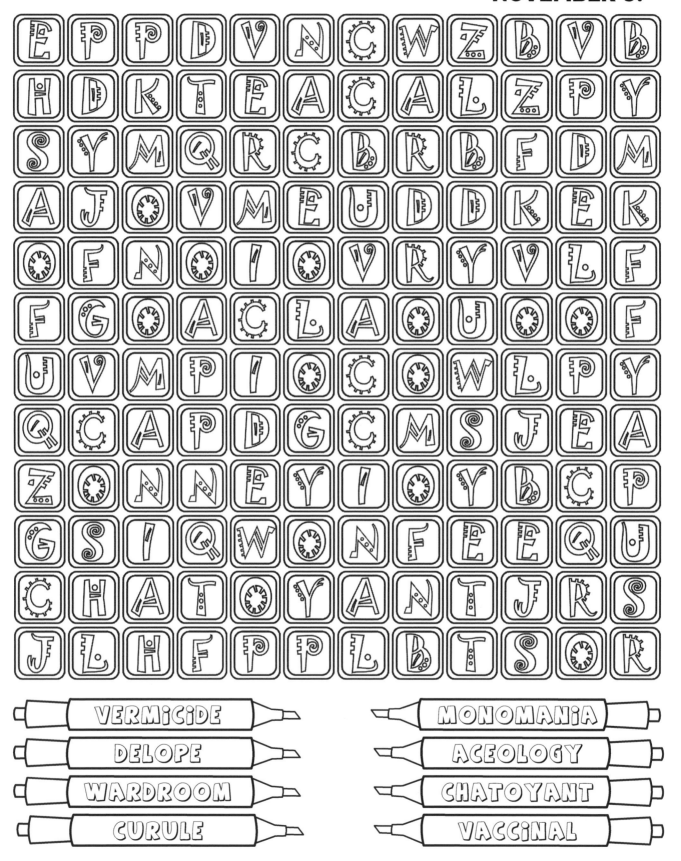

VERMICIDE

MONOMANIA

DELOPE

ACEOLOGY

WARDROOM

CHATOYANT

CURULE

VACCINAL

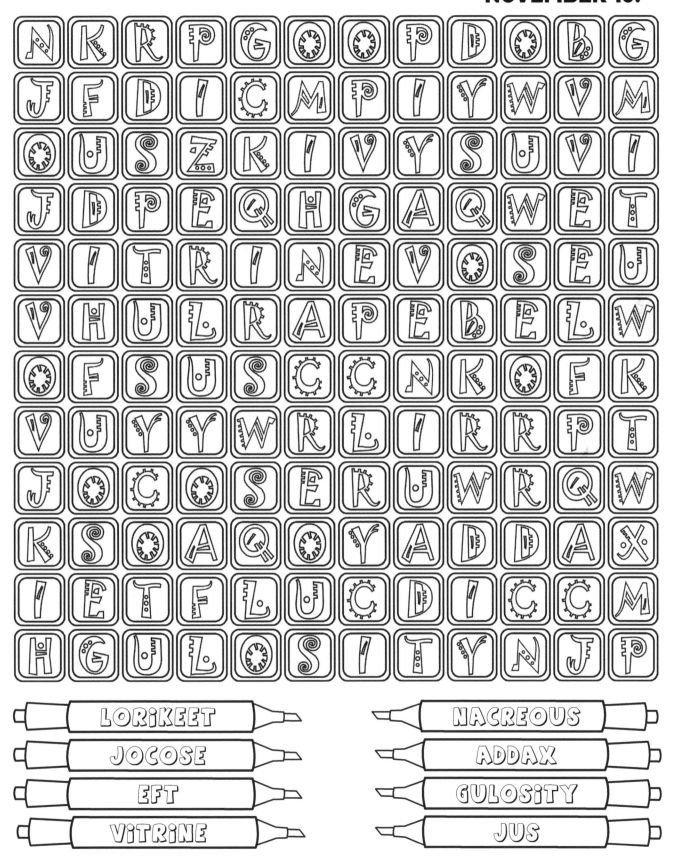

LORIKEET

JOCOSE

EFT

VITRINE

NACREOUS

ADDAX

GULOSITY

JUS

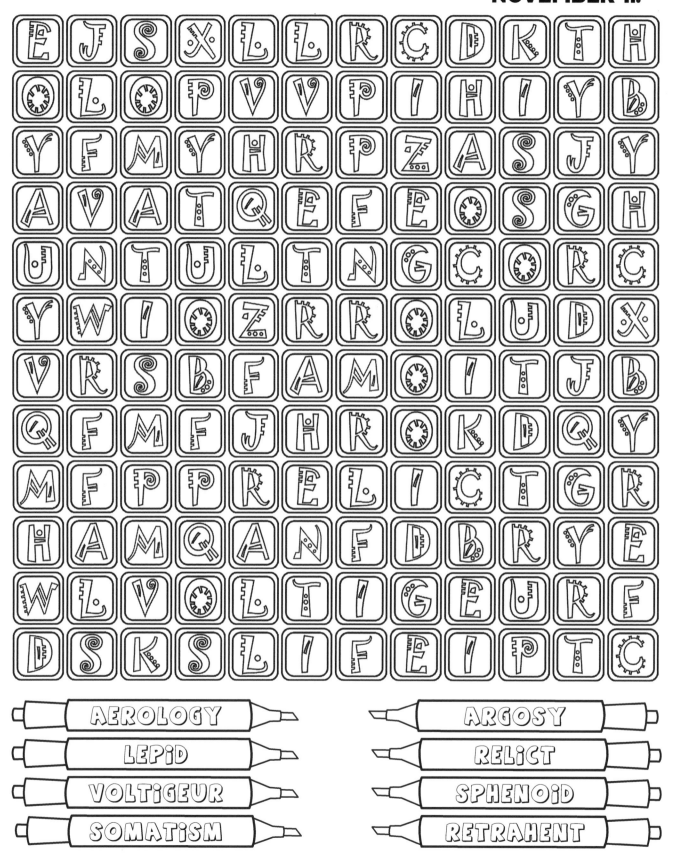

AEROLOGY

LEPID

VOLTIGEUR

SOMATISM

ARGOSY

RELICT

SPHENOID

RETRAHENT

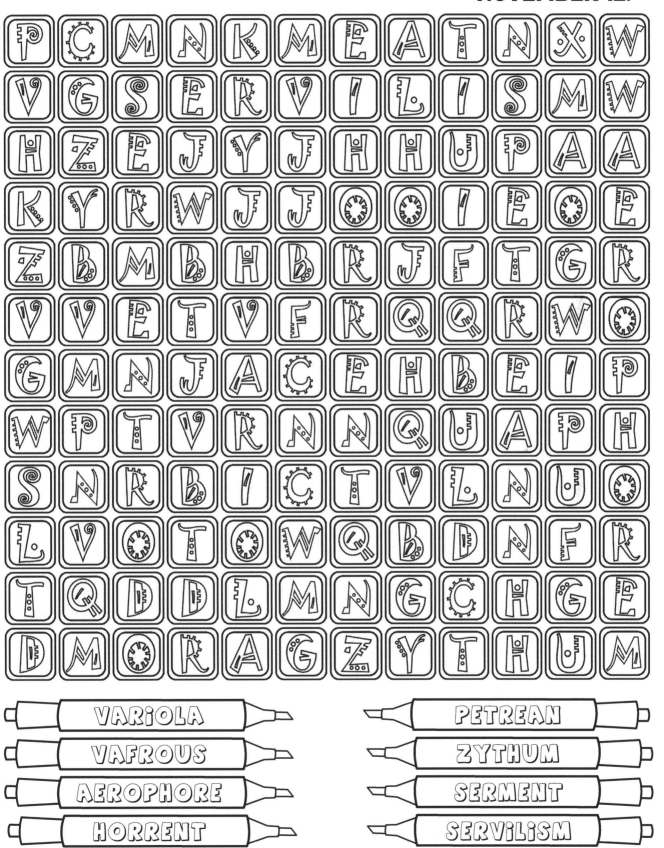

VARIOLA

VAFROUS

AEROPHORE

HORRENT

PETREAN

ZYTHUM

SERMENT

SERVILISM

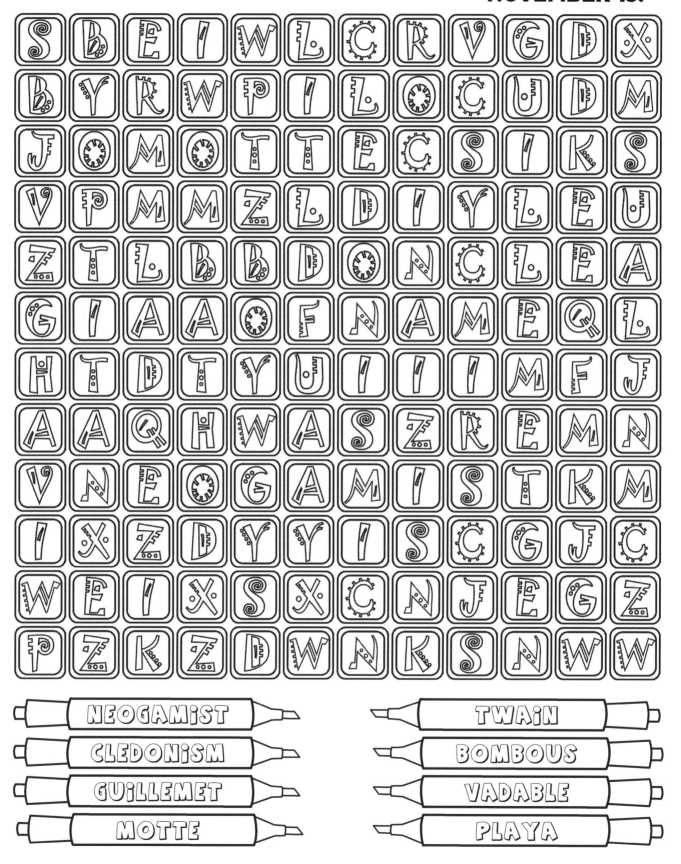

NEOGAMIST

CLEDONISM

GUILLEMET

MOTTE

TWAIN

BOMBOUS

VADABLE

PLAYA

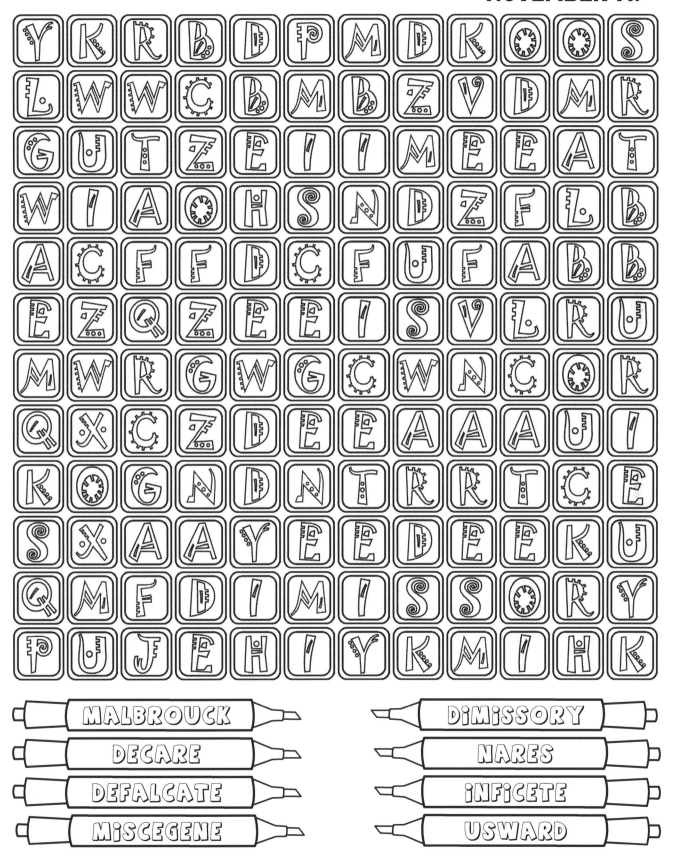

MALBROUCK

DECARE

DEFALCATE

MISCEGENE

DIMISSORY

NARES

INFICETE

USWARD

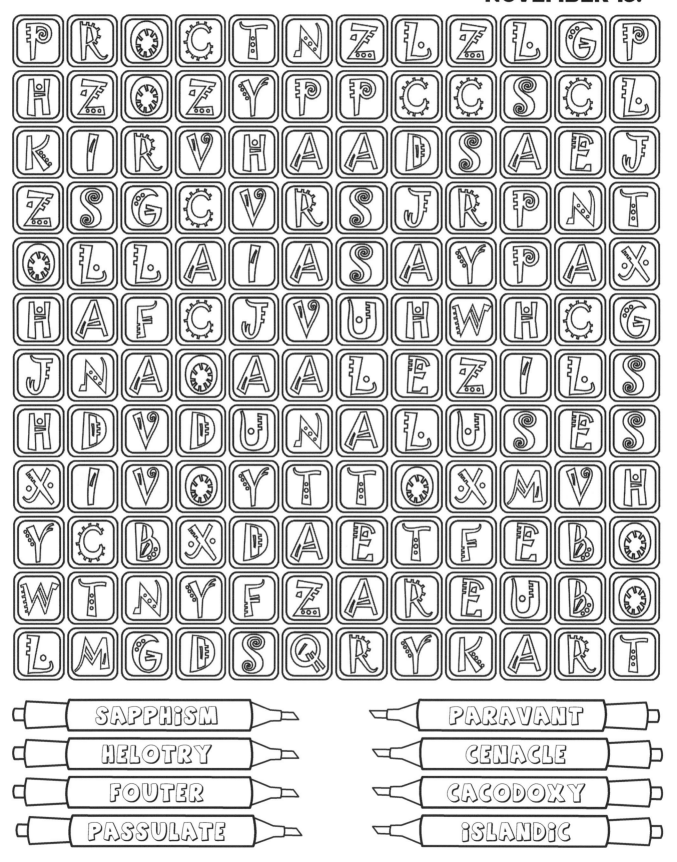

SAPPHISM

HELOTRY

FOUTER

PASSULATE

PARAVANT

CENACLE

CACODOXY

ISLANDIC

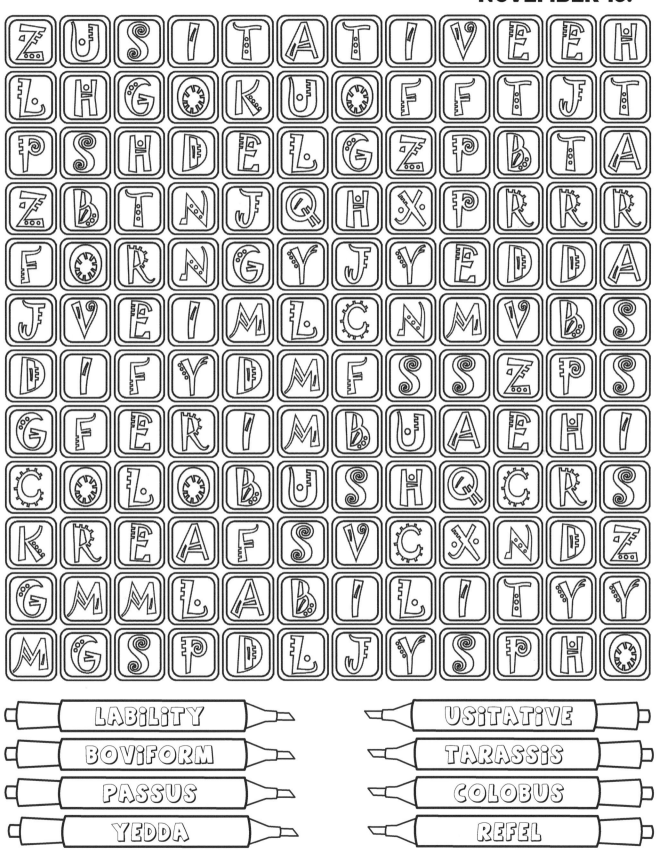

LABILITY

BOVIFORM

PASSUS

YEDDA

USITATIVE

TARASSIS

COLOBUS

REFEL

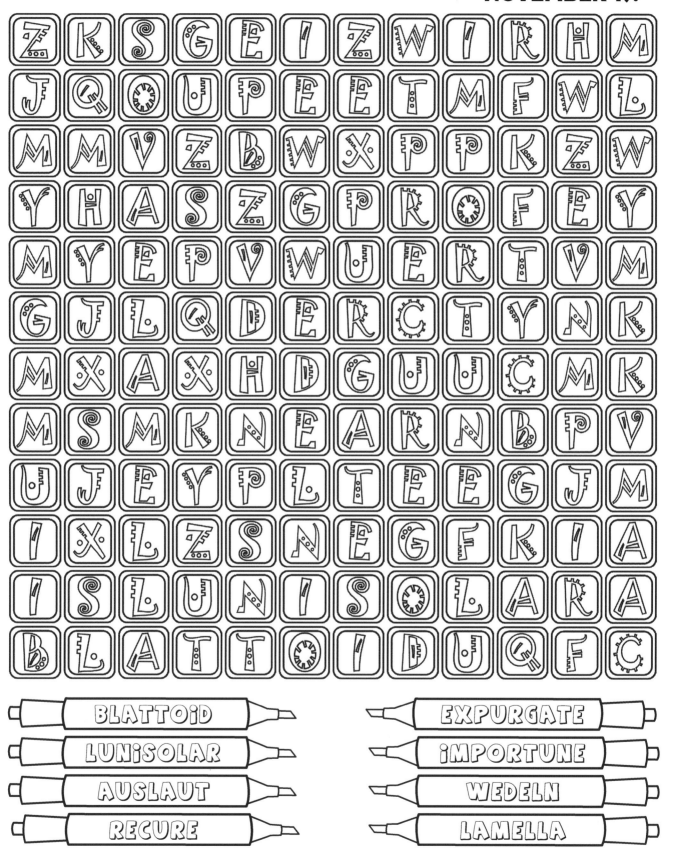

BLATTOID

LUNISOLAR

AUSLAUT

RECURE

EXPURGATE

IMPORTUNE

WEDELN

LAMELLA

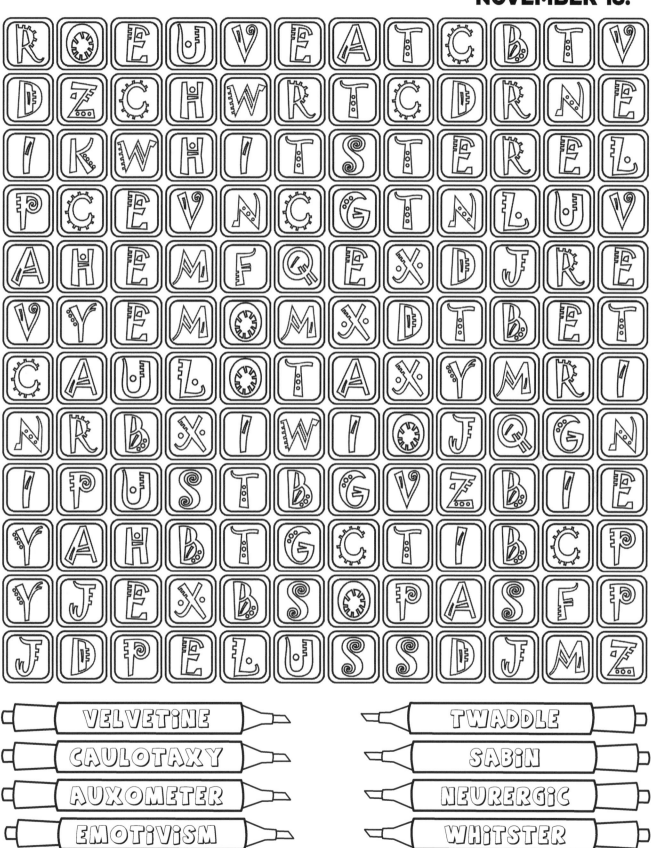

VELVETINE

CAULOTAXY

AUXOMETER

EMOTIVISM

TWADDLE

SABIN

NEURERGIC

WHITSTER

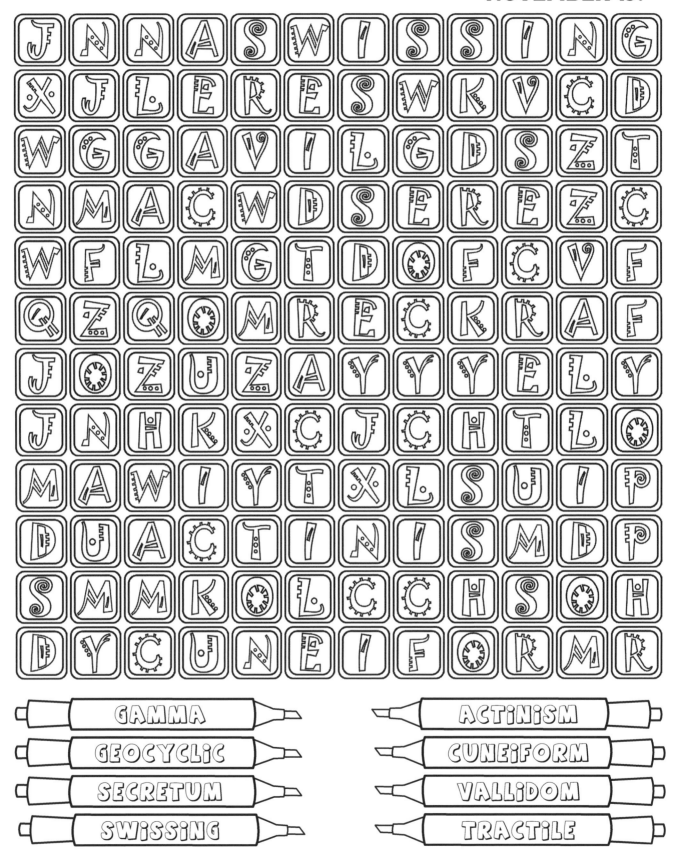

GAMMA

GEOCYCLIC

SECRETUM

SWISSING

ACTINISM

CUNEIFORM

VALLIDOM

TRACTILE

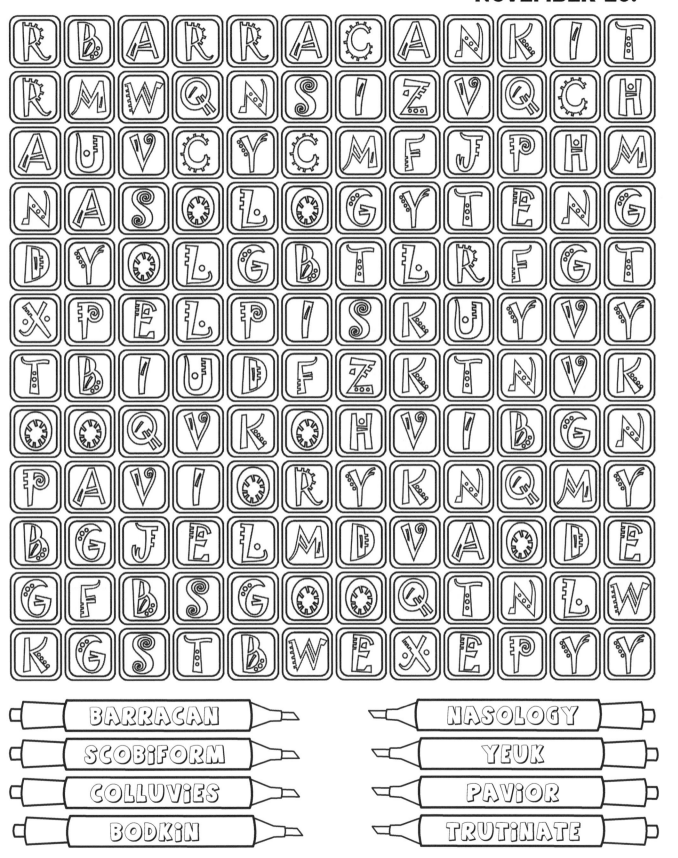

BARRACAN

SCOBIFORM

COLLUVIES

BODKIN

NASOLOGY

YEUK

PAVIOR

TRUTINATE

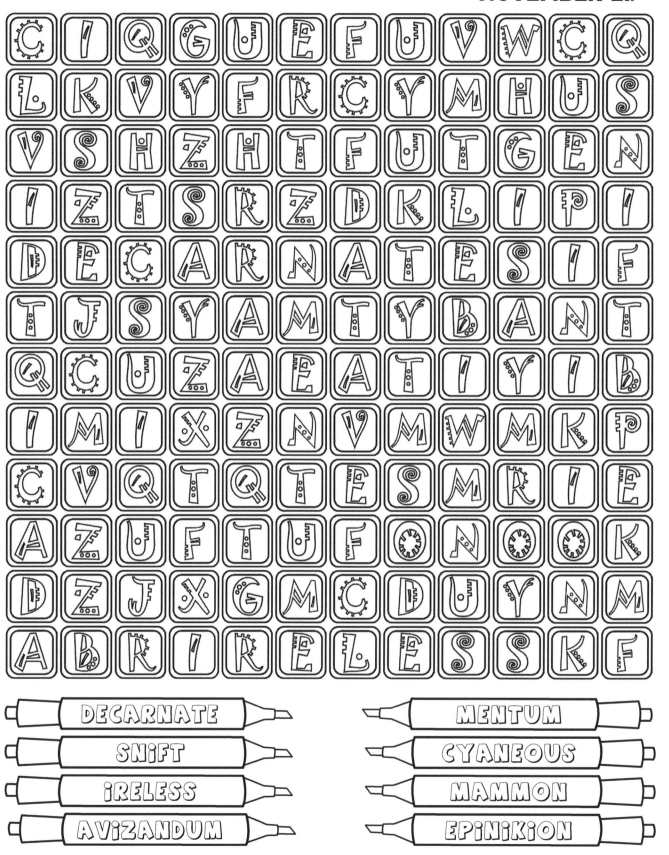

DECARNATE

SNIFT

IRELESS

AVIZANDUM

MENTUM

CYANEOUS

MAMMON

EPINIKION

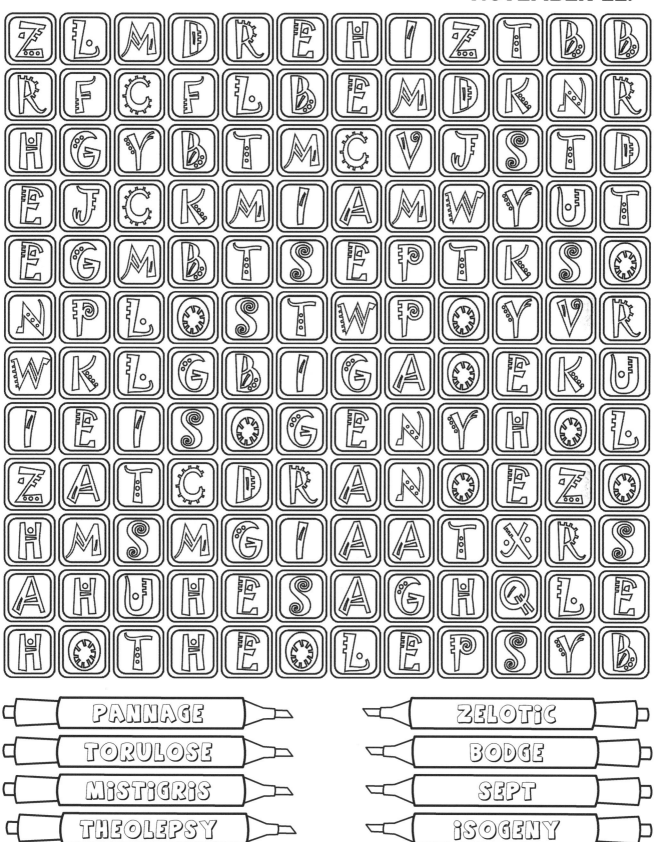

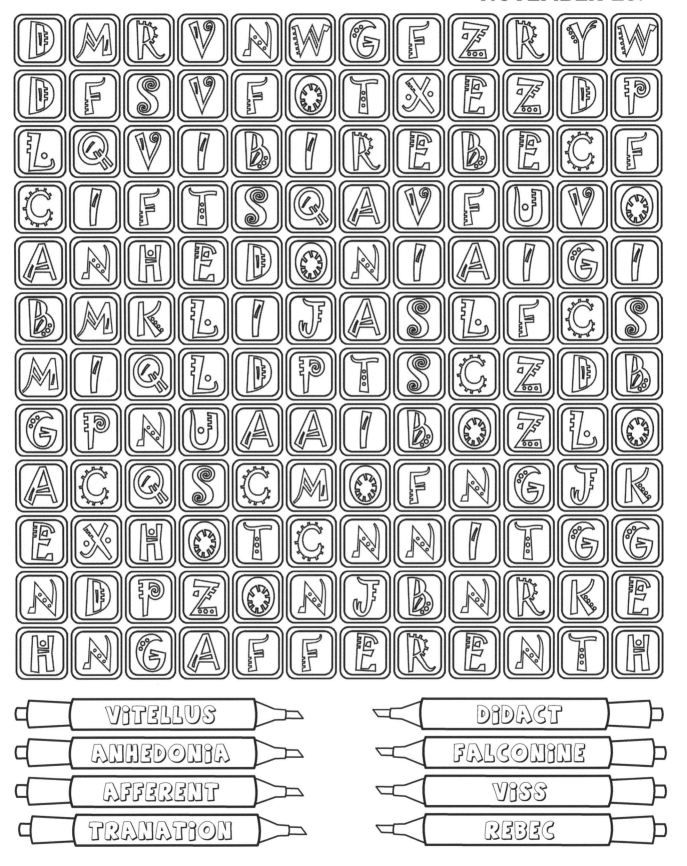

VITELLUS

DIDACT

ANHEDONIA

FALCONINE

AFFERENT

VISS

TRANATION

REBEC

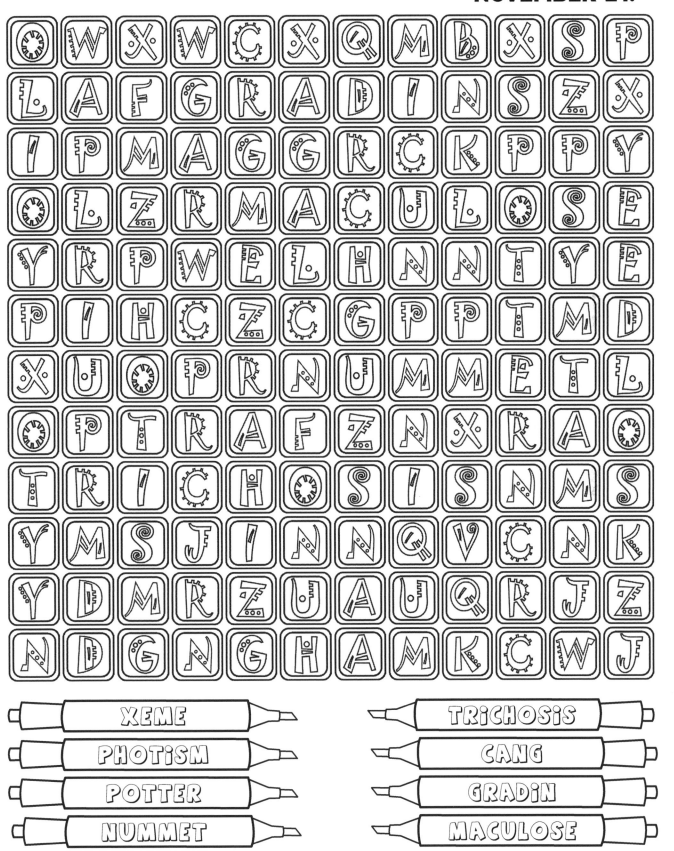

XEME

PHOTISM

POTTER

NUMMET

TRICHOSIS

CANG

GRADIN

MACULOSE

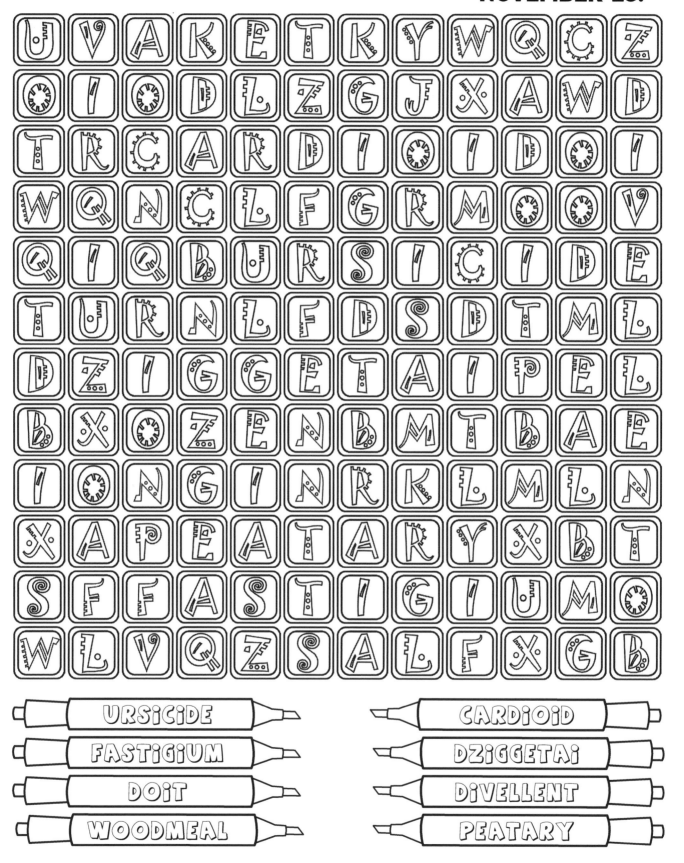

URSICIDE

CARDIOID

FASTIGIUM

DZIGGETAI

DOIT

DIVELLENT

WOODMEAL

PEATARY

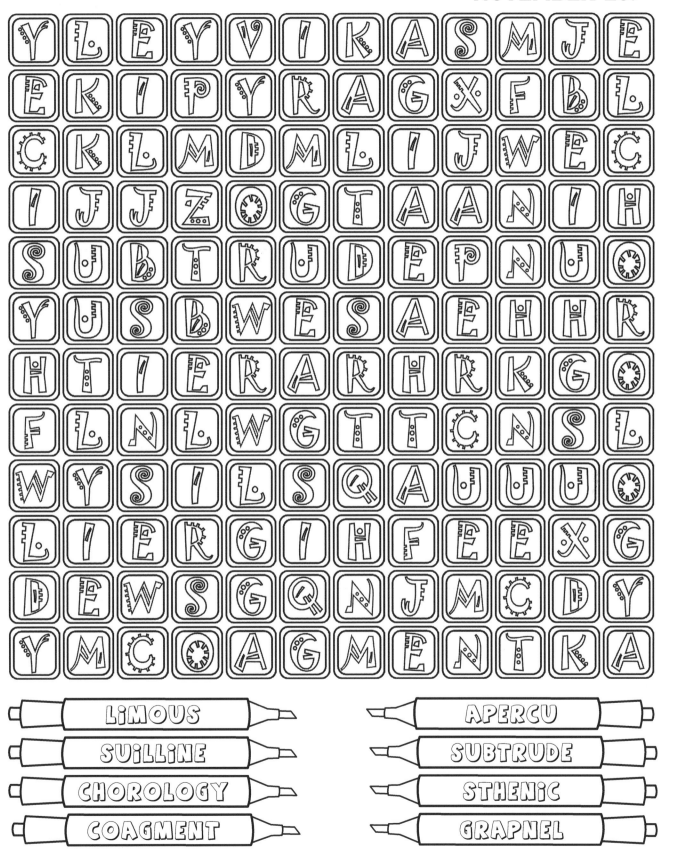

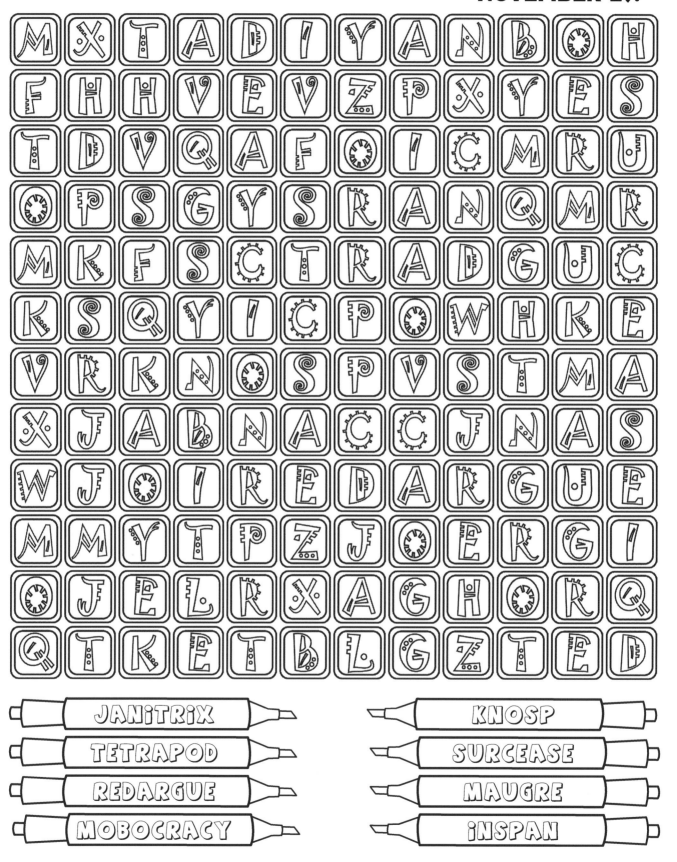

JANITRIX

TETRAPOD

REDARGUE

MOBOCRACY

KNOSP

SURCEASE

MAUGRE

INSPAN

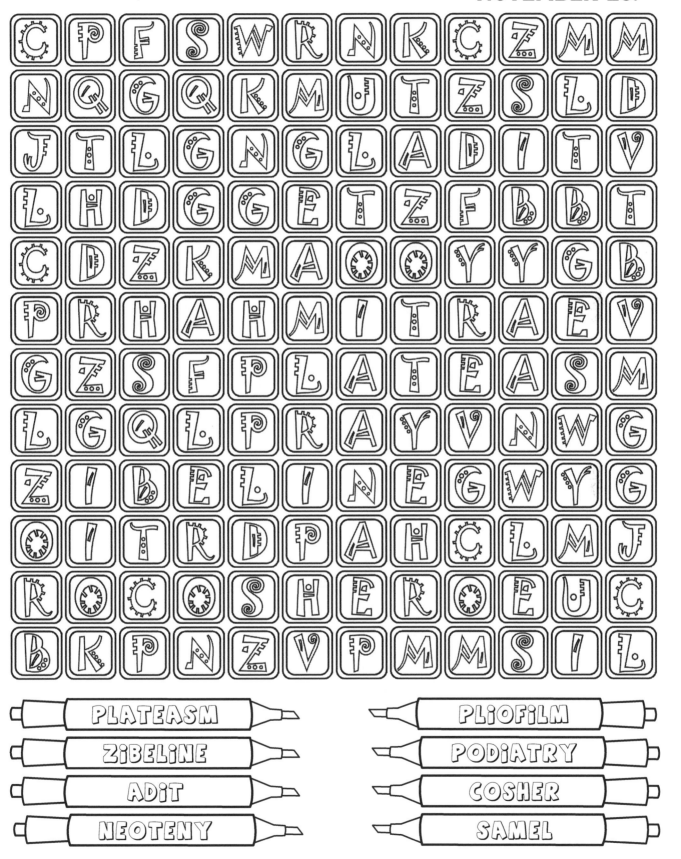

PLATEASM

ZIBELINE

ADIT

NEOTENY

PLIOFILM

PODIATRY

COSHER

SAMEL

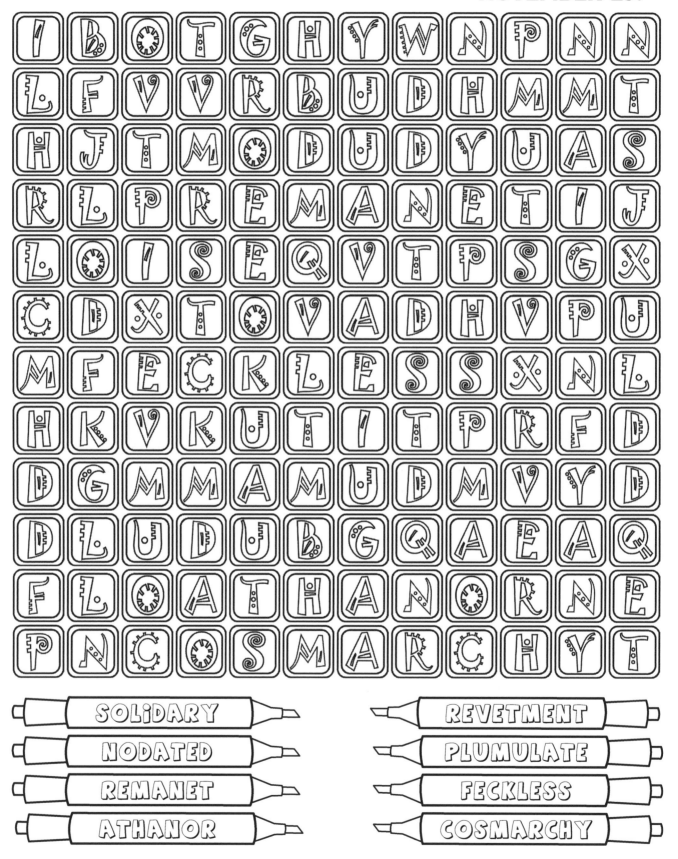

SOLIDARY

NODATED

REMANET

ATHANOR

REVETMENT

PLUMULATE

FECKLESS

COSMARCHY

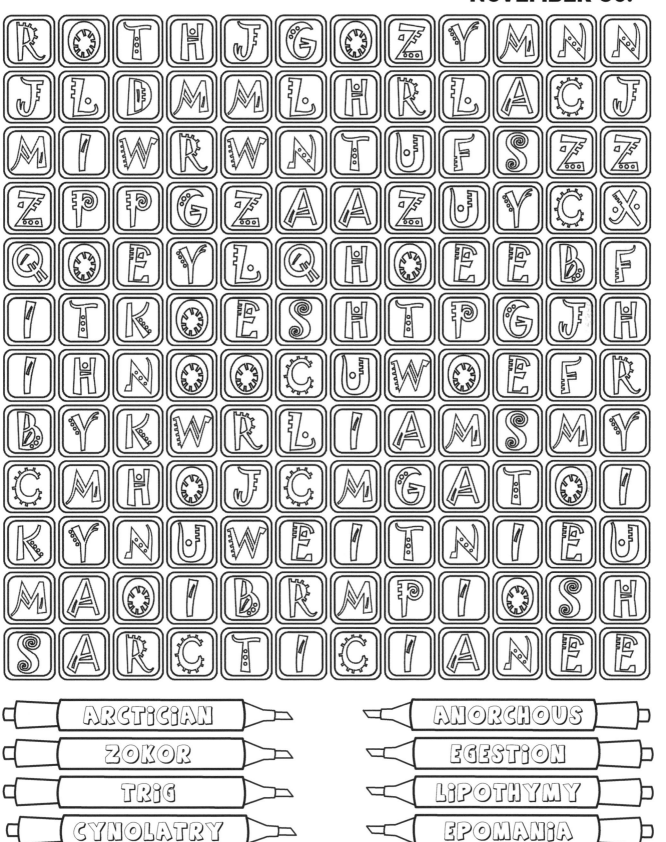

ARCTICIAN

ZOKOR

TRIG

CYNOLATRY

ANORCHOUS

EGESTION

LIPOTHYMY

EPOMANIA

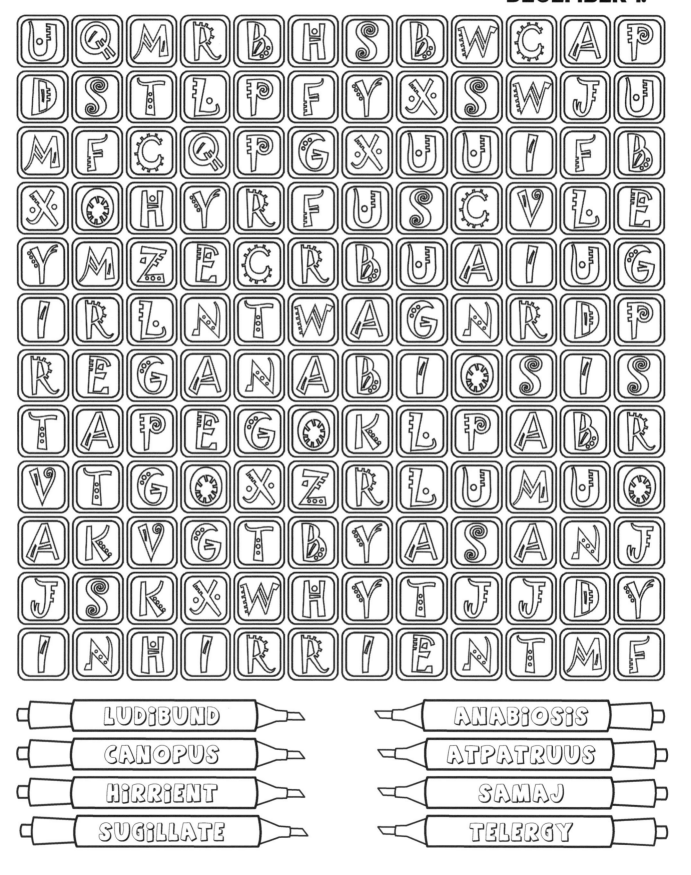

LUDIBUND
CANOPUS
HIRRIENT
SUGILLATE

ANABIOSIS
ATPATRUUS
SAMAJ
TELERGY

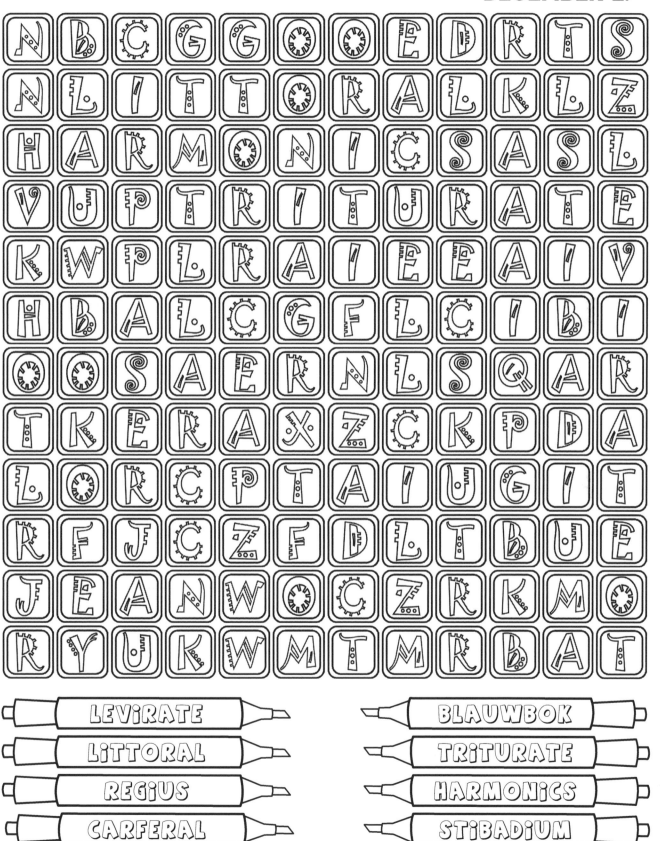

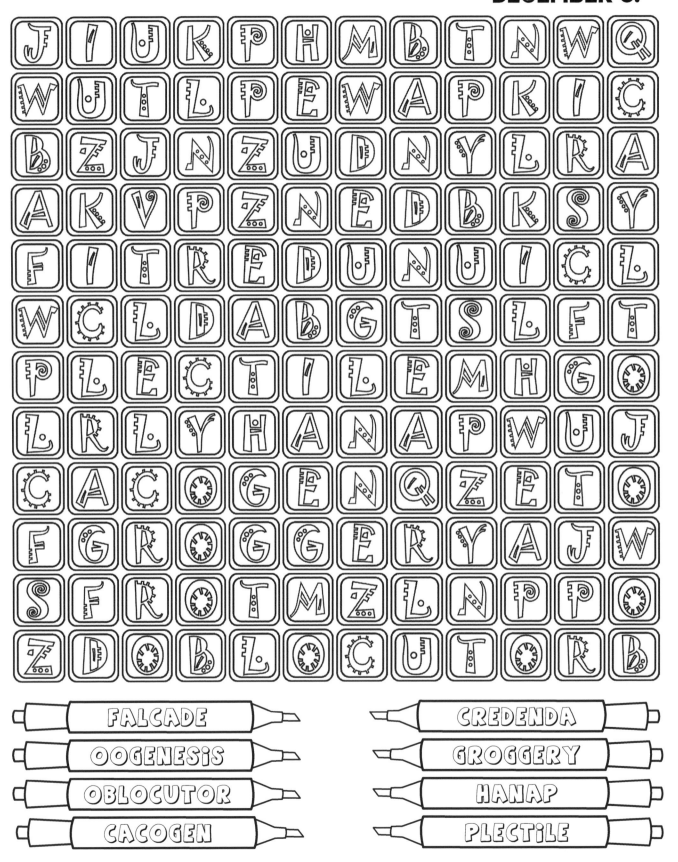

FALCADE

OOGENESIS

OBLOCUTOR

CACOGEN

CREDENDA

GROGGERY

HANAP

PLECTILE

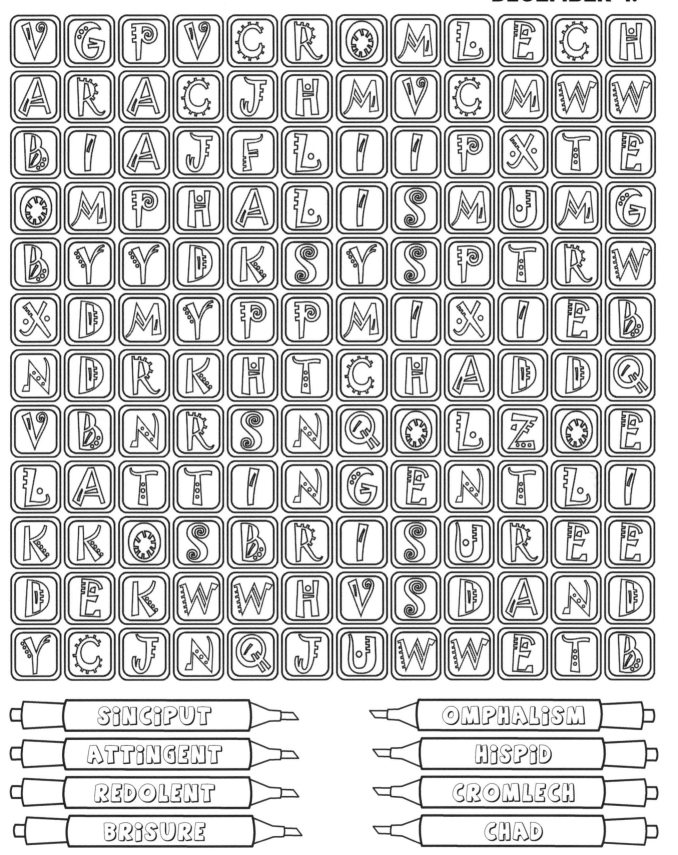

SINCIPUT

ATTINGENT

REDOLENT

BRISURE

OMPHALISM

HISPID

CROMLECH

CHAD

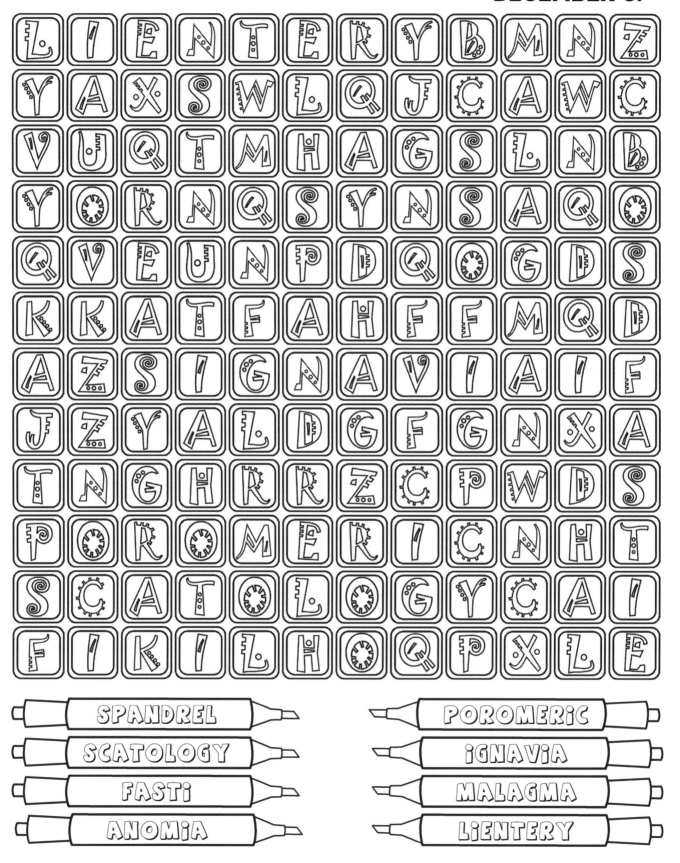

SPANDREL

SCATOLOGY

FASTI

ANOMIA

POROMERIC

IGNAVIA

MALAGMA

LIENTERY

OPSIGAMY

DISAGIO

ANNECTENT

DIASTEMA

NEXAL

KINKLE

NESIOTE

VEDALIA

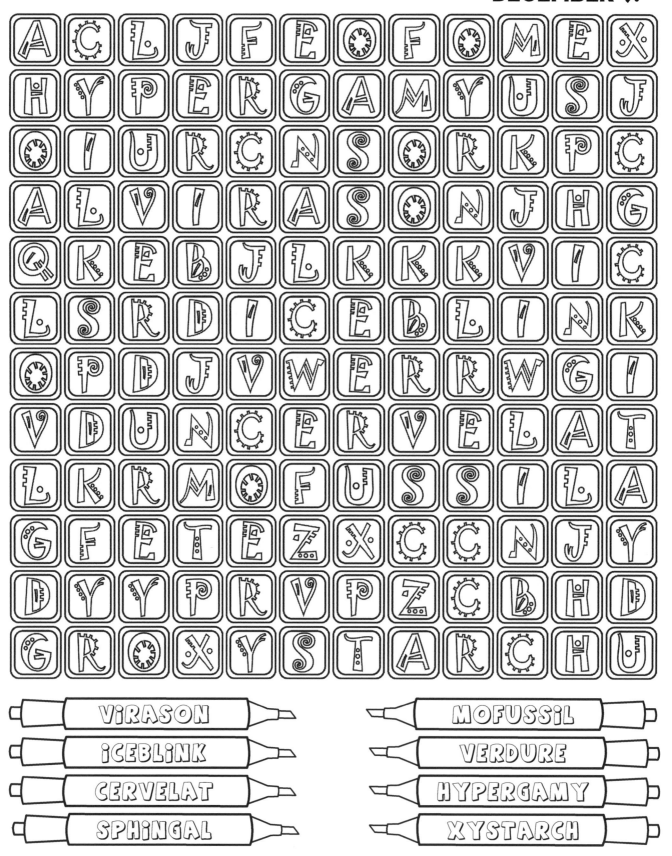

VIRASON

ICEBLINK

CERVELAT

SPHINGAL

MOFUSSIL

VERDURE

HYPERGAMY

XYSTARCH

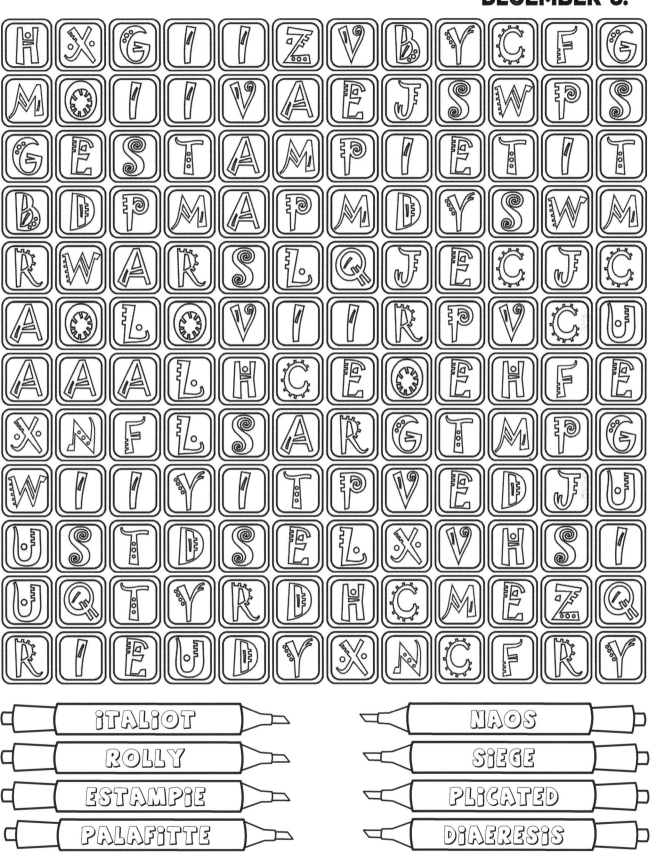

ITALIOT

ROLLY

ESTAMPIE

PALAFITTE

NAOS

SIEGE

PLICATED

DIAERESIS

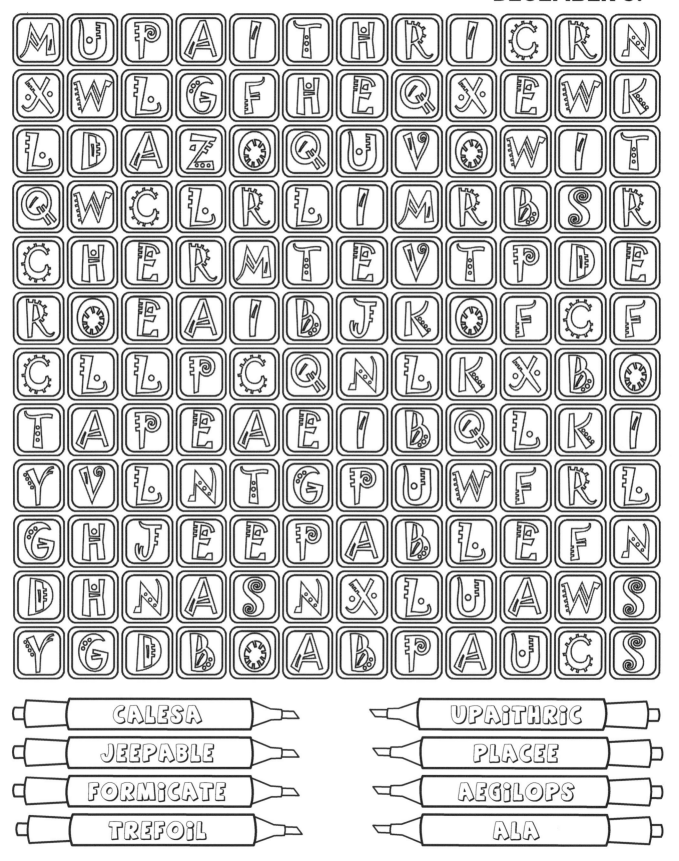

CALESA

JEEPABLE

FORMICATE

TREFOIL

UPAITHRIC

PLACEE

AEGILOPS

ALA

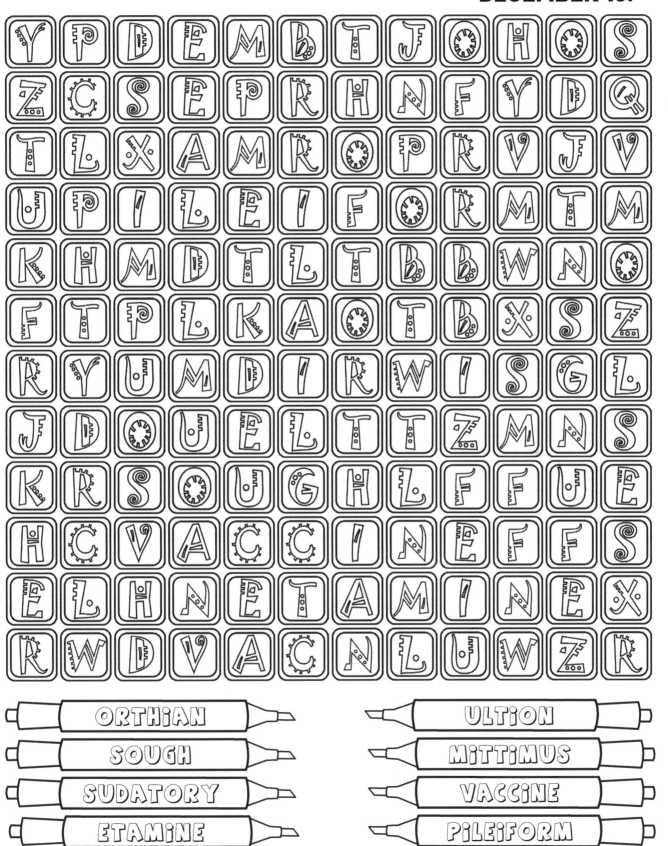

ORTHIAN

SOUGH

SUDATORY

ETAMINE

ULTION

MITTIMUS

VACCINE

PILEIFORM

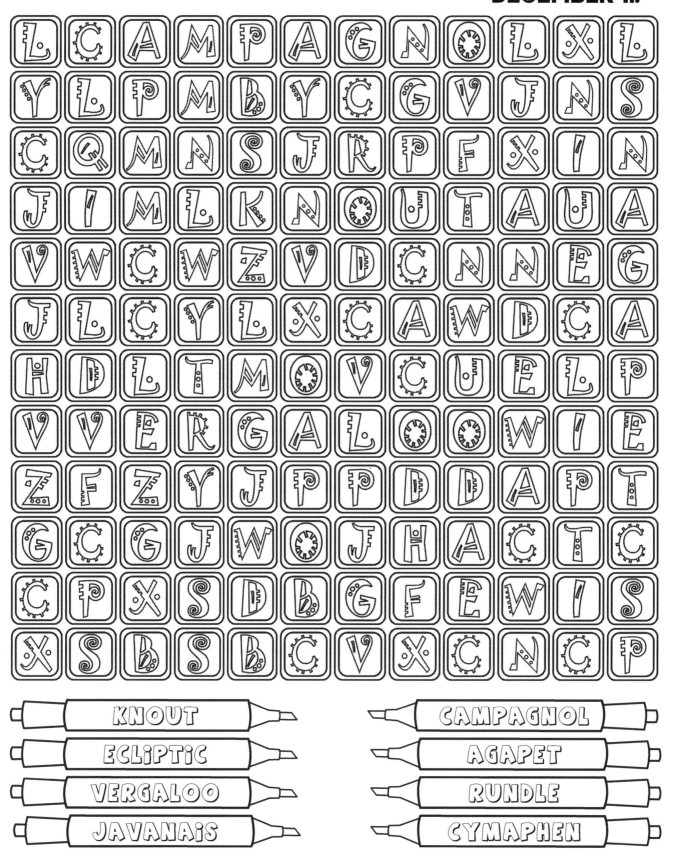

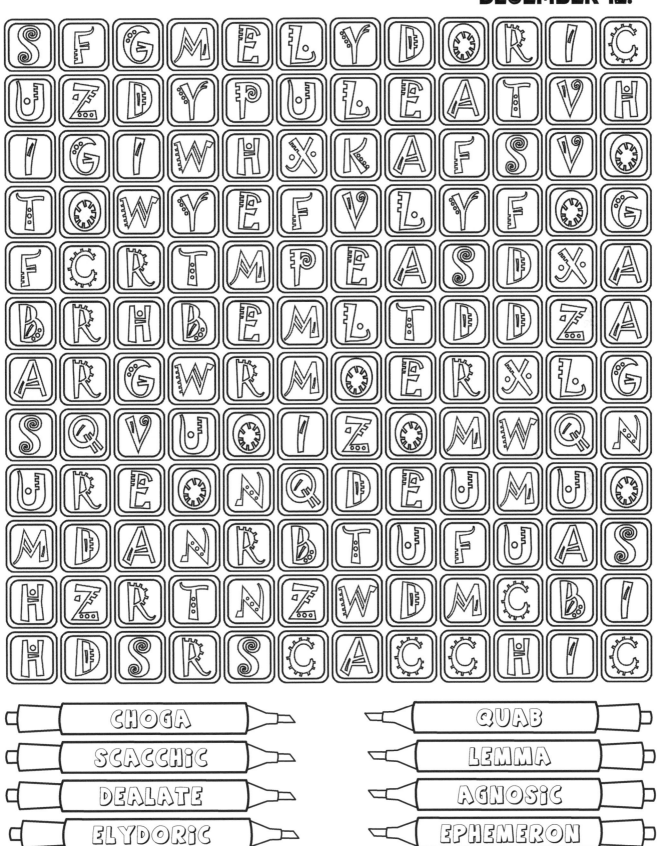

CHOGA

SCACCHIC

DEALATE

ELYDORIC

QUAB

LEMMA

AGNOSIC

EPHEMERON

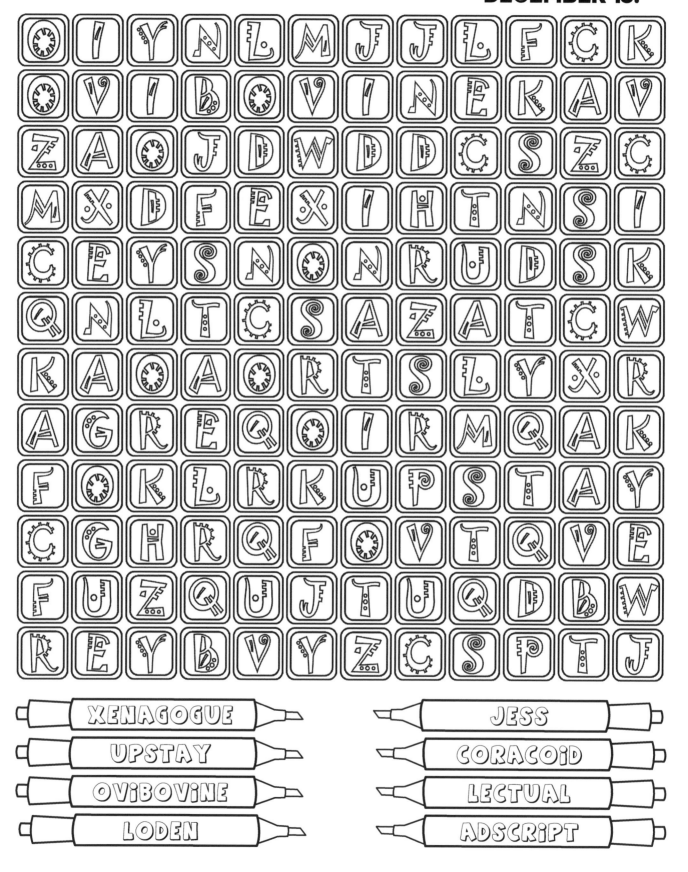

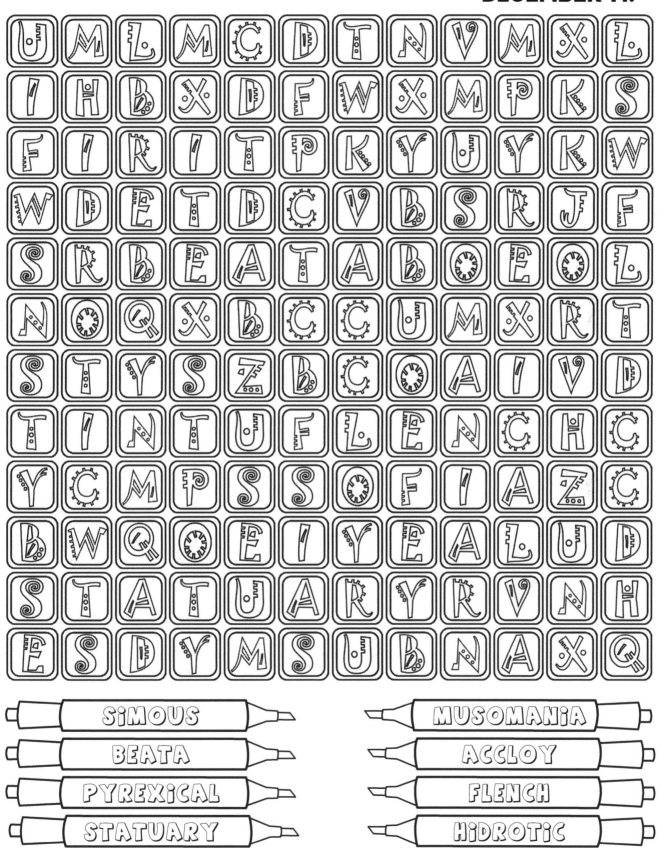

SIMOUS

MUSOMANIA

BEATA

ACCLOY

PYREXICAL

FLENCH

STATUARY

HIDROTIC

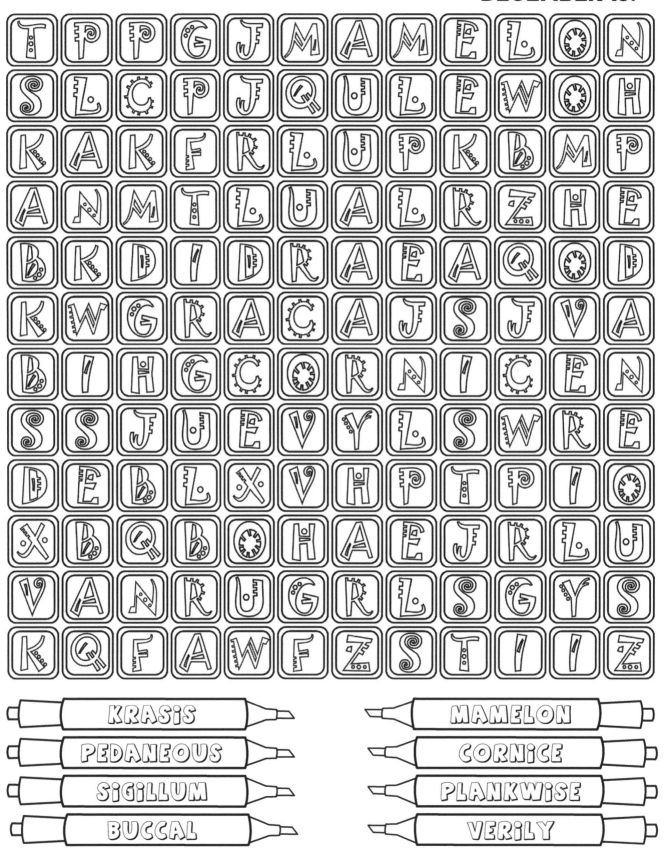

KRASIS

PEDANEOUS

SIGILLUM

BUCCAL

MAMELON

CORNICE

PLANKWISE

VERILY

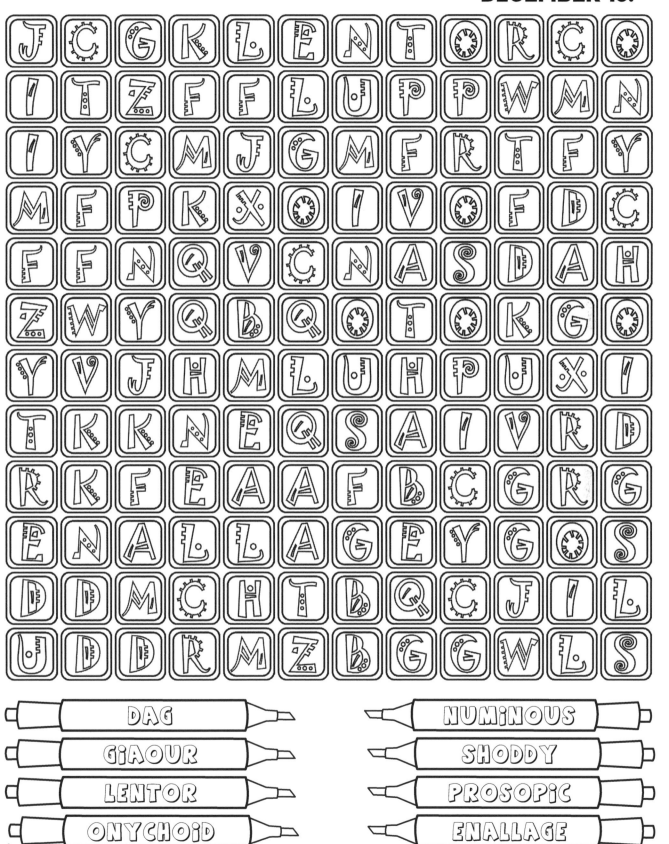

DAG

NUMINOUS

GIAOUR

SHODDY

LENTOR

PROSOPIC

ONYCHOID

ENALLAGE

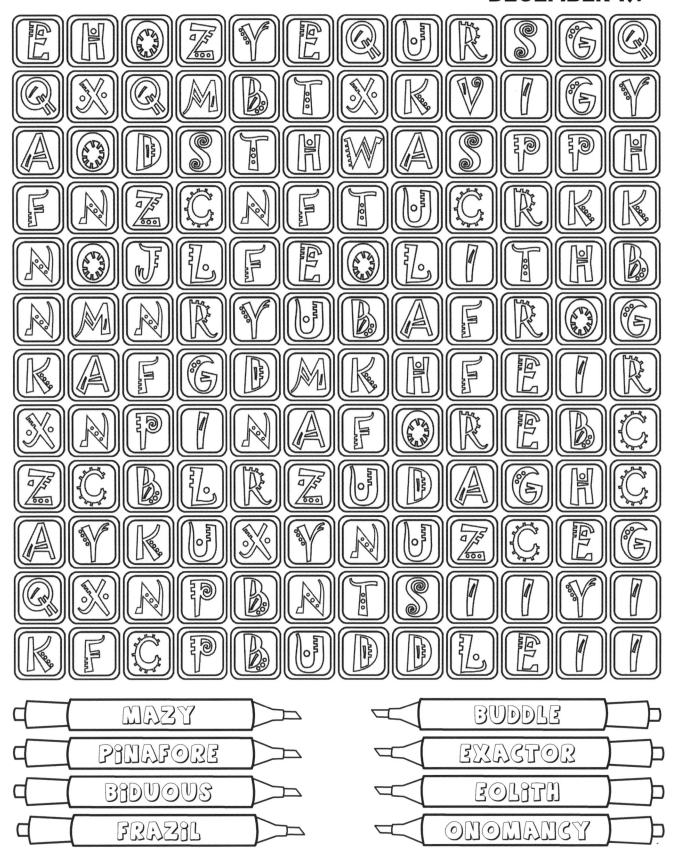

MAZY

PINAFORE

BIDUOUS

FRAZIL

BUDDLE

EXACTOR

EOLITH

ONOMANCY

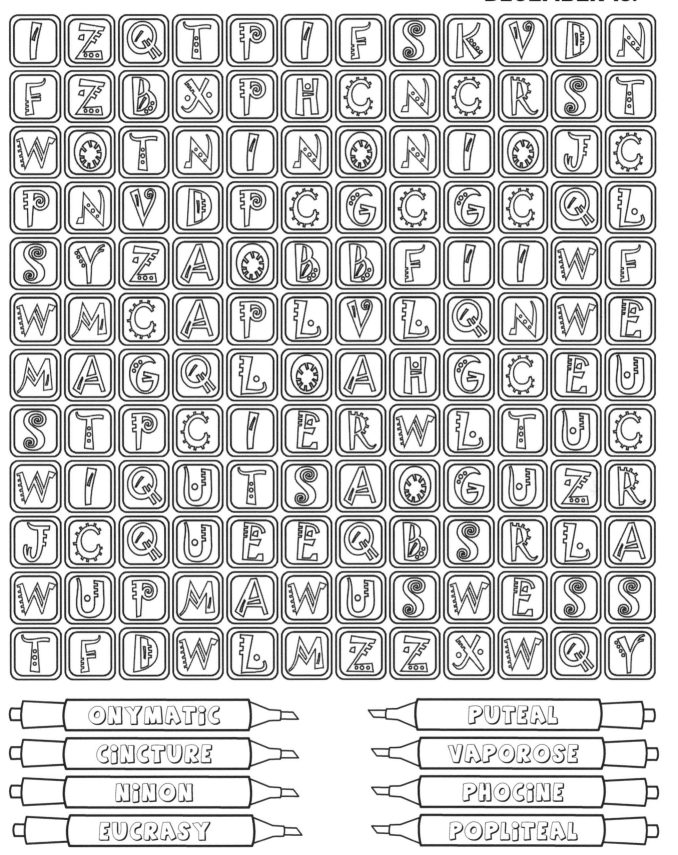

ONYMATIC
CINCTURE
NINON
EUCRASY

PUTEAL
VAPOROSE
PHOCINE
POPLITEAL

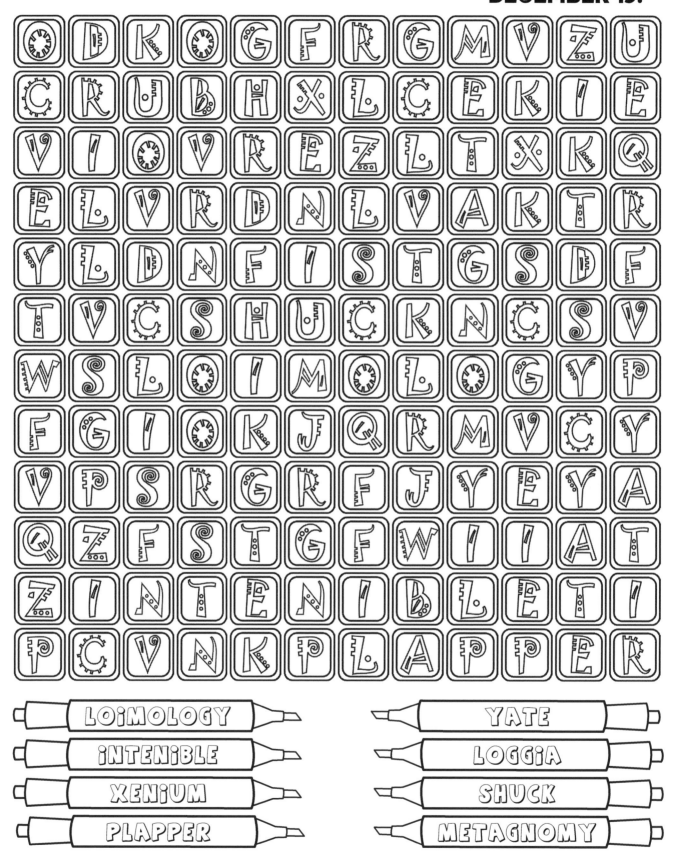

LOIMOLOGY

INTENIBLE

XENIUM

PLAPPER

YATE

LOGGIA

SHUCK

METAGNOMY

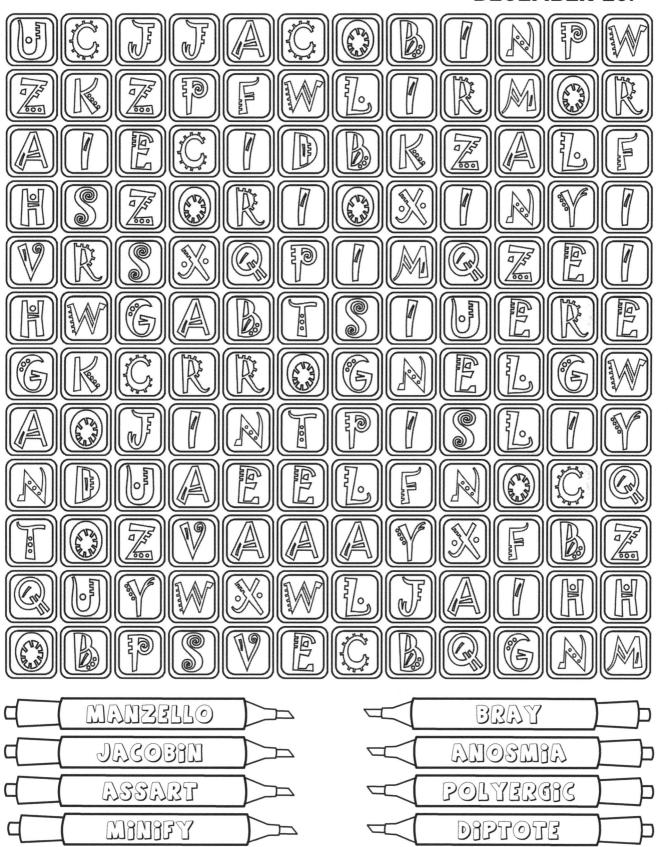

MANZELLO

JACOBIN

ASSART

MINIFY

BRAY

ANOSMIA

POLYERGIC

DIPTOTE

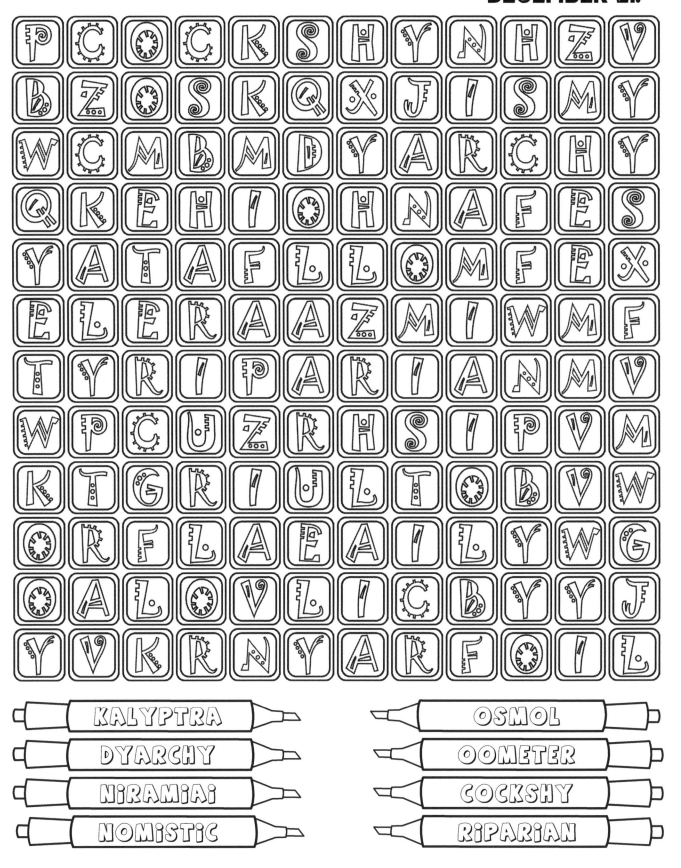

KALYPTRA

DYARCHY

NIRAMIAI

NOMISTIC

OSMOL

OOMETER

COCKSHY

RIPARIAN

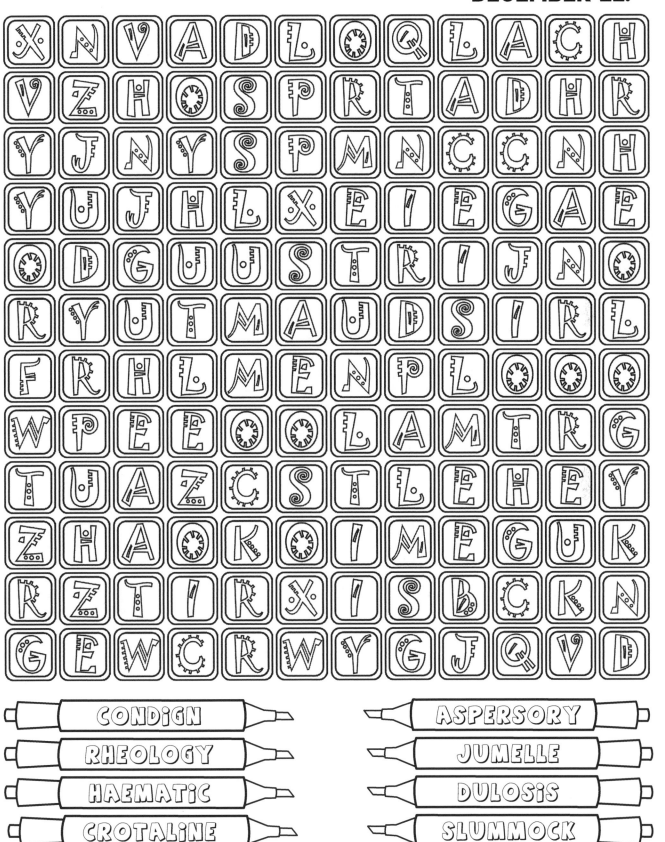

CONDIGN

ASPERSORY

RHEOLOGY

JUMELLE

HAEMATIC

DULOSIS

CROTALINE

SLUMMOCK

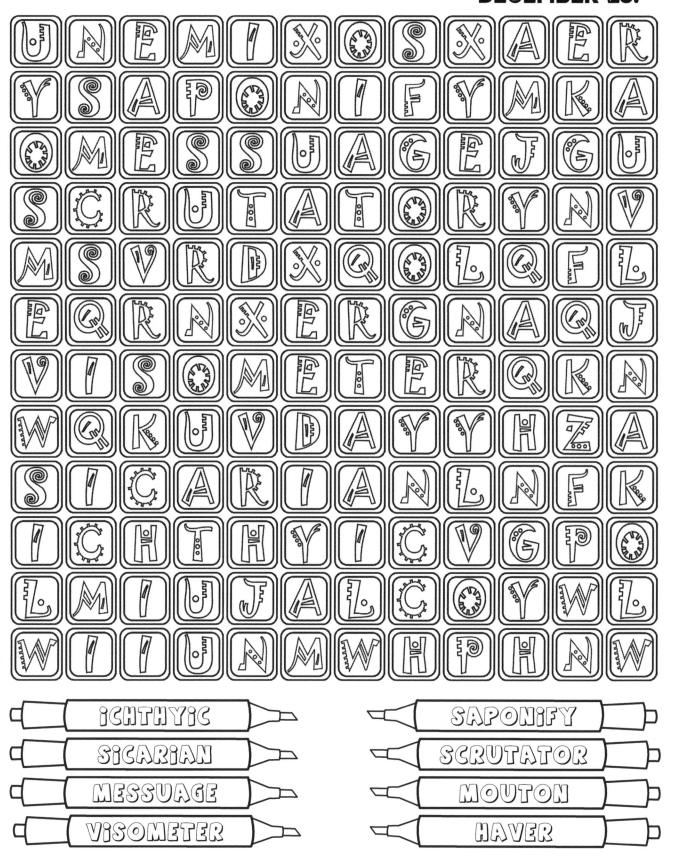

ICHTHYIC

SICARIAN

MESSUAGE

VISOMETER

SAPONIFY

SCRUTATOR

MOUTON

HAVER

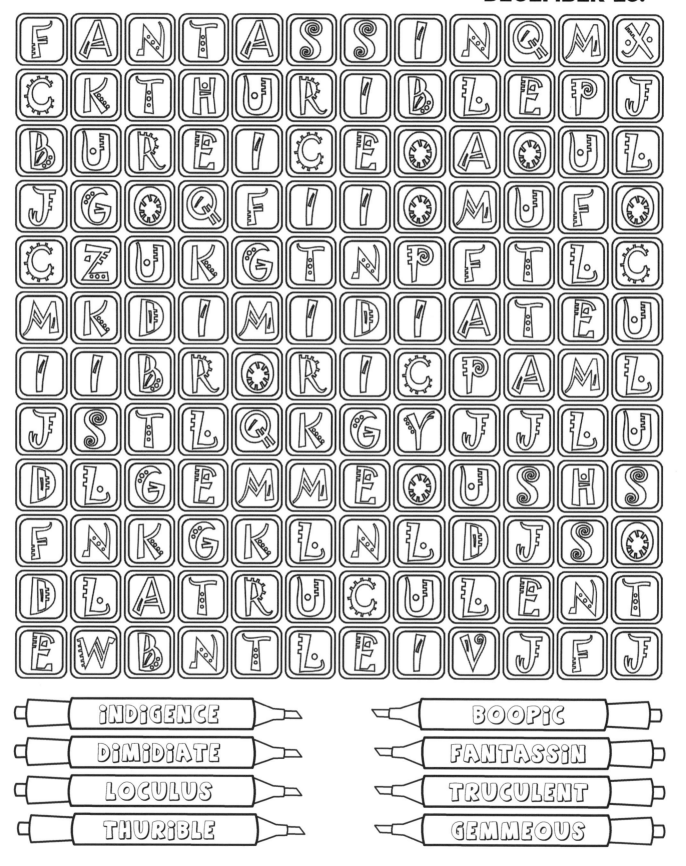

INDIGENCE

DIMIDIATE

LOCULUS

THURIBLE

BOOPIC

FANTASSIN

TRUCULENT

GEMMEOUS

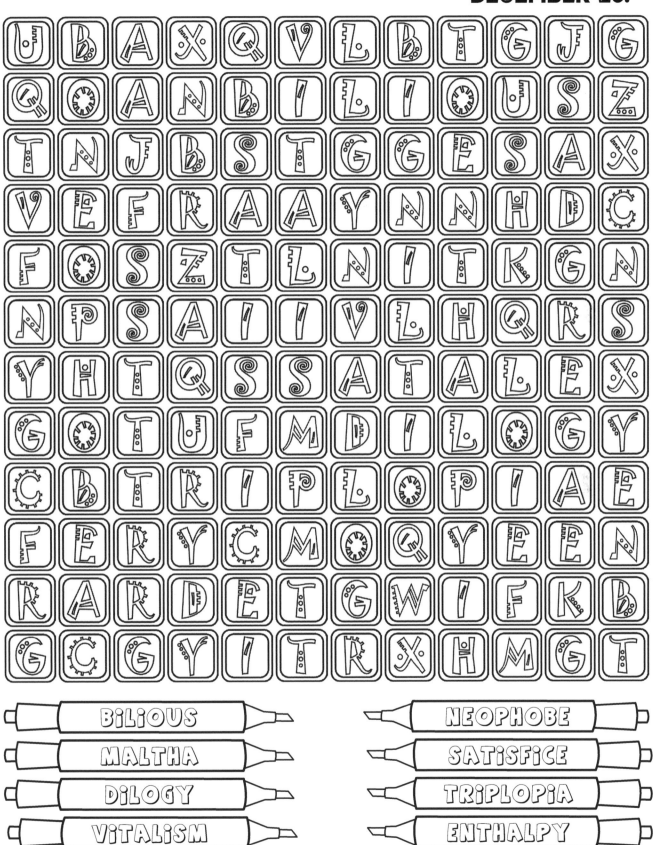

BILIOUS

MALTHA

DILOGY

VITALISM

NEOPHOBE

SATISFICE

TRIPLOPIA

ENTHALPY

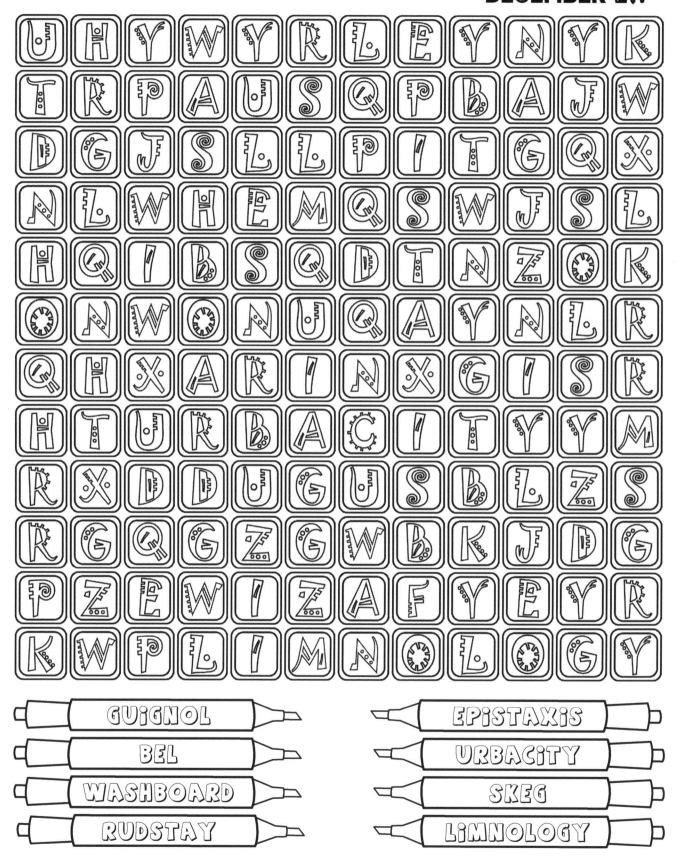

GUIGNOL

BEL

WASHBOARD

RUDSTAY

EPISTAXIS

URBACITY

SKEG

LIMNOLOGY

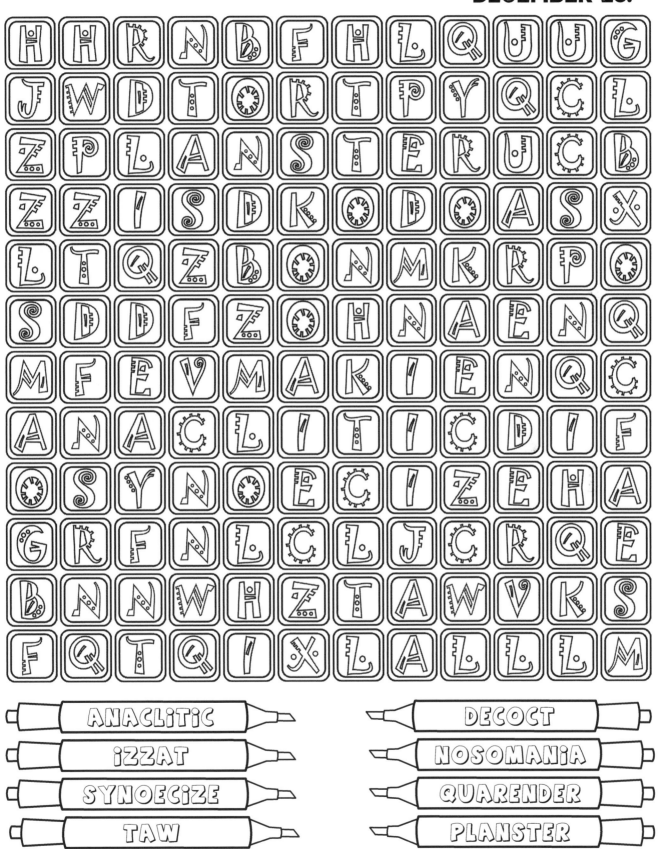

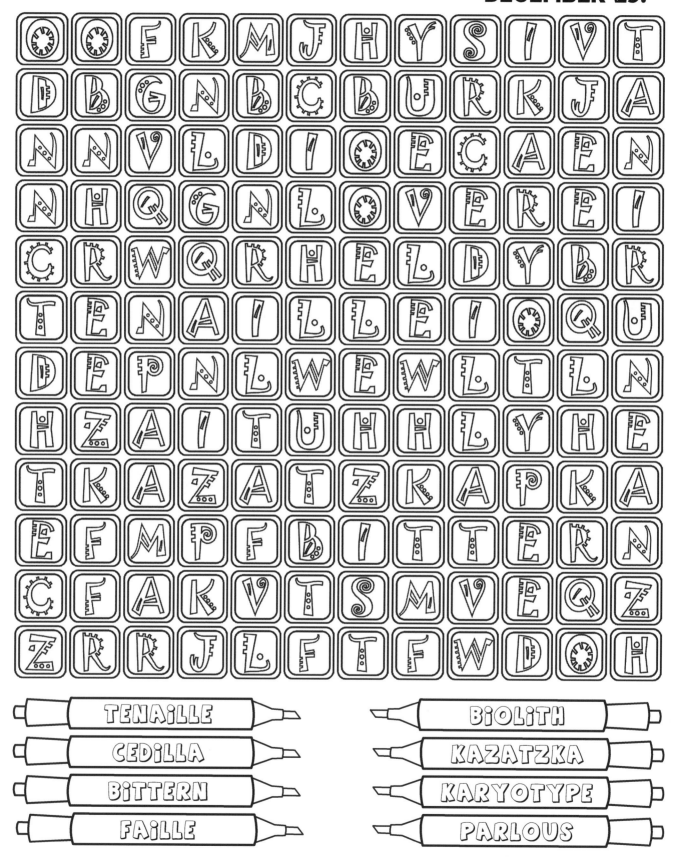

TENAILLE

CEDILLA

BITTERN

FAILLE

BIOLITH

KAZATZKA

KARYOTYPE

PARLOUS

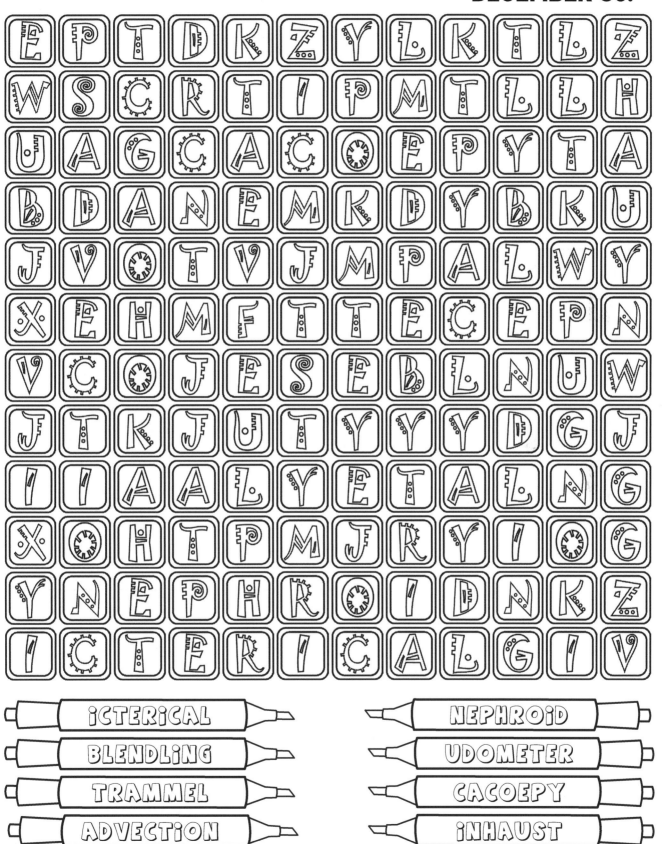

ICTERICAL

BLENDLING

TRAMMEL

ADVECTION

NEPHROID

UDOMETER

CACOEPY

INHAUST

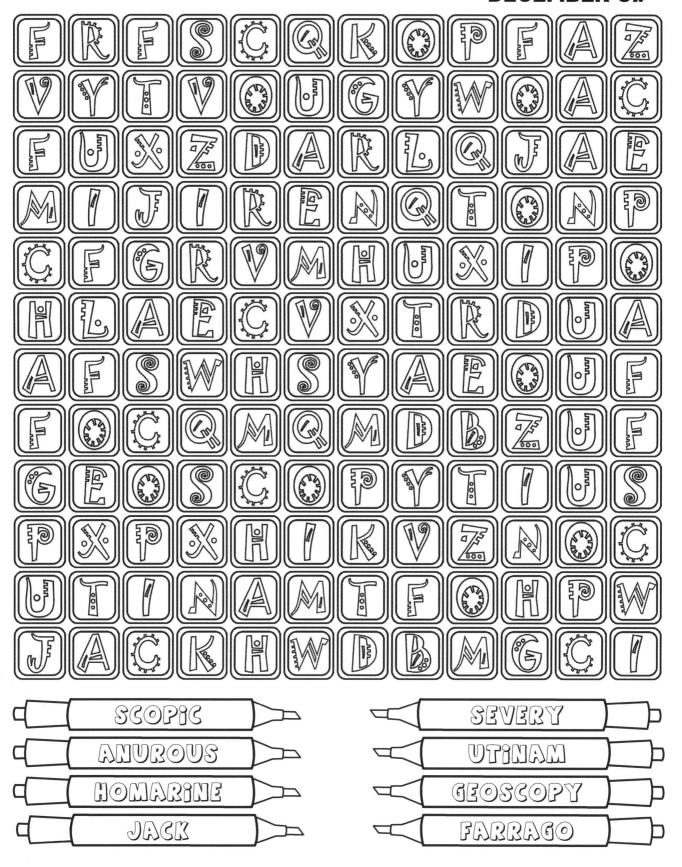

SCOPIC

ANUROUS

HOMARINE

JACK

SEVERY

UTINAM

GEOSCOPY

FARRAGO

Made in the USA
Middletown, DE
01 January 2023

19762080R00205